The Emerson Dilemma

The
EMERSON
Dilemma

ESSAYS ON EMERSON
AND SOCIAL REFORM

Edited by T. Gregory Garvey

UNIVERSITY OF GEORGIA PRESS   ATHENS AND LONDON

2001

© 2001 by the University of Georgia Press
Athens, Georgia 30602
All rights reserved
Set in Janson by G & S Typesetters
Printed and bound by Thomson-Shore, Inc.
The paper in this book meets the guidelines for
permanence and durability of the Committee on
Production Guidelines for Book Longevity of the
Council on Library Resources.

Printed in the United States of America
05 04 03 02 01 C 5 4 3 2 1

Library of Congress Cataloging-in-Publication Data
The Emerson dilemma : essays on Emerson and social reform /
edited by T. Gregory Garvey.
p. cm.
Includes bibliographical references and index.
ISBN 0-8203-2241-5 (alk. paper)
1. Emerson, Ralph Waldo, 1803–1882—Political and social views.
2. Literature and society—United States—History—19th century.
3. United States—Social conditions—19th century. 4. Social
problems in literature.   I. Garvey, T. Gregory, 1962–

PS1642.S58 E44 2001
814'.3—dc21   00-030217

British Library Cataloging-in-Publication Data available

Contents

Abbreviations

AW Emerson, Ralph Waldo. *Emerson's Antislavery Writings*. Ed. Len Gougeon and Joel Myerson. New Haven: Yale University Press, 1995.

C&R Thoreau, Henry David. Unpublished 1844 lecture on the conservative and the reformer, mistakenly labeled as an early draft of "Life Without Principle." Harvard University, Houghton Library, bMSAM 278.5, folder 18A.

CS Emerson, Ralph Waldo. *The Complete Sermons of Ralph Waldo Emerson*. Ed. Albert J. von Frank, Teresa Toulouse, Andrew Delbanco, Ronald A. Bosco, and Wesley T. Mott. 4 vols. Columbia: University of Missouri Press, 1989–92.

CW Emerson, Ralph Waldo. *The Collected Works of Ralph Waldo Emerson*. Ed. Alfred R. Ferguson, Jean Ferguson Carr, et al. 5 vols. to date. Cambridge: Harvard University Press, 1971–.

EL Emerson, Ralph Waldo. *The Early Lectures of Ralph Waldo Emerson*. Ed. Stephen E. Whicher, Robert E. Spiller, and Wallace E. Williams. 3 vols. Cambridge: Harvard University Press, 1959–72.

ELP Channing, William E. *Essays, Literary & Political*. Glasgow: James Hedderwick & Son, 1837.

EMF Fuller, Margaret. *The Essential Margaret Fuller*. Ed. Jeffrey Steele. New Brunswick, N.J.: Rutgers University Press, 1992.

ESR Kateb, George. *Emerson and Self-Reliance*. Thousand Oaks, Calif.: Sage Press, 1995.

ET Rowe, John Carlos. *At Emerson's Tomb: The Politics of Classic American Literature*. New York: Columbia University Press, 1997.

J Emerson, Ralph Waldo. *Journals of Ralph Waldo Emerson*. Ed. E. W. Emerson and W. E. Forbes. 10 vols. Boston: Houghton Mifflin, 1909–14.

JA Alcott, Bronson. *The Journals of Bronson Alcott*. Ed. Odell Shepard. Boston: Little, Brown, 1928.

JMN   Emerson, Ralph Waldo. *The Journals and Miscellaneous Notebooks of Ralph Waldo Emerson.* Ed. William H. Gilman, et al. 16 vols. Cambridge: Harvard University Press, 1960–82.

L   Emerson, Ralph Waldo. *The Letters of Ralph Waldo Emerson.* Ed. Ralph L. Rusk and Eleanor Tilton. 10 vols. New York: Columbia University Press, 1939–95.

LMF   Fuller, Margaret. *The Letters of Margaret Fuller.* Ed. Robert N. Hudspeth. 6 vols. Ithaca: Cornell University Press, 1983–94.

PJ   Thoreau, Henry David. *Journal.* Vol. 2, 1842–1848. Ed. Robert Sattelmeyer. In *The Writings of Henry D. Thoreau.* 12 vols. to date. Princeton: Princeton University Press, 1972–.

PN   Emerson, Ralph Waldo. *The Poetry Notebooks of Ralph Waldo Emerson.* Ed. Ralph H. Orth, Albert J. von Frank, Linda Allardt, and David W. Hill. Columbia: University of Missouri Press, 1986.

RP   Thoreau, Henry David. *Reform Papers.* Ed. Wendell Glick. In *The Writings of Henry D. Thoreau.* 12 vols. to date. Princeton: Princeton University Press, 1972–.

TAB   von Frank, Albert J. *The Trails of Anthony Burns: Freedom and Slavery in Emerson's Boston.* Cambridge: Harvard University Press, 1998.

TN   Emerson, Ralph Waldo. *The Topical Notebooks of Ralph Waldo Emerson.* Ed. Ralph H. Orth, Glen M. Johnson, Susan Sutton Smith, and Ronald A. Bosco. 3 vols. Columbia: University of Missouri Press, 1990–94.

TUE   Emerson, Ralph Waldo. *Two Unpublished Essays* ["The Character of Socrates" and "The Present State of Ethical Philosophy"]. New York: Lamson, Wolfe, 1895.

VH   Gougeon, Len. *Virtue's Hero: Emerson, Antislavery, and Reform.* Athens: University of Georgia Press, 1990.

W   Emerson, Ralph Waldo. *The Complete Works of Ralph Waldo Emerson.* Centenary Edition. Ed. E. W. Emerson. 12 vols. Boston: Houghton Mifflin, 1903–4.

Acknowledgments

MANY PEOPLE were instrumental in bringing this project to completion. The patience of the contributors deserves particular comment because they bore with the project as it was reimagined and made more comprehensive over a two-year period. The reports of the two readers whom the University of Georgia Press asked to review the original manuscript were very important in helping me to see the project in its broadest perspective. Malcolm Call, senior editor at the Press, gave sensible and reasonable guidance, as did Kristine Blakeslee and Stephen Barnett. I also owe important debts to faculty and staff at Michigan State University and SUNY-Brockport. I want to thank Doug Noverr, Valerie Milligan, and Judy Westerbrook at Michigan State University. Here at SUNY-Brockport, I want to thank Bernice Graham, Paul Curran, Yuko Matsukawa, Roger Kurtz, and Colleen Donaldson. Thanks also go to Marie-Helen Gold at the Schlesinger Library, Christopher Steele at the Massachusetts Historical Society, and Thomas Ford at the Houghton Library. Personal thanks to Len Gougeon and Jeffrey Steele for serving as honest brokers to plans and ideas. I am grateful for the generosity of Heather King, Rocco Marinaccio, Mark Rice, Carl Eby, Linda Avila, Mark Howell, Phoebe Jackson, Tersh Palmer, and Leon Jackson. My most special gratitude is for Kathleen McGarvey.

Introduction:
The Emerson Dilemma

EMERSON CLOSES HIS ESSAY "Experience" with a remark that does much to illustrate the dilemma that social reform posed for him. After evaluating his observation that "the world I converse with in the city and in the farms, is not the world I *think*" (cw 3:48), Emerson encourages himself to be patient with this disjunction and takes a lesson that would sound like a cliché if it were not made poignant by the depth of feeling that the discrepancy between thought and action evokes from him. This discrepancy speaks to Emerson, instructing, "never mind the ridicule, never mind the defeat; up again, old heart?—it seems to say—there is victory yet for all justice; and the true romance which the world exists to realize will be the transformation of genius into practical power" (cw 3:49). In Emerson's ideal world, the philosophy that motivates action would be indistinguishable from the practical power that flows from it.

The essays in this collection explore the relationship between Emerson's understanding of "genius" and "practical power" as a means of integrating the substantial body of scholarship that explains Emerson's transcendentalism with recent scholarship that has begun to recover his advocacy of abolitionism and other social reform movements. At the heart of the connection between the essays in this volume is the authors' desire to understand how Emerson's reform activism emerges out of his transcendentalism and how the transcendentalism that he developed early in his career shaped his involvement in reform movements during later periods.

The goal of transforming "genius," which Emerson tends to associate with psychological insight, spirituality, and art, into "practical power," which he associates with politics and business, was at the very heart of Emerson's aspiration. Yet he also had reservations about reform movements because participation in them would force him to align himself with a sect or party and thus undermine his ability to speak to the regeneration of society as a whole. Thus, he continually sought a mode of advocacy that would merge his ideal of individual autonomy with the practical political power that is gained through collective action.

After William Lloyd Garrison founded *The Liberator* in 1831, the antislavery movement developed an increasingly compelling public voice through the press and through organizations that sponsored lecture tours and meetings. The women's rights movement emerged as an organized public presence in the years following the convention at Seneca Falls, New York, in 1848. Emerson followed the progress of utopian societies such as Fruitlands and Brook Farm that formed communities in which to incubate the model of a perfect society.[1] Prison reform, temperance, societies to "redeem" prostitutes, and "foreign" missions to convert Indian nations and protect the integrity of their territory also emerged as significant organizations during the three decades that preceded the Civil War. More than the committees that organized political dissent during the Revolution, the reform organizations of antebellum America defined the pattern that is currently followed by civil, reproductive, and women's rights movements.

As consistent as many of the reform movements that Emerson saw around him were with his own vision for society, the associations that emerged to advocate each individual cause violated what may have been Emerson's most fundamental ethical belief: that authentic change cannot occur through piecemeal tinkering with the mechanics of society but must originate in a locus so fundamental that any change in it will also change the structure of society as a whole. For Emerson, this locus is the individual. Much of his writing thus apprises individuals of sources of personal power through which they can create model selves and thereby provoke reform in their societies.

Emerson's commitment to this indirect mode of achieving social reform created a dilemma. How could he speak as a reformer if he was unwilling to act as one? How could he promote his most ambitious and perhaps most circuitous method of reform and at the same time avoid involvement in movements that represented changes that he desired? Couldn't his aloofness be construed as subtle complicity in oppression? Couldn't it also be understood as an admission that his voice would have no impact on his society? The motivations to act that these questions might have provided, however, were counteracted by Emerson's conviction that joining reform movements would be to practice a method of advocacy that he considered symptomatic of the factionalization and fragmentation of society.

This dilemma produced the sense of ridicule and defeat that Emerson articulates at the end of "Experience." His comments there reflect his sense that up to that point in his career, he had failed to bridge the gap between his intellectual commitments to reform and the modes of public action that were available to him. By expressing a sense of being personally defeated and even a little ridiculous, Emerson defines the psychological costs of living in the space between a world in which he can "converse" and one in which he can only "think." In 1844, when he wrote "Experience," the difference between the two and the straitened limits of the world of thought must have been made even more vivid by the loss of his young son.[2]

By marking his own alienation, Emerson himself becomes the first in a long line of commentators who express the view that Emerson's writing and career lack political force or relevance. This tradition has dominated critical interpretation of Emerson's relationship to politics and has provided the strongest indictment of Emerson's contribution to American cultural history. It is worth pointing out that Emerson is a participant in what Michael Lopez refers to as "The Anti-Emerson Tradition."[3] Emerson's repeated denunciations of his own career, exemplified by the brief, personal jeremiads that he writes in his journals, underscore the depth of his own concern with the relevance of his writing and lectures. Cornel West offers an insightful reading of this dimension of Emerson's career. As a means of introducing his analysis of the American evasion of philosophy, West points out that the defeat Emerson communicates publicly in "Experience" is characteristic of a pattern of self-ridicule that also pervades Emerson's private writings. For West, the key to Emerson's "critique of" as well as his "minimal resistance to U.S. capitalist society" is to be found in Emerson's "guilt and shame" about his own "inaction and impotence."[4]

West underscores Emerson's feeling of impotence in relation to political involvement by citing a letter that Emerson wrote in 1837 to President Martin Van Buren to register his opposition to the removal of the Cherokee Indians from western Georgia. With the exception of the brief comments that Emerson makes on slavery and Indian removals during his ministry—a topic that Susan Roberson explores in her essay in this volume—Emerson's letter to Van Buren is his first public act as a reformer. This episode, and West's reaction to it, does much to reveal a set of basic patterns that characterize the frame of mind through which Emerson approached politics as well as the extent to which critical reception of Emerson's political writing has turned ambivalence toward political action into concrete rejection of it.

In his letter to Van Buren, Emerson begins by politely apologizing for intruding on the time of the "Chief magistrate." But he then explicitly situates his voice in an ongoing public debate by asserting that "At the instance of my friends and neighbors, I crave of your patience, through the medium of the press, a short hearing for their sentiments and my own" (AW 1). Although Emerson sent his letter to the President, he also released it to newspapers in Massachusetts and Washington.[5] The letter was not private correspondence; it was part of a long-running and deeply divisive debate.[6] Emerson introduces his topic by explaining the evolution of his community's understanding of the Cherokee situation:

> Even to our distant State, some good rumour of their worth and civility has arrived. We have learned with joy their improvement in the social arts. We have read their newspapers. We have seen some of them in our schools and colleges. In common with the great body of the American People, we have witnessed with sympathy the painful endeavors of these red men to redeem their race from the doom of eternal inferiority, and to borrow and domesticate in the tribe the inventions and customs of the Caucasian race. (AW 2)

Notwithstanding Cherokee progress toward assimilation—which Emerson uncritically regards as the appropriate goal of federal policy—the government had chosen to force the tribe onto land west of the Mississippi. By the time Emerson wrote his letter, the removals were a fait accompli. The negotiating was over and the nation's policy was set.[7] Emerson was aware that nothing he could do was going to avert or even delay the forced removal. As he brings his letter to a close, he self-consciously notes the "burlesque character" of a correspondence in which the holder of the highest office in the nation must be reminded of the most basic requirements of humanity.

As I was developing this collection of essays, carefully considering the trajectory of Emerson's psychology in relation to reform, I had hoped that the facts would permit me to avoid treating Emerson's opposition to the Cherokee removals as a dry run for his more substantial involvement in abolitionism. However, though it does not give the Cherokee their due, I think this incident remained in Emerson's imagination primarily because of the negative lessons he learned from it. Through his involvement in the removals crisis, Emerson learned how he ought *not* to practice reform in the future. Although he was undoubtedly concerned that something resembling justice be done for the Cherokee and proved willing to speak on their behalf, the conditions under which he wrote this letter left him feeling diminished by his own involvement.

Shortly after publishing the letter to Van Buren, Emerson made a trip to

New York, where he visited Bryant and Dewey and some of the other lights of New York society. On his return to Concord, Emerson notes in his journal that seeing these people helped him "to have hopes of the Republic." But he also immediately reinterprets his hopes in the context of the removals, lamenting that, "then is this disaster of Cherokees brought to me by a sad friend to blacken my days & nights. I can do nothing. Why shriek? Why strike ineffectual blows?" (*JMN* 5:475). His letter, in the end, as Emerson implicitly recognized, was a self-reflexive gesture that brought his political powerlessness into the foreground. His involvement was ultimately less about opposing the Cherokee removals than about going on the historical record as an opponent of the removal policy.

Cornel West concurs, pointing out that writing and publishing the letter "left [Emerson] feeling frustrated and powerless. Although he had protested, it seemed futile."[8] West is right to emphasize the sense of powerlessness that this incident impressed on Emerson. But like many critics before him, West also concludes that this incident set the pattern that Emerson would follow throughout his career. In West's words, Emerson "seems to have felt unable honestly to engage in sustained activism with agitators or reformers," or even more emphatically, "Emerson's 'American religion' renders his moral objections and cultural criticisms of America virtually impotent and politically ineffective."[9]

West's reaction to the implications of Emersonian "American religion" reflects a kind of frustration that mirrors Emerson's own ambivalence about the efficacy of his work. At the heart of Emerson's "religion," West finds a preoccupation with autonomy and purity of self that permits dissent but does not permit activism. Though it is adaptable to the kind of lifestyle choices exemplified by Thoreau, it is less adaptable to the organizational commitments of people like George Ripley, Theodore Parker, or Lydia Maria Child. Nonetheless, West situates Emerson in the "prehistory of American pragmatism" and identifies him as the crucial originary figure in the evolving relationship between American intellectuals and questions of public justice. Though West's conclusions have been undermined by recent historical research, they represent one of the most lucid assertions of a point of view that has characterized the assessment of Emerson as a reformer. West reiterates a tradition of Emerson interpretation that treats his career as a monolithic whole and ignores the patterns of development in his thought that led him to become more deeply involved in reform movements as the nation moved toward the Civil War.

Biographies by James Elliot Cabot and Oliver Wendell Holmes stand at the beginning of this tradition and are especially important in defining conventional treatments of Emerson's relation to political activism. Holmes's 1884 biography presents Emerson as an exemplary self characterized by a kind of perfect continuity of thought and action. This impressionistic goal, perhaps, motivated Holmes to emphasize harmony over conflict or intellectual contradiction as he describes the development of Emerson's career. In fact, Holmes closes his biography with a section titled "Life Judged by the Ideal Standard," and his final words indicate his sense of the continuity of Emerson's inner and outer lives:

> There are living organisms so transparent that we can see their hearts beating and their blood flowing through their glassy tissues. So transparent was the life of Emerson; so clearly did the true nature of the man show through it [that] . . . if He who knew what was in man had wandered from door to door in New England as of old in Palestine, we can well believe that one of the thresholds which "those blessed feet" would have crossed, . . . would have been that of the lovely and quiet home of Emerson.[10]

Though as Len Gougeon explains, Holmes was aware of Emerson's involvement in reform, the early biographer nonetheless displaces Emerson's activism onto contemporaries such as Theodore Parker to preserve the image of the scholar whose soul was in concord with his works.[11] In his discussion of "The Divinity School Address," Holmes contrasts Emerson's silence amid the uproar that his lecture created by including a description of Theodore Parker. He characterizes Parker as "A man of very different mental constitution, not more independent or fearless, but louder and more combative, whose voice soon became heard and whose strength soon began to be felt in the long battle between the traditional and immanent inspiration—Theodore Parker. If Emerson was the moving spirit, he was the right arm in the conflict." This separation of Emerson from any active participation in reform remains consistent throughout Holmes's biography and gets increasingly emphatic as Holmes addresses the period of Emerson's deepest involvement in antislavery.

Holmes introduces Emerson's relation to reform movements by noting that "Nothing is plainer than that it was Emerson's calling to supply impulses and not methods. He was not an organizer, but a power behind many organizers, inspiring them with lofty motive, giving breadth to their views [because they were] always tending to become narrow through concentration on their special objects." This assumption about Emerson's persona controls Holmes's interpretation, even to the point of conditioning his response to Emerson's 1844 address on emancipation in the British West Indies. Holmes claims that "This discourse would not have satisfied the Abolitionists" and accounts for this conclusion by pointing out that "It was too general in its propositions, full of humane and generous sentiments, but not looking to their extreme and immediate method of action." [12]

In describing Emerson's career in the 1850s, when Emerson was most public in his reform activism, Holmes reasserts the distance between the transparent sage and the din of the antislavery rally. Holmes sums up Emerson's reform activities by saying that "His sympathies were all and always with freedom. He spoke with indignation of the outrage on Sumner; he took part in the meeting at Concord expressive of Sympathy with John Brown. But he was never in the front rank of the aggressive anti-Slavery men." [13] Holmes thus tends to discount Emerson's involvement in reform by framing his participation as supportive or inspirational rather than administrative or institutional. This early portrait established a pattern that has often been reproduced. It reveals Emerson's liberal sympathies and even notes his public expression of them, but in order to sustain the pristine impartiality that Emerson created when he stepped beyond the institutional confinements of the ministry, it refuses to commit Emerson to a partisan movement.

In the biography that James Elliot Cabot published three years after Holmes's, Emerson's participation in reform is more fully explored. Yet while Holmes creates distance between Emerson and reform activism by maintaining a distinction between the thinker and the actor, Cabot tends to treat Emerson's reform commitments as a series of quixotic ventures that were praiseworthy but doomed to failure from the start. Cabot includes a substantial chapter on Emerson's reform activism that balances Emerson's sympathy with the goals of the reformers with his anxiety about their methods. Cabot emphasizes Emerson's annoyance with reformers, especially abolitionists, and presents an Emerson who feels that the specifics of reform are a kind of nuisance. Following a quotation of Emerson's best articulation of his own ambivalence about reformers—"They are partial, and apt to magnify their own. . . . Yet I feel that under him and his partiality and exclusiveness is the earth and the sea and all that in them is, and the axis around which the universe revolves passes through his body there where he stands"—Cabot asserts that "it was not fastidiousness nor inertia that made Emerson averse to active participation in the philanthropic schemes, so much as a necessity of his nature, which inclined him always to look for a relative justification of the offending party." [14] This "necessity of his nature," Cabot argues, kept Emerson on the sidelines, or at least at one remove from the hard-core political activism that characterized the 1850s.

Cabot's treatment of Emerson's involvement in reform is encapsulated in a chapter titled "Reform," in which he domesticates Emerson's involvement in political movements by sequentially subordinating them to Emerson's intellectual mission. He begins by discussing Emerson's ambivalence about racial equality and then explains Emerson's sympathy with, but reasons for demurring from, participation in the utopian communities Fruitlands and Brook Farm. Finally, Cabot subsumes the issues of oppression and egalitarianism that he sees underpinning Emerson's interest in reform into a section titled "Emerson's Own Experiments." In this section, Cabot discusses Emerson's effort to reshape his household economy by inviting his domestic servants to eat at the same table as the Emerson family. This incident serves as a paradigmatic example of Emerson's efforts to adapt his principles to daily life.[15] But Cabot's treatment of this experiment creates the impression of a man out of time who can see and articulate images of justice but who poses no serious threat to orthodox practices because his world of theory can never effectively adapt to the world of experience. Cabot quotes Emerson's letter to his brother William about the experiment:

> You know Lidian and I had dreamed that we would adopt the country practice of having but one table in the house. Well, Lidian went out the other evening and had an explanation on the subject with the two girls. Louisa accepted the plan with great kindness and readiness; but Lydia, the cook, firmly refused. A cook was never fit to come to table, etc. The next morning, Waldo was sent to announce to Louisa that breakfast was ready; but she had eaten already with Lydia, and refused to leave her alone.[16]

Emerson's effort at reform becomes a domestic farce in which the conservative servant outsmarts the liberal master and reasserts the status quo. Cabot emphasizes a similar subversion of Emerson's reform impulses in a discussion of women's rights at the end of the chapter. He ends the chapter by including Emerson's 1850 letter to Paulina Wright Davis, who had invited him to participate in a women's rights convention. In the letter, Emerson explains that "whilst I should vote for every franchise for women, . . . I should not wish women to wish political functions, nor, if granted, assume them. I imagine that a woman whom all men would feel to be the best would decline such privileges if offered, and feel them to be rather obstacles to her legitimate influence."[17] As Cabot's treatment of Emerson's reform activism indicates, there is a strongly conservative strain in his presentation of Emerson the reformer.[18] In relation to each of the major reform movements—antislavery, utopianism, egalitarianism, and gender equality—Cabot presents an Emerson who supports reform but whose deepest commitment is to maintaining the integrity of the self. In Cabot's view, this commitment blunts the effectiveness of his participation in reform activism.

Despite their blind spots, both Holmes and Cabot pay more attention to Emerson's reform activities than do later commentators like Perry Miller, who recontextualizes him into an intellectual tradition, or F. O. Matthiessen, who situates Emerson in a politico-aesthetic tradition. Holmes and Cabot establish the tradition that has minimized the importance of Emerson's activism by drawing the portrait of a man who posits radical individualism in the spiritual realm but who demurs from exploring the implications of that position for his own political and professional life.

The revival of interest in Emerson that occurred in the wake of Miller's reconstruction of American intellectual history revolved around a recognition of the importance of Transcendentalism in understanding the relationship between spirituality and individualism in the development of American thought. This new area of concentration directed Emerson's critics away from his political writing and toward explaining Transcendentalism as a spiritual and intellectual movement.[19] No doubt the richness of Emerson's effort to adapt Puritan spiritual rigor to a romantic concept of the self also helped dampen interest in his reform writing. The effort to understand the cultural history of Emerson's writing about the self was characterized by a dialogue in which critics such as Stephen Whicher and Jonathan Bishop argued for Emerson's increasing relevance while those such as Yvor Winters and Arthur Schlesinger dismissed Emerson as, in Winter's words, a man "interested primarily in thought about mystical experience, and whose attitude toward thought was self-indulgent."[20] The participants in this dialogue subordinated Emerson's reform activism to his transcendentalism to such an extent that the real subject of the debate became the contribution that Transcendentalist thought has made to American culture.

Those who asserted Emerson's importance did so by intense study of a relatively few essays from the mid-1830s. As critics emphasized the early works, Emerson emerged as the dominant American intellectual of the 1830s, and the 1830s emerged as the dominant period of Emerson's career. In Stephen Whicher's *Freedom and Fate*, for example, the psychological and spiritual power that Emerson defines in essays such as *Nature*, "Circles," and "The American Scholar," all written between 1835 and 1840, create the axis around which the other elements of Emerson's inner life revolve.[21] Though Whicher's Emerson intimates worlds of spiritual freedom, he also recognizes that transcendence is fated to be temporary. Emerson himself, like others, is destined to spend most of his time in the quotidian realm of daily affairs. Whicher makes an important step beyond the work of Holmes and Cabot by reemphasizing the internal conflict of Emerson's career through Emerson's effort to steer a course between transcendental solipsism and materialist pragmatism.

Arthur Schlesinger situated Emerson in a similar fashion, but unlike Whicher, he treats him as a noteworthy but negative exemplar. In *The Age of Jackson*, Schlesinger condemns Transcendentalism by arguing that as a group, the Transcendentalists stood aloof from the social institutions that transformed American politics during the 1830s. Schlesinger judges that politics represents Emerson's "greatest failure," but he also gives him a partial reprieve by portraying Emerson as a man caught between two worlds. In Schlesinger's view, Emerson had the integrity not to "succumb to verbal panaceas" offered by the Jacksonians, but he also "fundamentally did not care" about the pragmatics of democracy, "and thus he was betrayed, almost without a struggle, into the clichés of conservatism which had surrounded him from birth."[22]

In effect, the critical revival that began with Miller reestablished Emerson as a central figure in American cultural history; but that revival was also focused exclusively on his transcendentalism and consequently contained his significance within narrowly circumscribed boundaries. For critics of Whicher's and Schlesinger's generation, Emerson had historical and ideological importance. His thought defined a host of contradictions between religious and political definitions of selfhood that were especially salient during the Jacksonian period. He represented a moment in American cultural history and articulated an ideal of selfhood that was particularly appealing to those who understood America as a homogeneous nation characterized by consensual agreement about public priorities and personal values.

Scholars who have approached Emerson in the last fifteen years or so, motivated at least partly by a desire to understand American society in multicultural and pluralistic terms, have also found Emerson's writing to be surprisingly fertile. As Stanley Cavell notes in *This New Yet Unapproachable America*, criticism of the 1980s began to "recanonize" Emerson both by reevaluating his construction of selfhood and by asserting the significance of distinctly untranscendental strains of Emersonian thought.[23] This mode of criticism, which Lawrence Buell calls the "de-transcendentalizing" of Emerson, consists of stressing the material motives underpinning Emerson's writing and thus situates his transcendentalism within critical agendas that emphasize contextual and social issues.[24] The paradigmatic example of the de-transcendentalized Emerson is that of Len Gougeon's *Virtue's Hero: Emerson, Antislavery, and Reform* (1990), which explores Emerson's involvement in reform movements, especially abolitionism. While Gougeon provides substantial readings of texts such as "The American Scholar" and "The Divinity School Address" that were basic to Emerson's reputation as a Transcendentalist, equally influential texts such as *Nature* and "Circles" are not even listed in the index. What is noteworthy about the absence of these texts is that Gougeon was able to avoid them. His painstakingly researched book covers Emerson's entire career and relies significantly on material that has been widely available but nonetheless has lain fallow for a century.

Fueled by new social motivations and theoretical points of view, contemporary critics are once again undertaking a thorough revaluation of Emerson's cultural significance. Issues as basic as Emerson's construction of selfhood, the relative places of social heterogeneity and homogeneity, and the relationship of contemplation to action are being reexamined. The de-transcendentalizing of Emerson has given him unexpected purchase in a wide range of critical debates. Thus far, though, the debate is also characterized by a kind of dual image—Emerson is portrayed as a philosopher of independence, spiritual autonomy, and psychological power, and he is represented as an ardent family man and a reformer zealous enough to help finance John Brown's guerrilla war in Kansas.[25] The coexistence, often within the same text, of these two representations—Emerson the Transcendentalist and Emerson the reformer—is sustaining a unique dynamism within Emerson studies.

Emerson remains a linchpin figure in the American romantic movement and a key representative of antebellum intellectual culture, but he does so less as the embodiment of transcendental romanticism and more as a representative man struggling with conflicting philosophical and social commitments. As products of this dynamism, the following essays bring a familiar "Emerson the Transcendentalist" face to face with a now-recognizable "Emerson the reformer." They explore the psychological and cultural forces that influenced Emerson's involvement in politics and sound the extent to which his long career as a reformer emerged from the principles and priorities he developed during the 1830s and the early 1840s.

The first part of *The Emerson Dilemma*, "Emerson's Other Inner Life" extends Stephen Whicher's "inner life" of Ralph Waldo Emerson to include the intellectual impulses that pulled Emerson toward and away from active participation in reform. While Whicher focuses on the problem of action in itself, especially on the possible efficacy of action, Emerson's inner life was also propelled by thought about the ethics of different forms of action, including political action. The three essays in this part focus on the psychological issues that influenced Emerson's participation in reform and also on the impact of particular events—his wife's illness and death and Thoreau's arrest—on his willingness to participate in reform movements.

In "Reform and the Interior Landscape: Mapping Emerson's Political Sermons," Susan L. Roberson analyzes Emerson's discussion of Indian removals and slavery in sermons preached in 1830 and 1831. These early and tentative statements show Emerson displacing his grief at his wife's illness from the private to the public realm. He transforms the private reality of his wife's tuberculosis into a public metaphor of a diseased body politic. This brief interval, a period of just a few months in Emerson's career, dramatizes the deeply personal context from which Emerson first expressed views on reform, a context of impotence that may well have shaped his lifelong concern about finding methods of public action that could maintain the integrity of the self and demonstrate practical power. The implication of Roberson's essay is that Emerson's hesitance to participate actively in reform was partly a result of his experience with personal tragedy and his powerlessness to prevent it.

Garvey's essay, "Emerson's Political Spirit and the Problem of Language," describes an obstacle that Emerson had to overcome before he could fully commit himself to participate in the public debates over reform issues. This essay compares the organic theory of language that Emerson develops in 1835 and 1836 with the assumptions about language and signification that underpin the concept of the representative that he develops after finishing *Essays: Second Series* in 1844. The essay also links Emerson's organic theory of language to his early efforts to model reform through images of a perfectly transparent spokesperson for the spirit. The shape of Emerson's ethical commitments, which in the 1850s compelled him to seek a position of impartiality even if it meant remaining silent on issues of vital importance, shifted in the 1840s as he grew beyond the theory of language that motivated his early visions of poet-prophet figures. This essay begins to account for the internal logic that allowed Emerson to shift his attitude away from universal reform and toward the partisan reform movements that he had avoided during the early part of his career.

Linck C. Johnson focuses on the period between the Amory Hall lectures of 1844 and Emerson's work during the mid-1850s to explain the problem that Emerson and Thoreau faced as they worked to adapt the persona of the individualistic scholar to active participation in reform. The question that "Emerson, Thoreau's Arrest, and the Trials of American Manhood" poses is, did Thoreau's arrest offer Emerson a form of moral power, or did it demonstrate his powerlessness before the state? For Emerson, Thoreau's arrest seemed ill-directed and futile. For Thoreau, the reverse was true: suffering the indignity of arrest reaffirmed principles that compliance with unjust laws would compel one to suppress. Johnson reads Emerson's reaction to the arrest in relation to romantic ideals of masculinity. The ideal of the self-governing individual was both exemplified and negated by Thoreau's imprisonment. Emerson's reaction to the dilemma that Thoreau's arrest posed does much to dramatize his psychological priorities at a time when he was turning toward increasingly active participation in reform movements.

The second part of this volume takes up Emerson's views on the status of women in the public sphere. Not only do these three essays clarify important relationships in Emerson's life, the positions that the authors take frame a debate that is likely to continue for some time. Phyllis Cole's "Pain and Protest in the Emerson Family" addresses the impact that Lidian Emerson's and Mary Moody's reform activism had on the Emerson household. Contrasting what Cole calls the idealist reform rhetoric that Emerson's aunt began inculcating in the 1820s against his wife's sentimental rhetoric of protest, this essay defines the intensity with which the Emerson household was infused with discussion of reform throughout Emerson's career. On a more subtle level, Cole's essay explores how Lidian's and Mary Moody's activism shaped the dynamics of the Emerson home. Though Waldo spoke in favor of women's rights, he also treated Lidian's reform activism as a purely sentimental expression that lacked intellectual substance. Cole thus points to an important gap between Emerson's commitment to reform and his ability to hear positions that were consistent with his own but that were expressed in a feminized discourse.

In "Pierced with the Thorns of Reform: Emerson on Womanhood," Armida Gilbert historicizes Emerson's thought about women's rights between the 1850s and the 1870s. By comparing Emerson's rhetoric and thought about gender with that of organizers of women's rights conventions in 1850 and 1855, Gilbert concludes that by the ideological standards of the mid–nineteenth century, Emerson has to be considered a radical feminist. From this context, Gilbert explores how women's rights created a conflict between Emerson's ideals of womanhood and of justice. Justice, Emerson recognized, demanded equality, but his ideal of womanhood continued to require selflessness. As this process of exploration developed, Gilbert reveals Emerson struggling to remain the strongest possible advocate of women's rights despite his own essentialist understanding of gender and his recognition of the profound disruptions that would result from equality.

While Gilbert's essay emphasizes elements of Emerson's career that enabled early feminists to adopt him as an honorific mentor, Jeffrey A. Steele's "The Limits of Political Sympathy: Emerson, Margaret Fuller, and Woman's Rights" defines a psychological boundary that Emerson was never able to cross. Emphasizing that Emerson ignores women's claim to the authority of the pulpit, Steele compares Emerson's constructions of spiritual power with Margaret Fuller's. Steele concentrates on Fuller's efforts to achieve personal spiritual transcendence in 1840 and 1841 as a turning point that dramatizes the limitations of Emerson's feminism. The essay compares Emerson's concept of Spirit with Fuller's feminist myth-making and analyzes their differing interpretations of the Persian goddess Lilla, concluding that while Fuller reinvents Lilla as a figure of feminine empowerment and liberation, Emerson domesticates her into a model hostess. Emerson's inability to recognize the purpose of Fuller's project, Steele explains, indicates both a blind spot in Emerson's ability to see women as the spiritual equals of men and a gendered understanding of creative power that made the ordination of women ministers incompatible with his concept of agency.

The three essays in "Transitions in Antislavery" describe turning points in Emerson's abolitionism and indicate the extent to which Emerson's antislavery activism is less a deviation from his early transcendentalism than it is a logical extension of it. Michael Strysick's "Emerson, Slavery, and the Evolution of the Principle of Self-Reliance" reconstructs the changing role that the image of slavery played in the development of Emerson's model of selfhood. Beginning with Emerson's journals of the 1820s, Strysick traces the parallel development of slavery and self-reliance as images in Emerson's thought. He demonstrates that as Emerson's meditations on self-reliance become more concrete, his understanding of slavery as a material reality becomes more concrete as well. The psychological transformation of slavery from the metaphoric opposite of self-reliance into a social institution in which all Americans are implicated once again compelled Emerson to reevaluate his attitude toward political action. The impact of Emerson's growing awareness of the inextricability of self-reliance from slavery is most vivid in Emerson's 1854 address "The Fugitive Slave Law," which Strysick interprets as a translation of "Self-Reliance" into the discourse of the radical abolitionists.

In "Emerson's Abolition Conversion" Len Gougeon describes the impact that preparing his 1844 lecture on emancipation in the British West Indies had on Emerson's personal commitment to antislavery. By emphasizing Emerson's careful study of the history of slavery and his correspondence with people who were involved in litigating human rights cases, Gougeon makes the case that the preparation for this lecture catalyzed Emerson's antislavery sentiments and changed him from a sympathizer into an active abolitionist. The demands that Emerson's research placed on his sense of ethical responsibility changed his relation to antislavery activism, and did so largely as a result of private rather than public action. Given the moral imperatives that Gougeon shows Emerson discovering, the question of action is less one of whether he would avoid or participate in politics and more one of how he would participate in a public debate that was characterized by cant on both sides.

Harold K. Bush's "Emerson, John Brown, and 'Doing the Word': The Enactment of Political Religion at Harpers Ferry" uses Emerson's response to John Brown's raid on Harpers Ferry to explain the integration of spiritual and political action that was central to Emerson's reform methodology. In sharp contrast to his response to Thoreau's arrest, Emerson played a central role in the cultural interpretation that made Brown a martyr to the abolitionist cause. After situating the raid on Harpers Ferry in a tradition that includes Nat Turner's rebellion, David Walker's *Appeal,* and the assassination of Abraham Lincoln, Bush reads Emerson's "Speech at a Meeting to Aid John Brown's Family" as a text that exemplifies the role of the Declaration of Independence in American civil religion. Bush argues that Emerson's response to Brown indicates Emerson's sense of the transcendent possibilities of radical dissent. This speech, especially in its relationship to Emerson's response to Thoreau's arrest, dramatizes how much Emerson's thought about reform had changed between 1846 and 1859.

The final part of this collection interprets Emerson as a political theorist whose work became progressively more focused on the public realm.

David M. Robinson's "Emerson's 'American Civilization': Emancipation and the National Destiny" reads Emerson's 1862 essay "American Civilization" as an effort to situate the Civil War in a developmental theory of civilization. Robinson argues that Emerson draws an analogy between the physical principles that allow technological advancement and the moral principles that allow cultural advancement. By Emerson's logic, American slavery not only denoted the absence of civilization but also threatened to undermine other advancements toward civilization. Robinson's essay underscores the extent to which the Civil War compelled Emerson to adapt the interest in spiritual integrity and selfhood that characterize his transcendentalism into a general theory of the nature and purpose of civilization.

Stephen L. Esquith's "Power, Poise, and Place: Toward an Emersonian Theory of Democratic Citizenship" explores Emerson's legacy in relation to a resurgence of interest in citizenship among political theorists. By drawing on recent reinterpretations of Emerson's understanding of Nature as a force that establishes boundary conditions within which individuals live, Esquith explains how Emerson's attitude toward Nature is analogous to social environments in which we try to understand each other honestly and sympathetically. Esquith's model of Emersonian citizenship translates Emerson's traditional theory of selfhood as a quest for harmony with Nature into a quest for harmony within society. Esquith also brings into focus a problem that looms on the horizon: like recent critics who have addressed the compatibility of Emersonian thought with collective action, Esquith begins to explore questions about the adaptability of Emerson's thought to the global context in which contact among citizens occurs through increasing levels of technological mediation.

These eleven essays assert a dimension of Emerson's thought that it has only recently been possible to address. The reconstruction of Emerson's involvement in political action, the extent of his lecturing on reform topics, and the consistency with which political issues are discussed in his letters and journals have only recently been recovered to an extent that permits sustained analysis of the internal relationship between his career as a reformer and his more famous transcendentalism. Though antislavery fully compelled Emerson to set aside his ambivalences, his wide-ranging thought about and discussion of reform underscores that the tensions in his thought were not occasional or early aberrations. As these essays indicate, imagining ideals of public commitment and coupling them with active participation in reform movements is only one dimension of Emerson's career as a reformer. In the differences between Emerson's treatment of Thoreau's arrest and the execution of John Brown, in the irreconcilable contradictions of his writing on women's rights, and even in his theoretical approaches to the nation in his early sermons and his late "American Civilization," each chapter in this volume reveals an Emerson grappling with and modifying positions in a fundamental ethical dilemma with which he struggled from the very beginning to the very end of his career.

NOTES

1. Carl J. Guarneri, *The Utopian Alternative: Fourierism in Nineteenth-Century America* (Ithaca: Cornell Univ. Press, 1991), pp. 47–49.

2. Robert D. Richardson, *Emerson: The Mind on Fire* (Berkeley: University of California Press, 1995), pp. 355–58.

3. See Lopez's chapter titled "The Anti-Emerson Tradition" in *Emerson and Power: Creative Antagonism in the Nineteenth Century*, ed. Michael Lopez (De Kalb: Northern Illinois Univ. Press, 1996).

4. Cornel West, *The American Evasion of Philosophy: A Genealogy of Pragmatism* (Madison: University of Wisconsin Press, 1989), p. 21.

5. John McAleer, *Ralph Waldo Emerson: Days of Encounter* (Boston: Little, Brown, 1984), pp. 240–45; *VH* 57–58; Richardson, *Emerson*, pp. 275–79.

6. See John A. Andrew, *From Revivals to Removal: Jeremiah Evarts, the Cherokee Nation, and the Search for the Soul of America* (Athens: University of Georgia Press, 1992), pp. 229–58; and *VH* 57–58.

7. Reginald Horsman, *The Origins of Indian Removal* (East Lansing: Michigan State Univ. Press, 1970); Ronald Satz, *American Indian Policy in the Jacksonian Era* (Lincoln: University of Nebraska Press, 1975).

8. West, *American Evasion*, p. 21.

9. West, *American Evasion*, p. 22, 20.

10. Oliver Wendell Holmes, *Ralph Waldo Emerson* (1885; reprint, Detroit: Gale Research, 1967), p. 421.

11. Gougeon describes Holmes's notes for his biography and explains that in his research notes Holmes had listed Emerson's major antislavery speeches in chronological summaries of earlier biographies by George Willis Cooke, Moncure Conway, and Alexander Ireland (*VH* 10–12).

12. Holmes, *Emerson*, pp. 127, 141, 181.

13. Holmes, *Emerson*, pp. 211.

14. James Elliot Cabot, *A Memoir of Ralph Waldo Emerson*, 2 vols. (1887; reprint, New York: AMS, 1965), 2:427, 428.

15. Barabara Ryan offers an especially interesting reading of these domestic experiments in relation to Emerson's development as an abolitionist. See "Emerson's 'Domestic and Social Experiments': Service, Slavery, and the Unhired Man" *American Literature* 66 (fall 1994): pp. 485–508.

16. Cabot, *Memoir*, 2:446.

17. *L* 4:230; Cabot, *Memoir*, 2:455–56.

18. Nancy Simmons concludes that this was a conscious strategy that Cabot pursued out of a desire to write a biography of which Emerson would approve. Simmons writes that Cabot "stressed the conservative elements in Emerson's enterprise, depicting his career as one more stage in the successive unfolding of the universal mind rather than as an iconoclastic break with the past. Cabot watched Emerson carefully cultivating acceptance, working within the tradition, not against it. Cabot had no wish to destroy this image." See Nancy Craig Simmons, "Philosophical Biographer: James Elliot Cabot and a Memoir of Ralph Waldo Emerson" in *Studies in the American Renaissance*, ed. Joel Myerson (Charlottesville, VA: University Press of Virginia, 1987), pp. 365–92.

19. This mode of approaching the importance of the Transcendentalists is most vividly apparent in Anne C. Rose's *Transcendentalism as a Social Movement, 1830–1850* (New Haven: Yale Univ. Press, 1981), a book that insightfully explores the problems of adapting religious authority to the secular realm, but which treats issues such as antislavery and women's rights only in passing.

20. Yvor Winters, *Maule's Curse: Seven Studies in the History of American Obscurantism* (Norfolk, VA: New Directions, 1938), p. 135.

21. Stephen L. Whicher, *Freedom and Fate: An Inner Life of Ralph Waldo Emerson* (Philadelphia: University of Pennsylvania Press, 1953).

22. Arthur M. Schlesinger, *The Age of Jackson* (Boston: Little, Brown, 1945), pp. 384–85.

23. Stanley Cavell, *This New Yet Unapproachable America: Lectures after Emerson and Wittgenstein* (Albuquerque, NM: Living Batch, 1989), p. 3.

24. Lawrence Buell, "The Emerson Industry in the 1980's: A Survey of Trends and Achievements," *ESQ* 30:2 (1984): 117–36.

25. Recent books by George Kateb and Michael Lopez substantially reinvent traditional methods of reading Emerson's transcendentalism by emphasizing the importance of dialectical forms of psychological energy in his thought. See Kateb's *Emerson and Self-Reliance* (Thousand Oaks, CA: Sage, 1995); and Lopez's *Emerson and Power*.

Richardson describes the intensity of life in the Emerson household and Emerson's delight in the hubbub that long-term guests produced—a delight that was heightened, no doubt, by his easy access to a private study. See Richardson, *Emerson*, 313–17. Emerson's contributions of money to Kansans were ostensibly to aid settlers who opposed the westward extension of slavery. However, as Gougeon explains, Emerson knew that his contributions would be used for arms and that Emerson defended this aspect of the disbursement of funds. See *VH* 222–24.

Ralph Waldo Emerson, c. 1850. By permission of the
Houghton Library, Harvard University.

The Second Church, Boston. From David Greene Haskins, D. D., *Ralph Waldo Emerson: His Maternal Ancestors*, 1887.

WHILE EMERSON served as a minister at the Second Church of Boston between 1828 and 1832, social reform movements became increasingly visible in New England public and intellectual life. In 1831 William Lloyd Garrison started *The Liberator*, an antislavery newspaper that also took positions on other reform movements. Over time, the influence of William Ellery Channing, whose combination of spirituality with intellectual liberalism influenced Emerson's early career, waned as Emerson adopted more radical positions on reform.

Engraving of William Lloyd Garrison by T. F. Stuart, no date. Courtesy of the Massachusetts Historical Society.

Portrait of William Ellery Channing, by Washington Allston, 1811. Courtesy of the Massachusetts Historical Society.

Above: 1838 Woodcut representing the murder of Elijah P. Lovejoy, editor of the Alton, Illinois *Observer*, on November 7, 1837. Courtesy of the Library of Congress.
Right: The World Anti-Slavery Convention, London, 1840. By permission of the Library of Congress.

As antislavery activists became more visible in the late 1830s, two incidents were especially important in radicalizing Emerson and his community. In 1837, Emerson denounced the murder of Elijah P. Lovejoy, an antislavery newspaper editor in Illinois. Three years later, the refusal of the London World Antislavery Convention to seat woman delegates motivated the emergence of the women's rights movement and added rancor to schisms between advocates and opponents of women's rights within the antislavery movement. In this painting of the convention, note that the women, though present, are standing in the aisles.

Emerson's career as a reformer was shaped as much in the domestic realm as it was by public events. His aunt Mary inculcated the connection between spirituality, ethics, and reform early in his life. His wife, Lidian, and daughter, Ellen, were also active reformers who ensured that political discussion characterized conversation in the Emerson house.

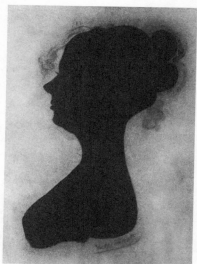

Above: The Emerson House in Concord, no date. By permission of the Concord Free Public Library.
Right: Silhouette of Mary Moody Emerson, no date. Courtesy of the Concord Free Public Library.

Above: Lidian Jackson Emerson as vice-president of the New England Women's Club, 1868. By permission of the Schlesinger Library, Radcliffe College.
Right: Ellen Tucker Emerson, 1860. By permission of the Houghton Library, Harvard University.

Crayon portrait of Henry David Thoreau, by Samuel Worcester Rowse, 1854. By permission of the Concord Free Public Library.

Bronson Alcott, no date. By permission of the Houghton Library, Harvard University.

Emerson's circle of friends provided a wide variety of committed reform practices. Thoreau's desire to express a perfect autonomy represented a lifelong commitment to the possibilities of liberal individualism. Bronson Alcott represented a perfect idealism that found methodological outlets in communitarian and educational reform. Emerson's ambivalence toward both of these influences underscored the difficulty of integrating ethical political action and comfortable social integration. Margaret Fuller's partly unheard challenge to Emerson's conventionalities marks the

Margaret Fuller, no date. Gift of Edward Southworth Hawes in memory of his father, Josiah Johnson Hawes. Courtesy of the Museum of Fine Arts, Boston.

John Brown, 1856. Daguerreotype by Amos A. Lawrence.

most searching tensions in Emerson's relationship to the reform movements of his time.

Although John Brown was at the center of the guerrilla war in Kansas, he gained lasting fame for his raid on Harpers Ferry, Virginia. Brown became one of the most important symbolic figures in Emerson's imagination. The daguerreotypist who made this image considered it worthy of memorializing: thirteen years after he took the image, the artist attached a paper label to the case that reads, "Mr. John Brown sat for this likeness for

"Heralds of Freedom," published by C. H. Brainard, Boston, 1857. Clockwise: Emerson, Wendell Phillips, J. R. Giddings, Theodore Parker, Gerrit Smith, Samuel J. May, and Garrison.

me in 1856 here in Boston after the Ossowatomie affair. Boston Feb. 12, 1869 Amos A. Lawrence." After speaking out against the expansion of slavery into Kansas, Emerson was invited to add his portrait to a poster of prominent abolitionists. The "Heralds of Freedom" poster was produced by C. H. Brainard of Boston in 1857. The original measures 53.5 cm by 40.3 cm.

Part One

EMERSON'S OTHER INNER LIFE

SUSAN L. ROBERSON

Reform and the Interior Landscape: Mapping Emerson's Political Sermons

IN THE AUTUMN of 1830 and on into the early months of 1831, Ralph Waldo Emerson, minister of the Second Church of Boston, does something very unusual for him, something he did at no other period during the six years of his ministry—he spoke out against slavery and the treatment of the Southern Indians who were being forced off their lands. Not readily given to such pronouncements during his ministry or indeed until his active involvement in the antislavery movement in the 1840s, Emerson gained the mistaken reputation of being detached from social and political reform. Len Gougeon has recently corrected this image of Emerson, demonstrating that Emerson was "a concerned, sometimes frustrated, but always committed social activist" (VH 14). Even so, Emerson remained largely silent on political issues during much of his ministry and up until 1837, when he wrote his open letter to President Van Buren about the Indian situation, and then again until 1844, when he entered the slavery fracas with his West Indies speech. Gougeon suggests that during the 1820s until the early 1840s slavery was largely an abstraction to Emerson, something he used in sermons to illustrate a point like "'man's inhumanity to man'" (VH 70, 34). What is perplexing, however, is not so much Emerson's silence on social issues during his ministry, for his silence can be explained in a number of ways. Rather, it is the breaking of that silence in only a handful of sermons, all at about the same time.

The timing of these pronouncements is curious, for they interrupt the progression of his thought on subjects that would become cornerstones of his Transcendentalist philosophy. After writing some fairly conventional early sermons that still had the ring of an earlier Calvinism, by 1829 and on into 1830 Emerson had been steadily working out issues of self-reliance, authority, and self-empowerment in his sermons. In Sermon No. LIII, first delivered on October 24, 1829, for instance, he urged his congregation to pursue moral and intellectual independence apart from society, warning of the mediocrity and complacency of an "accommodation to the expectations of others" (cs 2:72). Advocating independence of thought and action, he declares that "A man is respectable only as far as his actions are his own" (cs 2:71). And he formulated a theory of cosmic as well as social self-reliance, telling his congregation that "God is not alone self existent" (cs 2:74). Throughout the next year, he continued to build on the themes of self-reliance and personal authority, and on October 3, 1830, delivered the sermon (XC) that most closely anticipates his later essay, "Self-Reliance." In words that he would use again, he urges self-trust: "Let him scorn to *imitate* any being. Let him scorn to be a secondary man. Let him fully trust his own share of God's goodness" (cs 2:266). And he tells his listeners of the individual's God-like potential. Expanding the meaning of his favorite Bible verse, Luke 17:21, "The Kingdom of God is within you," he says, "If a man would always as exclusively consult his own thoughts . . . he would always speak with the same force, a force which would be felt to be far greater than belonged to him or to any mortal, but was proper to immortal truth" (cs 2:266). Speaking from the lofty heights of his emerging Transcendentalism, Emerson finds that the voice of God and authority reside in the individual rather than in external institutions or truths, empowering the individual and setting him apart from a world that confines and crushes personal and intellectual freedom. At the same time that he begins to fashion a theory of self-trust, he also fashions the self-reliant hero who is detached from the physical, social world, a man who finds power by abandoning external evidence to discover himself and authority in the spirit that resides within.

But it is just at this point, when we least expect it, that Emerson's high idealism is interrupted by sermons that speak of death and suffering, of "the gloomy apprehension of annihilation" (cs 3:31), of God's judgment and hell, and of sin—personal and national. The Indian Removal and slavery issues appear not in sermons that speak of freedom and independence, where we might expect to see them, but in sermons about other debaucheries of intemperance—drinking, dueling, and brothel visiting—sermons that reckon the costs of sin. To discover why Emerson would change the tenor of his sermons so abruptly and why he would speak out on political issues in this context during the waning months of 1830 and not earlier or throughout his ministry requires us to map out the terrain of the body— the body of his sermons and the body in his sermons.

As anthropologist Mary Douglas points out, the ways cultures use images of the human body correlate to their images of the social body, for the human body is always treated "as an image of society." The image of the human body, she contends, operates as a metaphor or symbol for the social body, and discussions of appropriate social behavior and social boundaries are channeled through the body metaphor. Prescriptions for bodily control, for instance, occur in conjunction with "the valuing of culture above nature." Likewise, she suggests, theological issues are channeled through the mind-body dialectic, freedom often being correlated with the spirit or mind rather than with the body.[1] Given Douglas's insights into the interconnection between the rhetoric of the body and discussions of social and theological import, it is not surprising that the body metaphor is persistent in Emerson's sermons and journals.

Sounding more Calvinist than Unitarian, the fledgling minister in his very early sermons joined his contemporaries in viewing the body, with its passions and appetites, as the agency and register of sin. Reading himself as "a lover of indolence, & of the belly" (*JMN* 2 : 241) and wary of the untamed terrain of the self, Emerson writes the body and the negation of the body in his sermons, advocating a morality of control and self-denial. As Carroll Smith-Rosenberg argues, the American nineteenth century was a time of obsession with "categorizing the physical, and especially the sexual," and an "ocean of words . . . rhythmically beat" against discussion of the self. While this discourse may in fact emphasize a language of the body, the aim was not so much erotic as prescriptive, to advocate control, denial, and negation of the body. In doing so, the "opinion setters" constructed a theology and morality focused on the body, finding the bosom sin to be one of appetite and indulgence, and morality to be a matter largely of temperance and self-control.[2] Thus when Emerson preaches, "Temptation never ceases. Our passions never relax their hold. Our appetites are never satisfied" (*cs* 1 : 167), he is reiterating not only the Puritan inheritance but also the message heard from various sources that the body and its appetites are to be distrusted, that he who gratifies the appetites commits a sin and will receive due compensation, whether in this world or in the one to come.

Like the moral advisors of the day, Emerson urged not only resistance to temptation but also a practiced self-denial and the development of habits that would form a character lean and spare and strong. He preached in the early sermons that "at our best estate we are imperfect and frail" (*cs* 1 : 70), warning his audience that we learn vice with a "fatal facility" beyond our capacity for learning good, for society teaches more readily the lessons of vice than those of moral behavior (*cs* 1 : 72).

Emerson carried the program of self-denial to his own life, writing diatribes in his journal about the debilitating influence of temptation and pleasure and engaging in scattered attempts at curbing his own dinner in an
attempt to raise his intellectual or spiritual sensibilities. Playing out the
rhetoric of morality on his own body, Emerson's anorexic reaction to his
physical self registers in his efforts to disengage himself from the body and
to define and fashion himself as a man of the mind. In April 1824, he reminded himself "to curtail my dinner & supper sensibly & rise from table
each day with an appetite; & see if it be fact that I can understand more
clearly" (*JMN* 2:240). Later, in March and April of 1832, he again experimented with mastering his appetite by diminishing his food intake, this
time in a gambit to gain "personal purity" (*JMN* 4:6). Wary of the potential
usurpation of the mind or spirit by the untamed body, Emerson played out
the theme of the body in his journals and sermons in terms of detachment
and abandonment of the physical.

Even as the rhetoric of the body informs Emerson's own discourse and
theology, another body appears—absently and silently—behind the text of
the sermons: the disappearing body of Ellen Tucker. Engaged to the beautiful but frail Ellen on December 17, 1828, he knew from the beginning
that she was "too lovely to live long" (*L* 1:259 n. 3), that the consumption
that ate up her lungs would at last consume her. Though he identified her
with spirituality and his own spiritual regeneration, writing of her as his
"beauty" and "angel," his "guardian angel" who would intercede for him
with God (*L* 1:259; *JMN* 3:149, 148), he also made her into a metaphor and
an idea. Erasing her real, physical presence from his private texts, he converted her figure into an abstraction more easily to cope with the real deterioration of her physical self. Unable or unwilling to write much about
her condition and his fears for her in his private texts—his letters and journals—Emerson turns to the public texts, the sermons, to work out symbolically his personal and philosophical struggle with mortality and loss. In
Sermon No. XLI, for instance, written shortly after a relapse in Ellen's
health (July 2, 1829), he writes of the immortality of the soul and Christian
consolation for death. Imaginatively projecting a future state of eternal society in which his mind can have "an uninterrupted intercourse with the
majestic society of all souls," the minister looks forward to "the event that
releases [him] from the prison" of the flesh and sends him "to the presence
of all that is holy and ravishing in moral beauty" (*CS* 1:310–11). Though
he identifies that "presence" as Christ, he uses language—"holy," "ravishing," "moral," and "beauty"—that suggests that he also has his mind on

Ellen, whom he will marry on September 30, 1829. As this sermon suggests, the figure of Ellen (here an erotic one) often lies behind the body of the sermons, informing Emerson's treatment of themes connected to the life of the spirit, death, and consolation.

While he found hope for the eternal communion of "majestic . . . souls" in 1829, fusing images of death and marriage, by the autumn of 1830 his sermons on death and consolation were dark with images of sin and retribution. When the deterioration of Ellen's body was too evident to ignore, when frantic calls to Dr. Jackson and removal to the warmer Philadelphia climate in March 1830 could not stop the "red wheezers" (L 1:296), he brings into the text of his sermons yet another body, the body politic. Having emerged from early discussion of the temptations of the body to an abandonment or sublimation of the body for the mind, reinventing himself as a man of the mind, Emerson in the fall of 1830 unexpectedly returns to the Calvinistic rhetoric of sin and retribution and delivers jeremiads about the diseased social body—the nation—substituting it for the diseased body of the woman he loved "too deeply."[3]

Caught in the grips of depression, in a Melvillean "damp, drizzly November" of the soul, Emerson returned his focus to the troubled terrain of the body—the individual body and the social body—working out his personal anxiety in symbolic code. While the letters and journals do not demonstrate fear for Ellen's life, his very real and heartfelt concern for her situation is evidenced in the abrupt shift in the sermons from topics of self-trust and self-culture, from sermons that located the kingdom of God within the self, to sermons that dwell on death and sin and judgment. He enjoins his congregation in Sermon No. XCV, first delivered on November 14, 1830, to let "the great doctrines of the New Testament, of death, of judgment, of heaven and hell, be studied" (CS 3:35). With Ellen's illness, he feels the powerlessness of his own will against the all-powerful machinery of God's law, declaring in his very next sermon (No. XCVI) that "All laws are directed to enforce God's will, and it is self that always breaks them. If self was permitted to seek and gain its ends, it would turn the world into a hell" (CS 3:43).

In the jeremiads that mark this period of personal depression, Emerson speaks as he had not before of national sins. As Mary Douglas suggests, social discussion of behavior and identity take place in and through the symbolic language of the body. While Douglas has in mind the way societies channel discussion of political issues through images of the human body, Emerson inverts this paradigm, using the body politic as a metaphor or code for the human body. For Emerson, the social body acts as an image of the human body, providing him with a code for articulating an unnarratable personal anguish. In his discussion of the American jeremiad, Sacvan Bercovitch also recognizes this correlation between the private and the public. Bercovitch notes that "the American jeremiad was a ritual designed to join social criticism to spiritual renewal, public to private identity, the shifting 'signs of the times' to certain traditional metaphors, themes, and symbols."[4] According to Bercovitch, the jeremiad, or political sermon, is "part of a strategy designed to revitalize the errand" into the wilderness, the mission that, from its Puritan beginnings, had both sacred and secular goals. By decrying the shortcomings of society and predicting doom and destruction, the jeremiad hopes to point its listeners back to God and godliness. In traditional jeremiadic form, Emerson had sought a renewal of virtue and religious observance in his early sermons. In Sermon No. XVII (April 2, 1828), Emerson claimed, "The sins of the nation are *our* sins" (*cs* 1:171), but he also saw prosperity coming out of adversity and the real ability of community members to correct the sins of the nation. On July 15, 1827, he had reminded his congregation of the trials and triumphs of the Puritan forefathers and of the prosperity of the nation as he called for a more consistent observance of the Sabbath and warned against a "degenerate effeminacy." And in his next sermon he had predicted a personal and national millennium, an "approaching era of human bliss" marked by a religion that "is cheerful, social, masculine, generous" (*cs* 1:110, 112).

But in the sermons of 1830, Emerson's jeremiads have a more urgent tone; the assurance of the earlier jeremiads is replaced by a mood of desperation and impotence. As Bercovitch further notes, jeremiads "betray an underlying desperation—a refusal to confront the present, a fear of the future, an effort to translate 'America' into a vision that works in spirit because it can never be tested in fact."[5] As such, the jeremiad is a construct of the authorial self who inscribes onto the national paradigm his own "moods and motivations."[6] In other words, the jeremiad grows from perceived political and moral shortcomings and often tells us more about the society's or individual minister's perception of the state of things than things as they really are.

In Emerson's case, his personal sense of "desperation [and] a refusal to confront the present" are played out in jeremiads that focus on national rather than personal ills. With Ellen's disintegrating health and his corresponding depression and powerlessness to avert the disaster or find a satisfactory compensation for loss and separation, he expanded discussion of the diseased body to the national arena, warning of the consequences of the national evil perpetrated against the weaker inhabitants of the nation, primarily the Indian and the slave. The spring of 1830 had seen Congressional debates on the Indian Removal Act, and memorials had been sent to Congress protesting the abuse of the Cherokee and Creek Indians, who were being pushed from their lands in Georgia. Emerson's brother Charles even participated in "the nefarious Indian Subject" (*L* 1 : 316). Yet public discussion of the problems of slavery and other social ills, as evidenced in newspapers and magazines, do not appear to have escalated in the autumn of 1830 or to have predicted doom and destruction.

Although the popular literature of the period does evidence concern about the Indians, slavery, dueling, and other issues, this concern is often meliorated by a vision of progress and reform and does not seem to have been peculiarly insistent in late 1830. In the *Boston Evening Gazette* for January 2, 1830, the writer looking back on 1829 does indeed bemoan the victimization of the Cherokee Nation at the hands of "political intolerance of personal and local cupidity" and the perpetuation of slavery in the South, but he does so in an essay that looks more consistently at the progress of the nation and the liberating institutions of New England. If there are problems in America, this article suggests, they are distant from a progressive and enlightened New England. An article in the September 1830 issue of the *Christian Examiner* addresses the problem of the Cherokees, claiming that Georgia has no legal or moral right to force the Cherokees from their land and demonstrating that these Indians are not savage but are devoted to agriculture, education, and Christianity. While the author does plead for justice and the proper exercise of executive power by the president, his is the only piece in the 1830 *Christian Examiner* that notices the plight of the Indians.[7]

On July 3, 1831, in a speech that was an expanded version of the one he delivered from Emerson's pulpit on May 29, 1831, Samuel J. May, Unitarian minister, reform advocate, and brother-in-law of Bronson Alcott, indicted in stirring words the nation, the South, and New England for the injustice served black Americans and the Southern Indians. Although this particular speech was delivered months after the period in question, it can serve as a model for the antislavery rhetoric of the time and provides a means of contextualizing Emerson's own earlier pronouncements on social issues. May speaks of the "great sins we have committed [and] the foul stains . . . upon our national character," of the "lust for wealth," "unprincipled speculations," and "arts of dishonest traffic" evident in a country that held "*two millions* of our fellow men in the most abject servitude." His concern centers on the distortion of freedom, liberty, and the creed that all men are created equal, and he predicts, "Certain destruction will overtake us if we persist in our iniquity." Even so, May assumes that freedom and equality are human rights that will persevere, comparing the imminent struggle of blacks for freedom with the "power of oppressed humanity," which in Europe was upsetting "the thrones of tyrants." Unlike Emerson's indictments during the autumn of 1830, which echo May's rhetoric and yet are unrelieved by a vision of reform, May's jeremiad becomes a profession of faith that Americans can, if awakened, correct injustice and establish a union of harmony and equality. Indeed, the news from Europe, Mexico, and South America concerning the revolutions of 1830 affirmed the American belief that the desire for freedom and liberty was flourishing and that the revolts were a "splendid illustration of the inviolability of the rights of man."[8]

In the autumn of 1830 and into 1831, Emerson echoed the current worry about the state of the nation in his sermons. While concerns about the Southern Indians, slavery, and other national ills were certainly in the air and were disturbing to one committed to moral reform, for Emerson these topics are suggestive also of personal ills. While Emerson had solid ground for criticizing society and the politics that condoned injustice and would increasingly lend his voice to reform issues from the 1840s on, his outspokenness now and in only a handful of sermons, rather than consistently and throughout his ministry, bespeaks something other than moral anger. It reveals a personal sense of powerlessness aggravated by the declining condition of Ellen's health and his own depression in the face of personal trauma. It appears that he transfers and transforms his personal tragedy in the sermons, giving vent symbolically to his own moods in publicly acceptable ways and at the same time disguising from himself and his audience a tale unnarratable because it is inappropriate and painful. In this way, the narrative of national sin and injustice serves as a cipher of his private narrative, for the larger story mirrors his private despair and impotence. Unable to control the real catastrophe of his life, he enacts it in the jeremiadic sermons, distancing and controlling it through language that metaphorizes his own situation.

It may be that Emerson was himself aware of this rhetorical stratagem, for he hints that he understood the correlation between the private self and the national scene. When he indicted New England for its economic complicity in slavery in a journal entry for November 10, 1830, he found fault with those who "with their sinful eyes can not see society without slaves," and he addressed the need for reform, for the "progress of every soul." In this passage, Emerson correlates personal sin with the perpetuation of slavery and personal reform with the reform of society (*JMN* 3:209). Yet he also seems to map out an interior landscape by means of the political terrain. The old concern for the potential usurpation of the mind by the untamed body is translated onto the body politic. This concern is represented in the sermons by his discussion on November 14, 1830, of "the ferocious usages of savage nations,—War, Dueling, Assassination" (*cs* 3:37–38), and on December 12, 1830, of "nameless dens of intemperance and debauchery" that threaten the moral well-being and power of the nation as well as the individual (*cs* 3:59).

Throughout this period he brings mention of slavery, intemperance, war, and the treatment of the Indians into his sermons: he speaks of "the evils of Slavery" and "the man who sought . . . [to] enslave his brother" (*cs* 3:43), of the need to empathize with the enslaved and work for "the redemption of African or Indian slavery" (*cs* 3:47), and of Christianity's condemnation of "war and slavery and intemperance, and every vice" (*cs* 3:64). Unlike earlier jeremiads, his political sermons of 1830–31 have a sense of catastrophe about them, envisioning a civil war that breaks up the national family at a time when Ellen's illness threatens to break up his own family. He writes of the evil "we discern impending over us" and of a change that may "blow the trumpet of civil war" (*cs* 3:140). Anticipating the mournful change within his own household, Emerson finds in the images and rhetoric of antislavery propaganda a means for expressing the anxiety that he could not and did not make explicit. Painting a picture of a nation turned criminal and murderous, in April 1831 he claims: "It needs only certain change in the speculative principles which we ourselves entertain. It needs a preponderance of passion over reason, a little more violent preference of selfish interest over honest shame than now we permit in ourselves, a little more casting off of the restraints of Puritan principles and Puritan manners, a little greater progress of unbelief which springs from a bad heart" (*cs* 3:141).

As in his earlier diatribes against the body, he constructs a moral equation for the nation with the same factors—the war between the passions and self-control, between morality and sin, between impotence and power. The sign he sees of his nation's "bad heart," its "treatment of the Indian in one portion of the country, a barefaced trespass of power upon weakness, . . . and the general indifference with which this outrage passes before the eyes of the whole nation" (*cs* 3 : 141), indicates his concern with the dichotomy of power—with the impotence of the individual in the face of overwhelming and oppressive power held by the tyrant few, and of the tyrant universe whose power spelled out most agonizingly to him the word "death."

Weighed down by the burden of personal anxiety and national guilt, Emerson in the closing months of 1830 saw little to hope for in the final judgment. His predictions are uncharacteristically gloomy and sound more like an Edwardsian prophesy than an Emersonian one. Emerson warns that to disobey God's principles is "to seal our doom . . . to incur the reproaches of our conscience . . . to ruin our peace of mind" (*cs* 3 : 38–39). The image of the sinner, the one fallen away from the "overflowing bounty of the benevolent Father" who carries "a fire . . . lighted from hell" in his soul, resonates with the personal anguish and pain of the young minister who too felt separated from happiness and whose future promised only doom and "painful thoughts" (*cs* 3 : 53, 39). As Emerson's vision darkened, his forecasts sounded the same note that they had in his first sermons. Echoing the warnings of an earlier Calvinism and at the same time giving voice to his own mood, Emerson proclaims the operation of Satan in the world: "Thus out of the bosom of every good comes forth the hand of the Adversary of God and man beckoning us backward with pleasant invitations to give up the good we have so hardly bought" (*cs* 3 : 58). Like his image of the individual, Emerson's homiletic narrative again retreats back to "representati[ons] of savage life," signaling his own psychic and intellectual retreat as he retells the story of man's fall, itself a narrative mirror of Emerson's personal subtext (*cs* 3 : 53).

As life around him—at least the life that really counted—was falling apart and disintegrating, Emerson found expression not in the original, risky thought about self-reliance he had been developing, but in the safety of the widely accepted tradition of God's omnipotence and human weakness and in diatribes against a diseased national body. Although Emerson never mentions Ellen's situation in his sermons and refers to it only elliptically in his personal texts, Ellen's ill health nonetheless provides the subtext for his philosophical position during the last months of her life.

After Ellen's death and during his long period of recuperation, he returned to discussions of self-reliance and of the body, finding that the "genuine man" (*cs* 4: 203) frees himself from the body—the human body with its demeaning appetites, the social body with its herdlike mentality, and, finally, the religious body with its insistence on ritual. Having experienced attachment to the body with his love for Ellen, Emerson also learned the need for an abandonment of the physical for the spiritual, for that which really counts and lives on beyond the death of the body. These lessons he brought with him to his resignation sermon, "The Lord's Supper" Sermon, in which he declared his religious independence from mere forms and institutions, once again incorporating the metaphor of the body into the larger discussion. Critiquing the symbolic ritual of eating and drinking the body and blood of Jesus, Emerson indicts a religion that has forgotten the true meaning of Christianity in its concerns for the outward, physical forms of worship. "My friends," he announces, "the kingdom of God is not meat and drink" (*cs* 4 : 192).

Likewise, when he turned his attention a decade later to the issue of slavery, he indicted the citizens of Massachusetts as "respecters, not of essential, but of external law, decorum, routine, and official forms" (*aw* 43). And as Jesus was the embodiment of spiritual truth, the Word made Flesh, so he calls upon citizens to become "yourselves Declarations of Independence" and to find in their "head and heart and hamstrings," rather than in mere legal forms, the truths of justice and freedom (*aw* 83). What he preached in 1832, that institutions and rituals must be rejected and reformed to more nearly constitute the true relation between moral substance and external form, he continued to preach in his antislavery writings.

NOTES

1. Mary Douglas, *Natural Symbols: Explorations in Cosmology* (New York: Pantheon, 1982), pp. 70, 71, 162.

2. Carroll Smith-Rosenberg, *Disorderly Conduct: Visions of Gender in Victorian America* (New York: Oxford Univ. Press, 1985), pp. 91, 25.

3. Jerome Loving, *Emerson, Whitman, and the American Muse* (Chapel Hill: University of North Carolina Press, 1982), p. 14.

4. Sacvan Bercovitch, *The American Jeremiad* (Madison: University of Wisconsin Press, 1978), p. xi.

5. Bercovitch, *American Jeremiad*, p. xiv.

6. Clifford Geertz, *Interpretations of Cultures: Selected Essays by Clifford Geertz* (New York: Basic Books, 1973), p. 90.

7. *Boston Evening Gazette*, January 2, 1830; *Christian Examiner*, New Series, 10 (1830): 107–60. The essay for the *Christian Examiner* summarizes and excerpts a variety of materials, including memorials presented to Congress in February 1830, on behalf of the Cherokee and Creek Indians, as well as Edward Everett's speech to the House of Representatives on May 19, 1830.

8. Samuel J. May, *Discourse: Slavery in the United States* (Boston: Garrison and Knapp, 1832), pp. 3, 4, 12, 16.

T. GREGORY GARVEY

Emerson's Political Spirit and the Problem of Language

Eloquence is *the power to translate a truth into language perfectly intelligible*
to the person to whom you speak. He who would convince the worthy
Mr. Dunderhead of any truth which Dunderhead does not see, must
be a master of this art. Declamation is common; but such possession of thought
as is here required, such practical chemistry as the conversion of a truth
in Dunderhead's language, is one of the most beautiful and cogent
weapons that are forged in the shop of the divine artificer.
"Eloquence"

EMERSON'S SENSE that reformers tended to speak to limited audiences from narrow points of view was one of the obstacles that prevented him from becoming active in social reform movements at the very beginning of his career. The frequently narrow focus of reformers motivated him to keep his distance from politically engaged movements because he hoped to discover a rhetoric that would transcend partisanship and have universal appeal. In "New England Reformers," the address that Emerson gave to the nonresistance meeting in Boston in 1844, he offers a kind of reception theory that does much to explain his sense of the relationship between language and the reformer: "The reason why anyone refuses assent to your opinion," Emerson explains, "or his aid to your benevolent design, is in you: he refuses to accept you as a bringer of truth, because though you think you have it, he feels that you have it not. You have not given him the authentic sign" (*cw* 3:164). In this passage, Emerson attributes the inability of reform movements to influence national policy to a failure in the reformer's voice. His use of the phrase "the authentic sign" not only marks his sense that the burden of change is on the reformers; it also denotes

Emerson's confidence that language can serve as a perfect medium of truth. When Emerson blames the reformers for failing to transform their audiences, he homes in on the gap between the values for which reformers speak and the language through which they promote their causes. By Emerson's logic, the "authentic sign" would close this gap by perfectly articulating the reformer's ideals. If a just cause is articulated with authentic signs, auditors will recognize it as just, "accept" the reformer as a "bringer of truth," and embrace the cause.

Since recent scholarship has done much to reconstruct the importance of external events in Emerson's emergence as a reformer, it is now possible to explore ways in which his reform activism also grows out of logics that are internal to his intellectual life.[1] Emerson's effort to discover the language represented by the "authentic sign" is important to his evolution as a reformer because his highest aspiration for reform was to generate broad-based belief in a transcendent "Spirit" that would be publicized by a prophetic public spokesperson such as a minister, scholar, or poet. Even though Emerson's analysis of transcendence is usually understood in relation to individual spiritual regeneration, he saw this underlying motivating force, whether he calls it Spirit, Nature, the Over-Soul, or just Soul, in both political and spiritual terms. The Spirit offered Emerson a nonsectarian locus of faith that held out the possibility of reconciling belief in the divinity of the individual with the desire to facilitate social harmony in the nation as a whole. The pattern of fragmentation through the development of sectarian and partisan associations that was gaining pace in the first third of the nineteenth century violated the basic ethical principle that Emerson believed should motivate reform activity.[2] Early in his career, at least through the mid-1840s, Emerson sought to promote a mode of reform that was premised on the possibility of infusing all of society with the same kind of insight that the individual gains at the moment of inspiration.

In addition to defining a romantic ideal of private divinity, the political dimension of Emerson's concept of the Spirit represents a set of core values that he believed able to provide the ideological foundation of a consensus society. However, according to the principles that he asserts in essays such as "Self-Reliance" and "Circles," dissent from majority opinion is a perfectly normal—perhaps even a necessary—position for the individual to adopt. Despite the importance of ideological dissent to Emerson's thought, he rejects the idea that the individual's obligation to follow his or her innermost convictions implies a public sphere that is filled with conflicting voices in never-ending debate.[3]

As Sacvan Bercovitch and Christopher Newfield have recently explored, Emerson's view of democracy is thus paradoxical in the sense that he assumes the possibility of combining radical autonomy for the individual with radical consensus within society as a whole. Bercovitch cites a journal passage from late 1842 to emphasize Emerson's investment in this apparent contradiction. In the entry, Emerson meditates on the relationship between the individual and the body politic. He concludes that "The Union is only perfect when all the Uniters are absolutely isolated. Each man being the Universe, if he attempts to join himself to others, he instantly is jostled, crowded, cramped, halved, quartered, or on all sides diminished of his proportion. And the stricter the union the less & more pitiful he is" (*JMN* 8 : 251).[4] Bercovitch takes this description of the paradoxical assumptions underpinning the relationship between American corporatism and American individualism as a statement of "Emerson's hesitation about adopting or rejecting either extreme [which] indicates a search for the proper paradox that would connect the two."[5] The problem that Bercovitch works to explain is Emerson's effort to reconcile radical autonomy with his conviction that all people share a universal spirit.[6]

Christopher Newfield approaches the same problem in Emerson's thought from a somewhat different point of view. Newfield situates Emerson at the heart of a tendency in American psychology that resolves the romantic model of liberal selfhood into a model of selfhood through which the individual willingly makes himself or herself submissive to abstract quasi-supernatural powers such as the state, public opinion, or large private institutions. By subordinating individualism to faith in the transcendent spirit to which all people must ultimately submit, Newfield argues that Emerson promotes a form of "submissive individualism." This model of self, Newfield argues, is the template of a model of submission that characterizes American thought. Emerson's impulse to argue for submission to the demands of the Spirit has been generalized to encourage submission to other, secular institutions. Ironically, Newfield argues that Emersonian quests for transcendence have promoted habits of ritualized submission to corporate authorities.[7] Both Bercovitch's explanation of Emerson's effort to reconcile autonomy and consensus within the boundaries of liberal thought and Newfield's articulation of the behavioral legacy of Emersonian spirituality reveal some of the political implications of Emerson's effort to bridge the gap between his belief in private autonomy and his desire for public consensus.

Emerson's changing understanding of the nature of language is also an important element of this process. In his early essays, especially in "English

Literature" and *Nature*, Emerson propounds a theory of language that did much to define his hope that consensus could be provoked by a perfect spokesperson for the Spirit. This confidence in language as a medium of reform influenced his attitude toward political activism because it implied that his highest political obligation was to seek the voice that could transcend partisanship and bring about consensus.

At the end of "The American Scholar," Emerson offers an image that describes the connection between individual and political consensus. He emphatically asserts that "if the single man plant himself indomitably on his instincts, and there abide, the huge world will come round to him . . . [Then] a nation of men will for the first time exist because each believes himself inspired by the Divine Soul which also inspires all men" (cw 1:69–70). The same "Divine Soul" that he describes here not only inspires "each" person, it also inspires "all" people. In political terms the Emersonian Spirit, or, in this instance, the "Divine Soul," embodies a centripetal force that permits the emergence of a society that is simultaneously *democratic*, in that individual belief serves to validate the authority of the Spirit, and *consensual*, in that all citizens hearken to the beat of a single transcendent drummer. The seamless connection that Emerson imagines between "each" and "all" overcomes the individual's alienation from a factionalized collective because it motivates consensual recognition of a single, transcendent source of authority.

Although Emerson is most widely recognized for his articulation of the liberatory potential that romantic spirituality holds for the individual, it was all but impossible for him to envision the working of the Spirit independently from its application to the society as a whole. In his 1861 eulogy for Thoreau, for example, Emerson comments on the potential of Transcendentalist inspiration in a way that underscores the civic responsibility that spiritual insight confers on the individual. Emerson praises Thoreau as the type of the self-reliant man, but he also explicitly connects Thoreau's quest for autonomy with the public obligation that a project such as Thoreau's properly generates. Emerson remarks on the courage that it took Thoreau "to refuse all accustomed paths, and keep his solitary freedom at the cost of disappointing the natural expectations of his family and friends." Almost in the same breath, however, Emerson expresses an equally clear dissatisfaction with what he perceived to be the half-heartedness of Thoreau's effort to carry his vision onto the public stage: "With his energy and practical ability he seemed born for great enterprise and for command; and I so much regret the loss of his rare powers of action, that I cannot help counting it a fault in him that he had no ambition. Wanting this, instead of engineering for all America, he was the captain of a huckle-berry party. Pounding beans is good to the end of pounding empires one of these days; but if, at the end of years, it is still only beans!"[8]

The distinction between pounding beans and pounding empires involves different scales of public ambition. Thinking, perhaps, of Thoreau's work in the bean field at Walden Pond, Emerson compares the process of pounding beans for individual nourishment to the process of pounding empires to liberate the people whose autonomy has been appropriated by an "imperial" political power. This analogy offers a measure of the difference between a Thoreauvian Transcendentalism, which Emerson understands to be pursued primarily as a self-reflexive ethical ideal, and an Emersonian Transcendentalism, which is explicitly oriented toward the public realm.

Though actual historical examples of the Spirit working as a principle of political inspiration prove difficult for Emerson to isolate, he does occasionally intimate its presence as a unifying and motivating force for entire communities. In his essay "Politics," Emerson echoes the closing lines of "The American Scholar" by asserting that "a nation of men unanimously bent on freedom, or conquest, can easily . . . achieve extravagant actions, out of all proportion to their means; as, the Greeks, the Saracens, the Swiss, the Americans, and the French have done" (*cw* 3:120–21). Earlier, in his 1835 "Historical Discourse" on the bicentennial of Concord, Massachusetts, Emerson explains at greater length the potential achievements of a community that acts by consensus. In this essay, Emerson identifies "two great epochs of public principle" in America (*w* 11:48). The founding of the colonies and the Revolutionary era, Emerson holds, are periods in which the Spirit infuses entire communities. His treatment of colonial Concord clarifies the social relations that he considers ideal and longs to reestablish.

The emphasis that Emerson places on the unified nature of Concord's commitment to the revolutionary cause underscores the importance he places on consensual political action: "On the 27th of June [1775], near three hundred persons" agreed to suspend trade with Britain. This decision was "solemnized by acts of public worship." In August, the town "forbade the justices to open the court of sessions. This little town then assumed the sovereignty . . . On the 26th of the month, the whole town resolved itself into a committee of safety to preserve order" (*w* 11:71–73). Though Emerson had read the town records, he does not discuss the debates that took place in town meetings; rather, he emphasizes unity and consensus as characteristic qualities of the townspeople's discussions.

This episode also reveals the motivations that impel a unified community into action. As his description of Concord's role in the Revolution draws to a close, Emerson sums up the impulses that drove Concordians to reject British authority: "It was not an extravagant ebullition of feeling, but might have been counted on by anyone acquainted with the spirits and habits of our community. Those poor farmers who came up, that day, to defend their native soil, acted from the simplest instincts" (*w* 11:75). The townspeople do not need an inspired poet to exhort them to action because they respond to the internal demands of "instincts" that all members of the community share.

Emerson's use of the words "spirits" and "instincts" in this explicitly political context indicates the extent to which he assumed that the Spirit could function as a principle for collective social action. In "Historical Discourse" Emerson reveals characteristics of a social order that—in the light of the increasingly combative, partisan, and self-interested culture of nineteenth-century Boston—contrast sharply with the world of his experience. Eighteenth-century Concordians act in response to "simple instincts" in order to promote "public principle." This image of deeply personal impulses unifying communities and motivating them to act for the public good is Emerson's exemplum of what can be accomplished by a society that is infused with the Spirit. In positing the Spirit as a structuring principle for social relationships as well as for individual faith, Emerson sought to define a source of authority that transcended the differences in values, faiths, and material interests that were making American society more diverse and heterogeneous, as well as more fractious, partisan, and sectarian.

The problem that Emerson's theory of the political spirit presented, but which he was never able fully to overcome, lies in the mediation of Spirit from the realm of private inspiration to the realm of public expression. George Kateb, in his analysis of Emersonian self-reliance, cites "Historical Discourse" as Emerson's best integration of the individualist and corporate principles of self-reliance. But Kateb also uses this essay to underscore the problems that collective action poses in Emerson's political thought. Kateb argues that in Emerson's view, corporate power "was tolerable because it was decentralized, and in each lesser unit—that in each town—popular self-government existed in the form of the town meeting." But Kateb then raises a series of questions to explore the implications of collective action for Emersonian self-reliance: "Where is the individual in all this? Did he submerge himself in a unitary cause, or was he conscripted into making a moral contribution? If so, then the town meeting can be praised as true group self-government, but group self-government is not the same as an individual's active self-reliance. Can the latter be politically expressed?"[9] In order for the power Emerson attributes to the Spirit to gain political force, the experience of the individual has to be converted into a language that not only signifies for others but that others recognize as authentic, original, and authoritative. An act of mediation is at the heart of Emerson's theory of the political spirit. This mediation consists of transforming inspiration from the type of private experience that Emerson describes in the "transparent eyeball" passage of *Nature* to a public utterance that all can recognize as "the authentic sign."[10]

Emerson frequently describes the effects that the authentic sign will have, but he is evasive when it comes to describing the mechanics of mediation itself. The closest he comes to describing the actual process of mediation is in his "Divinity School Address," where he writes that "It is the effect of conversation with the beauty of the soul, to beget a desire and need to impart to others the same knowledge and love. If utterance is denied, the thought lies like a burden on the man. Always the seer is a sayer" (*cw* 1:84). The experience of discovery is itself intensely personal, but once the individual has discovered the Spirit and thereby become a seer, he is almost automatically re-created as a sayer.[11] Although the drive to express, in Emerson's eyes, is coequal with the event of inspiration, Emerson does not talk of a perfect verbal outflowing of the Spirit. In the brief description quoted above, Emerson tacitly erases the transition from insight to expression. A personal conversation with the soul creates a "need" to publicize. But in the next sentence—"If utterance is denied, the thought lies like a burden on the man"—it is the failure to express rather than the fulfillment of the need to do so that is foremost in Emerson's mind. In the final sentence "Always the seer is the sayer," the problem is solved not by describing the process of mediation, but by an act of alliterative sleight of hand. In "The American Scholar," Emerson briefly returns to the problem that mediation creates when he points out that "long he [the scholar] must stammer in his speech" (*cw* 1:62).

In "The Poet" Emerson explains mediation in a way that characterizes his ideal. He treats expression as a kind of angelic force and asserts that the soul "detaches" from the self in order to become the medium through which expression occurs:

When the soul of the poet has come to ripeness of thought, she detaches and sends away from it its poems or songs,—a fearless, sleepless, deathless pro-

geny, which is not exposed to the accidents of the weary kingdom of time: a
fearless vivacious offspring, clad with wings (such as the virtue of the soul out
of which they came), which carry them fast and far, and infix them irrecoverably into the hearts of men. (cw 3 : 14)

By concentrating not on the poet as the author of a text but on the process
of transmission through which Spirit passes from author to audience, Emerson incrementally eliminates the poet's presence. Ultimately, it is not the
poet that speaks, but the poem itself; and the poem, "clad with wings,"
becomes fixed "irrecoverably" in the "hearts of men." Through this tran-
substantiation of the Spirit from poet to poem to reader, Emerson meta-
phorically expresses his desire to transmit Spirit in a way that transcends
both human agency and the mediatory instruments through which communication takes place. In this passage, the form of mediation that Emerson envisions for the political spirit paradoxically transcends language. The
poet's inspiration moves directly into the hearts of his or her auditors.

Even though he does not explain the mechanics through which the poet
achieves this end, Emerson undoubtedly foresees a public role for the poet.
As he puts it, also in "The Poet": "The Poet is representative. He stands
among partial men for the complete man and apprises us not of his wealth;
but of the common wealth" (cw 3 : 4). The poet speaks not of himself but
of the things that all hold in common. Later in the same essay he reiterates
this point, this time emphasizing continuities between the poet's two functions, seer and sayer: "The Poet is representative of man in virtue of being
the largest power to receive and to impart." The poet's ability to merge
these two functions has immediate consequences for the way his contemporaries see their world:

> For as it is dislocation and detachment from the life of God, that makes things
> ugly, the poet, who re-attaches things to nature and the Whole,—re-attaching
> even artificial things, and violations of nature, to nature, by a deeper insight,—
> disposes very easily of the most disagreeable facts. Readers of poetry see the
> factory-village, and the railway, and fancy that the poetry of the landscape is
> broken up by these; for these works of art are not yet consecrated in their
> reading; but the poet sees them fall within the great Order not less than the
> beehive or the spider's geometrical web. (cw 3 : 11)

The poet's voice explains, justifies, and situates all elements of experience
in a "great Order." All things, even the most ugly, can then be recognized
as necessary, even as divine.

Emerson also describes the effect of this process in explicitly political terms. As the poet speaks, he exerts a force that has the potential to transform both self and society. In "The Uses of Great Men," Emerson explains that "letting in this element of reason" permits the great man to "abolish himself and all heroes, . . . irrespective of persons, this subtilizer and irresistible upward force, in our thought, destroying individualism;—the power so great, that the potentate is nothing. Then he is a monarch who gives a constitution to his people; a pontiff, who preaches the equality of souls and releases his servants from their barbarous homages; an emperor who can spare his empire" (cw 4 : 14). In the act of releasing the "irresistible upward force" of the Spirit, the poet is compelled to "abolish himself" along with all the others in his "empire" as he and they have their individualism destroyed and are liberated by the coalescence of Spirit and word. To make this transformation vivid, Emerson creates images of highly centralized political structures—monarchical, papal, imperial—being re-created in egalitarian or democratic forms.

By envisioning the public expression of the Spirit as a vehicle of social reform, Emerson raises the requirements for the language that motivates political action to the very highest level. The would-be poet cannot speak in a way that represents a sectarian religious or partisan political interest. He must always speak in tones that present universal truths. The difficulty of inventing a language that satisfies these two requirements—ideological impartiality and perfect transparency of meaning—takes the theory of the political spirit to its farthest limit. Needless to say, though, Emerson found no one who satisfied the demands of mediation and who could both "receive," or "see," and "impart," or "say," the authentic sign.

The lack of any such poet is important in relation to Emerson's effort to imagine the Spirit as a public force that might guide social reform movements. Without the actual presence of the poet, the Spirit remains largely inarticulate, even for Emerson. He can believe in a universal "Great Order," and even catch occasional glimpses of it as he had on the Boston Common. Emerson's sense of the lack of the great poetic reconciler and reformer becomes ominously apparent as he concedes that "I look in vain for the poet whom I describe. We do not, with sufficient plainness, or sufficient profoundness, address ourselves to life, nor dare we chaunt our own times and social circumstance. . . . Time and nature yield us many gifts, but not yet the timely man, the new religion, the reconciler, whom all things await" (cw 3 : 21). Emerson's admission that he dare not "chaunt" his own times is telling. It indicates the fundamental level on which he holds that the elements of experience lacked the kind of order and continuity that would permit him to see his society as an organic whole.

Yet, as Emerson recognized intermittently throughout his career, the private experience and the public expression of Spirit can never be merged perfectly. This conclusion crops up in Emerson's thought from the 1830s onward, though he often imagined that it could be overcome through acts of will.[12] He marks his recognition of the problem of mediation in two ways: first, by continuity between his statements on social conditions and on language, and second, by his effort to imagine language in organic terms. In "The Divinity School Address," he notes that the restrictions language imposes on expression compel certain divisions: "[I]n speech," he writes, "we must sever, and describe or suggest by painful enumeration of many particulars." The ideas that permit one to transcend material relations "refuse to be adequately stated. They will not . . . be written out on paper, or spoken by the tongue" (*cw* 1 : 77). He echoes this image of "painful" fragmentation a year later when he begins "The American Scholar" by describing the "*divided* or social state" of 1830s America as one in which "the members have suffered amputation from the trunk, and strut about so many walking monsters,—a good finger, a neck, a stomach, an elbow, but never a man" (*cw* 1 : 53). Language implies a division of semantic labor among different words much like that which occurs among different people in society. Each word has flexible but real semantic boundaries. These boundaries force the speaker to "sever" the overarching unity of spiritual laws. From very early in his career, Emerson recognized that the material limitations of words always threaten to prevent the emergence of a language that can express the Spirit without distortion.

During the 1830s, though, this recognition coexisted with Emerson's organic theory of signification. When he first began analyzing language in the early 1830s, Emerson held that language emerged directly out of nature, or at least, that language was mimetic rather than arbitrary. This approach permitted Emerson to see language as a phenomenon that had more in common with nature than with society. From this point of view, the problem that reformers were having in getting through to the people was the same as that which Emerson attributes to the "spectral" preacher of "The Divinity School Address." They spoke with a language of convention rather than one that was drawn directly from nature.

Emerson begins to develop his organic theory of language in the introductory section of his 1835 essay "English Literature." Already, Emerson is identifying verbal expression as the vital goal of life: "The Ideas in every man's mind make him what he is. His whole action and endeavor in the world is to utter and give an external shape to those thoughts . . . Of the various ways in which man endeavors to utter the great invisible nature which gives him life, the most perfect vehicle of his meaning is Language" (EL 1:219).

In this lecture, Emerson vacillates between the position that words represent ideas that have a psychological origin and the position that they represent images from external nature that are then applied to ideas. However, Emerson already understands language as a vehicle that can collapse inner and outer nature. He writes that "The objects without him are more than commodities. Whilst they minister to the senses sensual gratification, they minister to the mind as vehicles and symbols of thought. All language is a naming of invisible and spiritual things from visible things. . . . The use of the outer creation is to give us language for the beings and changes of the inward creation" (EL 220). Although the material of language may come from the realm of outer experience, the use of language requires that one seek the proper analogy between the inner object of representation and its outer manifestation.

In "English Literature," Emerson defines three key elements of his theory of language that would shape his approach to communication for the first half of his career: the word, a referent in the realm of nature, and a referent in the intellectual or spiritual realm. When Emerson revised this lecture for publication in the "Language" section of *Nature*, he integrated these three elements into a ranked list of the ways in which Nature is the "vehicle of thought:"

1. Words are signs of natural facts.
2. Particular natural facts are symbols of particular spiritual facts.
3. Nature is the symbol of Spirit. (CW 1:17)

This list describes a logical referential progression that moves from the verbal to the material, then from the material to the spiritual, and finally from the spiritual to the universal. In this list, Emerson defines a process of mediation that is the poet-prophet's task to perfect. He sees each of the elements on his list as a mimetic image of the others.

He also adapts the section of "English Literature" on the analogic nature of language for use in *Nature*, reiterating that "Every word which is used to express a moral or intellectual fact, if traced to its root, is found to be borrowed from some material appearance. *Right* originally means *straight*; *wrong* means *twisted*," and so on. But he also argues that signification is not arbitrary. After working his way from simple images through abstract concepts such as reason, Emerson concludes that "It is easily seen that there is nothing lucky or capricious in these analogies, but that they are constant, and pervade nature" (*cw* 1:18–19). In Emerson's view at this early stage of his career, problems in expression derive less from inherent characteristics of language than from the individual's inability to get the analogies right and to discover organic signs that will express Spirit without distortion. Failure to do so marks an internalized condition that reflects the institutionalized distance between society and nature:

> A man's power to connect his thought with its proper symbol, and so to utter it, depends on the simplicity of his character, that is, upon his love of truth and his desire to communicate it without loss. The corruption of man is followed by the corruption of language. When simplicity of character and the sovereignty of ideas is broken up by the prevalence of secondary desires, the desire of riches, the desire of pleasure, the desire of power, the desire of praise,—and duplicity and falsehood take place of simplicity and truth, the power over nature as an interpreter of the will, is in a degree lost. (*cw* 1:20)

The link that Emerson draws between character and the ability to utter authentic signs implies the problem of mediation. The fewer mediatory elements that intervene between nature and utterance, the more likely a speaker is to "connect his thought with its proper symbol." In the most forceful image that *Nature* offers of disconnection and of the potential power that organic signification holds, Emerson compares language to a volcano: "We are like travelers using the cinders of a volcano to roast their eggs" (*cw* 1:21). The perfect mediator could tap into the energy within the volcano and have an impact on his or her society that would both embody and mirror a volcanic irruption.

The radical opposite of this is Emerson's extreme denunciations of certain kinds of political rhetoric, most notably, perhaps, of Daniel Webster's March 7, 1850, speech in support of the omnibus bill that included the Fugitive Slave Law (*aw* 53–72). In both cases, the natural and the conventional, the fulcrum on which Emerson's opinion rests is his confidence in the theoretical possibility that inspired speakers can create organic images that irreducibly connect their inner signifieds to their outer signifiers. In this respect, F. O. Matthiessen was right when he argued that Emerson sought an organic language through which he can fuse words with things. In comparing Emerson's theory of language to Wordsworth's and Coleridge's, Matthiessen concludes that Emerson "would have agreed that when the poet is receptive to the divine effluence, his mind is endowed directly with the word that embodies the thing." [13] Conversely, when Emerson talks about the degradation of language, he is talking about the emergence of arbitrary rather than organic signification.

In his early essays that focus on the poet-prophet figure, he also, without fully recognizing the implications of it, points out problems in mediation that signal inconsistencies in his theory of the organic nature of language. In "The American Scholar," written one year after he propounded his theory in *Nature*, Emerson admits that the historicity of language hinders the would-be poet's ability to transmit Spirit without distortion. Just as "no air-pump can by any means make a perfect vacuum," Emerson points out, "so neither can any artist entirely exclude the conventional, the local, the perishable from his book, or write a book of pure thought, that shall be as efficient, in all respects, to a remote posterity, as to cotemporaries" (*cw* 1: 55–56). This poses a theoretical problem because even if a poet capable of uttering the authentic sign were to emerge, at the very moment that this poet fulfills his or her function as the "namer" and "re-attaches things to nature and the whole," he also, by fixing meaning in a quasi-material object, taints the perfection of the utterance and begins the process of devitalization. Emerson's own theory of language places the poet in a double bind: at the same moment that the poet expresses a truth that speaks with authority to his contemporaries, he creates a golden calf for succeeding generations.

Emerson's conflicting impulses to see signs as material objects that exist in historical contexts and as organic symbols that can bridge the gap between the material realm and a transcendent realm of universal truth work in a contrapuntal relationship. In combination they create what Michael Lopez calls "creative antagonism," permitting Emerson to modulate his voice and point of view among apparently contradictory positions. [14] Thus, in what is well recognized as the great dialogic moment of Emerson's career, he begins *Essays: Second Series* by placing "The Poet," the essay that marks his finest expression of the political spirit, next to "Experience," the essay that marks his finest expression of the anxiety that the political spirit may represent an unattainable ideal. As "Experience" does in so many other ways, it also marks a turning point in Emerson's confidence in organic language.

Through essays such as "Divinity School Address," "The American Scholar," and especially "The Poet," Emerson defines images of the mediator who can utter the authentic sign. The potential of the Spirit as a voice of reform in the public realm hinges on the relationship between the personal experience and the public expression of inspired individuals. This connection between private experience and public utterance places Emerson's images of archetypal mediatory figures such as poets, scholars, and ministers at the center of his aspiration for the political spirit. As Frank Shuffleton has recently put it, the "younger Emerson often preferred to think about biographical characters as agents of the sublime." [15] These characters are abstract, paradigmatic images who represent platonic ideals and contrast with the historical images of representative men that Emerson began after completing work on *Essays: Second Series* in the early autumn of 1844.[16] His emphasis on abstract models of poet-prophet figures in major essays of the 1830s is a displacement of the real stumbling block that lay between an experience of the Spirit and its public expression. The problem, as Emerson explains in "Experience," lay less in the lack of inspiration and more in the linguistic obstacles that prevented inspiration from achieving broad public expression.

In "Experience" Emerson confesses, "I know better than to claim any completeness for my picture. I am a fragment, and this [essay] is a fragment of me. I can very confidently announce one or another law, which throws itself into relief and form, but I am too young yet by some ages to compile a code" (cw 3:47). Though he will scold Thoreau for failing to "engineer for all mankind," Emerson not only asserts that his own highest aspiration is to write a "code" but also admits that he is not up to the task. At the heart of his failure he finds a problem with his instruments: "It is very unhappy, but too late to be helped, the discovery we have made, that we exist. The discovery is called the Fall of Man. Ever afterwards, we suspect our instruments" (cw 3:43). For Emerson, the discovery of one's own existence, self-consciousness, marks nothing less than alienation from the Spirit and severance from the cosmic "trunk" that he hoped to repair. Self-consciousness represents the original fault line, the first fissure in the process of fragmentation that the political spirit is meant to counteract. Exacerbating this primary alienation is a lesser one, the consequent alienation of individuals from other individuals. Language—as well as it might conform to the poet's desire—never achieves perfect universality of expression. It proves to be a human rather than a divine instrument. Worse, it proves to be a social institution more like a church or a political system than an organic phenomenon.

The "suspect instrument" that prevents undistorted, perfectly transparent communication makes alienation from humankind inevitable, at least when it comes to expressing one's most inspired, or deeply held, or tragic sentiments. As Barbara Packer and others have argued, the skepticism of Emerson's old age may partly have been a result of the linguistic and contextual hurdles that unavoidably lead to this form of alienation.[17] Though Emerson never lost faith in the universality of Spirit, in "Experience" he feels compelled to admit the possibility that human instruments may be incapable of making genius universally intelligible.

Though Emerson never explicitly renounces or repudiates the organic theory of language that he developed in the 1830s, in the years after 1844 he seems to be working from significantly different assumptions about the nature of language. Beginning with the lectures on representative men that he delivered beginning in January of 1845, Emerson is less inclined to construct theoretical ideals that are unrestrained by a recognition of human limitations.[18] Rather, he tends to speak about those who mediate spiritual insight for the masses in more pragmatic and historical tones.[19] Especially in *Representative Men*, but also to a lesser extent in *English Traits* and *The Conduct of Life*, Emerson compares his sense of the ideal with an equally strong sense of the real and the possible. Mark Patterson goes so far as to read a chiastic structure into the relationship between *Nature* and *Representative Men*, arguing that "one ought to approach this volume as *Nature* reversed; instead of beginning with commodity and ending in idealism and Spirit, it begins with Plato's idealism and progresses toward Napoleon's use of the world as commodity."[20]

Emerson's approach to the great-man figure in *Representative Men* is particularly important. In contrast to his early essays on the scholar and the poet, the essays that comprise this book focus on actual, historical figures. Each of the figures that he discusses represents an aspect or dimension of the character that Emerson had previously attributed to the poet. As one critic has insightfully pointed out, the idea of synthesis becomes a problem in the second half of Emerson's career.[21] Although the figures he describes in *Representative Men* give public expression to the Spirit, they differ from the ideal poet in that their public discourses remain "partial," or imperfect. Ironically, the partiality that is the defining characteristic of the representative symbolizes the type of social relation that had kept Emerson out of reform activism and that he sought to overcome through his theory of the political spirit. Emerson's idea of the relationship between the representative and his society also more closely resembles the form of Emerson's own participation in the antislavery movement from 1844 onward. As David Jacobson and David Robinson have emphasized, *Representative Men* marks a key turning point in the evolving ascendancy of the pragmatic over the idealistic strains of Emerson's thought.[22]

Emerson's essay "The Uses of Great Men," which serves as the introduction to *Representative Men*, is a good counterpart to earlier essays such as "The Poet" and "The American Scholar" because it defines the concept of the representative in the same kind of paradigmatic terms that the earlier essays defined the ideal spokesperson of the Spirit.[23] This essay marks the culmination of a process of thought about the problem of mediation that Emerson had been intermittently pursuing since the 1830s. As he remarked in his notebook in 1834, "I like well the doctrine 'that every great man, Napoleon himself, is an Idealist, a poet with different degrees of Utterance'" (*JMN* 4:363). The great men Emerson analyzes in *Representative Men* are characterized by their ability to communicate with and command the loyalties of discrete groups in society. But their motivations, like the truths of their discoveries, are imperfectly expressed and thus fall short of being universally felt. Like the members of the nonresistance society that he had advised in "New England Reformers," the representative speaks in tones that only a few people recognize as the authentic sign.

Nonetheless, the representative does have the power to communicate his insight in a way that strikes *some* members of the society to the quick. In Emerson's view, a figure such as Napoleon combines a source of power that is derived from imperfect insight into Spirit with an expressive power that is capable of winning a substantial public following. Thus, representatives are beneficial to their societies because they can exhort the members of society to a general uplift. As Emerson puts it, emphasizing the ability of great men to transcend the limitations of their historical moment: "Men resemble their contemporaries, even more than their progenitors. . . . We learn of our contemporaries what they know, without effort, and almost through the pores of the skin. . . . But we stop where they stop. Very hardly can we take another step. The great, or such as hold of nature, and transcend fashions, by their fidelity to universal ideas, are saviours from these federal errors, and defend us from our contemporaries. They are the exceptions which we want, where all grows alike" (*CW* 4:15). In this passage, Emerson alludes to key attributes of the poet. The "great" are somehow directly connected to nature, mainly through their "fidelity to universal ideas." Fidelity to the universal permits the great man to exemplify a better world, a world where historical and personal differences do not obtain. "One's contemporaries," on the other hand, create a kind of contextual ballast that works against the aspirations that great men provoke.

The Emersonian representative, though, must be considered a diminished figure, at least when measured against the standard of the poet. This
is so because the representative is partial both in the sense of exemplifying
a portion of society rather than the whole *and* in the sense of being incomplete. The great men Emerson describes in *Representative Men* embody the
spiritual essence of a certain group or subset of the nation as a whole.[24] In
this respect, perhaps ironically, Emerson posits a causal theory for the factionalization that he believed to be disrupting American society. The representative expresses partial, incomplete truth, albeit in a way that has a
paradoxically concentrated purity. Yet this imperfect representation, given
the fact that language is an imperfect instrument, may be the best that human ingenuity can devise. It may be the mode in which people are fated to
muddle along.

The figures of *Representative Men* define "partial" poets that mark Emerson's adjustment to the problems he encountered in "Experience." For
Emerson, Napoleon serves as the clearest example of the representative's
characteristic partiality.[25] "The middle class everywhere," Emerson asserts,
"has pointed out Napoleon as the incarnate Democrat." But Napoleon
stands as the incarnation of only the limited interests of the bourgeoisie:
"'God has granted,' says the Koran, 'to every people a prophet in its own
tongue.' Paris and London and New York, the spirit of commerce, of
money, and material power, were also to have their prophet, and Bonaparte
was qualified and sent" (*cw* 4:130).

Napoleon represents the interests of the bourgeoisie so fully that his own
personality comes to represent his social environment: "[A] man of Napoleon's stamp almost ceases to have a private speech and opinion. He is so
largely receptive, and is so placed, that he comes to be a bureau for all the
intelligence, wit, and power, of the age and country." Though he may signify the spirit of the age, it is also true that "a man of Napoleon's truth of
adaptation to the mind of the masses around him, becomes not merely representative, but actually a monopolizer and usurper of other minds" (*cw* 4:
130–31). As a monopolizer and usurper, the representative poses a danger
to his or her society. Rather than liberating people, "a man of Napoleon's
stamp" threatens to eclipse other people's autonomy. The representative,
in his ambiguous position as a demi-poet, thus embodies a tension between
self-negation in that he "almost ceases to have a private speech and opinion," an attribute of the true poet, and the kind of self-aggrandizement that
characterizes the demagogue.

As Emerson recognized in the representative, the combination of spiritual insight and compelling but imperfect expression can have dangerous consequences. "The imbecility of men," he writes, "is always inviting the impudence of power. It is the delight of vulgar talent to dazzle and to blind the beholder" (*cw* 4:11). Unless they transmit the power that their access to the Spirit offers, representatives end up creating cults that raise them to a quasi-divine status. By performing "miracles"—be they military as in Napoleon's case or artistic as in Shakespeare's—the representative offers public proof of his access to divinity. Ironically, however, through "partial" utterance the representative threatens to divert attention that properly should be directed toward the Spirit and array it around his or her self.

Though the representative's ability to communicate effectively supports the possibility of bringing the Spirit into the public realm, the representative also threatens to blot out the Spirit and substitute the self as the source of his own inspiration. In this respect he is an opaque rather than a transparent figure, and he speaks an opaque rather than a transparent language. Yet this opacity of self-expression, which is the crucial characteristic of the representative, marks more than the personal limitation of a Napoleon or a Shakespeare. It also marks an irreducible aspect of social life. In spite of Emerson's unwavering belief that transcendence can occasionally occur on an individual level, the fact that daily life is structured by material relations and social institutions makes it all but impossible for Emerson to believe that his own desire for an organic society can ever serve as a realistic model for reform. Whereas the poet cancels out himself and language through a seamless mediation of nature and expression, the representative retains all the problems that Emerson discovers in the mediatory function of language. Thus language itself, through the partiality of the word, is the mirror image of "the divided or social state" that Emerson laments in "The American Scholar." The representative is the poet accommodated to the problem of language.

The turning point in the process through which the poet is reinvented as the representative coincides with Emerson's emergence as an abolitionist. This process of intellectual development in Emerson's thought played a significant role in enabling him to participate in reform movements and to become an increasingly radical abolitionist in the 1850s. In a way, this progression marks another "fall" or skeptical turn in Emerson's thought. But it also has the advantage of rendering moot an important ethical dilemma. As long as Emerson could hold out the poet's ability to utter the authentic sign as a practical reality, for him to pick a side on social and political questions rather than to speak for universal reform would necessarily have felt like an ethical compromise. But once Emerson explicitly recognized the coexistence of fragmentation, language, and society as philosophical facts, political ethics became a question of speaking for the good rather than for the whole. In this respect, Emerson's failed effort to imagine a reform that emerged from a language that transcended partiality and could provoke consensus also marks a kind of liberation.

NOTES

1. Len Gougeon's book *Virtue's Hero* (Athens: University of Georgia Press, 1990) is the central text in the reconstruction of Emerson's career as a reformer. Gougeon reads Emerson's emergence as an abolitionist in the 1840s as the vital turning point in Emerson's career, one that eclipses in importance events such as his resignation from the ministry in 1832 or his turn toward pragmatism or skepticism in the later 1840s. Gougeon discusses the history of biographical commentary on the relationship between Emerson's transcendentalism and his reform activities in the chapter titled "Abolition and the Biographers" (2–23). Robert D. Richardson, in *Emerson: The Mind on Fire* (Berkeley: University of California Press, 1995) also emphasizes the influence of outside actors such as Emerson's wife and brother on his initial involvement in reform, especially his participation in the Cherokee removal crisis (see Richardson's chapter "The Peace Principle and the Cherokee Trail of Tears"). He asserts, however, that Emerson comes into his own as a reformer in the period following the passage of the Fugitive Slave Act in 1850 (see Richardson's chapter "The Fugitive Slave Act"). In *Emerson on the Scholar* (Columbia: University of Missouri Press, 1992), Merton Sealts also underscores the importance of the transition that takes place in the early 1850s and in his chapter titled "Other Slaves to Free, 1851–1860," reads Emerson's book *The Conduct of Life* as a study of challenges to human freedom that was shaped by his involvement in the antislavery movement.

2. Mary Kupiec Cayton identifies the emergence of this principle most strongly with the period just following Emerson's resignation from the ministry. In Cayton's view, while sectarianism was the keynote of Emerson's dissatisfaction with the clergy, factionalism was the keynote of his dissatisfaction with society as a whole. See *Emerson's Emergence: Self and Society in the Transformation of New England, 1800–1845* (Chapel Hill: University of North Carolina Press, 1989), pp. 164–65. Gougeon approaches the issue of sectarianism and factionalism as primarily a methodological dilemma. Though he lived in a family and community of active abolitionists, and in his private writings took an antislavery position from the 1830s onward, Gougeon argues, earlier in his career Emerson chose to advocate a "broad-based" respect for self-culture rather than to align himself with any particular faction (*VH* 35).

3. For readings of Emerson's attitude toward forms of political debate, see Daniel Aaron, "Emerson and the Progressive Tradition," in *Emerson: A Selection of*

Critical Essays, ed. Milton R. Konvitz and Stephen E. Whicher (Englewood Cliffs: Prentice-Hall, 1962), pp. 85–100; Perry Miller, "Emersonian Genius and the American Democracy," in Konvitz and Whicher, *Emerson*, pp. 72–85; William R. Hutchinson, *The Transcendentalist Ministers: Church and Reform in the New England Renaissance* (New Haven: Yale Univ. Press, 1959); and Mary Kupiec Cayton, *Emerson's Emergence*, pp. 58–69. For discussions that focus on Emerson's ambivalence toward an economy that was becoming both more robust and more fractious see Michael T. Gilmore, "Emerson and the Persistence of Commodity," in *Emerson, Prospect and Retrospect*, ed. Joel Porte (Cambridge, Mass.: Harvard Univ. Press, 1982) pp. 65–85; and John Peacock, "Self-Reliance and Corporate Destiny: Emerson's Dialectic of Culture," *ESQ* 29 (1983) pp. 59–72.

4. Sacvan Bercovitch, *The Rites of Assent: Transformations in the Symbolic Construction of America* (New York: Routledge, 1993), p. 311.

5. *Ibid.*, p. 318.

6. This sentence distorts Bercovitch's argument, which presents Emerson's participation in a process through which Jacksonian Americans invested a particular construction of individualism with salvific powers that undermined the possibility of developing socialist ideologies in America that are similar to those that were then taking hold in Europe.

7. Christopher Newfield, *The Emerson Effect: Individualism and Submission in America* (Chicago: University of Chicago Press, 1996), pp. 17–39.

8. Ralph Waldo Emerson, "Emerson's 'Thoreau': A New Edition From Manuscript" in *Studies in the American Renaissance* ed. Joel Myerson (Boston: Twayne, 1979), p. 53.

9. George Kateb, *Emerson and Self-Reliance* (Thousand Oaks, CA: Sage Publications, 1995), p. 182.

10. Sealts offers a history of the development of Emerson's thought about mediation in his discussions of "conversion." See Sealts, *Emerson on the Scholar*, pp. 90–92, 105–8, 235–40.

11. *Ibid.*, pp. 90–92.

12. Writings that exemplify this mode of mediation are the "Discipline" section on *Nature*, the essay "Circles," and the conclusion of "The Divinity School Address" where Emerson advises Harvard's aspiring ministers that the answer to waning public faith is "first, soul, and second, soul, and evermore, soul" (*CW* 1:92). Emerson's interest in the idea of a supernaturally powerful "will" has also produced a resurgent line of critical commentary. Both Michael Lopez and George Kateb emphasize Emerson's figuration of will as a form of power. This important line of thought about mediation marks a counterpart to the one I am developing in this essay. Analysis of the Emersonian will in books such as Stanley Cavell's *Conditions Handsome and Unhandsome: The Constitution of Emersonian Perfectionism* (LaSalle, IL: Open Court, 1990); Michael Lopez's *Emerson and Power: Creative Antagonism in the Nineteenth Century* (De Kalb: Northern Illinois Univ. Press, 1995); and Kateb's *Emerson and Self-Reliance* deal with the problem of constructing psychological power

on an individual level rather than with developing political power that is oriented toward reform. This line of thought is most important in its efforts to reconcile Emerson's romantic construction of selfhood with contemporary philosophical perspectives that emphasize the extent to which external normative pressures define selfhood. See especially Cavell's lecture "Aversive Thinking: Emersonian Representations in Heideger and Nietzsche" in *Philosophical Passages: Wiggenstein, Emerson, Austin, Derrida* (Oxford, UK: Blackwell, 1995); Lopez's chapter "The Rhetoric of War" (pp. 190–210); and Kateb's chapter "Redeeming the Frustrations of Experience" (pp. 37–60).

13. F. O. Matthiessen, *American Renaissance: Art and Expression in the Age of Emerson and Whitman.* (New York: Oxford Univ. Press, 1941 [1968]), p. 31.

14. Lopez, *Emerson and Power*, pp. 3–4.

15. Frank Shuffelton, "Emerson's Politics of Biography and History," in *Emersonian Circles: Essays in Honor of Joel Myerson*, ed. Wesley T. Mott and Robert E. Burkholder (Rochester: University of Rochester Press, 1997), p. 57.

16. Albert J. von Frank, *An Emerson Chronology* (New York: Macmillan Library Reference, 1994), pp. 188–92.

17. John Michael, *Emerson and Skepticism: The Cipher of the World* (Baltimore: John Hopkins Univ. Press, 1988); Stephen Whicher, *Freedom and Fate: An Inner Life of Ralph Waldo Emerson* (Philadelphia: University of Pennsylvania Press, 1953), pp. 109–22; Barbara Packer, *Emerson's Fall: A New Interpretation of the Major Essays* (New York: Continuum, 1982), pp. 181–204.

18. Von Frank, *Emerson Chronology*, p. 194.

19. Much of my understanding of the evolution of Emerson's theory of language derives from David Robinson's articulation of the evolution of the pragmatic strain of Emerson's thought. Emerson's increased attention to context in his thought about great men as exemplified in the transition from the abstractions of "The American Scholar" to the historicity of *Representative Men* reflects his effort to imagine communication through the filter of what Robinson calls "ethical pragmatism." See his *Emerson and the Conduct of Life: Pragmatism and Ethical Purpose in the Later Work* (Cambridge: Cambridge Univ. Press, 1993).

20. Mark Patterson, "Emerson, Napoleon, and the Concept of the Representative," *ESQ* 31 (4th quarter 1985): 237.

21. Gustaaf Van Cromphout, "Emerson and the Dialectics of History" *PMLA* 91 (1976), p. 59.

22. See David Jacobson, *Emerson's Pragmatic Vision: The Dance of the Eye* (University Park: Pennsylvania State Univ. Press, 1993); and Robinson, *Emerson and the Conduct of Life*, pp. 89–110.

23. Shuffleton, "Emerson's Politics of Biography," p. 58.

24. Patterson, "Emerson, Napoleon," pp. 230–42.

25. *Ibid.*, pp. 230–31; and Joel Porte, *Representative Man: Ralph Waldo Emerson in His Times* (New York: Oxford Univ. Press, 1979), pp. 108–10.

LINCK C. JOHNSON

Emerson, Thoreau's Arrest, and the Trials of American Manhood

FOR REASONS THAT REVEAL more about twentieth-century attitudes than nineteenth-century actualities, one of the most famous incidents in the history of antebellum reform was Henry Thoreau's arrest in July 1846, when he spent a night in jail for his refusal to pay a tax to the state of Massachusetts. In accounts of that event, Emerson's role is at best incidental and, at worst, ignoble. Bronson Alcott recorded that Emerson thought Thoreau's act was "mean and skulking, and in bad taste," thereby suggesting that for Emerson the main issues were manliness and gentility (*JA* 183). A celebrated bit of apocrypha casts Emerson in an even more unflattering light, as a kind of straight man to Thoreau's passionate idealist. In that often-repeated story, Emerson came to the jail, where, standing outside the bars, he disapprovingly asked, "Henry, why are you there?"—to which Thoreau triumphantly replied, "Why are *you* not *here*?" [1] The two friends thus fall naturally into the postures in which posterity has so often fixed them: Emerson, the social and political moderate who shied away from the actions his own radical philosophy seemed to dictate; and Thoreau, the unyielding man of principle who in "Resistance to Civil Government" later declared: "Under a government which imprisons any unjustly, the true place for a just man is also a prison." [2]

There is at least a germ of truth in that imagined confrontation, but Emerson's response to Thoreau's arrest was far more complex and ambivalent than such anecdotes suggest. Emerson did wonder why Thoreau was in prison; in fact, following his friend's arrest, Emerson jotted down an extended entry in his journal, where he sought to clarify the individual's proper relationship to the state. Emerson, however, was ultimately far less concerned with the rationale for the act than its consequences for Thoreau,

35

who he feared was in danger of losing sight of his proper work and primary vocation. Emerson's journal entry thus echoed a series of addresses he delivered during the early 1840s, when he sought to defend his own scholarly vocation against the pressing claims of reform, which had gained the allegiance of so many of his friends and associates. When Thoreau went to prison rather than paying his tax, Emerson clearly felt betrayed by the man who had previously been his strongest ally in the ongoing skirmishes with the reformers. Although in 1846 he and Thoreau found themselves on opposite sides of the bars, they had previously taken the same stand, most conspicuously at Amory Hall, Boston, where in 1844 Emerson had delivered "New England Reformers" and Thoreau had delivered a kindred lecture on the conservative and the reformer.

But Emerson, no less than Thoreau, found it enormously difficult to sustain the seemingly unassailable position they had defended at Amory Hall. The lectures they delivered there at once marked the culmination of their debate with the communitarians, the reformers who had absorbed most of their attention prior to 1844, and the beginning of a more complex and many-sided debate over slavery generated by the annexation of Texas and the Mexican War. From 1844 to 1846, Emerson and Thoreau found themselves increasingly drawn into the antislavery crusade, the claims of which they had earlier so strenuously resisted. The critique of Thoreau's actions Emerson offered in 1846 was part of a struggle to answer a question both men had been grappling with: what was the scholar's proper relation to reform and the reformers? Emerson obviously shared his views with Thoreau, who vigorously defended his own actions in a lecture delivered in 1848 and published in 1849 as "Resistance to Civil Government." As his emphasis in that lecture on issues of manhood and vocation suggest, the lecture was in large part directed at Emerson, to whom Thoreau also briefly responded in "The Village" chapter of *Walden*, published in 1854. As he probably recognized, however, his most compelling reply to Emerson was not contained in *Walden*; it *was* that book, the writing of which was made possible by his own unswerving dedication to his private work, even after the passage of the Fugitive Slave Law in 1850 ignited a firestorm of controversy in New England. In contrast, Emerson was increasingly involved in the political debates of the early 1850s. By the time *Walden* was finally published in 1854, it was Emerson, far more than Thoreau, who had moved away from the position they had defended with such wit and vigor at Amory Hall in 1844.

When Emerson published "New England Reformers," the final chapter

in *Essays: Second Series*, he identified it as "A Lecture Read Before the Society in Amory Hall, on Sunday, 3 March, 1844." That "Society" was
composed of a radical group led by William Lloyd Garrison, the editor
of the *Liberator*, which rented Amory Hall for a series of Sunday lectures
on the subject of reform.[3] Emerson was consequently not speaking simply
about reformers but to reformers, both those in the audience, which was
drawn from various reform societies in Boston, and more obliquely to his
numerous friends and associates engaged in the work of reform, especially
George Ripley and other members of the Transcendentalist community
Brook Farm. Describing the costs of conforming to the conventions of society, Emerson in "Self-Reliance" had countered, "But do your work, and
I shall know you" (*cw* 2:32). He lifted that passage from an 1839 journal
entry entitled "Reform," in which he had expressed his gratitude to "these
beneficent reformers of all colors & qualities," whose demonstration of the
false usages of society helped establish the centrality of the self (*jmn* 7:
225). During the early 1840s, however, reform, with its organizations and
associations, came to embody for Emerson some of the same dangers that
"society" had represented to him during the late 1830s.[4] Consequently, at
the end of "New England Reformers" Emerson once again proclaimed the
primacy of private "work," insisting that "our own orbit is all our task, and
we need not assist the administration of the universe" (*cw* 3:166). Emerson
offered to those in the "Society in Amory Hall," and especially to those at
model societies like Brook Farm, the same lesson he had once offered to
members of the larger society: the lesson of work and of obedience to the
very soul of the self, the individual's only secure and reliable guide.

In his lecture on the conservative and the reformer delivered at Amory
Hall on the following Sunday, Thoreau amplified Emerson's message. In
"New England Reformers," Emerson sharply criticized what he characterized as the two major faults of "the movement party": "partiality," their
obsessive concern with a single wrong; and "their reliance on Association"
(*cw* 3:155). Similarly, although Thoreau's lecture concerned the failures
of both conservatism and reform, Thoreau devoted most of his attention
to the faults of the reformers, especially those involved in association. Dismissing "the importance of this unity or community of action," as he described it, Thoreau observed: "It is not the worst reason why the reform
should be a private and individual enterprise, that perchance the evil is private also."[5] That sentence later provided the germ of his critique of philanthropy in *Walden*, where he also incorporated a passage from the lecture in
which he exhorted members of his audience at Amory Hall to retire within

themselves, exploring the recesses of the soul. For Thoreau, as for Emerson, such personal reform could only be achieved through self-culture, an inward and ongoing process in harmony with the universal law of change and metamorphosis. Emphasizing that an individual's true calling is "a call upward, a voice from the heavens and not from society," he continued: "There is but one Great Cause. There are a million petty causes—and with every moment one such comes to an end. We ask for some pure product of man's hands—some life got in this old trade of getting a living—Some work done, which shall not be a mending—a cobbling—a reforming— . . . It is the delight of the ages, the free labor of man—even the creative and beautiful arts" (*C&R* 21, 22).

Like Emerson, Thoreau resisted the claims of those "petty causes" by appealing to the first cause of the universe. Ironically, however, by the time they spoke at Amory Hall in March 1844 both Emerson and Thoreau were being drawn into the cause of abolitionism, which began to challenge the "Great Cause" to which they had proclaimed their allegiance at Amory Hall. The antislavery crusade proved far harder to resist than association, the cause that had previously posed the greatest threat to their way of life and of work. Consequently, shortly after their appearances at Amory Hall, they offered their first public support of the abolitionists: Thoreau published a tribute to Nathaniel Rogers, the fiery editor of the antislavery newspaper *Herald of Freedom*, and Emerson delivered a major antislavery speech, "Address on the Emancipation of the Negroes in the British West Indies," on August 1, 1844. Further radicalized by the growing controversy over the annexation of Texas, Thoreau in 1845 wrote "Wendell Phillips Before Concord Lyceum," which was published in Garrison's *The Liberator*, while Emerson delivered another address commemorating emancipation in the West Indies on August 1, 1845.

Despite their public flirtation with the abolitionists, Emerson and Thoreau continued to devote most their energies to private labors. By the time he wrote his tribute to Phillips, Thoreau was already building his cabin at Walden Pond, where he moved on July 4, 1845. Following the abolitionists, who treated the national holiday as a day of mourning, Thoreau no doubt intended his withdrawal as a symbolic protest against a country that had abandoned the ideals of the Declaration of Independence and had consequently lost the right to commemorate the signing of that revered document. As the evangelical Garrison exclaimed in the final lines of "Fourth of July," a sonnet published in 1844:

But we will fall upon our bended knees,
And weep in bitterness of heart, and pray
Our God to save us from his gathering wrath;
We will no longer multiply our boasts
Of Liberty, till *All* are truly free.[6]

Thoreau, of course, did not withdraw to Walden Pond in order to weep or pray; certainly his move served personal and literary needs more than political ends. With the collapse of *The Dial* after the April 1844 issue, in which his tribute to Nathaniel Rogers had appeared, Thoreau lost his last ready outlet for his writings, including his unpublished lecture on the conservative and the reformer. By moving to the pond he hoped to gain the leisure and the freedom from financial concerns he needed in order to devote himself to even more ambitious literary projects. He immediately began to write his first book, *A Week on the Concord and Merrimack Rivers*, and to draft material for *Walden*, an account of his withdrawal from society to nature, from the public world of the reformers to the private realm of innocence and originality he had celebrated in his lecture at Amory Hall.

Emerson also retained a clear vision of his own distinct role as a writer and a speaker. In a journal entry drafted in a notebook containing extended passages for his 1844 address on emancipation, where he expressed admiration for the abolitionists, Emerson offered a sharply different estimate of their services to the country. "Does not he do more to abolish Slavery who works all day steadily in his garden, than he who goes to the abolition meeting & makes a speech?" he asked, implicitly comparing his forthcoming address with the kind of private labor he had recently celebrated in his lecture at Amory Hall: "The antislavery agency like so many of our employments is a suicidal business. Whilst I talk, some poor farmer drudges & slaves for me. It requires a just costume then, the office of agent or speaker, he should sit very low & speak very meekly like one compelled to do a degrading thing. . . . Let them do their own work. He who does his own work frees a slave. He who does not his own work, is a slave-holder" (*JMN* 9:126–27). Similarly, in his journal of 1845, immediately after jotting down a passage for his second address on emancipation, Emerson reminded himself of the dangers of being "headlong & abandoned to this one mania," as he referred to abolitionism (*JMN* 9:195). His determination to retain his own detachment and control was also revealed by his lecture series for 1845–46, "The Uses of Great Men," in which his political concerns found only oblique expression. Significantly, the central figure in the series was Plato, or the Philosopher, whom Emerson described as a "balanced soul" who "cannot forgive in himself a partiality, but is resolved that the two poles of thought shall appear in his statement" (cw 4 : 3 1).

As that passage suggests, Emerson still rejected what at Amory Hall he had characterized as the "partiality" of the reformers. In a brief speech delivered at an antislavery picnic in Dedham on July 4, 1846, six weeks after the declaration of war on Mexico, Emerson expressed his disgust "with the singular spectacle which our recent politics exhibit," congratulating the abolitionists for resisting "the political apathy of Massachusetts, and New England" (AW 41, 43). Nonetheless, he concluded the speech with a veiled critique of their narrow concerns, declaring: "There are other crimes besides Slavery and the Mexican war, and a more comprehensive faith, I hope, is coming, which will resolve all the parts of duty into a harmonious whole" (AW 44).

Even as he spoke at Dedham, Emerson clearly sought to distance himself from the other speakers, including Garrison, Phillips, and perhaps most particularly his friend William H. Channing, a tireless reformer who had recently turned his attention from Brook Farm and other communal experiments to the antislavery crusade. Emerson had addressed a similar message to reformers in his "Ode Inscribed to W. H. Channing," drafted a few weeks earlier, when he was completing work on *Poems*. The fact that Emerson had devoted so much time and effort to that volume during 1845–46 was itself an eloquent response to single-minded reformers like Channing, ironically hailed in the second line of the "Ode" as "The evil time's sole patriot." The poem has consequently most frequently been read as Emerson's apology for pursuing his private studies at a time of national crisis. For Emerson, however, the word "patriot" was rarely laudatory, whether it referred to zealots like Channing or to the jingoistic supporters of "the famous States / Harrying Mexico / With rifle and with knife" (w 9 : 76).

In fact, as Len Gougeon has convincingly argued, the "Ode" is neither a self-critique nor primarily an indictment of the country. Instead, it is a vigorous critique of the abolitionists, whose disunion policy had been fervently embraced by Channing (vh 1 14–15). In carefully chosen words that offer a lively illustration of his finely controlled irony throughout the poem, Emerson thus rhetorically queried: "What boots thy zeal, / O glowing friend, / That would indignant rend / The northland from the south? / Wherefore? to what good end?" In Emerson's view, the proponents of disunion naively believed that by cutting itself off from the South the North might escape the source of evil. He also perhaps implied what Channing's movement from cause to cause suggested, that such a restless seeker was unknowingly seeking his own liberation from sin. In response, Emerson suggested that slavery was only one outcropping of evil, which was inherent in the very nature of things. "Things are of the snake," he strikingly observed. If he exaggerated for effect the evil tendencies of things and of those who served the "law for thing," Emerson also affirmed the ultimate triumph of the "law for man"—of love, truth and harmony—which men like Channing had forgotten, but which Emerson vowed to serve (*w* 9:77–78).

His attitude toward militant activists like Channing, as well as his high hopes for Thoreau, helps explain why Emerson was so shocked and disapproving when his friend went to jail in July 1846. As sudden and seemingly unexpected as that event was, at least to Emerson, it nonetheless had a long foreground. In 1842 Bronson Alcott had been arrested for refusing to pay his poll tax, a tax levied on all adult males in Massachusetts. Apparently inspired by Alcott, Thoreau began to withhold his tax as early as 1842 or 1843, initially as a protest against slavery.[7] After ignoring the fact for several years, Sam Staples, the local constable, finally demanded payment, possibly because he was about to give up his job as tax collector and would otherwise have been forced to pay the tax himself in order to balance his books.[8] A good Democrat, Staples may also have been inflamed by the patriotic fervor generated by the outbreak of the Mexican War and further inflamed by the jingoistic editorials in the local newspaper, the *Concord Freeman*. Certainly Thoreau's own stand had been hardened by the outbreak of the war, and he flatly refused to pay the tax. After several warnings, he was finally arrested on July 22 or 23 and spent a night in the Middlesex County Jail. He was released the following morning after someone else, probably his Aunt Maria, paid the tax. And, as Emerson later recalled, when the "like annoyance was threatened the next year" some of Thoreau's "friends paid the tax, notwithstanding his protest," after which "he ceased to resist" (*w* 10:458).

Emerson's later account gave no hint of how appalled he was by the incident. But his objections to Thoreau's protest were far more complex than his immediate and highly exasperated comments to Alcott indicated. He not only viewed Thoreau's actions as "mean and skulking, and in bad taste," but he also believed they were futile. Emerson, however, was ultimately far less concerned with appearances than with the apparent implications and possible consequences of Thoreau's protest. Earlier in July he had read portions of the first draft of *A Week* to Emerson, who in a letter enthusiastically described the book as "a seven days' voyage in as many chapters, pastoral as Isaak Walton, spicy as flagroot, as broad & deep as Menu," a reference to the Hindu scriptures both men so admired (L 3 : 338). The spirit of those scriptures was profoundly quietistic, and Emerson was no doubt delighted that his friend had forged ahead with his work on *A Week* through the political turmoil of the previous two years. He also clearly believed that his friend and disciple was finally about to fulfill his literary promise, an optimistic belief that was shattered when Thoreau was arrested a week later. Indeed, Emerson feared that by going to prison rather than paying his tax Thoreau, like so many of their friends and former associates, was in danger of losing sight of his proper work and primary vocation.

In a dramatic journal entry written a few days after Thoreau's imprisonment, Emerson desperately sought to sort out his ambivalent reactions to the event and to resolve some of the tensions inherent in his own political position.[9] "Is not America more than ever wanting in the male principle?" he contemptuously asked, casting a hard eye on its political leaders and bemoaning its lack of "great captains." He thus compared the "rabble at Washington," who have "a sort of genius of a bold & manly cast, though Satanic," with "the snivelling opposition," men like Governor Briggs, Congressman Winthrop, and even Senator Webster, obsequious and compliant Whigs upon whom the Democrats "calculated rightly." "My friend Mr Thoreau has gone to jail rather than pay his tax," he continued. "On him they could not calculate. The abolitionists denounce the war & give much time to it, but they pay the tax" (*JMN* 9 : 444–45).

Yet, much as he admired Thoreau's manly stand, Emerson could not accept the ground upon which his friend stood. Describing the state as "a poor good beast who means the best," he insisted that one should not grudge it a little feed: "You who are a man walking cleanly on two feet will not pick a quarrel with a poor cow. Take this handful of clover & welcome. But if you go to hook me when I walk in the fields, then, poor cow, I will cut your throat." Because of his confusing shift from "you" to "I," it is not clear whether Emerson was comparing Thoreau's act to that swift and violent response or suggesting that such a response would be justified if the state actually offered violence to the man. In either case, Emerson clearly believed that the act was not justified under the circumstances, in which Thoreau rather than the state was the aggressor. "Don't run amuck against the world," he pleaded. "Have a good case to try the question on. . . . Socrates was told he should not teach. 'Please God, but I will.' And he could die well for that. And Jesus had a cause. You will get one by & by. But now I have no sympathy" (*JMN* 9:446).

Instead of following the lead of those heroic individuals, Emerson suggested that Thoreau was simply adopting the spurious arguments and imitating the misguided actions of far lesser men. Observing that Alcott "thought he could find as good a ground for quarrel in the state tax as Socrates did in the Edict of the Judges," Emerson replied: "Then I say, Be Consistent, & never more put an apple or a kernel of corn into your mouth. Would you feed the devil? Say boldly 'There is a sword sharp enough to cut sheer between flesh & spirit, & I will use it, & not any longer belong to this double faced equivocating mixed Jesuitical universe.'" Emerson thus adopted and enlivened the argument of a lecture he had heard two years earlier, "The Annexation of Texas," in which James Freeman Clarke had also emphasized the futility of efforts to purify the self by separating from corrupt institutions: "If you wish to become pure in this way, you must not only come out of the State, but you must go out of the world." [10] Emerson's primary target, however, was not Alcott but the Garrisonian abolitionists, who lacked the courage of their convictions. In a passage that echoes "New England Reformers," he sharply distinguished between the abolitionists, "hot headed partialists," and men like Thoreau. "The abolitionists ought to resist & go to prison in multitudes on their known & described disagreements from the state," he continued. "But not so for you generalizers. You are not citizens. You are not as they to fight for your title to be churchmembers or citizens, patriots. Reserve yourself for your own work" (*JMN* 9:446–47).

Emerson also echoed his "Ode Inscribed to W. H. Channing," written only a month earlier. But his message had suddenly gained tremendous urgency. The "Ode" was hardly an effort to convince or to convert Channing, who as far as Emerson was concerned had long ago sacrificed his potential as a scholar to the partial and transient work of reform. Thoreau was an altogether different case, different from Channing and from Alcott, whose arrest in 1842 had not particularly threatened or perturbed Emerson. As his ambiguous "you" and "yourself" indicate, Emerson in 1846 was speaking to himself as well as to Thoreau, a close friend and kindred spirit facing similarly conflicting claims upon his energies and allegiance. Challenging both the consistency and the utility of refusing to pay the tax, a protest that "does not reach the evil so nearly as many other methods within your reach," Emerson once again sought to remove Thoreau from the ranks of the abolitionists, "literalists" who simply sought to remove "a few specified grievances." In contrast, Emerson insisted that no form of government could ever appease Thoreau, whose true quarrel was with "the state of Man," not with "the state of Massachusetts." Exasperated with Thoreau's implied inability to understand that fundamental distinction, Emerson exclaimed with a combination of impatience and truly patrician disdain, "But really a scholar has too humble an opinion of the population, of their possibilities, of their future, to be entitled to go to war with them as with equals." As he had earlier in the entry argued that no man should argue with the state, that poor and contemptible beast, so he finally argued that for the scholar to engage in the kind of political action that absorbed the attention of the abolitionists and other citizens of the state was to abandon the high ground of literary aspiration and endeavor. Then—in a statement that seems like a non sequitur, yet one that follows naturally if we recall his earlier critique of the "suicidal business" of antislavery agency—Emerson abruptly added, "The prison is one step to suicide" (*JMN* 9:447).

As that vivid aphorism reminds us, the prison had highly charged associations for Emerson. It was, of course, a place for criminals and outcasts, threats to a social order that he still affirmed. For him going to prison was consequently among the most extreme acts, a sacrifice that could be justified by only the most compelling reasons. In a mocking reply to the "foolish philanthropist," for example, Emerson in "Self-Reliance" had dismissed the claims "of such men as do not belong to me and to whom I do not belong," adding: "There is a class of persons to whom by all spiritual affinity I am bought and sold; for them I will go to prison, if need be" (*CW* 2:30–31). Significantly, those persons did not include George Ripley and other communitarians who tried to enlist Emerson in their cause. On October 17, 1840, following his discussion of "the new social plans" for Brook Farm with the Ripleys, Bronson Alcott, and Margaret Fuller, Emerson lamented in his journal: "I wished to be convinced, to be thawed, to be made nobly mad by the kindlings before my eye of a new dawn of human piety. But this scheme was arithmetic & comfort; this was a hint borrowed from the Tremont House and U.S. Hotel. . . . It was not the cave of persecution which is the palace of spiritual power, but only a room in the Astor House hired for the Transcendentalists" (*JMN* 7:407–8). He clearly had in mind the cave where David was confined, from which the psalmist prays for deliverance from his "persecutors," crying out to God: "Bring my soul out of prison, that I may praise thy name: the righteous shall compass me about; for thou shalt deal bountifully with me" (Psalms 142:7). In his working notes for "New England Reformers," Emerson jotted down "Astor House" and "G. and S. Ripley's visit. Oct 1840" (*JMN* 12:272, 570), a visit that anticipated a similar meeting at Emerson's house on November 10, 1842, when Ripley, Theodore Parker, and others were invited to hear Alcott and Charles Lane unfold their plans for Fruitlands. In response to that discussion, and evidently with the 1840 meeting also in mind, Emerson had jotted down in his private journal a lesson he finally delivered publicly at Amory Hall:

> We desire to be made great, we desire to be touched with that fire which shall command this ice to stream, and make our existence a benefit. If therefore we start objections to your project, o friend of the slave, or friend of the poor, or of the race, understand well, that it is because we wish to drive you to drive us into your measures. We wish to hear ourselves confuted. We are haunted with a belief that you have a secret, which it would highliest advantage us to learn, and we would force you to impart it to us, though it should bring us to prison, or to worse extremity. (*CW* 3:163; cf. *JMN* 8:253)

In effect, Emerson faulted the reformers for failing to convince him that the spiritual rewards of involvement outweighed the possible loss of personal freedom, physical autonomy, and material comforts. He also recognized what some modern students of antebellum reform have emphasized, that the fierce embrace of such militant causes was in part an effort at self-liberation, which Emerson insisted could not be achieved by external, mechanical means. "Obedience to his genius is the only liberating influence," he proclaimed in the penultimate paragraph of the lecture. "We wish to escape from subjection, and a sense of inferiority,—and we make self-denying ordinances, we drink water, we eat grass, we refuse the laws, we go to jail: it is all in vain; only by obedience to his genius; only by the freest activity in the way constitutional to him, does an angel seem to arise before a man, and lead him by the hand out of all the wards of the prison" (*CW* 3:167). Significantly, Emerson had jotted down that sentence in his journal in October 1842, probably in reaction to his discussions with Alcott and Lane about their plans for Fruitlands (*JMN* 8:282). But the sentence also faintly echoes his response to the discussion of the plans for Brook Farm in October 1840. "I do not wish to remove from my present prison to a prison a little larger," he explained on October 17, 1840. "I wish to break all prisons" (*JMN* 7:408).

Ironically, given his imprisonment two years later, Thoreau exploited the same trope in his lecture at Amory Hall. Insisting that no man or institution could force its thought upon him except through some fault of his own, Thoreau continued: "The prisoner who is free in spirit, on whose innocent life some rays of light & hope still fall, will not delay to be a reformer of prisons, an inventor of superior prison disciplines, but walk free on the path by which those rays penetrated to his cell" (*c&r* 19). He probably had in mind the work of men like Louis Dwight, the evangelical founder of the Boston Prison Discipline Society, whose ardor had been fueled by his harrowing experience as an agent of the American Bible Society commissioned to carry Bibles to prisoners in institutions throughout the United States.[11] That specific example also illustrated a more fundamental philosophical division between such reformers and both Emerson and Thoreau. Although it was in large part based on Christian precept—a Biblical text, "I was in prison and ye came unto me" (Matthew 25:36), was often cited—efforts on behalf of prisoners were also generated by the emerging idea that human beings were products of their environments. That idea that was also central to certain forms of association, including those proposed by the French theorist Charles Fourier, to whose doctrines Brook Farm was converted in 1844, shortly before Emerson and Thoreau spoke at Amory Hall.

In contrast, both of them stressed the insignificance of outward obstacles and social conditions to the freedom and growth of human beings. Emerson's reference to that angel who seems "to arise before a man, and lead him by the hand out of all the wards of the prison" recalls Peter's delivery from Herod's prison in chapter 12 of Acts: "And, behold, the angel of the Lord came upon *him*, and a light shined in the prison" (*cw* 3:167, 236 n.). Thoreau alluded to the same verses, thus emphasizing what Emerson suggested, that such a divine light will free the individual from even the most seemingly oppressive material circumstances, just as Peter's chains fall from his hands and he is led through the iron gate of the prison. Whereas the most frequently quoted Biblical passage among the abolitionists was "Remember them that are in bonds, as bound with them" (Hebrews 13:3), both Emerson and Thoreau at least implied that instead of freeing the slaves such a preoccupation simply placed the abolitionists in bondage, since it diverted them from the path to true liberation.

In their lectures at Amory Hall, both Emerson and Thoreau suggested that the reformers fell prey to the very errors they strove to amend. In Emerson's lexicon prison came to stand for everything from which he sought to free himself and others, including reformers imprisoned by their obsessive concerns and rigid institutions. By going to prison rather than paying his tax, Thoreau had not only accepted Alcott's specious arguments and adopted the narrow perspective of the abolitionists: in Emerson's eyes, he had also implicitly abandoned the quest for true liberation. Describing the act as a protest against the Mexican War, Emerson ignored the fact that Thoreau had first refused to pay the tax several years earlier, before the two of them had so eloquently affirmed the primacy of that quest and, with it, the centrality of the scholar's role, in their discourses at Amory Hall. Instead of converting the reformers, Thoreau in 1846 looked to Emerson suspiciously like a new convert to reform, one who like most new converts was in danger of becoming even more zealous than those whose beliefs he embraced. The night Thoreau spent in prison therefore was less significant than the seeming implications and the possible consequences of his stand. The "suicide," or self-inflicted ruin, Emerson most feared for himself and for Thoreau was the destruction of the individualistic scholar by the emerging social activist, whose loud public protests threatened to drown out the private voice within that said "Work."

Initially, at least, Emerson's concerns about Thoreau's increasing activism seemed to be at least partly justified. Despite the pose of cool control he assumed in his later accounts of his protest, Thoreau was apparently furious when he was arrested. Certainly his anger was revealed by a journal entry written shortly after his release from prison, an entry in which Thoreau seemed to withdraw from the position he had taken at Amory Hall. There, reminding the reformers "that all that is called hindrance without is but occasion within," he had blithely asked: "How can I have any fatal opponents, or be prevented from being myself—by the faults of society?" (*c&r* 28). In sharp contrast, shortly after his arrest Thoreau angrily observed in the journal: "In my short experience of human life I have found that the outward obstacles which stood in my way were not living men— but dead institutions." The "innocent institutions" of 1844 assumed a radically different guise in 1846, when Thoreau described the church and state as "grim and ghostly phantoms like Moloch & Juggernaut," the ancient deities to whom innocent children and pilgrims were thought to have been sacrificed. "I love mankind," he exclaimed; "I hate the institutions of their forefathers." The conservative's effort to preserve existing institutions, which Thoreau had earlier viewed as simply misguided and regressive, had also taken on a more threatening aspect. Echoing Garrison, he suggested that there "probably never were worse crimes committed since time began than in the present Mexican war," one result of man's deadly reverence for institutions, "the stereotyped and petrified will of the past."[12]

Thoreau's militant anti-institutionalism had an almost immediate impact on *A Week on the Concord and Merrimack Rivers*, his account of a tour he and his brother, John Thoreau Jr., had made to the White Mountains of New Hampshire in 1839.[13] The book was designed as a kind of pastoral elegy for John, who had died of lockjaw in January 1842, the same month Emerson had lost his beloved son Waldo, whom he mourned in "Threnody," the penultimate work in *Poems* (1846). In the first draft of *A Week*, portions of which he read to both Emerson and Alcott during the summer of 1846, Thoreau had sought to avoid polemics, never allowing the pressures of a troubled present to impinge on his evocation of an idyllic past. As he revised and expanded the book during 1846–47, he began to confront the dead and deadening institutions he had denounced in his journal. In addition to a scathing critique of the Christian church and its ministers added to the "Sunday" chapter of *A Week*, Thoreau inserted in the "Monday" chapter a vigorous indictment of the state.

Most of the digression was drawn from the journal entry Thoreau had written shortly after his arrest in 1846, though he apparently revised that entry with an eye on his 1844 lecture on the conservative and the reformer. Early in that lecture, emphasizing the "very problematical existence" of government, he had observed that "most revolutions in society have not power to interest still less alarm us, but tell me that our rivers are drying up or the genus pine dying out in the country, and I might attend" (*C&R* 5–6). He used the same sentence in the "Monday" chapter of *A Week*, where he introduced the digression on government with the detached remark, "To one who habitually endeavors to contemplate the true state of things, the political state can hardly be said to have any existence whatever." If the state could hardly be said to exist, it could hardly represent one of those "outward obstacles" he described in the 1846 journal. Consequently, when he revised that entry for *A Week* he added the proviso "if there were any such." Following the reference to his arrest, he also added a dismissive passage beginning, "Poor creature! if it knows no better I will not blame it," a remark that recalls Emerson's contemptuous description of the state as "a poor good beast who means the best" (*JMN* 9:446). Nonetheless, Thoreau was far less detached and indifferent than he sought to appear, since the critique vividly illustrates his lingering fury at "dead institutions," a phrase he altered to "institutions of the dead" in *A Week*. Although he insisted that such institutions were simply "trifling obstacles in an earnest man's path," the digression in "Monday" indicates how difficult Thoreau found it to reconcile the position he had taken at Amory Hall with his growing conviction that "countless reforms are called for, because society is not animated, or instinct enough with life." By stressing the need for "countless reforms," rather than simply for reform, Thoreau seemed to give his blessing to a broad range of efforts to reform society, in which "all men are partially buried in the grave of custom." As his imagery suggests, for Thoreau such reforms were not simply desirable, they were matters of life and death.[14]

He assumed a similar stance in his first lecture on his life at Walden Pond, delivered at the Concord Lyceum in February 1847. Thoreau had begun to plan that lecture a year earlier, noting in the journal, "When I lectured here before this winter I heard that some of my towns men had expected of me some account of my life at the pond—this I will endeavor to give tonight" (*PJ* 2 : 142). As that comment suggests, Thoreau evidently at least initially planned to focus on how he lived rather than on the so-called life of his neighbors. At the opening of that 1846 journal entry he observed that every lecturer should offer "a more or less simple & sincere account of his life," and he entitled the February 1847 lecture "A History of Myself." But Thoreau actually defined himself in terms of the community from which he had withdrawn, the failures of which had been vividly illustrated by his own arrest and imprisonment. What he read at the Concord Lyceum in February 1847 was apparently an early version of what later became "Economy," a sharp and satirical critique of the "mean and sneaking lives" of his neighbors, a phrase that recalls Emerson's characterization of Thoreau's "mean and skulking" actions in July 1846.[15]

Although he did not refer to his arrest and imprisonment, that event was well known to his audience, and their knowledge no doubt gave added edge to Thoreau's portrait of himself as the only free man among men enslaved by their false economic, social, and religious practices. "I sometimes wonder how we can be so frivolous almost as to attend to the gross form of Negro slavery, there are so many keen and subtle masters that enslave both north & south," he observed early in the lecture. "It is bad to have a southern overseer, it is worse to have a northern one, but worst of all when you are yourself the slave-driver." Since Thoreau had originally refused to pay the poll tax because of his opposition to slavery, that statement was all the more provocative and surprising. He seemed to ratify the argument of proslavery apologists, who insisted that the Negro servitude was less onerous than "wage slavery" in the North, which in an article published in 1848 was described as "the most intolerable slavery men can suffer—a slavery which throws them into a state where wealth and power exercise the worst oppressions." [16] Thoreau thus turned the tables on the men who had imprisoned him, exposing the far more formidable prison they had constructed for themselves. "Look at the teamster on the highway, wending to market by day or night,—how much divinity is there in him?" he contemptuously asked. "See how he cowers and sneaks, how vaguely and indefinitely all the day he fears—not being immortal nor divine, but the slave and prisoner of his own opinion of himself." If the lecture was primarily an apologia for his withdrawn way of life at Walden Pond, it was also implicitly both a defense of his refusal to pay the poll tax and an indictment of his "townsmen," to whom he addressed both "A History of Myself" and the first version of *Walden*. Observing that men had abandoned certain unjust practices, including "imprisoning for debt, and chattel slavery in some places," Thoreau pointedly added that "they are not inclined to leave off hanging men because they have not got accustomed to that way of thinking." [17]

Thoreau's friends responded to "A History of Myself" in divergent and revealing ways. "Mrs. Ripley & other members of the opposition came down the other night to hear Henry's Account of his housekeeping at Walden Pond, which he read as a lecture, and were charmed with the witty wisdom which ran through it all," Emerson wrote Margaret Fuller in February 1847 (*L* 3:377–78). Although he had initially disapproved of Thoreau's experiment—"Cultivated people cannot live in a shanty, nor sleep at night as the poor do in a bag," Emerson had grumpily observed in 1845 (*JMN* 9:195–96)—he was clearly delighted by the lecture, which he obviously viewed as a kind of spartan development of his old idea of self-culture and consequently as yet another broadside in the ongoing debate with "the opposition," George Ripley and his allies at Brook Farm. The lecture may also have struck Emerson as a reassuring sign that Thoreau had recovered both his sanity and his sense of calling following his suicidal protest the previous summer. In contrast, Bronson Alcott drew a political corollary from Thoreau's account of his "housekeeping," a mode of personal economy that freed him from the grasp of both an oppressive society and the market economy. "The State springs from man's inability to supply individually his animal wants, and rises into form with the rise of traffic between individuals to this end," Alcott observed in his journal after hearing "A History of Myself":

Why should I need a State to maintain me and protect my rights? The Man is all. Let him husband himself. He needs no other servant. Self-helping is the best economy. That is a great age when the State is nothing and Men are all.

He who founds himself in freedom and maintains his uprightness therein founds an empire.

*   *   *

Could a man be thrown upon his own resources for a year, he might happen to see, and in no way short of this can he come to feel, the partnership in iniquities of which society is formed—and the people, silent partners, are themselves upholding, to their own impoverishment and shame.[18]

By translating Thoreau's lecture on economic self-reliance into political terms, Alcott anticipated the argument of Thoreau's later lecture on the rights and duties of the individual in relation to the state. That 1848 lecture was also inspired by deeply personal and intensely local concerns. The lecture was written for and delivered to his friends and neighbors, most of whom no doubt disapproved of the protest that had landed him in prison. He also alluded to Alcott's earlier imprisonment for the same protest, though Thoreau omitted that reference from "Resistance to Civil Government," possibly because he did not wish his act to be seen as part of a mass movement.[19] But he retained a reference to Samuel Hoar, who in 1844 had been driven by threats of mob violence from South Carolina, where he had been sent as an agent of Massachusetts to investigate complaints that black sailors on ships from that state were being illegally seized and placed in slavery. In a letter to the *New-York Tribune*, Emerson had stoutly defended Hoar, who "has done all that a man can do in the circumstances and has put his own state in the best position which truth and honor required."[20] Thoreau, in contrast, ironically suggested that his "esteemed neighbor" would have done far more to combat slavery if he had become a prisoner in Massachusetts (*RP* 75–76). Similarly, Thoreau illustrated the ways in which being "an agent of the government" denies individual choice and personal autonomy by citing the example of his "civil neighbor, the tax gatherer," Sam Staples. Staples offered a particularly effective illustration of the point, since many members of the audience probably knew that he had a high opinion of Thoreau, though like many others in town he was very skeptical of Emerson and the intellectuals he had attracted to Concord.[21]

Some people who heard Thoreau's lecture possibly also understood that it constituted one side of an argument that had deeply divided that "Transcendentalist crowd," as they were known in Concord. The lecture was in large part addressed to Emerson, who in early 1848 was delivering lectures in London. When he learned that his friend had delivered the lecture on

"the Rights & Duties of the Individual in relation to Government—much
to Mr. Alcott's satisfaction," as Thoreau put it in a letter, Emerson almost certainly did not share that satisfaction.[22] As he surely recognized,
that seemingly casual bit of information actually represented a calculated
though fairly amiable riposte, a sign that Thoreau had not budged from the
militant position that landed him in jail in 1846. Significantly, Emerson did
not respond to the announcement or remonstrate with his friend, probably
because he had earlier made his views well known to Thoreau. Emerson
had evidently openly expressed much of the criticism he had offered in his
journal following Thoreau's imprisonment. It is also possible that he had
invited Thoreau to read that journal entry. In either case, the fact that
Thoreau wrote his 1848 lecture on the rights and duties of the individual
in relation to the state while living in Emerson's house is doubly ironic,
since the lecture seemed to represent a challenge to both Emerson and
the kind of withdrawn, scholarly life symbolized by his book-lined and
comfortably-appointed study just off the entrance to the large white house
on the Cambridge Turnpike.

Although Thoreau had by no means rejected that way of life and work,
he assumed a far more engaged posture in "The Rights and Duties of the
Individual in Relation to Government." Emerson had described government as a "poor beast," little more than an instinctual animal; Thoreau
initially depicted government as an inhuman mechanism that transformed
its servants and supporters into machines. Where Emerson cast him as the
aggressor, Thoreau dramatized his conflict with the state as a struggle between the individual and the majority, the conscience and brute force, spiritual freedom and physical coercion. Near the end of his lecture, however,
he justified his own protest by insisting that government was "not wholly a
brute force, but partly a human force," an aggregate of "millions of men"
to whom "appeal is possible, first and instantaneously, from them to the
Maker of them, and, secondly, from them to themselves" (*RP* 85). By affirming the possibility of such moral suasion, Thoreau implicitly answered Emerson's objection that the scholar had "too humble an opinion of the
population . . . to be entitled to go to war with them as with equals." If he
did not exactly confront his neighbors as equals, Thoreau at least sought
to find a common ground on which he might address them. "You are not
citizens," Emerson had impatiently exclaimed in 1846; Thoreau in 1848
spoke, as he put it, "practically and as a citizen" (*RP* 64). As in "A History
of Myself," delivered a year earlier, Thoreau in "The Rights and Duties of
the Individual in Relation to Government" spoke in his most populist

mode. Both lectures were consequently at once apologias and efforts to address the practical and pressing problems of life: how to earn a living, that is, how to gain the independence and autonomy that made true life possible; and how the true *individual* should relate to an unjust government.

Thoreau also rejected Emerson's view of the nature of the conflict between those opposed and opposing parties. Emerson argued that Alcott and Thoreau lacked the kind of cause that ennobled the actions of Socrates and Christ: slavery was only one problem, the proper and primary concern only of "partialists" like the abolitionists, "who ought to resist & go to prison in multitudes on their known & described disagreements from the state." Thoreau was equally critical of the abolitionists, but he did not and would not have used a word like "disagreements," which implied that the conflict over slavery was narrowly political. For him, of course, it was not a political issue, it was a matter of principle. Dismissing those who served the state with their bodies or their minds, early in the lecture he hailed those "heroes, patriots, martyrs, reformers in the great sense, and *men*," who "serve the State with their consciences also, and so necessarily resist it for the most part" (*RP* 66). Actually, the abolitionists shared his revulsion from the kind of compromises and delays the political process necessitated—the Garrisonians called for *immediate* abolition, for example, not gradual emancipation. Nonetheless, Thoreau suggested that they were deeply ensnared in that process, seeking to convince others of the justness of their cause rather than displaying the courage of their convictions. "I know this well, that if one thousand, if one hundred, if ten men whom I could name,—if ten *honest* men only,—aye if *one* HONEST man, in this State of Massachusetts, *ceasing to hold slaves*, were actually to withdraw from this copartnership, and be locked up in the county jail therefor, it would be the abolition of slavery in America," he proclaimed. With characteristic flair, Thoreau thus charted a narrowing path from mass movements through smaller associations of men working for a common end to a lone man acting in accordance with the highest moral principles. "But we love better to talk about it: that we say is our mission," Thoreau mockingly continued, perhaps with a glance at *The Liberator*. "Reform keeps many scores of newspapers in its service, but not one man" (*RP* 75).

As the repetition of *man* and *men* in such passages suggest, Thoreau's lecture was almost aggressively masculine. In part, he employed the word *man* much as Alcott used it in the sentence "The Man is all," to signify the autonomous and self-governing individual. Yet Thoreau's lecture more narrowly concerned the rights and duties of a *man*, or even more narrowly the proper definition of manhood. All of the questions addressed in the lecture—whether to vote, to pay taxes, or to serve the state in more direct ways—concerned men and men only. Since Thoreau dismissed the value and validity of those activities, it was hardly surprising that he did not promote the rights of women to engage in them. Certainly he seemed indifferent to the kinds of arguments and appeals contained in the "Seneca Falls Declaration of Sentiments and Resolutions," which was adopted only six months after Thoreau delivered his lecture. That declaration was an appeal from those who suffered under an unjust government; Thoreau's lecture concerned the consequences of such injustices for those who governed, that is, for men.

As in the first version of *Walden*, "Addressed to My Townsmen," Thoreau once again challenged those men, especially Emerson, offering an almost point by point rebuttal to the criticisms he had lodged in 1846. But Thoreau's lecture was not simply a justification of his actions, it was also an assertion of his manhood, one that perhaps revealed just how anxious he was on that score. The only reference to a woman occurs in a passage concerning his imprisonment, an illustration of the foolish and un-neighborly actions of his "townsmen," though he had of course been locked up by the unarmed and mild-mannered Sam Staples, not by a posse, as the passage suggests. Ironically, however, he expressed his contempt for the blundering behavior of his townsmen by observing, "I saw that the State was half-witted, that it was timid as a lone woman with her silver spoons, and that it did not know its friends from its foes, and I lost all my remaining respect for it, and pitied it" (RP 80). He thus underscored the absence in America of what Emerson in his 1846 journal entry had called "the male principle."

Emerson was clearly of two minds about the manliness of Thoreau's protest. On the one hand, Emerson contrasted it to the limp response of the Whigs, "the snivelling opposition," to the war policies of the Democrats, who at least had "a sort of genius of a bold & manly cast, though Satanic" (*JMN* 9:445). On the other hand, Emerson told Alcott that he considered Thoreau's actions "mean and skulking, and in bad taste." Thoreau depicted his own actions as noble and forthright, remarking that it was not he but his townsmen who had "behaved like persons who are underbred" (RP 80). Emerson in his journal insisted that "a man walking cleanly on two feet will not pick a quarrel with a poor cow"; Thoreau replied that *men* inevitably resisted the state. Emerson viewed imprisonment with revulsion, as a threat to the scholar's—that is, to a *man's*—power, potency, and autonomy. Thoreau in his "history of 'My Prisons'" emphasized what both of them at least in theory believed, that physical barriers were no obstacle to spiritual freedom. "I could not but smile to see how industriously they [his townsmen] locked the door on my meditations, which followed them out again without let or hinderance, and *they* were really all that was dangerous," he blithely observed (*rp* 80). Where Emerson described prison as "one step to suicide," Thoreau vigorously replied, "Under a government which imprisons any unjustly, the true place for a just man is also a prison" (*rp* 76).

Although he rather grandly conceived of his arrest and imprisonment as the possible beginning of a second American Revolution, Thoreau surely realized that revolutions were not brought about by an individual act or a single lecture, however eloquent or compelling. On the contrary, they were generated by sustained agitation by committed men and women, the kind of activism Thoreau firmly rejected, at least for himself. Despite the unyielding tone of his lecture, he made it clear that he was not about to do what Emerson had most feared, allow militant activism to deter him from pursuing his proper vocation. "It is not a man's duty, as a matter of course, to devote himself to the eradication of any, even the most enormous wrong; he may still properly have other concerns to engage him," Thoreau affirmed; "but it is his duty, at least, to wash his hands of it, and, if he gives it no thought longer, not to give it practically his support" (*rp* 71). As that revealing statement indicates, Thoreau's protest finally served personal rather than broadly political ends. Certainly his refusal to pay the tax revealed a craving for personal purity and a determination to escape the taint of corrupt institutions characteristic of various "come-outers," including the Garrisonian abolitionists. But they withdrew from such institutions to follow what they conceived to be the laws of Christ, dedicating themselves to eradicating social injustice and thus preparing for His kingdom on earth. Freedom from institutional bondage made it possible for them to work for the liberation of others, especially the slaves. Thoreau withdrew from the state in order simply to "wash his hands" of such injustices, a particularly unfortunate phrase given the references to the passion of Christ elsewhere in his lecture. In effect, he was finally less concerned with liberating the slaves than with freeing himself to pursue his own vocation with a clear conscience.

"The Rights and Duties of the Individual in Relation to Government" was less a rejection than an amplification and extension of his earlier lecture on the conservative and the reformer, portions of which he revised for his 1848 lecture. "It is not necessary that we should steadily set our faces against government and what are called law and order," he had observed early in his lecture at Amory Hall. "This would not be an agreeable prospect. We would have it, and, in any case, the fates and the laws of the universe will have it, that governments shall continue bad until their subjects are better. . . . But every man who regards himself as a citizen, and is ambitious to live not simply under a government but on a level with or above it, needs to be informed chiefly with regard to the nature of his own and of all government" (c&r 5). Speaking "practically and as a citizen," Thoreau echoed that passage near the beginning of his 1848 lecture, where he continued, "Let every man make known what kind of government would command his respect, and that will be one step toward obtaining it" (rp 64). Later in his 1848 lecture Thoreau drew even more directly on his lecture at Amory Hall. There, arguing that a good man is a better authority than government, which "can only be just as good as the average character of its members," he had continued:

> Thus under the name of order and civil government we are all made at last to pay homage to and support our own meanness. After the first blush and rank offense of sin comes its indifference, and from immoral it becomes as it were unmoral and a legitimate product & fruit not quite unnecessary to that life we have made.
>
> The broadest and most prevalent error requires the most disinterested virtue to sustain it. The wisest & best are the steadiest defenders of the disorder called government. And the slight reproach to which the virtue of patriotism is liable, the noble are most likely to incur. (c&r 9–10)

Thoreau revised and incorporated those paragraphs into his 1848 lecture, where he once again dealt with the authority of government. Significantly, he omitted the sentence concerning "the wisest & best," perhaps an indication of how much his attitude toward the defenders of government had hardened following the annexation of Texas, the outbreak of the Mexican War, and his arrest in 1846 (rp 71–72). Certainly Thoreau was far less detached and philosophical about government in 1848 than he had been in 1844, when he had satirized the conservatives for their misguided reliance upon institutions. In contrast, Thoreau in 1848 expressed his contempt for the servants of the state, from the "mass of men," who served it with their bodies, to "most legislators, politicians, lawyers, ministers, and officeholders," who served it with their heads and consequently were "as likely to serve the devil, without intending it, as God" (rp 66). In saying that, however, Thoreau simply gave heft and resonance to what he had suggested four years earlier, that the great fault of all such public men lay in their abandonment of private conscience, a result of their failure to see that human laws and government had no divine sanction. Discussing the limited authority of customs and institutions, Thoreau in 1844 had rather lamely observed that "it takes a clear and far seeing eye to discover that these are not wholly divine in their origin or continuance" (*C&R* 11). Near the end of his 1848 lecture he transformed that dead metaphor into a powerful allegory of man's quest to discover such origins: "They who know of no purer sources of truth, who have traced up its stream no higher, stand, and wisely stand, by the Bible and the Constitution, and drink at it there with reverence and humility; but they who behold where it comes trickling into this lake or that pool, gird up their loins once more, and continue their pilgrimage toward its fountain-head" (*RP* 88).

Despite the implied direction of that quest, Thoreau's own pilgrimage was literary rather than political. In fact, delivering his lecture on the rights and duties of the individual in relation to government seems to have freed him from deeper involvement in political issues. Although he slightly revised the lecture for publication as "Resistance to Civil Government" in 1849, he was then far more engaged in his work on *A Week* and *Walden.* Soon after the publication of *A Week* in 1849, he embarked on a series of other literary excursions. That fall, he visited Cape Cod, subject of a popular lecture he delivered several times and revised after revisiting the area in the summer of 1850. The debate over the provisions of the Compromise of 1850 had by then already generated heated controversy in New England, but Thoreau remained aloof from the fray. On September 25, a week after the Fugitive Slave Act was signed into law, Thoreau traveled to Canada, a tour he described in lectures and "A Yankee in Canada," portions of which were published serially in *Putnam's Magazine* early in 1853. Apparently cheered by that publication, his first since *A Week*, he visited Maine in September and swiftly began to work up a lecture on the trip, later published as "Chesuncook."

But his most significant work was *Walden*, which Thoreau had originally arranged to publish shortly after *A Week.* Because of the abysmal commercial failure of that book, Thoreau's publisher declined to print *Walden*, which he subsequently began to revise late in 1851. In a process that occupied him on and off until the book was finally published in August 1854, Thoreau radically expanded the manuscript, nearly doubling its size and altering its impact in significant ways.[23] Certainly the political turmoil of the early 1850s left some marks on *Walden;* nonetheless, its publication was the clearest evidence of Thoreau's refusal to devote his energy or his pen to the work of reform. It is therefore all the more appropriate that Thoreau finally in *Walden* found use for significant portions of his 1844 lecture on the conservative and the reformer. In the early versions of *Walden*, Thoreau drew upon the lecture for the critique of philanthropy in what later became the introductory chapter, "Economy." In the later versions, he gleaned from the lecture a few more passages on reformers for "Economy"; but his most significant addition in the sixth and final surviving manuscript version of *Walden* was to the final chapter, from the opening of "Conclusion" through the urgent imperative beginning, "Start now on that farthest western way."[24] Virtually the whole of that section was adapted from Thoreau's 1844 lecture at Amory Hall. Thus, ten years after he had exhorted the reformers to turn away from society and its institutions back to nature and the self, Thoreau reaffirmed his dedication to the private work that had ultimately produced *Walden*.

In contrast, Emerson was increasingly diverted from such work by the political controversies ignited in 1850. In January he rounded out an extraordinarily satisfying and successful period of writing and lecturing by publishing *Representative Men*, his lecture series on Plato, Swedenborg, Montaigne, Napoleon, and Goethe. A radically different set of representatives claimed his attention after March 7, 1850, when Webster delivered "The Constitution and the Union," an address in the Senate in which he supported the Compromise of 1850, including the passage of the Fugitive Slave Law. A year earlier, in some brief remarks at an antislavery meeting in Worcester, Massachusetts, Emerson had confidently anticipated the triumph of abolitionism, which, he optimistically declared, "is not in man to retard" (*AW* 49). Webster, however, demonstrated just how much one man could do to retard that movement, and he had done so as the major political representative of Massachusetts. "We shall never feel well again until that detestable law is nullified in Massachusetts & until the Government is assured that once for all it cannot & shall not be executed here," Emerson declared early in 1851 (*JMN* 11:344). Both he and Thoreau were outraged when the law was executed in the case of Thomas Sims, a fugitive slave returned from Boston to a Georgia plantation. But unlike Thoreau, who never delivered the lecture on the Sims case that he began to draft in his journal (*PJ* 3:202–9), Emerson soon spoke out publicly on the Fugitive Slave Act. "The last year has forced us all into politics, and made it a paramount duty to seek what it is often a duty to shun," he proclaimed at the opening of his "Address to the Citizens of Concord," delivered on May 3, 1851 (*AW* 53).

That address indicates how far the passage and execution of the Fugitive Slave Act had driven Emerson from positions he had taken only five years earlier. After Thoreau's arrest in 1846, for example, Emerson had urgently argued against such passive resistance; now, he contemptuously derided the "passive obedience" to the law among leading figures in Boston. Echoing the argument of "Resistance to Civil Government," he argued that "an immoral law makes it a man's duty to break it," since "virtue is the very self of every man." As Thoreau insisted that a man "cannot without disgrace be associated" with the government, so Emerson observed that "no man can obey, or abet the obeying [of the Fugitive Slave Law], without loss of self-respect and forfeiture of the name of gentleman." By urging opposition to a single immoral law rather than to an immoral government, and by adding the element of social opprobrium to the consequences of obedience, Emerson tempered Thoreau's argument in revealing ways. But where Thoreau's imprisonment had earlier seemed to him like a step toward suicide, Emerson now suggested that the law itself represented the greatest threat of self-destruction, for both the individuals who obeyed it and for the Union it was designed to preserve: "one thing appears certain to me, that, as soon as the constitution ordains an immoral law, it ordains disunion. The law is suicidal, and cannot be obeyed. The Union is at an end as soon as an immoral law is enacted" (AW 53, 57, 63, 67–68).

As his 1851 address indicates, Emerson began to assume a new burden as a writer and speaker, applying the lessons of self-culture to contemporary events. Yet he remained deeply ambivalent about his own efforts to correct and inspire his countrymen. He delivered his 1851 address several more times in campaigning for John Gorham Palfrey, a scholar and former dean of the Harvard Divinity School who was running for Congress on the Free-Soil ticket. Palfrey carried Concord but lost the May 25 election, after which Emerson's ardor for political activity began to cool. "In the spring the abomination of our Fugitive Slave-Bill drove me to some writing & speechmaking, without hope of effect, but to clear my own skirts," he diffidently wrote Thomas Carlyle in July 1851. "I am sorry I did not print, whilst it was yet time. I am now told the time will come again, more's the pity."[25] Emerson's regrets reveal both his growing needs to publish his political views and his disgust with times that demanded such writings from the scholar, whose highest duty was to educate his countrymen in other ways. Although he continued to grumble about politics and the American people, "with their vast material interests, materialized intellect, & low morals" (JMN 11:385), for the time being he felt free to confront the larger implications rather than the specific manifestations of their spiritual mal-aise. During the fall of 1851 he therefore resumed his busy speaking sched-ule, further developing the lectures begun after his return from Europe in 1848, most of which later formed the core of *English Traits*, published in 1856, and *The Conduct of Life*, which was finally published in 1860.

As Emerson had anticipated, the time for him to speak out on contem-porary political issues did come again. In January 1854 Senator Stephen Douglas of Illinois, a strong supporter of a transcontinental railroad and a champion of interest of the distant Northwest, which he called "the hope of this country," introduced a bill for the organization of the territories of Kansas and Nebraska. That bill sparked a three-month debate over the ex-tension of slavery, a debate unprecedented in its intensity and ferocity. Em-erson was almost immediately swept into the maelstrom. With either luck or masterful timing, the radical abolitionists had in December 1853 orga-nized a series of lectures at the Broadway Tabernacle in New York City, bringing together both moderate and radical antislavery speakers, includ-ing politicians like John P. Hale, presidential candidate of the Free-Soil Party in 1848 and 1852; ministers of various denominations and political views, from Henry Ward Beecher to Theodore Parker; reformers like Hor-ace Greeley and Lucy Stone, an activist in woman's rights and abolition; and the most prominent of the radical abolitionists, William Lloyd Garri-son and Wendell Phillips. Emerson delivered the final speech in the distin-guished series, a speech carefully timed to coincide with the fourth anni-versary of Webster's "The Constitution and the Union" address of 1850.[26]

In his address, "The Fugitive Slave Law," Emerson traced his own reluc-tant steps toward involvement in the struggle against slavery. "I do not often speak to public questions," he characteristically began. "They are odious and hurtful and it seems like meddling or leaving your work." He thus echoed earlier works like "New England Reformers," in which he had vigorously defended the scholar's private work against the inroads of public issues, whether political or philanthropic. But a great deal had changed since he delivered that lecture in 1844. For example, where he had earlier consistently depicted the scholar as part of an intellectual and spiritual elite whose primary audience was other scholars, Emerson in his address at the Broadway Tabernacle offered a surprisingly democratic definition of schol-ars, which he described as "a class which comprises in some sort all man-kind,—comprises every man in the best hours of his life:—and in these days not only virtually but actually." What Emerson called "the silent revo-lution which the newspaper has wrought" had created for the scholar a new audience of scholars, represented by his auditors at the Broadway Tabernacle and ultimately including the masses reading reports of such lectures in newspapers like Horace Greeley's influential *New-York Tribune*. Despite the hope Emerson placed in the spread of literacy and culture, we may doubt that his conception of the scholar's relative status had actually changed so dramatically. By extending his definition of the scholarly class, however, Emerson sought to resolve the question of how a private scholar could speak out on public issues without abandoning his own idiom and betraying his own vocation. Emerson had, of course, struggled with that question in several antislavery addresses delivered during the 1840s. But the question had become far more urgent for Emerson since 1850, when, as he put it, "Mr. Webster by his personal influence brought the Fugitive Slave law on the country" (AW 73–74).

For Emerson, Webster's fateful act and the dark period it ushered in had taught a stern lesson to scholars, the expanded class to whom he addressed his remarks at the Broadway Tabernacle. In a passage punctuated with the mocking—and self-mocking—phrase "you relied," Emerson exposed the failure of the Constitution, the Supreme Court, the Missouri Compromise, the doctrine of state sovereignty, and even the guarantees of the Compromise of 1850 to check the aggressions of the slave power, which in 1854 was once against imposing its will on a docile North. "To make good the cause of Freedom you must draw off from all these foolish trusts in others," he declared. "You must be citadels and warriors, yourselves Declarations of Independence, the charter, the battle, and the victory." Emerson thus decked out his old doctrine of self-reliance in a new and militant garb, insisting—as Thoreau had earlier insisted in "Resistance to Civil Government"—that the minority had no influence because "they have not a real minority of one." Although he retained his faith that nature could "rid itself at last of every wrong," a serene belief in the future he had also expressed at Amory Hall, by 1854 Emerson had become impatient of the delays accompanying that ultimate triumph of principle. He consequently demanded "of superior men that they shall be superior in this, that the mind and the virtue give their verdict in their day and accelerate so far the progress of civilization" (AW 82–83, 85, 87).

Emerson redefined not only the scholar's proper sphere and primary duties but also the responsibilities of manhood. Displaying his usual strong distaste for politics and politicians, Emerson in 1843 had fastidiously observed: "Any form of government would content me in which the rulers were gentlemen, but it is in vain that I have tried to persuade myself that

Mr Calhoun or Mr Clay or Mr Webster were such; they are underlings, & take the law from the dirtiest fellows. . . . they are not now to be admitted to the society of scholars" (*JMN* 9 : 17). In his 1854 address Emerson criticized the scholars for their failure to guide politicians, implying that Webster's failure was shared by those who, like himself, had failed to speak out more forcefully before 1850. Consequently, where Thoreau in the "Conclusion" of *Walden* exhorted his "vagrant countrymen" to turn inward, Emerson at the end of "The Fugitive Slave Act" insisted that the disastrous events of the 1850s made it the duty of all men to turn outward, involving themselves in politics and the antislavery crusade. He thus offered a graceful tribute to his host, the American Anti-Slavery Society, concluding: "I hope we have come to an end of our unbelief, have come to a belief that there is a Divine Providence in the world which will not save us but through our own co-operation" (*AW* 89).

His final words at the Broadway Tabernacle indicate how far Emerson had moved from 1844 to 1854. At the conclusion of "New England Reformers" he had expressed a similar faith in such a divine Providence. In that 1844 lecture, however, Emerson invoked Providence to clinch his argument against reformers, whom he urged simply to "trust" its power to ameliorate social ills. Although events like the annexation of Texas and the Mexican War altered his view of the claims of reform, his response to Thoreau's arrest in 1846 and other journal entries illustrated how strongly Emerson resisted full involvement in what he privately called the "suicidal work" of abolition. Even in his antislavery speeches, Emerson subtly challenged both the efficacy and centrality of that work. In his remarks at the antislavery meeting at Worcester in 1849, for example, Emerson suggested that "it is the order of Providence that we should conspire heartily" in the work of abolition, but he also emphasized that its ultimate triumph would be brought about through the inevitable operation of divine laws rather than by what he called "human exertion" (*AW* 49–50). Webster's role in the disastrous events of 1850 profoundly transformed Emerson's conception of both the capacity of individuals to shape the course of events and the responsibility of men to involve themselves in the work of Providence, which as he put it at the Broadway Tabernacle "will not save us but through our own co-operation." Indeed, by ending his 1854 address with the word cooperation, Emerson signaled what his decision to appear at the Broadway Tabernacle had already hinted at: his willingness to work actively with other men in the struggle against slavery.

NOTES

1. Joseph Wood Krutch, *Henry David Thoreau* (New York: William Sloane, 1948), pp. 130–31. As Krutch observes, there "is no contemporary evidence to support the often told story" (p. 130). But one of Thoreau's contemporaries, John Weiss, recorded a less dramatic variant of the story: after Thoreau's release, Emerson asked him why he had gone to jail, to which he replied, "Why did you not?" See Walter Harding, *The Days of Henry Thoreau: A Biography*, enlarged and corrected ed. (New York: Dover, 1982), p. 206.

2. *Reform Papers*, ed. Wendell Glick, in *The Writings of Henry D. Thoreau*, 12 vols. to date (Princeton: Princeton University Press, 1972–), p. 76.

3. For a detailed discussion of their lectures in the context of the series at Amory Hall, see Linck C. Johnson, "Reforming the Reformers: Emerson, Thoreau, and the Sunday Lectures at Amory Hall, Boston," *ESQ: A Journal of the American Renaissance* 37 (1991): 235–89.

4. Cf. Henry Nash Smith, "Emerson's Problem of Vocation—A Note on 'The American Scholar,'" *New England Quarterly* 12 (1939): 52–67.

5. Unpublished 1844 lecture on the conservative and the reformer, mistakenly labeled as an early draft of "Life Without Principle," bMSAM 278.5, folder 18A in the Houghton Library, Harvard University. The lecture, quoted by permission of the Houghton Library, is cited as *C&R*, by Thoreau's page numbers; the references here are to pages 25 and 27.

6. *Anti-Slavery Almanac* (Boston: Anti-Slavery Society, 1844).

7. For a discussion of Alcott's influence on Thoreau's stand, see John C. Broderick, "Thoreau, Alcott, and the Poll Tax," *Studies in Philology* 53 (1956): 612–26.

8. Harding, *Days of Henry Thoreau*, p. 202.

9. For a different reading of this entry, see *VH* 123–25.

10. At Emerson's invitation, Clarke delivered the lecture at the Concord Lyceum on March 13, 1844 (*L* 3:243–44). It was published in the *Christian World* on April 20, 1844.

11. For a discussion of Dwight's work and of prison reform in the antebellum period, see Alice Felt Tyler, *Freedom's Ferment* (Minneapolis: University of Minnesota Press, 1944), pp. 265–85.

12. *Journal*, vol. 2, 1842–1848, ed. Robert Sattelmeyer, in *The Writings of Henry D. Thoreau*, pp. 262–64.

13. For a detailed discussion, see Linck C. Johnson, *Thoreau's Complex Weave: The Writing of "A Week on the Concord and Merrimack Rivers," with the Text of the First Draft* (Charlottesville: University Press of Virginia, 1986), especially chapter 3, "The Abuses of the Past," pp. 85–121.

14. *A Week on the Concord and Merrimack Rivers*, ed. Carl Hovde et al., in *The Writings of Henry D. Thoreau*, pp. 129–32.

15. Thoreau later expanded the manuscript of the lecture into the first version

of *Walden*, the text of which is printed in J. Lyndon Shanley, *The Making of "Walden"* (Chicago: University of Chicago Press, 1957), pp. 105–208. Thoreau's lecture apparently constitutes the first 35 leaves, pp. 105–35, since the following leaf was probably written later and a second series of page numbers begins with leaf 37 and runs through the rest of the first version.

16. Quoted in Kenneth S. Greenberg, *Masters and Statesman: The Political Culture of American Slavery* (Baltimore: Johns Hopkins University Press, 1985), p. 100. The common analogy between Northern laborers and Southern slaves had also been made by Emerson, who in a letter written to Thoreau on September 8, 1843, had described the plight of the workers brought to Concord by the construction of the Fitchburg railroad, "Now the humanity of the town suffers with the poor Irish, who receives but 60 or even 50 cents for working from dark to dark, with a strain & a following up that reminds me of negro driving" (*L* 7:558).

17. Shanley, *Making of "Walden"*, pp. 108–9.

18. *JA* 189–90. The undated entry follows an entry dated February 7, 1846, three days before Thoreau first delivered "A History of Myself" at the Concord Lyceum.

19. Taylor Stoehr, *Nay-Saying in Concord* (Hamden, Conn.: Archon Books, 1979), p. 52.

20. Quoted in *VH* 93.

21. Harding, *Days of Henry Thoreau*, p. 202.

22. *The Correspondence of Henry David Thoreau*, ed. Walter Harding and Carl Bode (New York: New York University Press, 1958), p. 208 (February 23, 1848).

23. See Shanley, *Making of "Walden"*; and Robert Sattelmeyer, "The Remaking of *Walden*," in *Writing the American Classics*, ed. James Barbour and Tom Quirk (Chapel Hill: University of North Carolina Press, 1990), pp. 53–78.

24. *Walden*, ed. J. Lyndon Shanley, in *The Writings of Henry D. Thoreau*, pp. 320–22.

25. *The Correspondence of Emerson and Carlyle*, ed. Joseph Slater (New York: Columbia University Press, 1964), p. 470.

26. The speakers in the series were first announced in the *National Anti-Slavery Standard*, 14 no. 28 (December 3, 1853), p. 110. Accounts of most of the speeches were published in the *Standard*, which printed a report of Emerson's speech on March 18, 1854, as well as in other newspapers in New York City. For a fuller discussion of the context of the 1854 speech, see *VH* 187 ff. A stimulating reading of the speech in relation to Emerson's doctrine of self-reliance is offered by Gertrude Reif Hughes, *Emerson's Demanding Optimism* (Baton Rouge: Louisiana State University Press, 1984), pp. 116–25.

Part Two

EMERSON AND WOMEN'S RIGHTS

PHYLLIS COLE

Pain and Protest
in the Emerson Family

"YOUR FATHER is not combative—*with exceptions!*" Lidian Jackson Emerson wrote to her daughter Ellen in 1873, claiming that he had "exercised great moral combativeness in writing the Pres. of the U.S. in defense of the Cherokee Indians." Looking back at an event then thirty-five years past, Lidian remembered both Ralph Waldo Emerson's actions and his reservations. He had written "against the grain," and now she praised him for doing so. Lidian's praise indicates that she more than Waldo represented family militance, especially since her letter rushed on to tell Ellen of a comparable crisis in the present day's news. Federal powers were mobilizing to exterminate the Modoc tribe, including "men, *women & children*!!!" "If I had your father's powers and influence," Lidian insisted, "quickly would I make something public about the Modoc Indians." But she listed reasons why she could not write, "chief of which is that I am nobody & editors would not publish any thing I wrote."[1]

Lidian's letter suggests the dynamics of a conversation that contributed decisively to drawing forth Ralph Waldo Emerson's public voice as a reformer from his earliest gestures to his final pronouncements. Indeed, two family women, Waldo's aunt Mary Moody Emerson and his wife Lidian, urged him to moral combat, not only in the 1838 Cherokee protest but also in his more sustained support of the antislavery and women's rights movements. As both his letter to the president and the journal entry following it made clear, he wrote at the behest of "friends" rather than from personal conviction alone (*aw* 1). The stance of representing others would always, with more or less comfort, characterize his voice as a reformer. Avoiding any exclusive identification of these two women as the "friends" in question, I would like to explore their role in bringing the urgencies of reform into the private Emerson family circle.

To do so is to offer a new context for evaluating Ralph Waldo Emerson's reform writing itself. Recently, John Carlos Rowe has faulted Emerson for adopting the central nineteenth-century causes of antislavery and women's rights only with a damaging "intellectual schizophrenia" between his abstract, individualistic ideals and his embrace of political process. Meanwhile, Albert J. von Frank demonstrates that Emerson's idealism had a direct impact on Boston's antislavery "revolution" of 1854. But von Frank distinguishes such principled politics from the woman-identified sentiment of Harriet Beecher Stowe, maintaining that these moral styles would only become complementary later in history.[2] My reading of the Emerson family substitutes the openness of conversation for the pathology of schizophrenia, and I discover moments of contact as well as resistance between genders and styles.[3] Waldo remained both open to the words of women and capable of refusing or transforming their meanings. Mary was a deep, long-term source of his idealist principles, while Lidian established his daily context as one of sentimental feeling. Both women, moreover, identified with the pain of the powerless and raged at wrongful exercise of public power, somewhat as if Harriet Beecher Stowe herself were present in the family circle.

Of course neither woman was a reforming novelist, instead defining herself as merely private, a "nobody." Almost fifty years before that self-characterization by Lidian, Mary had declared her response to Daniel Webster's Senate speech on Greek liberty to be "useless" for one such as herself. She expressed her excitement only by urging nephew Charles to be an orator greater than Webster.[4] Male surrogates were the necessary vehicle of female ambition under circumstances of societal constraint. Yet over the two long lifetimes of Mary (1774–1863) and Lidian (1802–92), constraint gave way and active participation of women in public affairs rose steadily, producing many articulate conversationalists and letter-writers as well as a few public crusaders. Both Mary and Lidian participated in the formation of women's voluntary, religion-based associations, major engines of reform in nineteenth-century America. Both were highly literate, seizing for themselves, like Stowe, the privilege of clerical fathers and husbands. Both read not only religion and literature but also the daily press, so that across the decades they could form views of the nation's grand orations and iniquitous policies. Ralph Waldo Emerson's search for means to claim practical power as a private citizen was redoubled and even driven by the respective searches of these two noncitizens. They spoke privately from the brink of public voice, and such urgency fed his.

At the same time, Waldo resisted this urgency because he found it vitiated by temperamental excess. Aunt and fiancée had met each other in 1835 through "diamond cut diamond" arguments that made him tremble for the family peace. Even while finding Mary a genius, he faulted her for "always fighting in conversation." "'She was endowed with the fatal gift of penetration,'" he quoted from her own words, then added, "She disgusted every body because she knew them too well." In 1836, after a decisive quarrel over dinner at the Emersons' new home in Concord, Mary bolted for her retreat in Maine and promised never to enter his house again;[5] thereafter her dialogue with both Waldo and Lidian took place by letter or from a neighboring boardinghouse. Meanwhile, the new lady of the Emerson house also lived in a climate of negative emotion—without, in Waldo's view, the compensating genius of Aunt Mary. Waldo's comments about Lidian over the years, amidst general toleration and concern, had a decidedly caustic undercurrent. As he observed to the children, "Your mammy has no sense of measure," but instead a gift "to curse & swear"; she even had "many holes in her mind." Calling Lidian by the nickname "Asia," he said, was a tribute to her Christian orthodoxy; but daughter Ellen instead recalled his explaining that no other New Englander "had ever possessed such a depth of feeling that was continually called out on such trivial occasions."[6]

Grievous feeling, though not limited to public issues, colored the political views of both women. In their distinctive styles, Mary and Lidian both exercised a politics of pain, identifying with victims of oppression and violence. The female ethic of sympathy and care led in this direction, but personal experience intensified the impulse. Mary, though born the daughter of Concord's minister, William Emerson, had been raised after his death in the Revolution by impoverished female relatives. Multiple early losses attuned her to death and sorrow; she never hesitated to name her childhood as "slavery" and to identify directly with slaves. Lidian likewise had been shadowed early in life by her mother's long illness, and both parents died when she was sixteen. From childhood, daughter Ellen relates, she suffered acutely at even imagining the pain of cats and birds. With a sharp, self-identifying despair she would exclaim, "I used to wish I had never been born," and then, "I have suffered more from the sufferings of animals than I ever have from my own." A similar agony accompanied her fear that the government was exterminating women and children.[7] In his 1838 protest against Cherokee removal, Waldo asked rhetorically if citizens were forced merely to look away "until the last howl and wailing of these poor tormented villages and tribes shall afflict the ear of the world." Perhaps he was alluding to such language when he expressed discontent with the letter in his journal. "Why shriek?" he asked (AW 4; JMN 5:475). It is likely that Lidian's shrieking echoed in his ear as he wrote both the letter and the afterthought. Over the years following, Waldo Emerson sought as a male reformer to absorb these women's pain but also translate it to more measured terms. Perforce he was also drawn at last to represent women in their own cause. Though never satisfying the most passionate advocates surrounding him, including his own wife, he spoke for the rights of women.

Mary Moody Emerson was Waldo's earliest teacher of the idealist ethics that would carry him through the antislavery controversy. In her own younger days, during her nephew's infancy, she had been deeply influenced by British Enlightenment philosophers Samuel Clarke and Richard Price, pseudonymously contributing passages from Price and essay-letters of her own to the pages of Boston's *Monthly Anthology*. These early letters explicitly affirmed women's power to perceive transcendent reality. Only later did the mentoring of nephews become Mary's major vocation. By Waldo's senior year at Harvard, as he prepared to write his essay on "The Present State of Ethical Philosophy," she was writing to him of Price's claim that "*Right* and *wrong* have had claims prior to all rites—immutable & eternal in their nature."[8] In his public memorial to Mary after her death, Waldo concluded, "She gave high counsels," and he used the word "high" to mean holy and transcendent, not just noble. From his youth through this late essay he referred to her as "Cassandra," uttering "the arcana of the gods."[9]

Mary opened a conversation about slavery in the 1820s with both of her favorite nephews, Waldo and Charles. With Waldo she speculated philosophically, in keeping with their inquiry into right and wrong. How, Mary asked, could one human being so torment another and also be capable of "abstract love of God and being universal"? Writing a letter to him in the voice of Plato, she charged that the slaves of Christian America were "more miserable than ever my country made." With Charles the conversation was openly patriotic and confessional. Wishing him to surpass Webster, she urged her young man not to excuse the blot of slavery on the Greek ideal of freedom, to model himself instead on the British abolitionist William Wilberforce, and by so doing to fulfill her memory of a father whose "love of liberty & honor" had primarily endeared the nation to her.[10] The loss of her father to the Revolution, original source of a lifelong mourning, also drove Mary to intense idealization of Christian American service and oratory.

Even while urging Charles to become an orator, her own letters shared an oratorical style. Amidst criticism of Edward Everett's overly secular Harvard address in 1824, she asked coyly if she had not herself "imitated the Professor" in her allusive writing style, then rose in the cadences of formal rhetoric to her own American jeremiad:

> The spirit that goes now abroad on the earth asks not only for political free-dom—but for immortality— . . . and in some forms looks for the completion of that glorious scheme which will consolidate all the nations and all their honors into one perfect fabrick. . . . But think—our nation had her nativity cast beneathe the influence of the cross as no other nation—and . . . if she wander (as some of her sons) into the havenless and heavenless chaos of deism, the graves of our sainted fathers and their sons will be trodden by despots & slaves—if there be not worse retribution.

Such letters were not merely "private," but absorbed and redirected public rhetoric in the persuasive women's work of influencing a man. Later in life Waldo asserted that "in her prime" Mary had been "the best writer . . . in Massachusetts, not even excepting Dr. Channing or Daniel Webster." [11] He was staking her claim against the platform giants of church and state in the 1820s.

Mary's American rhetoric was Christian, millennial, and liberationist, anticipating the militance of Garrisonian abolitionism even before its for-mal beginning in 1831. Charles rather than Waldo carried this message into the new age, persuading himself that Garrison was right in demanding immediate emancipation, becoming trained as a lawyer and himself offering an antislavery lecture to the public. [12] But family members and public causes soon came together: in the course of 1835 Mary, Waldo, Charles, and their respective fiancées, Lidian Jackson and Elizabeth Hoar, gathered in Con-cord, just as Garrisonian agents were first agitating the town. Mary de-clared herself "zealous" in the cause, wrote letters to friends in its support, and in her diary declared a straightforward hope for Waldo's conversion: "Let him and C.[harles] C. lecture on this subject with zeal & I will rejoice like Simeon of old." Then, like the old man finally witnessing the Messiah, she could "depart in peace." [13]

The means to convert Waldo, in Mary's eye, was Lidian. Though the younger woman had shown no previous interest in the antislavery cause, Mary now urged presumptuously that Lidian convince Waldo "to leave the higher Muses to their Elysian repose and . . . enter those of living degraded misery and take the gauge of slavery." Six months later, apparently seeing too little response, Mary invited agent George Thompson to breakfast at the newlyweds' house. Waldo found Thompson able to hear only his own opinion, but he also recorded his first tentative commitment to the organized antislavery movement: "As Josiah Quincy said in the eve of Revolution, 'the time for declarations is now over; here is something too serious for aught but simplest words & acts.'" Lidian's response to Thompson went unrecorded, but by the end of the year she had joined the new Concord Female Anti-Slavery Society, guaranteeing that reform issues would continue to be aired over the Emerson breakfast table. Independently of Waldo she befriended local activist Mary Merrick Brooks as well as the Thoreau women. Aunt Mary recognized the new bond with Lidian, sending an antislavery report along with her own hopes "for the fulfillment of w'h the present times seem preparing." "These are the broad & deep things, my dear Mrs. Emerson, to w'h I would hail your devotion—to w'h I would (as a fellow traveler) consecrate your growing influence in a place sacred to the memory of Ancestors eminently spiritualised."[14] The influence of women might itself fulfill America's millennial and Revolutionary hopes.

There was no easy fulfillment of Mary's aspirations for an Emersonian union in the cause. In 1836 Charles died of tuberculosis, redoubling Mary's grief and desire for isolation from others. As she fled back to Maine, Waldo completed *Nature*, a founding statement that unapologetically listened to higher muses than those of human misery. Meanwhile Lidian entered motherhood after fear and illness during pregnancy. Her own pains and her care of children would thereafter be major, even obsessive, preoccupations.

Nonetheless Lidian seems to have taken on the role of representative abolitionist in the reduced and scattered family. In 1837, the week after Waldo's "American Scholar" address, she hosted not only his friends of the Transcendental Club but also antislavery agents Sarah and Angelina Grimké, in separate occasions at the Emerson house. Wife as well as husband were opening their home's hospitality to public use; and now Lidian also began, like Mary, to urge others into the cause. "I think I shall not turn away my attention from the abolition cause till I have found whether there is not something for me personally to do and bear to forward it," she wrote to a niece. "I hope you will read any books or papers on the subject that you may meet with—if you can do nothing more for the oppressed after you have considered their case and become interested in it you can *pray* for them." Persuasive purpose was opening the customary exchange of news between women into the public domain. Such a desire to persuade also spilled over into her conversation with Waldo. He was not receptive, but criticized this vocal grieving "about the wretched negro in the horrors of the middle passage." The crucifixions of slavery, he asserted, did not come to people with Lidian's sensitivities but to the "obtuse & barbarous to whom they are not horrid but only a little worse than the old sufferings." [15] Waldo was doubly denying Lidian's politics of sympathy, granting no capacity for pain to Africans and nothing but pain to Lidian—no insight, principle, or agency to be reached through it.

Waldo's resistance to antislavery feeling as voiced by Lidian did not prevent him from assimilating parts of her message into his own. When the Grimkés' campaign resulted in the closing of Massachusetts churches to all antislavery speeches, especially by women, he spoke in defense of free speech to a Concord audience—but without either attacking slavery or defending women. When Lidian, in the wake of this controversy, declared that it was "wicked to go to church Sundays," he incorporated the remark into his "Divinity School Address" but suppressed both her identity and her cause. Meanwhile, however, husband and wife came together in signing the antislavery petitions that Concord, like many other northern towns, was sending to Congress.[16] Whether or not Waldo felt effective in contributing to a group voice, he had enlisted in the nation's first joint protest by men and women together.

Lidian did not singly influence Waldo to write in protest against Cherokee removal in 1838 but probably concentrated in household conversation a public concern that encompassed them both. As she described the course of events, Garrison's *Liberator* had reprinted the tribal appeal to Washington that led the Concord antislavery community to gather in concern after church on a spring Sunday. A series of male speakers addressed the audience, and separate petitions for men and women were presented and signed. Waldo Emerson stood amidst the speakers, and both Waldo and Lidian joined the signers (*aw* xxvi). A day later Waldo composed his letter to Van Buren while Lidian wrote to her sister, Lucy, in Plymouth. Both letters were part of a community protest, consciously composed as persuasive rhetoric. His represented the community on the most public level, questioning with mock innocence whether the "sinister rumors" of an unconscionable deed were to be credited, rising to outrage at the resulting loss of trust in government. Hers began more directly, but also strategically, by presenting the need to "do a little good" in the old-fashioned way; then she told the history of news reports and actions in Concord, instructing Lucy "what Plymouth may and should do to bear her testimony against this

wickedness in high places."[17] Lidian's letter was a characteristic part of the
women's work of private dissemination of a movement—and offers some
hint of her emotionally wrought conversation at home. After reading the
news report, she told Lucy, "you will feel . . . that you *must* do what
you can."

For Lidian feeling was encompassing and difficult to bear. In retrospect
Ellen Emerson saw a definite link between her mother's absorption in the
antislavery papers and her descent into depression: "it was as if she continually witnessed the whippings and the selling away of little children from
their mothers." Lidian returned as well to her grief over animals, and for
thirty years, from approximately 1840 to 1870, spent many of her days sad
and isolated in her bedchamber. Such sorrow was deeply personal, its
sources in old grieving, the unanticipated death of first child Waldo, and an
increasingly painful sense of distance from her husband. We know this distress from Margaret Fuller's vivid account of the household in 1842. Lidian
burst into tears at being left out of the walks and conversation, but in that
conversation Waldo had been finding a wife's intense devotion injurious
to her husband and the institution of marriage open to question. From
her single woman's perspective, Fuller doubted Waldo's speculations but
agreed that Lidian overly stressed "the demands of the heart."[18]

Yet Fuller was not seeing the ideology, humor, and commitment that also
gave edge to Lidian's feelings. Lidian's fullest statement of the heart's demands was the satiric "Transcendental Bible," which she wrote from her
sickbed in 1845 amidst dreams of living and dead children. This was not
a remonstrance against all reformers, but a thrust at those who rejected
"sympathy" in favor of the "noble, self-sustained, impeccable, infallible
self." The Female Anti-Slavery Society would have agreed entirely with its
embrace of all fellow humans, including the sick and the unintellectual.
Neighbor Abby Alcott copied Lidian's "Bible" into her own journal that
year, so others beyond the Emerson house clearly read it. Waldo Emerson
also found it "a good squib."[19] Antislavery sentiment may have deepened
Lidian's sorrow, but it also offered a channel and community for feeling. In
the course of the 1840s, as scattered reports reveal, she took pride in the
vigor of the movement in her hometown Plymouth, accompanied Waldo
to the Chardon Street Convention, joined Fuller's conversation group, and
publicly discussed community with Bronson Alcott.[20]

Waldo Emerson kept sorrow at arm's length and in 1841 began exploring the possibilities of reform based upon individual conscience and idealist
ethics. At almost the same moment he solicited Mary Moody Emerson to

overcome the silence of five years and renew ties, rightly affirming the bond of their solitary souls in "perception of one Law in . . . adoration of the Moral Sentiment." Over the years following, Mary often visited Concord—though staying in a boardinghouse—and once more contributed directly to its family and community conversation. Visiting the Boston Female Anti-Slavery Fair in 1841, she wrote two letters for its "Post Office," one urging a husband to support his wife's reform work outside the house, the other grounding reform in the "voice within" and universal obligation to God. In most visionary style, she described an 1845 protest against the Mexican War at Boston's Faneuil Hall, declaring the Revolutionary portraits on its walls to smile down as the onrolling wheels of Providence brought Christ's kingdom to a needy world.[21] Mary's abolitionism stood on ground that mediated between Waldo and Lidian. As determined as he to base action upon intuition of abstract principle, she had also affirmed the collective antislavery movement and devoted herself to it with religious enthusiasm. Her feeling ran more easily to anger rather than to tears, and she saw reform work as a route beyond the domestic role rather than an expression of it. Still, she and Lidian always communicated through their antislavery zeal and within a common network of friends supporting the movement.

Both women and their group rejoiced when Waldo delivered his first major antislavery address to honor the tenth anniversary of West Indian Emancipation in 1844. The Concord Female Anti-Slavery Society, Lidian among them, sponsored the event and invited his participation as "orator of the day." Mary wrote to the speaker from Maine in terms that echoed her first hopes for his conversion in 1835, hailing an address on "the very ground where freedom first struck her noble blow" and praising his muse for descending to "the humble ground of human emancipation."[22] The oration had many sources and promptings besides his female kin, and it recited a history of British abolition through the initiative of heroic statesmen rather than female agitation. Yet its emphases included and in a sense spoke to both Lidian and Mary.

If he had faulted his wife eight years before for dwelling on the pain of middle passage, now he confessed to feeling "heart-sick" at reading how slaves came to the new world and how they were kept. Acknowledging a modicum of sympathy for the planters, he dwelt sympathetically on the graphic details of pregnant slave women set in treadmills for refusing work and men's backs flayed by whips. "If we saw these things with eyes," he insisted, "we too should wince. They are not pleasant sights. The blood is moral: the blood is antislavery: it runs cold in the veins: the stomach rises with disgust, and curses slavery." As one newspaper reported, tears flowed down the cheeks of "sturdy men as well as tenderhearted women" in the audience (AW 9–10, xxx). This oration took Lidian's politics of empathetic pain, affirmed its root in moral conscience as well as the feminine heart, and granted its realism.

But his grounding of antislavery conviction in conscience and idealist philosophy was not simply a move to masculine ground, because he had learned so deeply of these from Mary: "The sentiment of Right, once very low and indistinct, but ever more articulate, because it is the voice of the universe, pronounces Freedom," he proclaimed. Mary's patriotic insistence was also present, though not to praise the millennial progress of freedom in Massachusetts so much as to judge the "tameness and silence" of its representatives in defending freedom nationally. Finally Waldo Emerson turned to individual intellect as nature's greatest miracle, greater than all the "songs and newspapers and money-subscriptions and vituperations" that still did not appeal to him in antislavery campaigns, but he explicitly offered this miracle to all, the heroic "antislave" of Jamaica and the audience before him: "I say to you, you must save yourself, black or white, man or woman; other help is none" (AW 33, 25, 31). His muse had learned not only to speak for human freedom but to acknowledge and address those others with whom he had been speaking about it.

The family alliance of antislavery conviction, though anticipated by Mary in 1835 and affirmed by Waldo nine years later, rose to its fullest force from the 1850s to the Civil War. Senator Daniel Webster prompted a new vehemence in the Emersons and their Massachusetts neighbors in March 1850 by turning his eloquence and authority to support of the Fugitive Slave Bill. Writing from Maine, Mary condemned the "odious *Bill*" and grieved anew at the loss of her father to the American Republic. When she regretted not being in Concord for the patriotic speeches at North Bridge on April 19, Lidian in response decried the "National Shame in standing on the neck of the enslaved black man while we shout aloud in praise of Freedom": "Webster and the majority of the Whig party with him," she asserted, "have deliberately and barefacedly set up the 'Constitution of the United States'—against the Law of God as given in nature and in Holy Writ and on this glorious day of jubilation not a hint was given that any thing was amiss in the Land—except the danger of Disunion!!!"[23] In these months Waldo separately recorded his dismay at Webster, but he attended the April 19 orations without condemning them as Lidian had, and he recorded no contrast of divine and national law until that fall. Pinpointing a single origin of ideas in conversation is impossible; but Waldo may well have echoed Lidian when his eventual speech "The Fugitive Slave Law," offered to a Concord audience the spring following, mocked the "brag" of April 19 oratory and affirmed the authority of higher law over any merely human code.[24]

This shared intrafamily outrage came after—perhaps even helped resolve—a period of strained relationship among the Emersons. By 1850 Mary no longer owned the house or enjoyed the support allowing her fixed residence in the hills of Maine but was choosing a life of boarding and wandering instead of dependence on her kin in Concord. She and Waldo wrote rarely. In 1847, as he left to lecture in England, she had urged him to "go commissioned with thundering terrors to that government about these slavery plans to supply the west indies!" But Waldo returned no message to her from Europe, so his wife had to remind him of his aunt's need.[25] Lidian's own need was even more acute. Possibly at her lifetime depth of illness and depression in 1847, Lidian had in part precipitated Waldo's departure (he hoped his absence would be a "relief") but then felt abandoned without him. Her letters described personal suffering, blankness of mind, and failure of hope, while she also pleaded with him for personally intimate words rather than chronicles of meetings. Waldo wrote back of his incapacity for such communication, but a new mutual commitment seems nonetheless to have sprung up through this difficult time. By the spring of 1848 she was claiming a recovery of health, thanking him for long letters, and promising "to be a good wife . . . if I never was before." At the same time her letter told primarily of an Associationist meeting in Boston, where W. H. Channing and the "Seeress" Anna Parsons alike prophesied the regeneration of humanity; this, Lidian insisted, was "one cause to which we need not fear giving too large a share of our attention or aid."[26] Male and female reformers—as well as particular husbands and wives—could unite in this common cause.

Sympathizing with the pain of others both expressed and enabled Lidian's emergence from self-preoccupation. In these years she had sprung to the defense of her brother, Charles Jackson, whose claim to have discovered the medical process of etherization was being challenged by a competitor. Vindicating his achievement in itself seemed to her "a triumph of Right over Wrong," but in addition, etherization was a means of alleviating pain and therefore of forwarding the cause of humanity. To ten-year-old Ellen she wrote of hungry children, affirming her core belief "that our part, if not to suffer—is to *relieve suffering.*" Such a mentality found its fullest moment in the 1850 crisis, when she named America's crime as the preservation of union though "the Slave groan or the Slave-mother weep or the Slave Maiden shriek as they might." Her sympathy with suffering took an intensely domestic form. When cannons had announced Concord's patriotic day three years before, she recalled to Mary, the news of bombarding Vera Cruz, Mexico, "so wrought me up that I felt as if each discharge might have sent a bomb-shell to burst in my nursery and mutilate my children and fire their home." Possibly in 1847 these sympathetic feelings had merely tortured raw nerves. In the aftermath of the Fugitive Slave Bill, however, they could be controlled within a shared rhetoric of indignation. "Just now a friend came into my house," Waldo related in his 1851 address, "and said, 'If this law shall be repealed, I shall be glad that I have lived; if not, I shall be sorry that I was born'" (AW 55).[27] These words are almost surely Lidian's, converting her long lament over having been born into a new political protest.

Lidian was not the most directly active woman abolitionist in Concord after the passage of the Fugitive Slave Law, but the Female Anti-Slavery Society allied her with those who were. Women led in supporting the escape of fugitive Shadrach Minkins the following February, with Ann Bigelow providing refuge and breakfast while sending for help from her neighbor Mary Merrick Brooks. "Mr. Nathan Brooks and Mr. Ralph Waldo Emerson were always afraid of committal," Bigelow recalled years later, "we women, never." On the night of Shadrach's flight through Concord, Nathan Brooks followed his wife to the Bigelow house and soon gave up his opposition to "aiding and abetting," offering his own hat as a disguise.[28] At the Emerson house, where action took the primary form of generating influential words, Lidian's vehemence of protest fueled the new fire of Waldo's address. Whether or not Ann Bigelow considered it sufficiently committed, the speech explicitly recalled the rescue of Shadrach and derided the tame, terrified enforcers of law in Boston. "There is not a manly whig, or a manly democrat," he claimed, "of whom, if a slave were hidden in one of our houses from the hounds, we should not ask with confidence to lend his wagon in aid of his escape, and he would lend it. The man would be too strong for the partisan" (AW 54, 60).

Waldo's speech suppressed the gender of his "friend" Lidian and characterized the virtue of resistance as "manly." His concern was to define true masculinity in opposition to the "humiliating scandal of great men warping right into wrong." Webster had enjoyed the reputation of possessing "the best head in Congress," the male rationality sustaining his authority and eloquence, but now he was revealed as obedient only to "animal nature." This was only a boy's pretended power: "All the arguments of Mr. Webster are the spray of a child's squirt against a granite wall." As Waldo's rhetoric defined an alternative, more authentic masculinity, however, it also sought alliance with women. The immoral law of Congress was contravened first by "the sentiment of duty" and then by "all the sentiments." A term of feminine, potentially negative emotionality was now claimed for the law of conscience. Furthermore, not only men could act upon it: Webster's law, he asserted, "has brought all the honesty in every house, all scrupulous and good-hearted men, all women, and all children, to accuse the law. . . . It has been like a university to the entire people."[29] Dividing men according to presence or absence of heart, he attributed that quality essentially to women and children. His essentialism hardly made room for difference among women, but it nonetheless affirmed the bond between men and women of conscience.

This Emersonian sentiment preceded by a year the popular surge of interest in Stowe's *Uncle Tom's Cabin*, which defined the abolitionist alliance of heart from a female perspective. Now a woman author addressed women readers, white heroines enacted the rescue of black fugitives, and husbands shared the crusade insofar as their power of sympathy had been opened. "Have you ever lost a child?" runaway Eliza demands of Mrs. Bird. "Then you will feel for me." And when Mrs. Bird immediately goes in search of clothing for Eliza's child in the room of her dead son, the narrator turns on the reader: "And oh! Mother that reads this, has there never been in your house a drawer, or a closet, the opening of which has been to you like the opening again of a little grave?"[30] This rhetorical question must have cut to the quick for Lidian, who in 1852 had never stopped mourning her first son, who had heard the bombshells at Vera Cruz as bursting in her children's nursery. Soon she was insisting that Waldo read the book. Then Mary Moody Emerson joined in the enthusiasm for *Uncle Tom's Cabin*: "Is it not a gem?" she asked when sent a copy, and for years afterward considered Stowe a "favorite."[31] Long attuned to both the experience of mourning and the suffering of slaves, she also brought to her reading of Stowe a kindred sense of the coming kingdom. Her idealism easily incorporated sentiment if it bore religious weight and vision.

Waldo's response to *Uncle Tom's Cabin* suggests the extent and the limit of his interest in women's sentiment. Upon reading an article about Stowe's work in August 1852, he immediately proposed that Charles Eliot Norton reprint the promotion so as to benefit a novel on this "subject so primary to us." Yet he could report to Lidian, "I have read Uncle Tom's Cabin," only the January following, probably long after she had read and recommended it. He subsequently praised the novel's power, moreover, for its ability to reach women across class, not men and women together. "It is read equally in the parlour & the kitchen & the nursery of every house," he commented. "What the lady read in the drawing-room in a few hours, is retailed to her in her kitchen by the cook & the chambermaid, as, week by week, they master one scene & character after another." This was a powerful indirect portrait of Lidian and her household, but it left his own response unspoken. When Waldo soon thereafter began keeping a notebook on the theme of American Liberty, he listed "Mrs. Stowe," followed by the separate item "The heroes & orators truly American."[32] How he wished to elaborate a connection between the woman and her oratorical American novel remains unclear.

Mary, Lidian, and Waldo Emerson all expressed commitment to the antislavery cause through the 1850s, but not in a concert so much as a crossing of voices. Mary returned to Massachusetts in the summer of 1851, immediately joining in opposition to the Fugitive Slave Bill with Mary Merrick Brooks, Henry and Sophia Thoreau, and her own kin. She measured one orator according to his heroism on behalf of fugitive Thomas Sims, declared her interest in the moral crisis of America to lie deeper than Kossuth's Hungarian cause, and reminded Waldo, "I like a conscience war as did our kindred." Nearing eighty, however, she still insisted on separation from the influential community of Concord so much that, through subsequent years, she visited only temporarily while in search of residence elsewhere. As she wandered amidst boarding houses in western Massachusetts, she called the town of Savoy a "desert" because it lacked both church and antislavery society.[33] More commonly these organizations offered her temporary homes in a rootless old age.

Lidian continued, in Waldo's gently disparaging words, to "do antislavery," supporting bazaars and tea parties where abolitionist ideas were purveyed. The description in Garrison's *Liberator* of one such party, presented in Concord to the Middlesex County Anti-Slavery Society amidst the crises of 1851, suggests the dimensions of this work: Concord women provided tea, coffee, and edible "luxuries" for over two hundred, as "the flow of 'almighty talk' swept on in resistless current." Some of the talk would have been about Ralph Waldo Emerson's public letter of support to Mary Merrick Brooks, the preamble to his address on the Fugitive Slave Law (*AW* 51–

52).[34] Lidian and Waldo often met in the same public spaces. "Mother and Father were faithful attendants of Anti-Slavery conventions, lectures, &c.," daughter Ellen recalled. "Mother had several friends made on these occasions, Mr. Wendell Phillips, Mrs. George R. Russell, Miss Lucy Goddard, Mr. & Mrs. George L. Stearns. . . . With them she would hold pow-wows refreshing to her very soul, together they would pour forth their indignation and their forebodings, and blast with every epithet of contempt the South Side clergy and the treacherous statesmen." Lidian's most memorable symbolic action came on the Fourth of July in 1854 when, in the wake of the Kansas-Nebraska bill and the kidnapping of Anthony Burns, she considered the nation "wholly lost to any sense of righteousness." As Ellen told the story, "Seeing flags going up, she asked Father's leave to cover our gates with a pall. Father smiled and consented. So she got a quantity of black cambric, and made a great show of it on our front gate and gateposts." The Emerson children felt mortified, but the parents were of one accord. As Waldo had written that spring to commemorate the anniversary of Webster's fall, "the Fugitive Slave Law did much to unglue the eyes of men, and now the Nebraska Bill leaves us staring"(AW 89).[35]

Idealist and sentimental protest found common cause in their mutual opposition to the treacherous "South Side" rhetoric of church and state: both found an alternative to sermons and legal codes in intuitive knowledge, whether based on emotion or intellectual principle. Waldo became learned in the consonance and dissonance of civil law with moral principle, so that, as von Frank writes of the 1855 "Lecture on Slavery," personal sympathy for the black man was invisible.[36] Lidian put that sympathy foremost, and Mary ended her long diary with a prayer of complete identification: "God of mercy whose purposes are wise & perfect tho eclipsed look on thy coloured people. Behold their sufferings. Deliver me with thine own hand!"[37] Nonetheless, Waldo and the two women joined in invective, calling the nation's proslavery system evil, a calamity and a swindle. Even in his moral and legal abstraction, moreover, the female was usually present at least figuratively. Liberty, he claimed in 1854, was "the oppressed Lady whom true knights on their oath and honor must rescue and save." But then he shifted to representing woman as the prophet rather than object of the rescue mission: "I respect the Anti-Slavery Society. It is the Cassandra that has foretold all that has befallen."[38] Since his college days, "Cassandra" had been among private names for his oracle Mary Moody Emerson.

In these same years the rising movement for women's rights solicited his support, as was probably inevitable for a man affiliated with both the antislavery movement and the recently deceased Margaret Fuller. In 1850 and 1851 he declined, placing above the new cause both his work on Fuller's *Memoir* and his concern for the nation's crisis. Besides, as he wrote to Paulina W. Davis, he found the prospect of a public convention for women's rights "not very agreeable." "The fact of the political & civil wrongs of woman I deny not. If women feel wronged, then they are wronged. . . . [But] I should not wish women to wish political functions, nor, if granted assume them."[39] Here at last was the labored, difficult statement of reservation about the common cause that his antislavery speeches had assumed since 1844. Women might provide the unfailing heart of conscience, play Cassandra, or write novels to reach across classes, but they should not therefore become public citizens or organize publicly to demand rights. By 1855, the same year as his consummate "Lecture on Slavery," Waldo finally did address the Woman's Rights Convention in Boston, but his reservations and equivocations continued. These are illuminated with new clarity when seen in the context of the intrafamily, reformist conversation of Mary and Lidian.

Both women, coming from significantly different allegiances, were proto-feminists. Mary had read and substantially approved Wollstonecraft's *Vindication of the Rights of Women* before the turn of the nineteenth century, and as she turned in early adulthood to the pursuit of spiritual transcendence and ideal truth, she had repudiated marriage. A generation later Lidian idealized Swedenborg's idea of heavenly marriage rather than solitary self-fulfillment; she had "dared" to marry Waldo, she confessed, because she believed God had destined their union. But from these differing perspectives both Mary and Lidian looked critically at the shortcomings of actual marriages. In 1850, even as Mary wrote to Lidian about the year's "great question" of politics, she also evoked "the dark side of matrimony" in anticipation of a niece's wedding. Lidian answered Mary's request for an opinion: "[W]hat you said of marriage . . . is I am sure both true and false—that is it is most true of marriage without love—and I supposed the majority of marriages are so. . . . A true marriage is 'perfect freedom' there is no *yoke* there. But the yoke of an unfit marriage may I should say be more galling and degrading than that of the Negro slave."[40]

It is not clear where Lidian was placing her own marriage here. She had had a long education in the women's rights analogy between wife and slave; over the fifteen years previous she and Waldo had hosted at their house some of the age's leading feminist-abolitionist thinkers, including Harriet Martineau, Angelina and Sarah Grimké, and Fredericka Bremer.

There had been no moment in the history of Transcendentalism when the "woman question" was not, in one form or another, also on the table. Most of all, she had known Margaret Fuller as both a leader of thought and a houseguest, painfully feeling the insecurity of her competition for Waldo's regard. Lidian's letters are peppered with comments on the inadequacies of other women's husbands, and once she sarcastically demanded of Waldo the same sympathy for a recent wasp-sting "which you demanded and I gave you in your hour of like calamity."[41] Yet, as far as the surviving, admittedly incomplete record of these years goes, she never directly accused him, claimed the yoke of slavery, or ventured overt opinions of women's rights comparable to her abolitionist convictions. It is likely that in 1850—the year of Waldo's invitation to the women's rights meeting—she contained her troubles and held to the ideal of spiritual union. She does not seem to have attended either of the first public conventions in Massachusetts.

But another campaigner for women, Elizabeth Oakes Smith, reveals that by the end of 1851 the women's movement had caught up with Waldo and Lidian Emerson and their Aunt Mary. Possibly aware of Smith through their common friend Wendell Phillips, husband and wife together journeyed into Boston to propose a visit and speaking engagement in Concord. Before Smith's lecture on "Womanhood," Lidian warned Smith that Mary—now on one of her visits through town—might walk out if displeased. This confidentiality implies entire trust in the message and speaker on Lidian's own part, and in fact Mary stayed through the lecture to applaud it warmly as well. Soon thereafter Lidian was the only one of the circle to stay through an entire Lyceum lecture on temperance: Smith, as well as Mary and Waldo Emerson, Bronson Alcott, and Henry Thoreau, all abandoned the speaker to huddle in a downstairs room and hold their own rhapsodic conversation about romantic genius. The crossing of people and issues that Smith evokes—antislavery, temperance, Transcendentalism—evokes the complex setting in which questions about women's civil, spiritual, and marital privilege were being raised. "You must come and live in Concord," Waldo told the visitor, "and we shall have an oracle."[42] He seems to have been trying to recall the earlier presence of Mary Moody Emerson or Margaret Fuller for the 1850s, and when in September 1855 he actually addressed the Boston convention, he shared the stage with Elizabeth Oakes Smith.

To read Waldo's address "Woman" in the context of that year's shared intensities, however, is to hear what is missing from it. Though he spoke of

women's rights to education, property, and equality in marriage, he evoked
no concrete sense of injustice done in any of these areas. Certainly he echoed none of the analogy between wife and slave so quick to Lidian's pen a
few years before. At a time when he was baring the discrepancy between
the moral and civil law concerning slavery, he now settled for an unelabo-
rated, liberal gesture of permission: "Let the laws be purged of every barbarous remainder, every barbarous impediment to women." Most of all,
there was no sense of a national crisis, an impending evil, or a promise
betrayed in the address. His declaration that women rather than men
should decide on their public role sounded generous, but it was not advocacy, and indeed it was followed by a definition of the "true woman" as one
who worked only indirectly, decorating the home and seeking to "find in
man her guardian." This was a soft version of the domestic gospel that
abolitionist women, including Mary and Lidian Emerson and even the do-
mestically loyal Harriet Beecher Stowe, would not have accepted. He did
embrace the recent "antagonism to Slavery" as woman's best university.
But he carried none of the content of that antagonism from questions of
race to questions of gender. He voiced no pain and no protest. Later Elizabeth Oakes Smith, even while admiring in Waldo Emerson the "high humanities" that included alliance with women, contrasted his 1855 performance with another male advocate's: "He was one that did not seek contest,
did not snuff the battle with the heat of the war-horse, like Wendell
Phillips."[43]

In fact the address was not primarily political at all, but a reflection on
women's "oracular nature," its origins in his religious and literary romanticism much more than recent abolitionist thought. To say this in itself is
not to find fault. Since his youth Waldo had been powerfully characterizing
his mentor Mary as oracle, Cassandra, and "weird woman," as now he
quoted from the *Edda* that women were "Weirdes all." More recently the
role of prophetess had also been played in his life by Margaret Fuller, and
he had even hoped for the same power from Elizabeth Smith. But his terms
of characterizing women's intuitive power of mind did little honor to these
women of family and town, Transcendentalist and abolitionist circles. In
particular, Mary as oracle had been a single and intellectual enthusiast of
intuition. Now he separated women's native gift from primary intellect and
failed to imagine any woman outside of marriage. "Women are strong by
sentiment," he began; but then, rather than calling upon sentiment to lead
mind or conscience, he added, "The same mental height which their husbands attain by toil, they attain by sympathy with their husbands" (*w* 11:

338). Women were always and only wives, and the marital bond of sympathy went only from wife to husband. From this bland characterization one gains no hint of the seismic rumblings within his own marriage, either his critique of the bond as spiritually constricting or the hints from Lidian that he owed reciprocal sympathy. Waldo's address to the women's rights convention reads as a retreat—a deeply characteristic one—from both his personal dealings with women and his own abolitionist thought on the principles of liberty and equality.

Lidian was probably present at this convention but left no record of her thoughts about it; Mary remained in western Massachusetts. Indeed there is no immediately audible response to the address "Woman" in his closest circle, for in the years immediately following, family and town riveted their attention on the escalating conflict over slavery. Mary may not have commented on "Woman," but in 1857 she declared Waldo's Kansas speech the voice of truth.[44] By this time Charles Sumner, successor to Webster, had been physically beaten in reprisal for his speech "Crime against Kansas," and freedom fighter John Brown had first visited Concord. Henry Thoreau introduced him to the Emersons, and the Emerson house and Lidian's hospitality once more provided board and occasion for talk. As Ellen remembered Brown's visit, he spoke gently of his sheep and his Christian conversion when the children were present. In their absence, however, antislavery "pow-wows" were the order of the day. When Waldo spoke again on Kansas in September 1857, he directly solicited money for rifles from his audience (AW xlvi).[45] In a time of direct action against perceived evil, there could be no moral uncertainty. A year later Mary, finally willing to settle, returned to Concord and again joined the debate. At a conversation conducted by Bronson Alcott at the Emerson house in November, the eighty-four-year-old woman spoke her final piece on the idealist certainties of moral law, in so doing both grounding the day's politics and vindicating her own womanly power.

The group present on this occasion included women and men of both Transcendentalist and abolitionist allegiance. Waldo was out of town lecturing, but Lidian presided over the parlor, welcoming among others Henry and Sophia Thoreau, Mary Merrick Brooks, Ellery Channing, Samuel Ward, Franklin Sanborn, and the newcomer Henry James Sr. James did not understand that Alcott controlled an Alcott conversation, and soon he had taken over, attempting to exonerate criminals from their crimes and charge society instead. Such an assumption would have been horrific to these people of conscience: all had denounced Webster and the

attack on Sumner; some had aided Shadrach and braved the marshals seizing Anthony Burns; several would soon be defending John Brown's raid on
Harpers Ferry. But Mary seized the moment for them all. When James, as
Sanborn recalled, "spoke repeatedly and scornfully of the Moral Law," she
burst forth to the whole group:

> Rising from her chair at the west side of the room, . . . she clasped her little
> wrinkled hands and raised them toward the black band over her left temple (a
> habit she had when deeply moved), and began her answer to these doctrines
> of Satan, as she thought them. She expressed her amazement that any man
> should denounce the Moral Law,—the only tie of society. . . . She referred
> him to his Bible and to Dr. [Samuel] Clarke (one of her great authorities from
> childhood) and she denounced him personally in the most racy terms.[46]

Mary had not only known from "childhood" of Clarke's and Price's idealist
grounding of right and wrong in God's law; she had taught such lessons to
Waldo, returned to dialogue with him on this strength, and written for the
women's abolitionist fair about the universality of the voice within. So too
was she speaking of an intuition that equalized women and men, meanwhile
demonstrating her equality as she would not have demanded it, through
her public denunciation of James. Though Waldo was not present, she was
enacting the role of "oracle" that he himself had known—and significantly
misrepresented in "Woman." According to Alcott, all present praised the
performance.

John Brown became the single heroic figure who most united the ideal-
ists and activists, men and women, of this circle. He stayed again at the
Emerson house in May 1859, and though no one seems to have anticipated
the actual insurrection of five months later, they contributed to his legal
fees, supported the family after his execution, and defended Frank Sanborn
against charges of active conspiracy with Brown. "Have you seen the verses
of our favorite [Lydia] M.[aria] Childs on the Martyr Brown kissing a
coulered infant when going to death[?]" Mary asked Lidian from her final
home with a niece. "Do thank her for giving to print that most delightful
characteristic of the man." Waldo too memorialized Brown as a man of
feeling across race, whose boyhood sympathy upon witnessing a slave-
beating "worked such indignation in him that he swore an oath of resistance
to Slavery as long as he lived." Here not only was the black slave's pain
present in the address, but the principle of sympathy became its rhetorical
foundation. Slaveholders, Waldo asserted, could complain of abolitionist
sympathy with slaves no more than of gravity or ebbtide; and Brown him-

self, as champion of the slave, had drawn "all people, in proportion to their sensibility and self-respect," to sympathy with his cause. "All women are drawn to him by their predominance of sentiment. All gentlemen, of course, are on his side" (*AW* 122–23).[47]

The "John Brown" speech of January 1860 announced the militant feeling of the Civil War. Though slipping into a final dementia, Mary wrote Lidian sixteen months later thanking Providence for the war only "if it is to free the slaves." Waldo responded for himself and Lidian: "What a relief in the political convulsions, you must feel with us. The shame of living seems taken away, & to mature & old age the love of life will return, as we did not anticipate." Mary died in 1863, the spring following emancipation; possibly she had been able to greet the freedom of slaves that she had so long anticipated. Lidian's waiting for this watershed event took more explicit form. The most extreme radical in the family, she did not allow her son Edward to enlist until emancipation identified the goal as "holy war" against slavery; she regularly pronounced judgment upon the government's slow pace; and she consented heartily in 1863 to the newspaper story of a black soldier who found the American flag only now to "signify Liberty." Publicly responding to Lincoln's promise of emancipation in October 1862, Waldo declared all "hurts . . . healed" and defined the constituency rallying behind this moment: "every spark of intellect, every virtuous feeling, every religious heart, every man of honor, every poet, every philosopher, the generosity of the cities, the health of the country, the strong arms of the mechanics, the endurance of farmers, the passionate conscience of women" (*AW* 132).[48] If he had hesitated in 1855 to advocate women's full part in American democratic processes, his 1863 rhetoric of emancipation apparently found the change accomplished for women as well.

Of course public pronouncements rarely close issues definitively. In neither the nation nor the Emerson family were all hurts healed or all inequities resolved. Despite ongoing protestations of ill health, Lidian kept attending Wendell Phillips' antislavery meetings; in 1867 he singled her out to illustrate persistence in a failing cause, calling her "one of these ladies who sits by me when her husband objected to her coming, . . . replying that she could die but she could not not be there." After the war's close, when the widened franchise did not after all include women, Lidian also found energy for commitment to the renewed women's rights movement. When the New England Woman Suffrage Association was founded in 1868, she sat on the stage as a full and public supporter. Six months later Waldo was enlisted to speak once more on "Woman," as well as to serve as an honorary vice-president of the organization. Now more than before the war he was prepared explicitly to endorse women's suffrage; in his view "the great enterprise of recent civilization, the putting down of slavery" had shown women's capacity in public affairs. His fundamental sense of women's nature, however, had not changed: women showed themselves in the world "as affectionate, as religious, as oracular"; whether at home or in public, woman was a wife, an inspiring partner who "holds a man to religion."[49]

Ralph Waldo Emerson's view of women's rights had progressed with the women's movement and was probably well received by the moderate leaders of the New England Association. Still it acknowledged only part of the complexity of the women whose protests had urged him onto the stage. His memorial address on Mary Moody Emerson earlier the same spring recognized that a woman of religious feeling could be single, solitary, and difficult as well as inspiring. Even then, he failed to speak of either his aunt's antislavery politics or her particular influence on him. As for Lidian, this wife did not settle for holy and affectionate guidance alone, and however far Waldo had progressed in the cause was not sufficient for her. In 1871, when Ellen offered the "firebrand" of her own antisuffrage ideas over tea, both parents responded characteristically. Ellen described the scene in comic tones to her brother Edward: "Mother mounts her most bolting & snorting warhorse and leaves us all nowhere in less than no time. Edith on a pony of the same breed charges valiantly on her presuming sister. . . . Father won't speak one word till, particularly requested, he gives his views and as a reward has directly the fury of all his household leveled at them."[50] Waldo's moderation hardly had the last word in this circle of combatants.

NOTES

1. *Letters of Lidian Jackson Emerson*, ed. Delores Bird Carpenter (Columbia: University of Missouri Press, 1987), pp. 308–9.

2. John Carlos Rowe, *At Emerson's Tomb: The Politics of Classic American Literature* (New York: Columbia University Press, 1997), p. 21; Alfred von Frank, *The Trials of Anthony Burns: Freedom and Slavery in Emerson's Boston* (Cambridge: Harvard University Press, 1998.

3. Mikhail Bakhtin's sense of the novel as "social heteroglossia" applies to the Emersonian essay as well: the primary text is "impersonal, but pregnant with the images of speaking persons." Even language that appears unitary is polemical and apologetic, another party in conversation; and more often language itself reflects multiple voices in the environment. See Bakhtin, *The Dialogic Imagination: Four Es-*

says, ed. Michael Holquist (Austin: University of Texas Press, 1981), pp. 331–32. As I have written elsewhere, the availability of Emerson family papers (edited and in manuscript) offers a rare opportunity to recover actual voices from this author's most immediate environment. See "'Men and Women Conversing': The Emersons in 1837," in *Emersonian Circles: Essays in Honor of Joel Myerson*, ed. Wesley T. Mott and Robert E. Burkholder (Rochester: University of Rochester Press, 1997), 127–59; and *Mary Moody Emerson and the Origins of Transcendentalism: A Family History* (New York: Oxford University Press, 1998).

4. *Letters of Mary Moody Emerson*, ed. Nancy Craig Simmons (Athens: University of Georgia Press, 1993), pp. 180–81, cited hereafter as *Letters of MME*.

5. Ellen Tucker Emerson, *Life of Lidian Jackson Emerson*, ed. Delores Bird Carpenter (Boston: Twayne, 1980), pp. 72–73, cited hereafter as *Life of LJE*; *JMN* 5:64; *JMN* 4:53; *Letters of MME*, p. 428.

6. *Life of LJE*, pp. 68–69, *JMN* 8:88; *Letters of Ellen Tucker Emerson*, ed. Edith E. W. Gregg (Kent, Ohio: Kent State University Press, 1982), 1:607; *Correspondence of Emerson and Carlyle*, ed. Joseph Slater (New York: Columbia University Press, 1964), p. 184.

7. On Mary's early life and "slavery," see Cole, *Mary Moody Emerson*, especially pp. 56–57 and 71–79. *Life of LJE*, pp. 24–25, 42. The culmination of Lidian's advocacy of animals came after 1868, when she became an officer of the reorganized Massachusetts Society for Prevention of Cruelty to Animals; later she told Ellen that she had written unsigned articles for its publication *Our Dumb Animals* (*Life of LJE*, pp. 167–68, 250 n.) On the anti-pain politics of this organization in the context of other nineteenth-century reforms, see James Turner, *Reckoning with the Beast: Animals, Pain, and Humanity in the Victorian Mind* (Baltimore: Johns Hopkins University Press, 1980).

8. The Price excerpts are in *Monthly Anthology and Boston Review* 1 (Aug. 1804): 456–57, the two most important essay-letters as "Constance" in 1 (Aug. 1804): 453–54 and 1 (Dec. 1804): 646–47. *Letters of MME*, p. 139; cf. Cole, *Mary Moody Emerson*, 167 and 341 n. for the source in Price.

9. *W* 10:432; cf., for instance, *L* 1:104–5.

10. *Letters of MME*, pp. 176–77, 186, 180–81.

11. *Letters of MME*, p. 191; Ralph Waldo Emerson quoted in Franklin B. Sanborn, *Sixty Years of Concord, 1855–1915*, ed. Kenneth W. Cameron (Hartford: Transcendental Books, 1975), p. 48.

12. See Cole, *Mary Moody Emerson*, pp. 221–23, 234–35.

13. *Letters of MME*, pp. 355–56; Mary Moody Emerson, "Almanack," [March] 29, 1835 (manuscript, Houghton Library, Harvard University, bMSAM 1280.235 [385], folder 18).

14. Mary Moody Emerson to Lidian Emerson, [March 29, 1835] (manuscript, Houghton, bMSAM 1280.226 [770]); *Letters of MME*, pp. 364, 366; *JMN* 5:90–91; *Life of LJE*, p. 64.

15. *Letters of LJE*, pp. 60–61; *JMN* 5:382.

16. *JMN* 5:442; cf. *CW* 1:88. Len Gougeon discusses Ralph Waldo Emerson's 1837 address in *VH* 37–40, and presents the record of Emerson family support for antislavery petitions in the introduction to *AW*.

17. *AW* 1–5; *Letters of LJE*, pp. 74–75.

18. *Life of LJE*, p. 84; Joel Myerson, "Margaret Fuller's 1842 Journal: At Concord with the Emersons," *Harvard Library Bulletin* 21 (1973): 330–31, 338.

19. Lidian Emerson to Ralph Waldo Emerson, Dec. 21, [1845] (manuscript, Houghton, bMS AM 1280.226[556]); "Transcendental Bible" quoted in *Life of LJE*, pp. 81–83; Abby Alcott, "Journal 1845," pp. 2, 5 (manuscript, Houghton, *59M-311).

20. *Life of LJE*, p. 84; *Letters of LJE*, pp. 114, 125. Lidian's presence at the abolitionist-sponsored Chardon Street Convention is mentioned in Deborah Weston to Anne Warren Weston, Nov. 17, 1840 (manuscript, A.9.2.14.59, Weston Sisters Papers, Boston Public Library).

21. *L* 2:396-97; Mary Moody Emerson to "Albert," Dec. 9, 1841; Mary Moody Emerson to Anti-slavery Fair, Dec. 8, 1841 (manuscripts, Houghton, bMS AM 1280.226 [1299, 1300]); *Letters of MME*, pp. 475–76.

22. *AW* 206–7 n.1; *Letters of MME*, pp. 460–61.

23. *Letters of MME*, pp. 525, 519–20; *Letters of LJE*, p. 172. George Tolman, who read and transcribed Mary Moody Emerson's manuscripts in the late nineteenth century, wrote that "her grief and indignation were unbounded" at Webster's 1850 speech (*Mary Moody Emerson* [Cambridge: privately printed, 1929], p. 9); but her full statement of indignation apparently no longer survives.

24. *JMN* 11:249, 250, 279 ff.; *AW* 55, 59–60.

25. *Letters of MME*, p. 496; *Letters of LJE*, pp. 148, 152, 156.

26. *Letters of LJE*, pp. 141, 146, 157–58, 154–55. Cf. Harmon D. Smith, "At Home with Lidian: Henry Thoreau in 1847–48," *Concord Saunterer*, New Series 3 (1995): 35–48 for a nuanced portrait of Waldo and Lidian as well as her co-housekeeper Thoreau during Waldo's absence.

27. *Letters of LJE*, pp. 143, 155, 164, 173.

28. Gary Collison, *Shadrach Minkins: From Fugitive Slave to Citizen* (Cambridge: Harvard University Press, 1997), pp. 151–56; Bigelow quoted on p. 151.

29. *AW* 62–63, 66, 60, 57, 60, 64.

30. Harriet Beecher Stowe, *Uncle Tom's Cabin or Life among the Lowly*, ch. 9. Cf. Catharine E. O'Connell's analysis of this scene as a "sentimental paradigm" in "'The Magic of the Real Presence of Distress': Sentimentality and Competing Rhetorics of Authority," in *The Stowe Debate: Rhetorical Strategies in Uncle Tom's Cabin*, ed. Mason Lowance et al. (Amherst: University of Massachusetts Press, 1994), pp. 15–18.

31. *L* 4:343; Mary Moody Emerson to Elizabeth Hoar, Feb. 17, 1853 (manuscript, Houghton, bMS AM 1280.226 [1200]); *Letters of MME*, p. 295.

32. *L* 4:302-3, 343; *JMN* 13:121, 14:414.

33. See Cole, *Mary Moody Emerson*, pp. 281–84 on her 1851 conversations. *Letters of MME*, pp. 550, 553, 538; Mary Moody Emerson to Elizabeth Hoar, Oct 29, [1857] (manuscript, Houghton, bMSAM 1280.226 [1203].

34. *L* 4:239; Lidian Emerson to Ralph Waldo Emerson, Mar. 24, 1851 (manuscript, Houghton, bMSAM 1280.226 [563]); *The Liberator* 21 (April 3, 1851).

35. *Life of LJE*, pp. 130, 125.

36. von Frank, *Trials of Anthony Burns*, p. 333; cf. O'Connell, "Sentimentality," 18–29, on the contesting of religious and patriotic rhetoric by sentimentalism.

37. "Almanack," Jan 16, 1858 (manuscript, Houghton, bMSAM 1280.235, folder 25).

38. *AW* 93, 104, 88–89.

39. *L* 4:230; cf. *L* 8:288–89.

40. *Letters of LJE*, pp. 153–54, 174; *Letters of MME*, pp. 518, 521.

41. *Letters of LJE*, pp. 249–50; cf. 192, 194 and *Life of LJE*, p. 90.

42. *Selections from the Autobiography of Elizabeth Oakes Smith*, ed. Mary Alice Wyman (Lewiston, ME: Lewiston Journal, 1924), pp. 134–35, 137–38, 141. Mary Moody Emerson soon thereafter published an unsigned letter in the *Christian Register* that tried to be "rid of the notion" that she was "for the rights." See Cole, *MME*, pp. 281–82, for an assessment of this conservatism and her longer record of support for women's autonomy. There is no record of her directly speaking for or against women voting or preaching.

43. *W* 11:354, 355; Smith, *Autobiography*, p. 148.

44. Mary Moody Emerson to Ralph Waldo Emerson, Aug. [2? 1857?] (manuscript, Egbert Starr Library, Middlebury College). Gougeon names two probable occasions when Ralph Waldo Emerson addressed Kansas relief meetings, June and September 1857 (introduction to *Emerson's Antislavery Writings*, p. xlvi). The first is the more likely occasion for Mary Moody Emerson's comment.

45. *Life of LJE*, p. 131.

46. *JA* 308; Sanborn, "A Concord Notebook: The Women of Concord," *The Critic* 48 (1906): 158.

47. Mary Moody Emerson to Lidian Jackson Emerson, Dec. 31, 1859 (manuscript, Houghton bMSAM 1280.226).

48. *Letters of MME*, p. 599; *L* 5:249; *Letters of LJE*, pp. 216, 219–20.

49. *Letters of Ellen Tucker Emerson*, ed. Edith E. W. Gregg (Kent, Ohio: Kent State University Press, 1982), 1:426; Ellen Carol DuBois, *Feminism and Suffrage: The Emergence of an Independent Women's Movement in America, 1848–1869* (Ithaca: Cornell University Press, 1978), p. 168 on Lidian Emerson, and ch. 6 on the formation of two competing women's rights organizations in response to the failure of the Fifteenth Amendment to grant suffrage to women. The New England Women's Rights Association, forerunner of the Women's Rights Association, was moderate in accepting the primary need for black male suffrage and pursuing votes for women as a postwar agenda, whereas Elizabeth Cady Stanton's National Women's Rights

association refused to accept suffrage for blacks but not for women. The New England-American Association generally affirmed women's domestic sphere, whereas the National critiqued it more radically. Len Gougeon, "Emerson's Second Address on the Woman Question," *New England Quarterly* 71 no. 4 (December 1998): 588–89. My thanks to Len Gougeon for providing access to this article in manuscript.

50. *W* 10:397–433. Elizabeth Palmer Peabody's obituary essay on Mary Moody Emerson, by contrast, named her allegiance to Clarke and Price, found the antislavery movement "a counterpart of her religious devotion, a flaming fire," and declared that she had sacrificed "the meridian of her life" to raising nephews ("A Tribute to Mary Moody Emerson," *Boston Evening Transcript* [May 14, 1863]). *Letters of Ellen Tucker Emerson* 1:621.

ARMIDA GILBERT

"Pierced by the Thorns of Reform": Emerson on Womanhood

IN ORDER TO UNDERSTAND Emerson's developing attitudes toward the woman's rights movement, it is necessary to appreciate the way in which the movement began, grew, and changed and the issues around which the early debates were centered. Before even the earliest stages of the woman's rights movement in America, Emerson had been introduced to the ideas that would inform it, especially through the pioneering work of his friend Margaret Fuller. As explained by her, first in "The Great Lawsuit,—Man Versus Men, Woman Versus Women" in the Transcendentalist literary journal *The Dial* in 1843, then in expanded form in the first book written in America to argue for woman's rights, *Woman in the Nineteenth Century*, in 1845, Fuller's ideas, transmitted to Emerson through their frequent conversations and correspondence, came to form the core of his thinking on women. Fuller's carefully reasoned tactics would form the basis for the approaches and arguments that would later be adopted by the nascent woman's rights movement, as Elizabeth Cady Stanton, Susan B. Anthony, and Matilda Joslyn Gage acknowledged in their monumental *History of Woman Suffrage*, when they stated that Fuller's work "gave a new impulse to woman's life as a thinker."[1] Thus Emerson shared essential concepts and patterns of thinking about issues regarding women with the American woman's rights movement from the earliest days of its existence, inspiring suffragists to accept him as one of their champions.

Following on Fuller's prescient presentation of the issues of women's role in society, the woman's rights movement in nineteenth-century America emerged from the crucible of the abolitionist movement, in much the same way that the contemporary women's movement would later spring from the furor of the civil rights movement. The catalyzing event for the woman's rights movement was the 1840 World Anti-Slavery Convention in London. After women organized and planned the first international convention, a massive undertaking, when they arrived at the site they were informed that they could not be seated at their own conference due to their sex; all women were to be excluded from the platform and convention seating and allowed only to stand voiceless and silent in the aisles and gallery. Outraged, organizers Lucretia Mott and Elizabeth Cady Stanton agreed to hold the first woman's rights convention upon their return to America.[2]

By 1848, these American women had organized their historic first woman's rights convention, held in Seneca Falls, New York. As Julia Ward Howe, later leader of the suffragist American Woman's Party, observed, 1848 was considerably before "the claims of women to political efficiency had begun to occupy the attention . . . of the American public"; full recognition of the "woman question" came only after the Civil War.[3] Word spread quickly among women involved in social reform, however, and another National Woman's Rights Convention was held in Worcester, Massachusetts, in 1850, only two years after the historic Seneca Falls Convention. Emerson was invited to the convention and gave it his support. As was the common practice, the convention prepared a public declaration of principle that would be signed by the attendees, indicating their agreement with these principles. Emerson signed this statement of support, an unusually bold step for a writer who generally avoided identification with any formal organization for social reform and who tended to be extremely cautious about any public pronouncement. His willingness to be publicly included as a supporter of the convention indicated not only his awareness of the aims of the woman's movement long before most of the country realized its existence but also the strength of his agreement with its principles.[4]

Certainly Emerson was sincere in his letter expressing his wish to appear at the 1850 convention; it was not an excuse to avoid facing the issue. In 1855, Emerson would appear in person to address that year's Woman's Rights Convention. His address on that occasion was later revised to form the essay "Woman." In both the original lecture and the slightly emended essay, "Woman" was Emerson's most public and extended statement of his opinion on women's issues, a serious avowal of his dedication to woman's rights. Couched as it was in the terms of the nineteenth-century woman's movement, the essay may seem lukewarm to contemporary readers. Yet Emerson made his partisanship of woman's rights clear from the start, first by staking a claim for the importance of the issue, declaring that no reform movement was "more seriously interesting to every healthful and thoughtful mind" than the position of women (*w* 11:405).[5] Later in the essay he would contrast these "healthful and thoughtful" supporters of woman's rights with the presumably unhealthy and thoughtless detractors of the movement, whom Emerson attacked—in very strong language for him—deriding the "cheap" jokes at the expense of the campaigners for equal rights and the "monstrous exaggeration" of every misogynist writer from "Mahomet" and Aristophanes to Rabelais and the highly popular Tennyson (*w* 11:418). Previously, Emerson had deplored this tendency to denigrate women, and particularly, their intellectual efforts. Writing in his journal in 1841, he quoted the mayor of Lowell, Massachusetts, as saying disparagingly of a group of women arriving to testify in a trial, "There go the light-troops!" and criticized, "Neither Plato, Mahomet, nor Goethe have said a severer thing on our fair Eve. Yet the old lawyer did not mean to be satanic" (*JMN* 8:85). In 1848, while in France, he observed that "At the Club des Femmes, there was among the men some patronage, but no real courtesy. The lady who presided spoke & behaved with the utmost propriety,—a woman of heart & sense,—but the audience of men were perpetually on the look out for some equivoque, into which, of course, each male speaker would be pretty sure to fall; & the laugh was loud & general" (*JMN* 10:268).

Having established the significance of the issue and the superficiality of its opponents' arguments, Emerson consolidated his position by establishing woman's strengths. Unfortunately, the strengths he singled out for praise, however complimentary to nineteenth-century women, would come to seem problematic to late twentieth-century readers. As he had stated in the address to the 1855 Woman's Rights Convention on which "Woman" was based, "Women feel in relation to men as geniuses feel among energetic workers, that tho' overruled & thrust aside in the press, they outsee all these noisy masters." This praise of women's "oracular nature," their greater intuitive powers, has reminded many contemporary women of the cliché of "women's intuition." Whenever they used their intelligence more quickly or efficiently than the men around them, it was dismissed as "women's intuition," not recognized as a sign of women's equal intellectual capacity. In the address, Emerson had clarified this idea by suggesting that what appeared to be women's intuition was actually the result of a quicker thought process: "They learn so fast & convey the result so fast, as to outrun the logic of their slow brother."

Further, during this period, even the strongest suffragists clung to their claim for psychic and spiritual superiority. Fuller's *Woman in the Nineteenth Century* resounded with such rhetoric: "The especial genius of Woman I believe to be . . . intuitive in function" (*EMF* 309). Her influence on Emerson was evident here, as in so many of the other ideas in "Woman," particularly since he had been so recently at work on editing the *Memoirs of Margaret Fuller Ossoli*. Like Fuller, too, Emerson suggested that women's faster thought processes placed them in the vanguard of social reform: "Any remarkable opinion or movement shared by women will be the first sign of revolution" (*W* 11:406). In this firmer logic, women influenced the progress of society, as Emerson observed in his journal: "they buy slaves where the women will permit it; where they will not, they make the wind, the tide, the waterfall, the steam . . . do the work" (*JMN* 10:103). The French Revolution was another example (*JMN* 10:296).

Like Fuller and most other nineteenth-century feminists, Emerson did not take into account the effect of social conditioning in creating women's "strength" of "sentiment" and "sympathy" (*W* 11:406–7). However, awareness of the effects of gender role conditioning was decades away, with the nascent science of sociology, and Emerson's tropes here, however painful to postmodern sensibilities, were no different than those of his female and suffragist contemporaries. In fact, by following the paths of argument laid down by Fuller and her suffragist successors, Emerson proved how closely he adhered to her ideas.

Emerson's views as expressed in "Woman" were what contemporary critics would today term "essentialist," implying an innate, inborn difference between the male and female temperaments true across the bounds of cultural and historical conditioning. While today essentialism can be viewed as one among a variety of hotly contended feminist viewpoints, in Emerson's time, given this lack of awareness of social conditioning, it was the norm. In the nineteenth century it was truly the woman's—singular—movement, generally agreeing on an essentialist philosophy and a demand for equal legal rights, as compared to today's far more diversely oriented women's—plural—movement, in which a multiplicity of often clashing viewpoints have struggled for expression.[6] Emerson's assumption of intrinsic emotional and physical discrepancies in men's and women's strengths were aligned to his era. The most outspoken suffragists of Emerson's time would have agreed that women were, in his words, "More vulnerable, more infirm, more mortal" than men, in a time when women had an exceptionally high death rate, especially in childbirth. Fuller, in fact, had stated unequivocally in *Woman in the Nineteenth Century* that "Woman is the weaker party" (*EMF* 33). Emerson may also well have had the premature demise of his first wife Ellen in mind here. Indeed, Ellen Tucker Emerson was, with Fuller, the previously unacknowledged model for Emerson's vision of womanhood. As he mused in his journal, "I can never think of women without gratitude for the bright revelations of her best nature" (*JMN* 8: 381). He continued to contemplate her sayings and examples throughout his life.[7] As debatable as it may be in our time, few in the nineteenth century would have disagreed with Emerson's paraphrase of Swedenborg that "the difference of sex [runs] through nature and through thought" (*w* 11:416). Yet Emerson did at times approach a more androgynous ideal, as when he noted in his journals that "A highly endowed man with good intellect & good conscience is a Man-Woman, & does not so much need the comple-ment of Woman to his being as another. Hence his relations to the sex are somewhat dislocated & unsatisfactory. He asks in woman sometimes the Woman, sometimes the Man" (*JMN* 8:175 and 10:392). He concluded that "the finest people marry the two sexes in their own person. Hermaphrodite is then the symbol of the finished soul . . . in every act shall appear the married pair: the two elements shall mix in every act" (*JMN* 8:380). Else-where, he observed the "feminine element" was always to be found in "men of genius" (*JMN* 10:394). Emerson agreed with Fuller that both men and women contained a balance of traits that society called masculine or femi-nine, but neither he nor Fuller were able to apply this insight further to realize the effect of social conditioning in encouraging certain traits more highly in each gender.

Perhaps contemporary readers wish that Emerson could have leaped so far ahead of his era as to be aware of the effects of societal condition-ing precisely because, despite his consonance with the ideas of his time, "Woman" was a prescient statement of views that would not become cur-rent until recent times. When Emerson began to analyze the popular re-sponses to the woman's movement, he sounded remarkably like women who would not be writing until the twentieth century.

An example would be the hoary charge that women had produced no masterworks in the arts and sciences. In the original address on which "Woman" was based, Emerson's only response to this charge had been that women excelled instead at life. He admired what he called in his journals this "putting of the life into [women's] deed" and used as examples Mary Seton, "who put her arm into the bolt to save Queen Mary," and "the women in the old sieges who cut off their hair to make ropes & ladders" (*JMN* 10:346).[8] This was itself an advance on Emerson's earlier reflection of the social stereotype that women's role was simply to inspire men (seen in, for example, *JMN* 8:149–50). By the time of the essay "Woman" Emerson had gone a step further and realized that it had not been possible for female genius to be recognized "Till the new education and larger opportunities of very modern times" (*W* 11:408). Here he anticipated Virginia Woolf's classic essay "A Room of One's Own," which also refuted this charge by reference to women's historic denial of access to educational and occupational opportunities. In the original address Emerson had also followed the same line of argument as Woolf's lecture, often titled "Woman in the Professions," pointing out that, in Emerson's words, women "are better scholars than we [men] are at school & the reason why they are not better than we, twenty years later," was not because of an innate intellectual deficit but "because men can turn their reading to account in the professions, & women are excluded from the professions." Similarly, as he controverted the "monstrous exaggeration" of the misogynists, he noted their tendency to resort to stereotypes of women as mentally deficient and of femininity as an illness, anticipating the twentieth-century analyses of Charlotte Perkins Gilman, Simone de Beauvoir, and others.

Still, "Woman" has been questionable for modern readers because the essay was typical of Emerson's penchant in public statements to first summarize all the negative ideas on a topic, then turn to the positive—the technique his friend the feminist Caroline Dall called seeming "to lure the conservatives on over his flowers till all of a sudden their feet are pierced by the thorns of reform."[9] In the second half of the essay, if contemporary readers can bear through, they will find Emerson stating an agenda of women's rights that was extremely radical even for the late nineteenth century, much less for its midpoint. Emerson called openly for women to receive their "one half of the world . . . the right to [equality in] education" and "employment, to equal rights of property, to equal rights of marriage, to the exercise of the professions and of suffrage" (*W* 11:416). In essence, Emerson was here setting out the full agenda of the 1850 Women's Rights Convention for which he had signed the call, proving that he was fully aware of his actions in so doing and truly supported all of these then-radical reforms.

"Woman" encapsulated Emerson's support for full equality for women: "Let the public donations to education be equally shared by them, let them enter a school as freely as a church, let them have and hold their property as men do theirs." In a time when colleges were closed to women and the law forbade their owning property, Emerson's demands were extremely progressive. Emerson even went so far as to argue that if suffrage was denied to women, "You [must] also refuse to tax them," based on the American principle of no taxation without representation. That Emerson was aware of this central and most controversial principle of Susan B. Anthony's in only the first decade of her public work revealed how much he was abreast of the developing suffrage movement and how far ahead of his time he was, but it was not surprising, given that Anthony also cited Fuller as her source material.[10]

Another reason for contemporary readers to perceive "Woman" as lacking in enthusiasm for the suffrage movement is the fact that Emerson, like many among the relatively few Americans who first became aware of and involved with the woman's movement in the 1850s, experienced some confusion from listening to the women who constituted both the pro-suffrage and equally vocal anti–woman's rights campaigns. Emerson was influenced for a time by women who were anti-suffrage, and at first believed the anti-suffrage view that the majority of women did not want change and that it would thus be forced violently upon them. Later, other of the women around him, such as his aunt Mary Moody Emerson, while like Emerson himself repulsed by the materialism and lack of moral judgment in the political and commercial worlds women would be entering, would persuade him that change in their status was nonetheless essential. At the time, however, Emerson had not yet come to his later realization that even the most refined and intellectual women desired the vote, as he stated, "The answer that lies, silent or spoken, in the minds of well-meaning persons, to the new claims, is this: that though their mathematical justice is not to be denied"—a position Emerson held as given, extreme though it was at the time—"yet the best women do not wish these things" (*W* 11:418–19). Despite this belief, Emerson did not ameliorate the radicalism of his demands for equality, urging that even if the most favored women did not want or even need political equality, it must nevertheless be available for the benefit of the women who lacked their social and economic advantages. Emerson understood that all women were, as he stated in his journals, "Starved for thought & sentiment," but that the problem was most burdensome to the underprivileged: "In the labours of house & in poverty I feel sometimes as if the handiness & deft apparatus for household toil were only a garb under which the softest Cleopatra walked concealed" (*JMN* 10:78). Emerson often responded with strong sympathy to the plight of impoverished women.[11] He realized that change in women's financially dependent position was essential to their freedom; in his journals he observed: "Society lives on the system of money & woman comes at money & money's worth through compliment. I should not dare to be woman. Plainly they are created for that better system which supersedes money . . . on our civilization her position is often pathetic. What she is not expected to do & suffer for some invitation to strawberries & cream." At the time he wrote that passage Emerson consoled himself, "Fortunately their eyes are holden that they cannot see" (*JMN* 10:392). By the time he was writing "Woman," the woman's rights movement had made it plain that women did indeed see their subservient economic position and linked it directly to their deprivation of political rights and civic opportunities. This awareness of working-class women was relatively rare even in the woman's movement, as recent histories of the British and American suffrage movements have made clear.

Despite his belief that all women did not desire equality, then, Emerson made a strong case for it, stating boldly that women "have an unquestionable right to their own property. And if a woman demand votes, offices, and political equality with men . . . it must not be refused" (*W* 11:419). The change in number—from the plural "women" to the singular "a woman"—is interesting here, implying that even if only one woman desired the vote, it must be granted her. Further, Emerson determinedly refuted the objections to woman's suffrage. In reply to the common objection to women's political participation, their "want of practical wisdom" (*W* 11:411), he argued wittily that a less than perfect grasp of the issues had never disqualified men from voting. If men voted as they were told by their political bosses and parties without troubling to inform themselves on the issues, women could certainly do no worse. In response to the charge that women lacked worldly experience, Emerson quipped that this was "not a disqualification, but a qualification" (*W* 22:420). In a somewhat ironic tone, he pointed out that there would never be a shortage of voters who would represent "the expediency . . . the interest of trade or of imperative class interest" (*W* 11:422). Even if women did vote from a basis of naivete and aim "at abstract right without allowing for circumstances" (*W* 11:422), as many opponents of suffrage argued, they would serve to balance morally the voting populace who aimed only at material gain or maintaining a prejudicial status quo without allowing for right or justice. Emerson's implied argument was that granting women full political participation would improve the entire nation—again, an echo of Fuller's tactics, as they would be adopted by the suffrage movement.

Indeed, for Emerson, woman's civilizing influence was a major reason to give them the ballot. This argument, strong in "Woman," was even more emphasized in the address to the 1855 Woman's Rights Convention upon which it was based. Emerson made the equation plain—"Woman *is* the power of civilization"; woman "altered & mended" the "rough & reckless ways of men." Therefore, given the "election frauds & misdeeds" with which the land was rife, extending the suffrage to women to "civilize the voting" was "the remedy at the moment of need." This was a more specific application of the general principle, which Emerson stated in his journals as "the virtue of women [is] the main girth or bandage of society" (*JMN* 10:83).

Emerson took this argument further in answering the other common objection to woman's suffrage, that it would "contaminate" women and "unsex" them. He pointed out that this argument "only accuses our existing politics . . . It is easy to see that there is contamination enough, but it rots the men now." Rather than denying the vote to women in order to protect them from the dirty business of politics, he suggested, the wiser course was to clean up the political system. Again, Emerson here duplicated Fuller's tactics, as she was wont to argue—as were other suffragists such as Sojourner Truth—that if the system were inimical and harmful, then the system itself needed to be changed; banning women from it was only avoiding the problem. In fact, suggesting that to "Improve and refine the men" was to "do the same by the women," Emerson implied that the better educated and the more moral men became, the more they would become, in his phrase, "true men," and the more they would not only be willing to give women their "half of the world," but would insist, like Emerson himself, on women's right to it (*w* 11:423). Emerson saw a "real man" as one who was so secure that he did not need to force others into a subservient position in order to aggrandize his own status. To Emerson, a "real man" was one who actively advocated women's rights and equality; in today's terms, to be a real man was to be a feminist.

Despite his confirmed belief in the 1850s that most women did not desire suffrage, Emerson nonetheless insisted that it be available for those who did. Especially notable was how uncertain Emerson appeared to be about the true desires of women on this issue—notice the hedging language on the part of a writer who was usually so straightforward: "I do not *think* it *yet appears* that women wish this equal share in public affairs" (*w* 11:423–24, emphasis added). In the very next sentence, though, when Emerson returned to his call for equal opportunity, he again found his accustomed directness of voice: "But it is they and not we that are to determine it." While Emerson was uncertain of the wishes of the women about him—and he was apparently receiving a great deal of contradictory information at this time—he was certain that the right to choose rested with them, not with men. Emerson explicitly acknowledged women's right to decide for themselves the part they would play on the national and world stage; men's role, in his view, was simply to support them in enforcing their decision against the weight of entrenched prejudice and tradition. As he would write in a letter to Caroline Sturgis Tappan in 1868, "It is of course for women to determine this question! the part of men, if women decide to assume the suffrage, is simply to accept their determination & aid in carrying it out" (*L* 9:326–27). In his journals he had reached a similar conclusion as early as 1845: "To me it sounded hoarsely the attempt to prescribe didactically to woman her duties. Man can never tell woman what her duties are . . . Women only can tell the heights of feminine nature, & the only way in which men can help her, is by observing woman reverentially & whenever she speaks from herself & catches him in inspired moments to a heaven of honor & religion, to hold her to that point by reverential recognition of the divinity that speaks through her" (*JMN* 8:381). The language of "sacred womanhood" here was a means of expressing respect for women's strengths. Emerson's was a very progressive opinion even for the 1850s, anticipating contemporary feminism's emphasis that women not ask men for rights, thereby implying that those rights were men's property to give to women as a gift, but rather that women should grasp their rights for themselves. As Fuller, again, had stated, these were women's "birthright" (*EMF* 347), and Emerson's trust in Fuller's judgment was again apparent.

In fact, one could argue that Emerson followed Fuller with such implicit faith that he echoed her even in those ideas that contemporary feminism has discarded. Today's critics, who would not condemn Fuller for such concepts, have ignored her profound influence on Emerson when they have attacked him for following her lead. An example would be Emerson's statement that "a masculine woman is not strong, but a lady is" (*W* 11:425), echoing Fuller's sentiment that true women would "never wish to be men, or man-like" (*EMF* 276–77). Emerson sounded most like Fuller when he argued such ideas as that it was "impossible to separate the interests and education of the sexes." *Woman in the Nineteenth Century* was full of such pleas for the unity of women's and men's interests, as when Fuller stated that women's interests "were identical" with men's (*EMF* 344) or that "I believe that the development of the one cannot be effected without that of the other" (*EMF* 245). What has sounded to contemporary readers like an implication that women's interests were only important as they affected

men was to nineteenth-century readers a daring avowal of the equal significance of women on the world stage, as well as a politic way to appeal to
men's self-interest. Emerson emphasized his anticipation of this transformation in attitudes toward women's place when he concluded, perhaps
overly optimistically, "the aspiration of this century [for women's equality]
will be the code of the next" (*W* 11:424).

Regarding the timeline of the development of Emerson's thoughts on
women, and particularly on their right to political equality, Emerson was
already, at the beginning of the American suffrage movement in the 1850s,
convinced of and speaking out for its necessity. While his arguments, influenced by Fuller, were couched like hers in the essentialist nineteenth-
century language of sacred womanhood, gentility, and intuitive superiority,
his political demands on behalf of woman were as bold as hers.

Emerson's ideas of woman's role were also continually evolving, as seen
in the changes from the 1855 address to the essay "Woman." In addition
to the changes previously mentioned, the address dwelt far more fixedly on
women's manners,[12] on custom and ritual, and on women's self-sacrifice
and devotion, all stereotypes that were de-emphasized or removed from the
published essay "Woman."

The next major change in Emerson's developing awareness of women's
issues would come after the Civil War, when most Americans became
aware of the woman's rights movement. By this time, encouraged by such
women in his circle as Mary Moody Emerson and Louisa May Alcott, Emerson had realized that the one caveat he had withheld—that women themselves did not desire the vote—was untrue. Emerson commented upon this
change himself in the previously mentioned letter to Caroline Sturgis Tappan on 13 November 1868. In response to Sturgis Tappan's statement that
"All women should feel & say that they are suffering from being governed
without their consent," he explained that previously, he had "believed that
women did not wish [to enter into public life], that those whose decision
would be final, the thoughtful serene typical minds shrank from it," but, he
continued, "I have been much surprised to find that my saints or some of
them have a feeling of duty that however odious the new order may appear
in some of its details they must bravely accept & realize it" (*L* 9:326–27).
This process of transition in Emerson's views has not been previously recognized.[13] Emerson himself would see this recognition of women's desire
for emancipation as the point of his conversion to the woman's cause, even
though he had been actively supporting it since 1850, and in the 1860s and
1870s he would become an icon of the suffragist leaders.

Today's readers may be surprised that the suffragists would find any aspect of women's equality "odious." However, many women, and Emerson himself, valued some of the qualities that had arisen from women's socially enforced exile to a passive role in life: unselfishness, spirituality, cooperativeness, gentleness, caring. These women feared that when women entered into work and politics they would be forced to behave as men had been conditioned to so as to survive in the patriarchal outer world and would lose these attributes. Again, Julia Ward Howe, who by the time of Emerson's death had become a distinguished poet as well as a leader of the suffragist American Woman's Party, provided one of the most insightful analyses of this conflict between the appreciation of the more nurturing, "feminine" traits in both women and men and the need for fuller social and political freedom. She especially contrasted Emerson's attraction to the beauty of the feminine character as it had developed in a hothouse environment of artificial restrictions against his recognition of the justice of women's demand for a more equal and active part in defining their own lives. In analyzing this conflict, Howe accurately noted an essential Emersonian debate between Beauty and Justice, or Truth, as Emerson called the principle for which Howe used the term Justice.

In a more abstract fashion, this dialectic between Beauty and Truth rang throughout Emerson's works as it did those of other Romantics such as the English poet John Keats. Emerson respected Keats's "Ode to a Grecian Urn" practically alone among Keats's works because it addressed this Romantic problem of the proper relationship of Beauty to Truth. However, Emerson disagreed with Keats as to the exact equivalence of Beauty and Truth (Keats had claimed "Beauty *is* truth, truth beauty"). Emerson believed that Truth was even more important than Beauty. This belief was notable in, among other indicators, Emerson's placing the chapter on Beauty in his book *Nature* before that on Truth ("Discipline"), since the chapters were placed, in typical Romantic fashion, in rising order of importance.

Emerson, Howe noted, did not use stereotypical definitions of Beauty as feminine and Justice or Truth as masculine, but recognized that "justice, as well as beauty, was to him a feminine ideal." To Emerson, Beauty and Truth each embodied a "feminine" as well as a masculine "Ideal." Further, Howe recognized Emerson's stand, in declarations such as "Woman," that woman must have the power to decide for herself what her role in society would be: "He believed in woman's power to hold and adjust for herself the scales in which character is weighed against attraction."[14] As Emerson had stated to Caroline Sturgis Tappan, the power of self-determination must be given to woman even if her ultimate choice would involve less of "attraction"—Beauty—and more of "character"—Truth—than Emerson's personal aesthetic sense would find pleasing.

Emerson, who himself shrank from the public sphere, admired and appreciated the intensely spiritual unselfishness women had been forced to develop while sequestered as "the angel in the house." He also had, as seen in "Woman," deep doubts about the corruption inherent in participation in the world of politics and commerce. He would have preferred to see women remain, and men become, more inner-directed, aloof from the materialistic concerns of social life. While Emerson's democratic tendencies and his profound respect for the women in his own life forced him to support the movement for women's equality, he had an abiding distrust of the public and especially the political arena, which women were entering by their agitation for suffrage and would be entering even further by gaining the vote. Emerson feared that women, previously excluded and therefore protected from these areas, would make the same mistakes that he saw men as having made, losing their spiritual focus to the necessary compromises of politics (as had Daniel Webster, a prime example) and falling into the lure of materialism when they entered the workplace. Ultimately, Emerson questioned the feasibility of anyone, not only women, being what he had called in the lecture on which "Woman" was based "innocent citizens." To Emerson, the very possibility of being both "innocent" and a participating "citizen" of a flawed—at that time, even slave-holding—political system was highly questionable. Aspirations to innocent citizenship appeared to him to be laudable in principle but in the practice of the corrupt state regrettably oxymoronic. Yet he also recognized that the choice was not his to make, but women's own. If they believed that political and social equality was necessary to their spiritual development, his responsibility was to support them in their struggle. He would not keep them housebound in order to promote their spiritual beauty any more than he would keep the slaves in captivity in order to enjoy the harmony of their songs for freedom.

Emerson's position was thus characteristic of nineteenth-century feminists, female and male, and the suffragists were outspoken in their praise and gratitude to Emerson for his efforts on behalf of women's empowerment, education, and equality. In the suffragist organ *The Woman's Journal*, the leaders of the suffragist movement specifically addressed Emerson's role, as they saw it, in the woman's movement. While Emerson, with characteristic modesty, would not give himself credit for his early support of the

woman's rights movement, suffragists such as Julia Ward Howe were ada-
mant concerning Emerson's stand: "At more than one woman suffrage
meeting, he has entered his protest against the political inequality which
still demoralizes society." Howe was certain where Emerson's loyalties lay
on the suffrage question: "He was *for us*, knowing well enough our limitations and short-comings, and his golden words have done much both to fit
us for the larger freedom, and to know that it belongs to us." [15]

In 1882 Howe enlarged on Emerson's contributions, stressing his respect for women's intellect. Indeed, she went so far as to credit Emerson
with an important role in her own conversion from judging women by their
physical attractiveness to considering their true character, the very trait she
had emphasized in her analysis of Emerson in the *Woman's Journal*. As
she told it, when Emerson "asked me if I knew Margaret Fuller I told him
I thought her an ugly person. He then dwelt upon her mind and conversation." [16] Clearly, Emerson had transcended the Victorian valuing of women
solely for their ornamental role, to appreciate them on the same grounds
by which he did men—for their intelligence. To Emerson, the key attraction was inner, not outer beauty. Even in admiring the famous actress
Rachel, Emerson admired her "terror & energy . . . defiance or denunciation," and most of all her "highly intellectual air" and "universal intelligence" (*JMN* 10:269). Indeed, he counted seeing Rachel more highly than
hearing the renowned scientist Michelet lecture and as one of the high
points of his trip to France (*JMN* 10:323, 362).

Howe's perception of the value of Emerson as a teacher of women was
upheld by Ednah Dow Cheney, a leader of the Massachusetts Woman Suffrage Society and the School Suffrage Association and a prominent woman
writer. Cheney recalled, "When we were young girls, nothing in our list of
entertainments was to be compared with Emerson,—no party, no singing,
no theatre." Cheney went on to remark upon Emerson's total and eager
attention to every person he met, however young, making no distinction
between male and female. [17] As Cheney had suggested, Emerson persisted
in taking seriously his female audience despite the fact that they were a
hindrance to his public (male) reputation. Emerson's journals bear testimony to this respect for his youthful and female audience; in the late 1840s
or early 1850s he wrote, "No part of the population interests except the
children & the young women" (*JMN* 10:465). As Howe would recall later
in an article for the special issue of the *Critic* on Emerson's work, "The
distinguished jurist, Jeremiah Mason, said of [Emerson's] lectures: 'I cannot understand them, but my daughters do.' This dictum was at the time

considered a damning piece of irony."[18] Indeed, it could be argued that women, especially the suffragists, were among Emerson's earliest and most sympathetic audience because they shared his sense of alienation from the social sphere and were intimately acquainted with society's strictures against nonconformity. Howe continued to emphasize Emerson's respect for women as an important audience and his "sympathy with the new opportunities accorded to women. He spoke more than once in favor of woman suffrage, and was for many years an honorary member of the New England Women's Club, to whose gatherings he occasionally lent the charm of his presence and of his voice."[19] Cheney also recalled Emerson's honorary membership in the New England Woman's Club, noting that he became such immediately upon the club's formation in 1865: "He frequently came to its meetings and read some of his most personal and charming papers there," including the first draft of his reminiscences of his aunt, Mary Moody Emerson, a major figure in his intellectual development.[20]

Emerson was also concerned with the effect of his lectures on women, especially what would today be called "empowering" women, as one anecdote makes clear. Respected author, lyceum lecturer, and women's rights activist Elizabeth Oakes Smith recalled that after Emerson's lectures on "Power," he "approached the bright-minded Mrs. C.—I noticed he uttered the one word, 'Well?' interrogatively, and with an almost childish simplicity, to which she replied: 'Oh, Mr. Emerson, you make me feel so powerless, as if I could do nothing.'" At this expected response of stereotypical feminine helplessness, Emerson, in Oakes Smith's words, "looked grave and turning to me, repeated the enigmatical monosyllable, 'Well?' . . . to which I replied, 'In listening to you, Mr. Emerson, no achievement seemed impossible; it was as though I might remove mountains.' 'Ah, that is well,' he answered cordially."[21]

Oakes Smith remembered that while Emerson "did not seek contest, did not snuff the battle with the heat of the war-horse, like Wendell Phillips . . . he did . . . accept and give his testimony to all high luminaries, ideas, and movements, including that of suffrage for women; for he stood on the same platform with myself on more than one occasion."[22] Emerson's respect for Oakes Smith and her cause was reflected in his attendance at her lectures on the themes of women of history; womanhood, manhood, and our humanity; and her strong argument for women's rights.[23] Emerson responded with approval, telling her at one point, "you must come and live in Concord, and we shall have an oracle."[24] To be invited by Emerson to join his Transcendentalist community was a rare honor, and it was an even higher

sign of respect to be compared to the classic oracle, a simile usually reserved by Emerson for his friend, the philosopher Bronson Alcott. Emerson's attempts to include suffragists such as Fuller and Oakes Smith in his
literary community reflected his admiration and support of their cause.

The *Woman's Journal* continued to emphasize this perception of Emerson as a nineteenth-century feminist. As Henrietta H. Bassett observed,
"the psychic energy of our latter day women has drawn upon . . . [Emer-
son's] speech . . . Because of him, New England women who loved him will
be the wiser to determine issues." [25] Whether Bassett meant by "Emerson's
speech" the lecture "Woman" or his general ideas taken as a whole, she
emphasized the importance of Emerson to the suffragist readers of the
Woman's Journal, which was then underscored in the same issue by several
relevant announcements, as of a portrait of Emerson available for purchase
and James Elliot Cabot's appointment to write the official biography of
Emerson. The *Woman's Journal* saw Emerson specifically as a proponent of
women's rights. [26]

This response to Emerson by the suffragists has suggested a facet of his
work that has thus far been overlooked in the ongoing debate over Emerson's response to women's issues. Like Margaret Fuller before them, the
suffragists saw Emerson as one who encouraged women's intellectual independence and honored their literary status on fully equal terms with
men. They appreciated his respect for the women and young people in his
audience and his efforts to recruit brilliant women for his Concord coterie.
They had no difficulty in reconciling his respect for women's spiritual en-
dowments with his awareness of their need for entitlement and empowerment in society, since they themselves performed the same balancing act.
While they recognized that he would himself prefer to cultivate both men's
and women's souls even at the cost of their social participation, they knew
that he understood their need and right to make that decision for themselves and would support their choice.

Further, as more critics of nineteenth-century women writers have begun to recognize, they were deeply aware of stylistic concerns. Dall's
"thorns of reform" comment was a fine example. Julia Ward Howe stressed
that Emerson tended to qualify his public statements, suggesting in her
speech at the memorial meeting for the ninety-sixth anniversary of Emerson's birth that "Emerson was as great in what he did not say as in what he
said. Second-class talent tells the whole story, reasons everything out; great
genius suggests even more than it says." [27] Emerson, in Howe's analysis,
inspired the reader to consider for himself or herself the implications of a

particular idea. Women could then apply these implications to and for themselves, as Margaret Fuller had done in extending Emerson's concepts of self-reliance, individualism, and the primacy of spiritual or moral character to women and their conditioning in *Woman in the Nineteenth Century*.

Emerson's full ideas on women's rights were not stated publicly but must be inferred from the incidents of his life and his response to women who dared to carry out the radical ramifications of his ideas for women, such as Fuller and Howe. The suffragists comprehended Emerson's typical technique of laying forth all the negative sides of an idea before the positive and saw that he applied this technique even-handedly, as much for his criticism of Shakespeare, Milton, and Wordsworth as for women's issues. Indeed, they recognized, as few contemporary readers have, Emerson's strategy in using this advanced argumentation form to lure opponents of his ideas by apparent agreement, then trap them into considering reforms. There was no question in their minds that Emerson was, as they would have phrased it, a true friend and proponent of women's rights.

Emerson's periodical reading further illuminates his interest in women's issues. He did a great deal of reading on the issue of marriage, an institution with substantial impact on women's status, particularly in the nineteenth century. He had begun his investigation of these ideas as early as 1817, at the age of fourteen, when he borrowed Hannah More's *Strictures on a System of Female Education*, which argued that marriage should be a union based on an educated and mutual understanding, common interests, genuine respect, and sexual equality. In 1829 he read one of his major intellectual influences, Sampson Reed, whose unsigned "Introduction to Entomology" contained, surprisingly, a passage on celibacy.[28] The next year he followed this by reading in the same month two articles, Caleb Reed's unsigned article on the nature of affection[29] and John Hubbard Wilkins' unsigned "On Marriage."[30] In 1831 he returned to Sampson Reed with the unsigned "Guardian Angels," which like the previous articles stressed the permanence of spiritual ties between the sexes,[31] and in 1832 he read Reed's similar piece "Marriage in the Heavens."[32] In 1834 Emerson read Caleb Reed's unsigned "Supposed Extinction of our Proper and Peculiar Loves at Death," which reinforced the argument that human affections are eternal;[33] and in 1835, he read a last unsigned piece by Sampson Reed concerning marriage in heaven.[34] These articles, published in the *New Jerusalem Magazine*, an organ of the church founded by the philosopher Emanuel Swedenborg, conditioned Emerson to its view of marriage as a state of spiritual relation rather than a social institution. This outlook would predispose him to see women as souls rather than chattel and to assume their equal rights in marriage, for which he would argue so strongly in "Woman."

Emerson's personal feelings about the legal institution of marriage appeared to be ambivalent. If marriage were a spiritual state, its official and legal codification by the state was suspect. Emerson observed, "The wave of evil washes all our institutions alike," especially marriage (*JMN* 8:185). In the journals he mused, "None ever heard of a good marriage from Mesopotamia to Missouri and yet right marriage is as possible tomorrow as sunshine. Sunshine is a very mixed & costly thing as we have it, & quite impossible, yet we get the right article every day. And we are not very much to blame for our bad marriages." Emerson seemed almost to be aware of the negative results of social conditioning and gender roles on marriage:

> We live amid hallucinations & illusions, & this especial trap is laid for us to trap our feet with, & all are tripped up, first or last. . . . Into the Pandora-box of marriage, amidst dyspepsia, nervousness, screams, Christianity, comes poetry, & all kinds of music, [and] some deep & serious benefits & some great joys . . . And in these ill assorted connections there is ever some mixture of true marriage. The poorest Paddy & his jade, if well-meaning & well tempered, get some just & agreeable relations of mutual respect & kindly observation & fostering of each other. & they learn something, & would carry themselves wiselier if they were to begin life anew in some other sphere. (*JMN* 10:351–52)

The influence of Hannah More's work, with its emphasis on the need for "mutual respect" to constitute a "true marriage," and the Swedenborgian emphasis on the positive effects of marriage on the after-death state, or "other sphere," were both evident in Emerson's views. Indeed, he echoed Swedenborg frequently in his desire for "the true nuptials of minds" (*JMN* 8:94).

On the other hand, Emerson recognized that marriage as a social institution rather than a spiritual partnership, an "unfit marriage," could paralyze individual growth (*JMN* 8:69). But the drawbacks of divorce for women's security prevented him from supporting its legalization:

> We cannot rectify marriage because it would introduce such carnage into our social relations. . . . Woman hides her from the eyes of men in our world: they cannot, she rightly thinks, be trusted. In the right state the love of one, which each man carried in his heart, should protect all women from his eyes, and make him their protector & saintly friend, as if for her sake. But now there is in the eyes of all men a certain evil light, a vague desire which attaches them

to the forms of many women, whilst their affections fasten on some one. Their
natural eye is not fixed into coincidence with their spiritual eye. Therefore it
will not do to abrogate the laws which make Marriage a relation for life, fit or
unfit. (*JMN* 8:95)

Indeed, Emerson had great respect for fidelity in marriage, noting in 1841:
"Permanence is the nobility of human beings. We love that lover whose
gayest of love songs, whose fieriest engagement of romantic devotion is
made good by all the days of all the years of strenuous, long suffering, ever-
renewing benefit. The old Count said to the old Countess of Ilchester, 'I
know that wherever thou goest, thou wilt both trust & honor me, and thou
knowest that wherever I am I shall honor thee'" (*JMN* 8:134). Emerson
continued to try to solve the riddle of marriage, considering the ideas of
Swedenborg and Percy Bysshe Shelley (*JMN* 8:174), whose idea of marriage
for love, he noted, removed the scent of the Inquisitor's oppression (*JMN* 8:
187), and even such unlikely solutions as "For marriage find somebody that
was born near the time when you were born" (*JMN* 8:168). At least partial
approval was suggested by the many matchmaking attempts into which
Emerson entered with regard to younger male and female acquaintances
such as Anna Barker and Samuel Gray Ward. Indeed, the very frequency
of Emerson's attempts at devising matrimonial pairs from among his single
friends suggests that his opinion of marriage was positive enough for him
to attempt to bestow its benefits on the unattached members of his circle.

Emerson's involvement with women's issues, then, developed in stages,
from his support of the movement despite some doubts in the 1850s—in
itself a radical position for the time—through the resolution of his doubts
after the Civil War and his wholehearted "conversion" to woman's suffrage.
His correspondence with and support of key leaders of the woman's rights
movement, such as Stone and Howe, has been minimized, although his
relationship with Fuller made such associations mandatory. While plagued
by the same disparity between the ideal world of innocent citizenship and
the real world of political infighting, Emerson's advocacy of the woman's
movement created a heretofore unrecognized crosscurrent of influence between Emerson and the major thinkers and writers of the suffrage associations. It is now our responsibility to see that he is, finally, given the credit
that his forward-thinking efforts deserve.

NOTES

1. Elizabeth Cady Stanton, Susan B. Anthony, and Matilda Joslyn Gage, *History
of Woman Suffrage*, 2 vols. (New York: Fowler & Wells, 1881), 1:40.

2. Stanton et al., 1:53ff.

3. Julia Ward Howe, *Reminiscences 1819–1899* (Boston: Houghton, Mifflin, 1899), p. 158.

4. Stanton et al., 1:820. See also Thomas Wentworth Higginson's 1876 article on Emerson's participation at the convention, "Tested By Time," in the suffragist organ the *Woman's Journal* 7, p. 1.

5. For more information on Emerson and the Woman Right's Convention, see Higginson, "Tested By Time."

6. I am indebted to an audience member at the American Literature Association Thoreau Society Panel in 1996 for this cogent observation. While in the late nineteenth century the woman's suffrage movement split over regional and political issues, these controversies occurred largely after Emerson's active involvement in the movement, and so I will not address them here.

7. See, for example, *JMN* 8:29, 339.

8. It is interesting that Emerson misremembered this deed (actually Katherine Douglas's) as being undertaken to aid another woman, when in actuality Douglas acted to protect James I of Scotland (*JMN* 10:345 n.).

9. I am indebted to Helen Deese for providing me with information from her forthcoming edition of the Dall journals. This is from the journal of September 23, 1855.

10. Stanton et al., 1:40.

11. See, for example, *JMN* 10:181 and *L* 3:443.

12. As reflected in the earlier journals; see *JMN* 8:149.

13. In fact, the editor of the volume in which this letter appears, Eleanor M. Tilton, in a footnote terms Emerson's statement "evasive" and observes, "In Emerson's own household, only Ellen took his position" (9:327), thus assuming, despite the content of the letter concerning the change in his position, that Emerson was anti-suffrage. So pervasive has been the assumption of Emerson's monolithic and static opinion on women's rights that the evidence to the contrary, even in his own words, has been ignored.

14. J[ulia]. W[ard]. H[owe]., "Ralph Waldo Emerson," *Woman's Journal* 13 (May 6, 1882), p. 140.

15. Howe, "Ralph Waldo Emerson," p. 140.

16. Julia Ward Howe, "Reminiscences," in *Concord Lectures on Philosophy* (Cambridge, Mass.: Moses King, 1882), p. 63.

17. Ednah Dow Cheney, "Reminiscences," in *Concord Lectures on Philosophy* (Cambridge, Mass.: Moses King, 1882), p. 74.

18. Julia Ward Howe, "Ralph Waldo Emerson as I Knew Him," *Critic* 42 (May 1902), 411–15. The importance of this anecdote to nineteenth-century women was evident in the many times they recorded, repeated, and analyzed it. Ednah Dow Cheney, for example, mentioned it in her lecture "Emerson and Boston," printed in F. B. Sanborn, ed., *The Genius and Character of Emerson: Lectures at*

the Concord School of Philosophy (Boston: James R. Osgood, 1885), p. 19, and in her *Reminiscences of Ednah Dow Cheney* (Boston: Lea and Shepard, 1902), pp. 232–33.

19. Howe, "Ralph Waldo Emerson as I Knew Him," 413.

20. These public reminiscences of Aunt Mary were typical of Emerson's respect for the women of his circle. He often quoted their bon mots and insights in his journal, citing Mary Moody Emerson (*JMN* 8:530, 10:26, 29, 39, 69, 178, 363, 385, 390), his second wife, Lidian (*JMN* 8:88–89, 134, 173, 195, 238, 260, 365), and his daughter, Ellen (*JMN* 8:178–80, 205). Emerson especially praised Elizabeth Hoar (*JMN* 8:25, 49, 161, 164, 165, 178, 385, 351, 10:385, 398, 399), whom he called "immortal . . . an influence I cannot spare" in his journals (*JMN* 8:105) and may have considered a fit contributor to the Transcendentalist literary journal *The Dial* (*JMN* 8:498). Emerson also frequently cited Sarah Alden Ripley, whose "high & calm intelligence" (*JMN* 8:94) he admired, as he did that of Rebecca Black (*JMN* 8:202, 204, 235, 347, 385). He admired the unconventionality and original thinking of Black and Aunt Mary (*JMN* 8:391). Jane Welsh Carlyle, wife of English author Thomas Carlyle, he regarded at least as highly as her husband (*JMN* 10:227). He also quoted and praised Anna Barker Ward (*JMN* 8:76) and Caroline Sturgis (*JMN* 8:22, 51, 122, 165, 174, 368) as well as lesser known women (*JMN* 8:36, 181–82, 3:205, 129), women writers (*JMN* 8:388), and women no longer remembered today (*JMN* 8:25, 49, 178, 161, 164–65, 388, 10:129, 205, 379, 428, 532–33).

21. *Selections from the Autobiography of Elizabeth Oakes Smith*, ed. Mary Alice Wyman (New York: Columbia Univ. Press, 1924), p. 145.

22. *Ibid.*, p. 148.

23. *Ibid.*, p. 14.

24. *Ibid.*, p. 141.

25. Henrietta H. Bassett, "The King Is Dead," *Woman's Journal* 13 (May 20, 1882), 159.

26. In this the *Woman's Journal* differed from the more general epitaphs written by women as well as by men, such as Mary Clemmer's in the *Independent* (Mary Clemmer, "*A Woman's Letter From Washington*," *Independent* 34 [May 11, 1882], 2–3).

27. Laura E. Richards and Maude Howe Elliott, *Julia Ward Howe, 1819–1910*, 2 vols. (Boston: Houghton, Mifflin, 1916), 2:263–64.

28. [Sampson Reed,] "Introduction to Entomology (4)," *New Jerusalem Magazine* 2 (May 1829): 274–82 (listed in Cameron, p. 43).

29. [Caleb Reed,] "The Love of the World," *New Jerusalem Magazine* 3 (Mar. 1830), 199–206 (listed in Cameron, p. 45).

30. [John Hubbard Wilkins,] "On Marriage," *New Jerusalem Magazine* 3 (Mar. 1830), 217–19 (listed in Cameron, p. 45).

31. [Sampson Reed,] "Guardian Angels," *New Jerusalem Magazine* 5 (Nov. 1831), 112–19 (listed in Cameron, p. 48).

32. [Sampson Reed,] "Marriage in the Heavens," *New Jerusalem Magazine* 5 (May 1832), 321–28 (listed in Cameron, p. 49).

33. [Caleb Reed,] "Supposed Extinction of our Proper and Peculiar Loves at Death," *New Jerusalem Magazine* 8 (Oct. 1834), 50–53 (listed in Cameron, p. 54).

34. [Sampson Reed,] "Changes Effected at Death—Personal Form and Appearance (5)," *New Jerusalem Magazine* 8 (May 1835), 296–300 (listed in Cameron, p. 55).

JEFFREY A. STEELE

The Limits of Political Sympathy: Emerson, Margaret Fuller, and Woman's Rights

In 1855, EMERSON GRATIFIED the audience at the Boston Woman's Rights Convention with the stirring declaration that "the times are marked by the new attitude of Woman; urging, by argument and by association, her rights of all kinds,—in short, to one-half of the world;—as the right to education, to avenues of employment, to equal rights of property, to equal rights in marriage, to the exercise of the professions and of suffrage" (*w* 10:416).

Such public advocacy of much of the official woman's rights platform culminated a lengthy intellectual development for Emerson. In her recent book, *Feminist Conversations: Emerson, Fuller, and the Play of Reading*, Christina Zwarg persuasively argues that this move toward feminism reflects the influence of Margaret Fuller, who helped Emerson refine a style of radical critique.[1] Fuller's spectral presence in his lecture (delivered five years after her death) is unmistakable, since she had helped to convince Emerson that "the laws" (as he phrases it) should "be purged of every barbarous remainder, every barbarous impediment to women" (*w* 10:424). But if Emerson found himself profoundly influenced by Fuller's ideas and methodology, he did not share the scope of her feminist vision. In this regard, his 1855 lecture can be viewed as a strong misreading of Fuller (in Harold Bloom's sense of "misreading").[2] The lecture subtly acknowledges Fuller's influence while transforming it, by embracing *part* of Fuller's feminist program while suppressing other aspects. Specifically, it leaves out the demand that women be given an equal role in the religious institutions and theological practices of nineteenth-century America. While this omission allowed

Emerson to acknowledge women's demand for equality, it deprived him of the means to theorize the ideological foundations of gender inequality in America. As we shall see, this absence also marked the limits of his political sympathy towards the woman's rights movement and one of its strongest advocates, Margaret Fuller.

Although Emerson glossed over it, the question of religion was of great urgency for nineteenth-century leaders of the woman's rights movement, who clearly recognized the ways in which theology, ideology, and social power were intertwined. Among the concluding resolutions of the 1848 "Declaration of Sentiments and Resolutions," adopted at Seneca Falls, New York, was a condemnation of the way in which "perverted application of the Scriptures" had been used to justify the "circumscribed limits" of women's lives and the assertion that women should have equal opportunity to teach "the great subjects of morals and religion . . . both in private and in public, by writing and by speaking."[3] The close ties, in the nineteenth century, between social practice and religious authority were not lost on the organizers of the Seneca Falls Convention, Lucretia Mott (a Quaker preacher) and Elizabeth Cady Stanton. Later in her life, Stanton became "convinced that the church and its interpretation of the Bible were the greatest obstacles to the progress of women."[4] As early as the 1820s, Frances Wright had addressed the ways in which Biblical justifications, "conjured from the prolific brain of insatiate priestcraft," were used to rationalize the secondary position of women.[5] A decade later, Sarah Grimké wrote about the debilitating effects for women of the narrative of Eve's fall, which had been used "for nearly six thousand years" to justify the "dominion" of man.[6] Early woman's rights leaders clearly saw the link between the male interpretation of scripture, the gendering of ecclesiastical authority, and the subordinate position of women.

Emerson's omission of the religious plank of the woman's rights platform is all the more surprising, given his own central role as a critic of institutionalized religion in America. In his 1855 lecture, he refers favorably to the prophetesses found in various religious traditions as evidence of woman's "power of divination" and "leading position" but does not suggest that woman's "religious character" carried over into areas of church leadership or theological interpretation (*w* 10:414). In addition, Emerson's characterization of "the new attitude" toward women does not include a consideration of the feminist demand for equal rights in the interpretation of scripture and in the right to preach. Such omissions must have been noticeable to Paulina Wright Davis, the woman's rights leader who had been instrumental in convincing Emerson to speak at the 1855 convention; for Davis had "her interest in feminism . . . first aroused by a church discussion over the impropriety of letting women speak during religious sessions where men were present."[7] Davis had been working on Emerson since 1850, when she urged him to attend the Woman's Rights Convention in Worcester, Massachusetts. In his 1850 reply, Emerson had granted the "fact of the political & civil wrongs of woman," but he qualified his support with the proviso that "I should not wish women to wish political functions" (*L* 4:230). Five years later, Emerson modified his views to the extent of accepting the political function of public conventions, but he still shied away from accepting the idea that women should serve as public authorities, either in government or in church. On the question of women's holding public office, he claimed that "I do not think it yet appears that women wish this equal share in public affairs." But, with equal educational opportunities and equitable property laws, he suggested, the situation might change, "and in a few years it will easily appear whether they wish a voice in the laws that are to govern them" (*W* 11:423–24). But on the question of women's holding ministerial positions, he is silent.

In this context, Emerson's references to the "religious character" of woman are highly problematic. For example, he cites Eve, the Virgin Mary, and "the deification of Woman in the Catholic Church" as positive evidence of woman's religious role without commenting upon the interpretive narratives surrounding such figures (*W* 11:415, 413). As most woman's rights leaders knew, the image of Eve's fault, as the temptress of Adam, had been used for centuries to justify women's secondary position. Apparently oblivious to such connotations, Emerson blithely asserts that "the omnipotence of Eve is in humility" (*W* 11:413). Given his premise that "the starry crown of woman is in the power of her affections and sentiment," his reference to "the equality in the sexes" found in the Quaker and Shaker religions is also unsettling; for it fails to mention any of the strong women leaders in either tradition—individuals like the Quaker preacher Lucretia Mott or the Shaker leader Mother Ann Lee, who asserted "that God had a dual nature, part male and part female" (*W* 11:412, 415). Ironically, Emerson's list of religious women seems to replicate many of the examples used by Margaret Fuller in *Woman in the Nineteenth Century*. But an important element is missing in his references to Eve, Mary, and prophetesses—a consideration of woman's power to interpret scripture, to preach religious doctrine, and to revise the sacred myths of her culture. Fuller, in contrast, had supplemented her portraits of the "religious character" of women (a nineteenth-century commonplace) with discussions of their power *within* religious institutions as nuns, saints, and religious leaders with "disciples" (*EMF* 299, 301). This supplementation played an important cultural role in her argument, since it suggested alternatives to the status quo. Emerson, on the other hand, eliminates from consideration the leadership of women in religious affairs and thus does not grant them the same radical theological position that he had constructed for himself.

In order to understand the full dimensions of Emerson's opposition to female spiritual authority, it is necessary to go back to the fall and winter 1840–1841, to the moment when Fuller began shaping her own vision of self-reliance. Forced by personal circumstances into an unwonted isolation, Fuller began to explore in her writing a posture of independence in which—like Emerson—she attuned the self to its inner spiritual resources. Like Emerson, Fuller believed that self-fulfillment depended upon firm intuitive connections to the divine depths of the self, but she departed from his theories by representing this divine ground through powerful myths that moved far beyond his frame of reference. "I grow more and more what they will call a mystic," Fuller confided to her journal; "Nothing interests me except listening to the secret harmonies of nature."[8] Writing in September 1840 to her friend Caroline Sturgis, she referred to "the mighty changes in my spiritual life. . . . All has been revealed, all foreshown yet I know it not. Experiment has given place to certainty, pride to obedience, thought to love, and truth is lost in beauty."[9] "All things have I given up to the central power," she wrote Emerson several days later, "myself, you also" (*LMF* 2 : 160). By mid-October she was describing the "sweet harmony" flowing through her; and, on October 22, she assumed the mantle of prophecy with the declaration that "I would sound a trumpet note clear as light now that you are ready for the Genesis" (*LMF* 2 : 163, 167).

Fuller's spiritual illumination, she confided in a letter to William Henry Channing, motivated her desire to preach. Echoing but revising the language of Emerson's "Divinity School Address," she recounted her recent experience of an uninspired male preacher who "uprose . . . to deny mysteries, to deny the second birth, to deny influx, and to renounce the sovereign gift of insight, for the sake of what he deemed a '*rational*' exercise of will" (*LMF* 2 : 172). Like Emerson, who had denounced such lifeless and spiritless ministry, Fuller advocated a religion of spiritual insight. But her application of Emerson's position crossed a boundary that he never examined. "Yet the time seems now to have come," she continued, "for reinterpreting the old dogmas. I would now *preach* the Holy Ghost as zealously as they have been preaching Man, and faith instead of the understanding and mysticism" (*LMF* 2 : 172–73, my italics). Fuller's desire to preach, we may surmise, was at least partially fulfilled in some of her Conversations for Boston women, judging from the evidence of Sophia Peabody's undated manuscript poem to Fuller entitled "To a Priestess," which contains the lines:

> My priestess! thou hast risen through thought supreme
> To central insight of eternal law
> Thy golden-cadenced revelations seem
> From that new heaven that John of Patmos saw.[10]

"When she named me her Priestess," Fuller wrote Channing in December 1840, "that name made me perfectly happy. Long has been my consecration; may I not meet those I hold dear at the altar?" (*LMF* 2 : 187). Eventually, Fuller came to understand that "the era of illumination in my mental life" represented the turning point in her career (*LMF* 3 : 55). Beginning in the fall of 1840, she began to define a feminized model of self-reliance that was supported in part by the mystical theories of Jacob Boehme, Emmanuel Swedenborg, and Louis Claude de Saint-Martin.[11] She found in such writers something lacking in Emerson—a valuation of the divine feminine, Sophia, and the assertion that spiritual enlightenment necessitated a harmonious balancing of both male and female principles within the self.[12]

In contrast to Fuller's sense of enthusiasm and prophetic power, Emerson felt that the changes taking place in his friend were strange and uncanny, evidence that she had been "self-deceived by her own phantasms" and was dabbling in an unhealthy "mysticism."[13] In an October 1840 letter to Caroline Sturgis, for example, he complained that "there are new sects in heaven who teach an occult religion" and which lead to "flights in the sky" (*L* 2 : 346–47). As an antidote to such unorthodox views, he advocated "acts of faith & courage" that "will be audible & musical to *all* ears" (*L* 2 : 347, my italics). Unable to hear the tones of spiritual authority in Fuller's voice, Emerson eventually dismissed her ideas as limited and "pagan."[14] He later concluded in the posthumous *Memoirs of Margaret Fuller Ossoli* that, during her spiritual "ecstasy" of 1840–41, she failed to "come to any experiences that were profound or permanent." Instead, he saw in her "an occasional enthusiasm, which gave a religious dignity to her thought."[15] But we look in vain for any recognition that spiritual ecstasy, enthusiasm, or even "religious dignity" had important ideological functions for a woman committed to woman's rights—that they provided a platform from which to address the founding patriarchal myths of the age.[16]

As Fuller began defining a theological framework for her own vision of self-reliance, the differences between her views and Emerson's came sharply into focus. Turning to Emerson for support, she found that he was reluctant to follow her most original and profound insights. At the time, Fuller complained to Emerson that he had failed in "the highest office of friendship, by offering me the clue to the labyrinth of my own being" (*LMF* 2:159). Part of this breakdown in communication resulted from her development of a language of self-reliance that deeply challenged the foundational terms of Emerson's thought. As a result, Emerson found it difficult to follow the reaches of Fuller's enthusiasm, asserting in one of his letters that man "is no match for the Oracle in Woman" (*LMF* 2:334). "I understand your language better, I hear my native tongue," he wrote her in September of 1840, "though still I see not into you & have not arrived at your law" (*L* 2:336). But, as he struggled to identify Fuller's language as his own, Emerson was forced to admit that the two of them were "not inhabitants of one thought of the Divine Mind, but of two thoughts, that . . . meet & treat like foreign states, one maritime, one inland, whose trade and laws are essentially unlike" (*LMF* 2:336). The two of them, he eventually recognized, spoke different languages: "There is a difference in our constitution. We use a different rhetoric[.] It seems as if we had been born & bred in different nations. . . . You cannot communicate yourself to me. I hear the words sometimes but remain a stranger to your state of mind" (*L* 2:353). Fuller, we surmise from Emerson's letters, was making him aware of what he called the "wild element in woman"—a "volcano" that "outdares, outwits, & outworks man" (*LMF* 2:345). Emerson's defensive reaction to Fuller's new position suggests that she was developing a model of transformation that modified his model of self-reliance by shifting it onto a different psychological and theological terrain.

One of the major differences between Emerson and Fuller lay in their competing models of the self's motive power. In contrast to Fuller's development of profound female myths, Emerson conceptualized agency in terms of the expression of an innate masculine power that actualized itself through the manipulation of feminized matter. The self, Emerson maintained, contained a divine core of unconscious energy that authorized individual creative and spiritual expression. At the heart of each person's being, he located a core of "elemental power" that "is not conscious power" (*CW* 1:42). While Emerson multiplied the terms he used to characterize this inner power, he rarely wavered in his gendering of the mind's potential and its expressive effects.[17] The "universal soul" that each person carries within, he asserted in *Nature*, is the center of creative "Spirit": "Spirit is the Creator. Spirit hath life in itself. And man in all ages and countries, embodies it in his language, as the FATHER" (*cw* 1:18–19). At many moments in his career, Emerson equated the expression of this inner spirit with an increase in "manliness." The "spiritual element," he argues in *Nature*, "can be loved without effeminacy" (*cw* 1:15). One of the problematic areas in Emerson's thought, Eric Cheyfitz has shown, was the relationship between such masculine power ("the sacred realm of the FATHER") and the region of sensuous being and matter that he gendered female.[18] Although Emerson attempted to reconcile "masculine 'will'" with "feminine 'intuition,'" it was difficult for him to escape from a dualistic ontology in which masculine power and will was given priority over a feminized region of material reality.[19]

At times, Emerson's image of the natural world took on the contours of a nurturing mother. "Nature stretcheth out *her* arms to embrace man," he wrote in *Nature*, "only let his thoughts be of equal greatness. Willingly does she follow his steps with the rose and the violet, and bend her lines of grandeur and grace to the decoration of her darling child" (*cw* 1:16, my italics). But at other moments, the image of a maternal Nature fades into a vision of passive matter, waiting for the impress of masculine energy: "Nature is thoroughly mediate. It is made to serve. It receives the dominion of man as meekly as the ass on which the Saviour rode" (*cw* 1:25). Emerson's commitment to male "dominion" culminated in a triumphant vision of the "kingdom of man over nature" (*cw* 1:45). In *Nature*, his models of "dominion" were Adam naming all of the living things in the garden and Julius Caesar ruling his massive empire: "All that Adam had, all that Caesar could, you can have and do" (*cw* 1:45). Eight years later, in his essay "The Poet," Emerson celebrated the "poet" as "a sovereign" who "stands on the centre" of the self and nature (*cw* 3:5). As a model of such creative power, he turned to the figure of Noah: "Nothing walks, or creeps, or grows, or exists, which must not in turn arise and walk before him as exponent of his meaning. . . . All the creatures, by pairs and by tribes, pour into his mind as into Noah's ark, to come forth again to people a new world" (*cw* 3:23). Committed to the masculine expansion of "dominion," Emerson easily slipped into historical (Caesar) and Biblical (Adam, Noah) models that marginalized or excluded female agency. In the popular mind, the female analogues of such figures—Eve, Caesar's wife, and Noah's wife—were all equated with female weakness and fallibility.

Even more problematically, because of its implications for the emerging discourse of woman's rights, Emerson's conception of the self's impulse toward "dominion" skewed his conception of "friendship." It was difficult for him to extend his model of self-reliance to those who did not share his own privileged situation; for, in his eyes, self-reliance was a personal affair that tended to detach the individual from burdensome social relations. "Society," he asserted in "Self-Reliance," "everywhere is in conspiracy against the manhood of every one of its members" (*cw* 2:29). Because of his commitment to a concept of individual expansion, Emerson found it difficult to theorize social relations as a reciprocal process of interpersonal relationship. In his writing, the movement seems to be one way—toward an expansion of the imperial self. "The soul environs itself with friends," he observes in "Friendship," that it may enter into a grander self-acquaintance or solitude" (*cw* 2:116–17). Later in the same essay, he chillingly asserts that even the most intimate friend is "not my soul, but a picture and effigy of that" (*cw* 2:116). As a result the "friend . . . is a sort of paradox in nature": "I who alone am, I who see nothing in nature whose existence I can affirm with equal evidence to my own, behold now the *semblance of my being* in all its height, variety and curiosity, reiterated in a foreign form" (*cw* 2: 120, my italics). Looking for the soul's reflection in his friends, Emerson was unable to theorize the unique personal differences that motivate the need for human relationships. At the same time, his solipsistic view of human identity left little room for the recognition of personal limitation—the very foundation of the movement for woman's rights. Aspiring to liberate the soul's divine potential, he was often impatient with the banal chains that bound the self to earth.

But what Fuller, as well as early woman's rights leaders knew all too well, was that the chains so easily scorned by Emerson shackled many women to diminished lives. Rather than advocating the imperialistic expansion of personal power, Fuller thus argued for the recognition of difference. During her 1840–41 crisis, this idea became one of the leading themes in her correspondence with Emerson. Like Emerson, who later alluded to their letters in his essay "Friendship," Fuller used their relationship as a yardstick against which to measure her evolving ideas of social being. In the process, she came to the conclusion that self-development could not be detached from social responsibility to others. In contrast to Emerson's unidirectional model of friendship (which stressed the benefits derived *from* one's friends), she thus developed a reciprocal model of friendship in which "both seem to rise" (*emf* 41). Theorizing the importance of friendship in her 1840–41 "Autobiographical Romance," for example, she highlighted the ways in which self-reliance depended upon the support of friends: "These not only know themselves more, but *are* more for having met, and regions of their being, which would else have laid sealed in cold obstruction, burst into leaf and bloom and song" (*EMF* 40–41).

Ultimately, Fuller came to see that the achievement of equal rights for women was impossible without attending to unjust social relationships and institutional structures. As they struggled for greater independence, she eventually argued, women needed to expand the ideal of friendship into the public sphere, shaping networks of nurturance and support in which they helped each other. Working out the political implications of such views in *Woman in the Nineteenth Century*, Fuller exhorted the middle-class women of New York to "seek out" the "degraded women" released from prison and "give them tender sympathy, counsel, employment." "Take the place of mothers," she continued, "such as might have saved them originally" (*EMF* 329).

In contrast to Emerson's intense commitment to the individuation of the solitary self, Fuller aimed at nurturing of the "flower of love" whose "roots" would be fed by the articulation of "mutual aims," "tasks," and "ideals." Unlike Emerson (who found it difficult to theorize the personal needs of others), she insisted upon the "cognizance of one another's laws." Her recognition that self-actualization can only be achieved *with* others leads to the valuation of "mutual action energizing love." A society based upon such principles could not value "the one" over "the two."[20] This is a great distance from Emerson's unitary vision of "dominion" and begins to explain why Fuller's favorite term for personal and social perfection is "harmony"—a term that highlights a person's complex relationships to the inner self, to the natural world, and to others.[21] In Fuller's vision, there can be no rebirth of the self, no harmony, without division and doubleness. The greatest harmony of being is achieved when "Life and peace bloom at once and the One divides itself to win the last divinest birth of Love" (*LMF* 2:167). The attempt to resolve everything down to a metaphysical, psychological, or social unity is doomed; for the quest for unity inhibits the recognition of otherness needed to balance the self in all of its domains. Decentering Emerson's advocacy for a strong creative center to the self, Fuller thus advances the "harmonious development of mind by mind, two souls prophesying to one another, two minds feeding one another, two human hearts sustaining and pardoning one another."[22] In her vision of self-reliance, other-reliance is a necessary component; for without the other, one exists in a vacuum filled with beautiful dreams.

As in the case of Emerson, Fuller's model of social relations was mirrored in the religious and mythical narratives that she used to ground her sense of self. But while Emerson was attracted to figures of masculine accomplishment such as Adam, Noah, and Orpheus, Fuller developed reciprocal images of *female* power to justify women's claims for spiritual authority. As we have seen, Fuller's feminist mythmaking was deeply unsettling for Emerson, who was shocked by her declaration of a profound religious awakening that gave her access to what she termed "the central power" (*LMF* 2 : 160). Opposed to Emerson's sense that the expression of spirituality is a masculine prerogative, Fuller defended the right of women to apprehend and to share authentic experiences of the divine. It is intriguing to consider whether Emerson was fully aware of Fuller's theological aspirations (which she confided to Channing), since they meshed with the very plank of the woman's rights platform that he later omitted from his 1855 lecture "Woman." [23] But what we can establish with more certainty are his reactions to the female myths that began emerging in Fuller's writing around 1840. In some of her *Dial* essays, which Emerson read, she experimented with a succession of female myths that embodied alternatives to his paternal model of Spirit. Over the next four years, refracted images of Fuller's mythical images found their way into Emerson's letters and essays.

One of Fuller's most important works is "The Magnolia of Lake Pontchartrain," published in the January 1841 issue of *The Dial*. This essay constructs a dialogue between a male narrator (modeled partly on Emerson) and a female speaker (the Magnolia) who dramatizes Fuller's new vision of selfhood. This work, which represents Fuller's declaration of spiritual independence, culminates in a profound vision of the divine feminine, embodied in the assertion that "All the secret powers are 'Mothers.' There is but one paternal power" (*EMF* 48). But in 1841, Fuller recognized, this vision of divine female power could not be comprehended by her friend Emerson: "A moment more and I was before the queen and guardian of the flowers. Of this being I cannot speak to thee in any language now possible betwixt us" (*EMF* 48). That Fuller was correct in her estimation is made clear by Emerson's response to the essay. Writing to Fuller in January, he acknowledged the commentary on their relationship: "Depart ye profane this is of me & mine" (*L* 2 : 377–78). Significantly, his characterization of the essay's central character completely missed its theological dimensions, substituting in their place a personalized narrative of Fuller's biography (a strategy of reading replicated by many of Fuller's critics). "The Magnolia," he observed, "is a new Corinna with a fervid Southern eloquence that makes me wonder as often before how you fell into the Massachusetts"

(*L* 2 : 378). Beginning with Emerson, Perry Miller explains, many of Fuller's acquaintances found irresistible the connection with Madame de Staël's Romantic heroine Corinne. As a figure of what Miller terms "sentimental ecstasy," Corinne provided an image of unconventional womanhood and genius that seemed to capture Fuller's elusive personality.[24]

But as Miller's commentary makes clear, the image of Corinne also allowed Fuller's interpreters to avoid the larger, theological dimensions of her thought. Miller, for example, reduces Fuller's vision of self-reliance to what he terms "the hyperbolically female intellectualism of the period."[25] The question that neither he nor Emerson asked was why female intellectuals in the 1840s were attracted to hyperbolic forms, or why the figure of Corinne represented such a compelling model for Fuller's male interpreters. Providing an image of emotional intensity and improvisational excess, the image of Corinne enabled Fuller's acquaintances and critics to dissociate her unsettling social effects from their theological underpinnings. A much more fruitful point of departure (at least for the reader interested in Fuller's ties to the emerging discourse of woman's rights) is provided by the Magnolia's declaration, near the end of the essay: "Nor shall I again detain a wanderer, luring him from afar, nor shall I again subject myself to be questioned by an alien spirit to tell the tale of my being in words that divide it from itself" (*EMF* 49). Having taken "a step inward" and "become a vestal priestess," the Magnolia dedicates her life to a region of female spiritual power lying far outside nineteenth-century America's mainstream religions (*EMF* 49). In place of God the Father, she encounters a "goddess," the "form that took me home" (*EMF* 48). Neither Emerson nor Perry Miller seem to have taken seriously the significance of Fuller's image of the Goddess. That such a figure might have important theological and ideological functions was simply not an idea available to them.

Between 1840 and 1844, Fuller developed in her writing a number of goddess-figures (such as Isis, Diana, and Ceres) to exemplify what she came to call the "idea of woman" (*EMF* 269). Representing idealized images of female power, such figures allowed her to remap her society's vision of female potential. The most important of these divine images was a syncretic goddess-figure who functioned as the subject of Fuller's most radical *Dial* essay, "Leila." Celebrating Leila as "a bridge" to "the infinite," Fuller represented this goddess-image as a personification of the divine depths of the self. As a feminized counterpart to Emerson's god within, Leila became Fuller's most powerful female myth, counteracting Emerson's image of masculinized "Spirit" as the motive power of the psyche. Pursuing "Leila,

Saint of Knowledge," the narrator connects with an ecstatic female energy that turns all solid barriers "fluid," transforming the "prison walls" inhibiting her development "into Edens" (*EMF* 56, 57). Most radically, Fuller represents Leila as a female Christ-figure, waiting to be incarnated in human form. Instead of proposing the imitation of Christ as a standard for human conduct, she offers her female readers the imitation of a *female* savior, who combines spiritual ecstasy and suffering. As Julie Ellison has reminded us, what is important is not Fuller's belief in such a figure (which never can be ascertained with any certainty), but rather its performative value as a cultural construction.[26] Like the utopian images of the contemporary French philosopher Luce Irigaray, Fuller's myth of Leila allows her to intervene in and realign the symbolic relations of her society, mapping a narrative space that reconfigures the theological foundations of America's dominant ideologies.[27]

As we have seen, Emerson found unsettling what he termed "the wild element in woman." Thus, it should not surprise us that his vision of Leila is much tamer than Fuller's. Fuller encountered the prototype for her image of Leila in Persian poetry, either in the famous love poem *Lailí and Majnun*, (translated in 1836 by James Atkinson) or in Hafiz's famous cycle of mystical love poems, *The Divan*, books contained in Emerson's library. In both texts, Laili/Laila represents the ideal woman capable of stirring the poet to rapt mystical adoration. Although Emerson barely mentions the figure of Leila in the *Memoirs*, it is noteworthy that he refers to a related figure, "Lilla," in his essay "Manners." Near the end of this essay, in a famous paragraph calling for male "chivalry in behalf of Woman's Rights," he returns to the question of Fuller's influence on his life (although she is not mentioned by name). "The wonderful generosity of [woman's] sentiments," he writes, "raises her at times into heroical and godlike regions, and verifies the picture of Minerva, Juno, or Polymnia; and, by the firmness with which she treads her upward path convinces the coarsest calculators that another road exists, than that which their feet know" (*CW* 3:88). But this apparent acknowledgement of Fuller's mythmaking (recognized through the allusion to "Minerva") is quickly subsumed beneath a more familiar image of womanhood. "But besides those who make good in our imagination the place of muses and of Delphic Sibyls," Emerson continues, "are there not women who fill our vase with wine and roses to the brim, ... who unloose our tongues, and we speak; who anoint our eyes, and we see?"[28] In a domesticated parody of prophetic and messianic power (unloosed tongue and anointed eyes), Emerson diminishes the image of female power from the mythic dimensions of Leila to that of the gracious and inspirational true woman.

Then, in what seems a pointed reference to Fuller's "Leila," Emerson clinches the commentary on Fuller's mythmaking by identifying his model-woman as "Lilla" (a move that directly contradicts the image of woman-hood in Fuller's "Leila"). "What Hafiz or Firdousi was it," he writes, "who said of his Persian Lilla, She was an elemental force, and astonished me by her amount of life, when I saw her day after day radiating, every instant, redundant joy and grace on all around her. She was a solvent powerful to reconcile all heterogeneous persons into one society: like air or water, an element of such great range of affinities, that it combines readily with a thousand substances" (*cw* 3:88). In this passage, Emerson displaces the *theological* significance of Leila through a series of materialized metaphors that depict Lilla as an "elemental force," a powerful "solvent," "like air or water," and a universal "element."

Like Fuller, Emerson perceived in the Persian Laila a figure who lent herself to imaginative reveries on ideal womanhood. But we notice a strik-ing difference: where Fuller transforms the Persian Laila into an image of independent female spirituality, Emerson identifies her as the perfect host-ess, able to smooth individual differences by radiating "joy and grace." Linking woman and nature, he constructs in his account of Lilla a materi-alized image of female being that keeps in place male spiritual mastery and interpretive power. Several years later, we find a similar pattern in the essay "Uses of Great Men."[29] "Each man," Emerson observes, "is, by se-cret liking, connected with some district of nature, whose agent and inter-preter he is." "It would seem," he continues a few lines later, "as if each waited, like the enchanted princess in fairy tales, for a destined human de-liverer" (*cw* 4:6).

As Fuller's thought developed, she began to resist such narratives of male heroism through an important expansion of her mythmaking. Rather than constructing solitary images of divine female power (such as the Mag-nolia or Leila), she began to conceptualize the female psyche in terms of the harmonious balancing of "masculine" and "feminine" powers found within.[30] This androgynous model of the psyche counterbalanced Emer-son's masculinized model of Spirit through the representation of both pa-ternal and maternal powers within the self.[31] Contending that "man and woman . . . are the two halves of one thought," Fuller replaced Emerson's solitary image of male power with what she termed "The Sacred Mar-riage," a symbol of psychological equilibrium in which "masculine" Spirit is paired with an equally powerful female energy (*EMF* 378). Arguing, in *Woman in the Nineteenth Century*, that "Male and female represent the two sides of the great radical dualism," she identifies the "feminine" and "masculine" sides of the female psyche as the "Muse" and "Minerva," respectively.[32] While many of Fuller's contemporaries probably connected with her image of the "Muse" (with its familiar connotations of female influence and emotionality), her image of "Minerva" (Athena) presented a real obstacle. The virginal and warlike daughter of Jove (Zeus), Minerva embodied a series of traits that—in the nineteenth-century—were not considered womanly: aggression, heroism, will, and intellectuality. Even Emerson, in his address to the 1855 Woman's Rights Convention in Boston, asserted that "a masculine woman is not strong, but a lady is" (*w* 10:425). Since most Americans were content to relegate women to muse-like roles, it was Fuller's explicit intention "to call" women "to the Minerva side," so that their "incarcerated souls" might be stirred to a "religious self-dependence." Asserting the need for woman to achieve "the power of self-poise," she declaimed: "Grant her, then, for a while, the armor and javelin. Let her put from her the press of other minds and meditate in virgin loneliness" (*EMF* 311, 313).

Appropriating and transforming Emerson's ideas, Fuller's image of Minerva represented female spiritual independence as the foundation of self-reliance. In a sense, she claimed for herself and her American sisters an independence of spirit, a "religious self-dependence," as profound as that asserted by Emerson. Given Fuller's revisions of Emerson's model of self-reliance, it is noteworthy that he directly responded to her paradigm of Muse and Minerva in his 1844 essay "Experience."[33] Retreating from the view that the psyche's energy is coextensive with paternal power, he asserts that "there is that in us that changes not." "Fortune, Minerva, Muse, Holy Ghost," he continues, "—these are quaint names, too narrow to cover the unbounded substance. The baffled intellect must still kneel before this cause, which refuses to be named" (*cw* 3:42). Although it is philosophically appealing, Emerson's argument adroitly sidesteps the political issues contained in Fuller's mythmaking. What is missing in his argument is any recognition that, as theologized images of the psyche's power, figures such as Minerva, Muse, and Holy Ghost were implicated in nineteenth-century ideologies. Countless men and women knew from weekly sermons of the agency of Father, Son, and Holy Ghost (or "Spirit," as Emerson had termed this power in *Nature*). They imbibed with such religious instruction a vision in which authority and power were gendered male. Only a few leading thinkers in the nineteenth century, Fuller among them, understood the ways in which ideologies of male domination were perpetuated by such religious imagery. But by refusing to distinguish "Minerva" and "Muse" from "Holy Ghost," Emerson negated the important gender distinctions between them. Indeed, his argument moves to an ungendered plane of "unbounded substance" that defines out of existence one of the most important political arguments of the woman's rights movement—the idea that the image of gender transcendentally projected in religious figures and narratives is replicated in social relations.

In Fuller's eyes, it made a world of difference whether spiritual agency was identified with the Holy Ghost or Minerva. Like Emerson, she anchored her hopes for society in the faith that the self could be reconfigured. But what Emerson saw less clearly than Fuller was that this reformation of the self would not just shift the cognitive and spiritual boundaries of a person; it also would realign the mental categories shaping the performance of gender. Once a new imaginary pathway defining the "soul" had been opened, it was impossible to control the avenues of their unfolding. Bringing to the surface what had been unexpressed in Emerson's theory, a female god-language authorizing woman's empowerment, Fuller began to realign both men and women in terms of a gendered continuum of mythically defined energies. By restructuring the terms that mapped the self and its productive energies, she intervened directly in the gender myths of her society. It should not surprise us that her more radical interventions in nineteenth-century theology were misunderstood by virtually everyone. One 1845 reviewer of *Woman in the Nineteenth Century* exclaimed in horror: "She is greatly taken with Isis, Sita, Egyptian Sphinx, Ceres, Proserpine. Would she recall these ancient heathen deities, their ancient worship, filled with obscene rites and frightful orgies?"[34] Rather than suggesting strange new rites, Fuller combed classical mythology for effective models of female agency to counteract the negative connotations of figures like Eve.

Although Emerson was able to acknowledge the importance of Fuller's influence and of the new woman's movement, he could not wholly resist the seductive role of the powerful male "deliverer" interpreting and releasing "the enchanted princess" from her prison. But as Margaret Fuller and many of the early leaders of the woman's rights movement knew all too well, patterns of male interpretation (located, for example, in Biblical exegesis) rarely removed the bars from women's enchantment. Like "princesses captive in the prison of a barbarous foe," to switch to Fuller's evocative phrasing of this process, women needed to gain control of the means of ideological reproduction.[35] These means were located in what Louis Althusser has called the "ideological state apparatuses"—in the home, in the school, in the workplace, in government, in laws, and in the church.[36]

Perhaps the most powerful ideological apparatus of all was found in a site that Emerson could leave but which he could never entirely remove from his political imagination—the pulpit. Thus, it is highly significant that Fuller's writings contain something that few of her readers have perceived—passages of revisionary Biblical interpretation. Over fifty years before Elizabeth Cady Stanton organized the publication of *The Woman's Bible*, Fuller highlighted the ways in which "conservative religious ideologies and institutions tended to legitimate the oppression of women."[37] Like Stanton, Fuller recognized that traditional patterns of nineteenth-century theology represented "the ideological basis for women's subordination."[38] At Seneca Falls, Stanton had paraphrased Fuller in her stirring assertion of the need for female spiritual independence: "Let her live *first* for God, and she will not make imperfect man an object of reverence and awe."[39] Such idolatry, both Stanton and Fuller realized, perpetuated the glorified image of manhood found in weekly sermons.

Despite her radical theological use of classical mythology, Fuller shared with the early leaders of the woman's rights movement a deep concern with the ways in which the language of the Bible, codified in religious practices, had shaped the masculinist stereotypes of her culture. This connection between theology and sexual stereotypes is immediately apparent in the responses of Fuller's early reviewers. In his 1845 review of *Woman in the Nineteenth Century*, Charles F. Briggs presented what he considered an irrefutable argument. "The true position of woman," he pronounced, "is not a disputable point; the universal sentiment of mankind has determined it; God himself has said 'her desire shall be unto her husband, and he shall rule over her.'"[40] In similar terms, Orestes Brownson's review attacked Fuller's advocacy of woman's rights by adducing Paul's alleged support of male "dominion" in his assertion that wives should "love and *obey* their husbands."[41] In the eyes of Briggs and Brownson, the secondary status of women was divinely sanctioned. Fighting against such a climate of opinion, Fuller found it necessary to make strategic use of the Bible in *Woman in the Nineteenth Century*, for the transformation of social structures, she realized, necessitated a realignment of the theologized ideology supporting them.

Fuller opened *Woman in the Nineteenth Century* with a familiar figure—that of the prodigal son awaiting his inheritance. But in her ensuing argument, she displaced this claim onto American women, arguing for their equal right to a cultural and spiritual inheritance. At the same time, Fuller suggests that man's birthright is intimately linked to the condition of women. Man is "still a stranger to his inheritance," because the suppression of women has submerged both the female side of himself and of American culture (*EMF* 249). To overcome this schism, she argues, it is necessary to see the ideological conditions that have perpetuated women's inequality. In a radical appropriation of Christ's words in the Sermon on the Mount, she envisions this process as a process of spiritual reorientation: "Whatever the soul knows how to seek, it cannot fail to obtain. This is the law and the prophets. Knock and it shall be opened, seek and ye shall find." In a further appropriation of the Christian narrative, Fuller imagines the social consequences of such ideological reorientation as the emergence of "a love that cannot be crucified" (*EMF* 249, 250).

Fuller's radical appropriation of Biblical narratives is even more evident in her striking revision of one of Christ's most famous parables. The original passage, in the tenth chapter of John, begins: "He that entereth not by the door into the sheepfold, but climbeth up some other way, the same is a thief and a robber. But he that entereth in by the door is the shepherd of the sheep." The standard interpretation, provided in succeeding verses, is that Christ is the good shepherd guarding his flock. Rewriting this narrative, Fuller focuses on the ways in which opponents of woman's rights have used Biblical language to buttress their arguments. "The numerous party," she observes, "whose opinions are already labelled and adjusted to their mind to admit of any new light, strive, by lectures on some model-woman of bride-like beauty and gentleness, by writing and lending little treatises, intended to mark out with precision the limits of woman's sphere, and woman's mission, to prevent other than the rightful shepherd from climbing the wall, or the flock from using any chance to go astray" (*EMF* 257). The "model-woman" in this passage seems unerringly similar to Emerson's image of Lilla, the ideal woman (probably modeled on his wife Lidian) "radiating . . . redundant joy and grace on all around her." As a result, her discussion of the male shepherd provides a devastating commentary on his unexamined view of wifely devotion. In Fuller's revision, the "rightful shepherd" who climbs the wall is placed in the position of the thief in the original parable. Fuller's shepherd is the traditional guardian of "the limits of woman's sphere"—the husband who defends his marital interests and works to prevent his wife from going "astray." The image of thievery suggests a degree of sexual depredation that Fuller examines more completely elsewhere in *Woman in the Nineteenth Century*, especially in her discussions of the sexual double standard and the sexual exploitation of New York City's fallen women. With extraordinary efficiency, she shows her audience the ways in which nineteenth-century theology supported unequal gender ideologies and social conditions.

Like the early leaders of the woman's rights movement, Margaret Fuller knew that it would be a difficult process for women to "vindicate their birthright" (EMF 347). The struggle for equality entailed much more than the passage of new laws or, as Emerson imagined, the chivalrous granting of equal property or marital rights. For such social changes were dependent upon a difficult ideological struggle. They involved the transformation of public opinion, which had crystallized into symbolic structures that replicated unexamined assumptions about women's incapacity and inferiority. Many of these ideological patterns had been naturalized, being taken as "the way things are," and had fallen beneath the epistemological threshold of visibility. Fuller's goal—like that of Lucretia Mott, Elizabeth Cady Stanton, and other woman's rights leaders—was to make that threshold visible. What made this process especially difficult (and especially hard for Emerson to see) was that mainstream American churches reinforced the status quo, lending an aura of sanctity and the weight of doctrinal inertia to woman's secondary social position. Only when that ideological threshold became visible could the American public witness the human expense of the troubling alliance between its religious values and its social structures.

In conclusion, we must give full credit to Emerson for developing a model of personal transformation that opened the door toward female liberation. But, in terms of its gender politics, Emerson's model of self-reliance was deeply flawed. By gendering the motive power of the psyche in masculine—or, at times, neutral—terms, he overlooked the powerful role that theological myths play in shaping the gendered awareness and social roles of their recipients. Despite his own heterodox theology, it was ultimately difficult for Emerson to move outside of a world ruled by God the Father and His male representatives on earth. Writing and thinking from within a position of gender privilege, he was not able to evaluate the sexual politics contained within the theological terms and narratives that he was using. From the perspective of the woman's right's movement, Emerson's disregard of the gendering of theological language prevented him from seeing one of the most important ideological foundations of women's oppression in America. Ironically, Emerson could leave the church behind out of the profound conviction that religious institutions stifle the human spirit. But he was never able to ask whether women in nineteenth-century America experienced the same kind of doctrinal and institutional enclosure.

NOTES

1. Christina Zwarg, *Feminist Conversations: Fuller, Emerson, and the Play of Reading* (Ithaca: Cornell Univ. Press, 1995).

2. Harold Bloom first outlined his theory of misreading in *The Anxiety of Influence: A Theory of Poetry* (London: Oxford Univ. Press, 1973). Studying the relationship of male writers to their forerunners, Bloom develops a dynamic model of inter-authorial ties based upon varying degrees of appropriation and distortions.

3. "Declaration of Sentiments and Resolutions, Seneca Falls" in Miriam Schneir, ed., *Feminism: The Essential Historical Writings* (New York: Vintage, 1972), pp. 81–82.

4. Alma Lutz, "Elizabeth Cady Stanton," in *Notable American Women: A Biographical Dictionary*, ed. Edward T. James, Janet Wilson James, and Paul S. Boyer, 3 vols. (Cambridge, Mass.: Harvard Univ. Press, 1971), 3 : 346.

5. Frances Wright, "Course of Popular Lectures" in *Feminism: The Essential Historical Writings*, p. 20.

6. Sarah M. Grimké, "Letters on the Equality of the Sexes and the Condition of Woman" in *Feminism: The Essential Historical Writings*, p. 38.

7. Alice Felt Tyler, "Paulina Kellogg Wright Davis" in *Notable American Women*, 1 : 444.

8. Fuller Papers, Boston Public Library, MSAm 1450 (119).

9. Margaret Fuller, *The Letters of Margaret Fuller*, ed. Robert N. Hudspeth, 6 vols. (Ithaca: Cornell Univ. Press, 1983–94), 2 : 158. Subsequent references to this set will use the abbreviation *LMF*.

10. Fuller Papers, Harvard University, Houghton Rare Book Library, bMSAm 1086.

11. More attuned to Fuller's mystical antecedents, William Henry Channing linked her spiritual crisis "to the doctrine of the wise Jacob Boehme." Perceiving in Fuller a mystical conjunction of opposites, he resorted to a highly figurative mystical discourse in order to summarize the change that took place in her: "the fierce, hungry fire had met in embrace the meek, cool water, and was bringing to birth the pleasant light-flame of love." *The Memoirs of Margaret Fuller Ossoli*, ed. Ralph Waldo Emerson, James Freeman Clarke, and William Henry Channing, 2 vols. (Boston: Phillips, Sampson & Co., 1852), 2 : 93.

12. See "The Divine Sophia," chapter 10 of Arthur Versluis, *TheoSophia: Hidden Dimensions of Christianity* (Hudson, NY: Lindisfarne Press, 1994).

13. Fuller, *Memoirs* 1 : 279.

14. *Ibid.*, 1 : 219.

15. *Ibid.*, 1 : 308, 309.

16. In chapter 8 of *Feminist Conversations*, Zwarg argues that Emerson used his sketch of Fuller's life, in this edition, to distance himself from his earlier opposition to her radical ideas. In her reading, Emerson's portrait of his reaction to Fuller's spiritual crisis is an ironic parody, measuring the extent to which he had begun to accept Fuller's influence after her death. But whether or not Emerson ever accepted Fuller's model of critique (as Zwarg contends), there is little evidence that he completely understood the ideological resonance of her theological aspirations.

17. In a single paragraph in his essay "Self-Reliance," for example, he describes it as: "the aboriginal Self," "the essence of genius," "Spontaneity," "Instinct," "the fountain of action and thought," and "the lap of an immense intelligence" that radiates illuminating "beams" (*CW* 2:37).

18. Eric Cheyfitz, *The Trans-Parent: Sexual Politics in the Language of Emerson* (Baltimore: Johns Hopkins Univ. Press, 1981), p. 41.

19. *Ibid.*, p. 61.

20. "The Sacred Marriage," *EMF* 378.

21. The idea of "harmony" first emerges in "The Great Lawsuit," where it functions as a complex model of spiritual, social, and psychological balance. This concept is found throughout "The Great Lawsuit"; for example on pp. 3, 16, 24, 28, 29, 38. *The Dial* 4, no. 1 (July 1843).

22. "Autobiographical Romance," *EMF* 67.

23. Fuller confides her theological aspirations in her letter of Oct. 25/28, 1840, to William Henry Channing. For example, she asserts, "I would now preach the Holy Ghost as zealously as they have been preaching man" (*LMF* 2:173).

24. Perry Miller, "Foreword" to *Margaret Fuller, American Romantic: A Selection from Her Writings and Correspondence*, ed. Perry Miller (1963; reprint, Ithaca: Cornell Univ. Press, 1970), p. xix.

25. *Ibid.*, p. xvii.

26. Julie Ellison, *Delicate Subjects: Romanticism, Gender, and the Ethics of Understanding* (Ithaca: Cornell Univ. Press, 1990), p. 243.

27. Margaret Whitford provides an excellent analysis of this process in *Luce Irigaray: Philosophy in the Feminine* (London: Routledge, 1991).

28. Zwarg notes that Emerson's references to Minerva, the muses, and the Delphic Sybils clearly refer to some of Fuller's favorite myths (*Feminist Conversations*, pp. 159–60).

29. Zwarg reads this essay as a disguised tribute to Fuller's influence. But this tribute is complicated by the masculinized vision of interpretation presented earlier in the essay.

30. *EMF* 343. Just after using these traditional gender terms, Fuller complains that "we have not language primitive and pure enough to express such ideas with precision."

31. Unwilling to validate mythic female power (which he demonized as "the wild element in woman"), Emerson found it nearly impossible to envision the enlightened and empowered self in terms of androgynous spiritual harmony.

32. EMF 310, 311. It is important to note that these figures map woman's psychic being through *female* rather than male myths.

33. Fuller first presented her conceptions of Muse and Minerva in her 1843 *Dial* essay, "The Great Lawsuit," which was published the year before Emerson's essay.

34. Orestes A. Brownson, "Miss Fuller, and Reformers," *Brownson's Quarterly Review* (April 1845); reprinted in *Critical Essays on Margaret Fuller*, ed. Joel Myerson (Boston: G. K. Hall, 1980), p. 22.

35. The cited phrase is from "The Magnolia of Lake Pontchartrain," EMF 45.

36. Louis Althusser, "Ideology and Ideological State Apparatuses," in *Lenin and Philosophy and Other Essays* (New York: Monthly Review Press, 1971), p. 143.

37. Maureen Fitzgerald, "Foreword" to *The Woman's Bible* (Boston: Northeastern Univ. Press, 1993), p. vii.

38. *Ibid.*, p. viii.

39. Cited by Fitzgerald, "Foreword," p. xv. The original passage in *Woman in the Nineteenth Century* reads: "I wish woman to live, *first* for God's sake. Then she will not make imperfect man her god, and thus sink to idolatry" (EMF 346). I want to thank Phyllis Cole for drawing to my attention Fuller's influence on Stanton.

40. Charles F. Briggs, review of Margaret Fuller, *Woman in the Nineteenth Century*, *Broadway Journal* (March 1845); reprinted in Myerson, *Critical Essays*, p. 14.

41. Brownson, "Miss Fuller and Reformers," p. 22.

Part Three

TRANSITIONS IN ANTISLAVERY

MICHAEL STRYSICK

Emerson, Slavery, and the Evolution of the Principle of Self-Reliance

> Society everywhere is in conspiracy against the manhood
> of every one of its members.
> —RALPH WALDO EMERSON, "Self-Reliance"

EMERSON'S RELATION to pressing social issues such as slavery has been frequently addressed in recent criticism, most notably in Len Gougeon's *Virtue's Hero: Emerson, Antislavery, and Reform* (1990). Gougeon's ground-breaking study challenged the prevailing opinion that Emerson was a disinterested scholar who appealed to broader philosophical questions at the exclusion of particular social issues. The dust has not yet settled over this issue, however, and it will likely be engaged for many more years. Two camps have emerged: those who portray Emerson's activism as an anomaly, inconsistent with his larger transcendental project, and those who portray Emerson's activism as a natural extension of this project. The publication of *Emerson's Antislavery Writings* (1995), edited by Gougeon and Joel Myerson, has helped support the latter position, precisely because of the sheer number of passionate essays, letters, and speeches devoted to the topic.

The debate has its own history, and the renewed interest in Emerson's relation to the antislavery movement has followed a course nearly similar to that set almost half a century ago by his twentieth-century biographers. The first chapter of Gougeon's book charts the influence of the two most prominent biographers: Ralph Rusk, whose *Life of Ralph Waldo Emerson* (1949) presents Emerson "as an active social reformer," and Stephen Whicher, whose *Freedom and Fate: An Inner Life of Ralph Waldo Emerson* (1953) depicts Emerson as someone who "separated himself, intellectually and emotionally, from the various crises of the hour throughout the 1840s and 1850s" (*VH* 2).

By way of example, even after the publication of *Virtue's Hero*, recent studies such as George Kateb's *Emerson and Self-Reliance* (1995), the work of a political scientist, and John Carlos Rowe's *At Emerson's Tomb: The Politics of Classic American Literature* (1997) argue that "Emersonianism," a trope for Transcendentalism broadly, is incompatible with social activism, finding this so-called aesthetic dissent a weak attempt at best to effect social change. This is made clear in a representative passage from Rowe, who suggests that "transcendental and practical politics continue to collide in his essays from 1844 to 1862, demonstrating the inappropriateness of Emersonianism for any practical social reforms."[1] This essay takes the opposite approach, suggesting that with the message of self-reliance in place, Emerson sought to be more than its messenger: he sought its application.

Albert J. von Frank's *The Trials of Anthony Burns: Freedom and Slavery in Emerson's Boston* (1998) shares sympathy with Gougeon, particularly because von Frank sees that Emerson's essays and speeches are "a remarkable instance of his ability to address the topic without retreating from his characteristic idealism, which is just the challenge that slavery is supposed to have set for him."[2] In further addressing this "remarkable instance," von Frank hits the crux of the current debate that I intend to address here: "How could this dealer in abstractions, with his reputation for keeping aloof from the real world, confront effectively (or at all) a problem so manifestly human and social? The assumption has generally been that in order to do so he would have somehow to forget that he was a Transcendentalist and repudiate or retreat from the principles that won him his first audience" (*TAB* 327).

After noting the "lack of consensus among historians and students of Emerson" over this issue, von Frank offers his own distinction. On the one hand, "a great many hold that Emerson simply could not suspend his idealism before the vulgar dispute between slave and master and so made himself and his followers irrelevant to the struggle." More important for my purposes here, von Frank also recognizes those who "suppose that his career in the 1850s was a more or less steady *retreat from* important early beliefs, and that while he indeed spoke forcefully and influentially on slavery, he did so *at the cost of consistency* and because material circumstance now bulked larger in his thought" (*TAB* 327, emphasis added).

Emerson's earliest writing reveals that his attention to slavery in the 1840s and 1850s was not a retreat from but a return to early beliefs that stayed with him throughout his life. Referring to the world as "this wide prisonhouse" at one point, Emerson believed all of us to be similarly imprisoned. What dawned on him as the century wore on is the radical difference between literal and figurative prisons, those of the mind and those of the body. Enslavement, after all, was the mortal and moral enemy of self-reliance, and he spoke of slavery as "the worst institution on earth" (*JMN* 2 : 57). By tracing this early material, it becomes clear that Emerson's inevitable antislavery activity did not mark the beginning of his evolution as an abolitionist, but was instead the evolution of the principle of self-reliance—indeed, an *extension* of self-reliance.

While activism was an important part of Emerson's overall message, rather than looking merely at his message, Emerson's very *motivation* as messenger must figure into the equation. Ever since his years as a student at Harvard, Emerson realized a pronounced sense of duty to his fellow human beings, and over time he evolved his sense of how best to fulfill that duty, not merely as creator of the message but as messenger, too. After all, nowhere in his early journals did he struggle over whether or not to improve the world: the question was always how to do so.

Duty and self-reliance can be seen as compatible only if we understand self-reliance to be a dynamic concept, not a static one. A static reading of his principle offers the strongest justification for viewing Emerson's attention to social issues as an anomaly, what Rowe would characterize as short-sighted aesthetic dissent. This is what von Frank is referring to when he suggests that some critics believe Emerson spoke out against slavery "at the cost of consistency" (*TAB* 327). Emerson insists in "Self-Reliance," however, that a "foolish consistency" is "the hobgoblin of little minds," and that "a great soul has simply nothing to do" with consistency (*CW* 2 : 57). Self-reliance is through and through a dynamic principle, one that avoids the hobgoblin of even its own foolish consistency. While it took considerable intellectual and moral vision to promote such a principle, what makes it even greater is that the messenger was not satisfied simply to deliver his message. Instead, he went further by addressing the conditions under which it would be heard.

As all great ideas are tested by time and experience and strengthened in the crucible of specific forces, the issue of slavery helped transform the practical application of the doctrine of self-reliance for Emerson.[3] The Concord sage refused to speak out on this issue for many years, in large part because of his trust in the principle of "moral suasion" imparted by his Harvard professor, William Ellery Channing. A man philosophically sensitive to imprisonment, Emerson came to realize that the principle of self-reliance is meaningless if society does not recognize the agency of all of its members; indeed, it is impossible for an individual to be self-reliant if a society maintains a constitutional and legal interpretation of inferiority regarding the status of some of its citizens. Ultimately, Emerson realized the degree to which speaking out against slavery would not compromise his singular, self-reliant stance but would complement it by working to achieve the greater potential of others to work toward their own self-reliance.

Politics in Emerson's Earliest Writing

Investing all hope in the individual, Emerson believed any lasting alteration of the whole could only be achieved through alteration of each part. Individuals could change society only by changing themselves. But this could occur only if they possessed the agency to do so.

Readers of Emerson have long associated him with a more intellectual than physical individualism, what George Kateb distinguishes in *Emerson and Self-Reliance* as the difference between "mental self-reliance and active self-reliance."[4] Some critics have seen "active self-reliance" as an oxymoron. Kateb takes up the issue of self-reliance and social action in a chapter entitled "Self-Reliance, Politics, and Society." He begins by asking, "What provision does Emerson make for a self-reliant individual to work with others, to cooperate and collaborate?" (*ESR* 173). The attacks Emerson made on slavery, especially in the 1840s and 1850s, seem to be the proving ground for this question.

Kateb believes, however, that Emerson's antislavery activities are an aberration in the larger picture: he asks, "Are there not institutions so dreadful that what matters is their reform or abolition, not any other consideration?" Kateb concedes that passage of the Fugitive Slave Law in 1850 altered the equation for Emerson, arguing that "This spreading evil—this evil which is truly evil, not only apparently so—forces him [Emerson] to change his attitude on the subject of associating for reform" (*ESR* 177). Yet Emerson's attitude toward slavery evolved rather than being forced to change, since Emerson could have never seen self-reliance as a hard and fast principle not open to alteration. Kateb allows that "we can say that Emerson accepts the sacrifices of every sort—including the abandonment of aspirations of free persons to self-reliance—which are needed to give all Americans, not just some, the chance for self-reliance." Kateb justifies this by continuing, "Perhaps a society has no self-reliance anywhere in it if there are slaves anywhere in it. But before this change in, or suspension of, Emerson's teaching takes place, he discountenances association as solidarity" (*ESR* 178). Yet Emerson did consciously engage in antislavery activity, and this "association as solidarity" need not be seen as opposed to or separate from the rest of his thinking.

The crucible of time—and especially experience, that great guide for Emerson—led him to extend and expand the principle of self-reliance. Although the principle originally maintained that the individual remained the primary agent of social change, Emerson realized that self-reliance was hollow if particular individuals had no access to or concept of their agency. For Emerson, self-reliance was bound up with duty. Had he not felt any duty to his fellow individuals, had he not felt a sense of community, he would scarcely have bothered to lecture, preach, and write.

While Emerson's evolution took place most evidently between 1841, the date of "Self-Reliance," and his 1855 "Lecture on Slavery," the development of this principle began before 1841. Not only did his 1836 *Nature* begin the outline of self-reliance but so did his student work, particularly his 1821 Bowdoin Dissertation Prize essay at Harvard, and passages in his "Wide World" journals, specifically those from late 1822. What occurred over the course of Emerson's lifetime was an increasing awareness of and sensitivity to those held in literal prisons who did not have individual agency and subjectivity from which to act self-reliantly. This awareness altered the way in which he mediated individual and society, self-reliance and duty.

The issue of enslavement had long occupied Emerson, specifically as a trope for the limited manner in which individuals live their lives. As is evident in some of his earliest writings, Emerson believed the past to represent the strongest of shackles: in the introduction to *Nature*, for example, the past is represented through the trope of the "fathers" (*cw* 1:7). Emerson's early writings and speeches concentrate on how America can and must be different from the hegemony of the so-called paternal Old World. By referring to the building of "the sepulchres of the fathers" in *Nature*, Emerson was intent on burying the past rather than constantly trying to revive it. He believed strongly that "we should also enjoy an original relation to the universe" rather than groping "among the dry bones of the past." He demanded, in no uncertain terms, "new lands, new men, new thoughts" (*w* 3:7). The degrees of this newness, however, and the lengths to which it would extend, were themselves at issue in Emerson's own original relation to his vision of America's brave new world.

Lacking all confidence in external reforms, be they governmental, legal, political, or even religious, Emerson left reform to the individual, and he sought to empower individuals through increased reliance upon themselves. However, individual action was laden with an overwhelming responsibility in Emerson's vision. Self-reliance meant more than simply being and doing for oneself; it required individuals to create and live by a set of internal laws that were open to external scrutiny.

Emerson's criticism of the "fathers," the defiant statement that opens the *Nature* essays of 1836, was a project Emerson began much earlier. He wrote two Bowdoin Prize essays while at Harvard, and I would like to concentrate on his 1821 effort titled "The Present State of Ethical Philosophy." This essay traces the lineage of the "fathers" as far back as the Greeks, pausing to be especially critical, as one might guess from the anti-Calvinist young Unitarian, of the Catholic church fathers of the Middle Ages. In this early work Emerson recognized slavery as a great scourge on the present state of ethical philosophy: "The plague spot of slavery must be urged thoroughly out before any one will venture to predict any great consummation."[5] At about the same time, he began his so-called "Wide World" journals, depositing his thoughts in these self-described savings banks. In 1822, in "Wide World" 8, Emerson declared that enslavement was the most important question for the nineteenth century, writing that the "secrets" of slavery "darken the prospect of Faith, and teach us the weakness of our Philosophy" (*JMN* 2 : 42).

Emerson's Bowdoin essay shows the influence of Channing, specifically through the importance placed upon duty, the hallmark of Channing's philosophy.[6] Emerson begins by talking about "the social human condition" as composed of "man's first sense of duty to his Maker and to his fellow man" (*TUE* 43). Throughout his life and work, Emerson struggles to understand and mediate the relationship between duty and his fierce emphasis upon individuality. The challenge is that duty and individuality are not mutually exclusive, but must be constantly mediated. The individual, except in rare cases, must live in society; while individuals may like to do as they please, they are ultimately bound to an external code of behavior.

In his assessment of philosophy, Emerson chose to look at the history of philosophy itself, a task he would take on as part of his first series of public lectures.[7] Emerson asserts that early philosophy was limited, largely because "The world was not old enough to have accurately parceled and distributed her science into professions," and because Greek thinking was influenced by a limited worldview that believed "that an inscrutable fate overruled their destinies" (*TUE* 45). When people did think about ethics, this thinking consisted of dictating laws for the government of kings and empires or locking up their results and conclusions in costly manuscripts, so that their influence upon the whole of society was "remote and insignificant." Socrates changed all this: "from him is derived the modern custom of grounding virtue on a single principle" (*TUE* 48). Emerson's fascination with this custom and with Socrates cannot be missed. Was he being Socratic by trying to ground his own sense of virtue on the single principle of self-reliance? Ultimately, what Emerson took from Socrates is that virtue and justice were convertible, informing the premium he placed upon his singularly just principle.

After the rise of the Roman Empire, and the *translatio imperii*, Emerson sees a decline in the quality of ethical philosophy, for "the obscurity of the monastic cell, and the narrow views which were entailed upon each succession of the Roman priesthood, were unfavorable to grand apprehensions of moral science." Expecting much more from these early philosophers, mostly priests, Emerson comments: "Neither domestic relations nor labors to obtain a livelihood interfered to deter them." Despite this relative leisure and isolation, however, Emerson sees that the inability to create a truly practical ethical system had a kind of blindness as its source: "The difficulty seems to have been lodged in the very spirit which pervaded and characterized the whole church, that of choosing darkness rather than light,—a perverse obstinacy of ignorance." He finally calls "bigotry" the "besetting sin of the Roman church" (*TUE* 54).

Emerson paints this historical picture because he believes that ethical laws and truths must be eternal and universal, outside temporal and spatial limitations. He asserts that "The truths of morality must in all ages be the same. . . . Its fundamental principles are taught by the moral sense, and no advancement of time or knowledge can improve them" (*TUE* 58). Perhaps anticipating his opening of *Nature* fifteen years later, he then comments on the paternal character of Rome: "by investing the father with the power it tempts him to become a tyrant, and the son of a domestic tyrant was rarely virtuous himself" (*TUE* 63). As he looked ahead toward future generations, Emerson found one overriding similarity among all so-called modern philosophers: "a conformity to the law of conscience" (*TUE* 67). This conscience would become the inner, eternal law on which the individual must alone be reliant.

The "Wide World" Journals

The sources for these and future essays can be found in Emerson's "Wide World" journals.[8] Their very breadth show an intense, inquiring mind, and their very existence indicates that Emerson felt that he had something to say to the world. He ranged among a variety of topics, offering careful foot-ers on the journal pages indicating that he was currently writing about SLAVERY or JUSTICE or OMNIPOTENCE. Emerson started keeping these jour-nals while in his second year at Harvard, intending them to be a kind of commonplace book. They spanned almost four years, from January 25, 1820, until August 11, 1824. Nearly every separate journal bears a dedica-tion. In the first journal he calls on the assistance of "witches" to "enliven or horrify some midnight lubrication or dream (whichever may be found most convenient) to supply this reservoir when other sources fail" (*JMN* 1:4). Several months later, on April 10, he repeats the entreaty: "Ethereal beings to whom I dedicated the pages of my 'Wide World' do not I entreat you neglect it; when I sleep waken me; when I weary animate!" (*JMN* 1:15).

The purpose of the journals is clear, a point Emerson acknowledges at the end of "Wide World" 1: "it has been an improving employment decidedly . . . & has afforded seasonable aid at various times to enlarge or enliven scanty themes &c" (*JMN* 1:25). The journal has "enriched my stock of language for future exertions," Emerson adds, primarily because "Much of it has been written with a view to their preservation as hints for a peculiar pursuit at the distance of years" (25). Scholars have documented how sub-sequent speeches and essays grew from entries in these early notebooks, but his social motivations are present as well.

While the passages devoted specifically to slavery are found in "Wide World" 8, the various topics throughout young Waldo's journals establish a background for these comments. Particularly, he devotes attention to the relation between good and evil and the hindrance evil places upon human perfection, the relation between scholarly abstraction and moral obligation (duty), and the influence of Socrates in the development of ethics.

From the start, Emerson's idealism shines through. In the summer of 1820 he remarks that "it is joyful change to see human nature unshackling herself & asserting her divine origin" (*JMN* 1:18). Several months later, in December, Emerson suggests that he believes humanity is successfully on the path of progress: "the human soul, the world, the universe are labour-ing on to their magnificent consummation" such that "Man shall come to the presence of Jehovah" (*JMN* 1:46). By "Wide World" 4 he suggests that current and past imperfections help reveal what challenges remain: "Hu-man wisdom sees the imperfections of the past, and labours to make out the perfection of the whole from the analogies of the universe which fall under its eye" (*JMN* 1:92). But in further pondering this consummation, he admits that even "if the filmed eye of human understanding were purged to perceive clearly, it would only discern insurmountable obstacles in the way of perfection" (*JMN* 1:185). Rather, Emerson adds, "The proper mode of pursuing this train of thought, would be to state, in a more definite manner, the advantages and conditions of that state of society which would result from an entire harmony and cooperation of its parts, and, to show why this effect has not, & cannot, be brought about" (*JMN* 1:106). This said, the need for a singular principle is established.

This idealism is not naïve. Emerson devotes many passages to discussing the role and derivation of evil, commenting early on that "People prate of the dignity of the human nature. Look over the whole history of its degradation & find what odious vice, what sottish & debasing enormity the degenerate naughtiness of man has never crouched unto & adored?" (*JMN* 1:18). Any doubt, he offers months later, can be answered "from every corner of this globe. . . . The enslaved, the sick, the disappointed, the poor, the unfortunate, the dying, the surviving cry out It is here [*sic*]" (*JMN* 1:93).

The first example of evil Emerson lists is enslavement. The most memorable slave, in his eyes, is Socrates, of whom he writes, "In prison he was directed in vision to seek the favor of the muses" (*JMN* 1:213). Seeing Socrates as his own great inspiration, he too sought to think from prison, a trope that arises nearly two decades later when Emerson first declines to speak out publicly against slavery. However, his personal and philosophical evolution occurred when he appreciated the difference between internal and external prisons, between those that were figurative and those that were literal.

Emerson found Socrates to be a curious figure. At once aloof and at the same time always working among the people, Socrates operated at a certain level of moral abstraction but always as a means to impart some principle, some idea to those with whom he was gathered. At one point, Emerson ponders the role of such scholarly disinterestedness, part of which is implicit in self-reliance: "How immensely would a scholar enlarge his power could he abstract himself wholly, body & mind from the dinning theory of casual recollections that summon him away, from his useful toils to endless, thankless, reveries" (*JMN* 1:40–41). Yet several days later, without batting an eye, Emerson also remarks, after a sermon delivered by Everett on charity at the Old South Church in Boston, that human interaction is necessitated by "the duty of charity" (*JMN* 1:45). Socrates' singular principle was virtue, and Emerson, still musing on duty, asks "what is Charity—Patriotism—Benevolence, Prudence, but the exercises of Duty toward fellow-beings?" (*JMN* 1:68). These activities, he continues, "form the atmosphere and the bond of unison to *social*, cultivated and active Man." He adds, "Great actions, from their nature, are not done in a closet"—the latter a reference to the scholarly isolation of the priesthood of the Middle Ages— "they are performed in the face of the sun, and in behalf of the world" (*JMN* 1:98). Speaking out against slavery, as von Frank suggests, was the proving ground for Emerson, and we can see that Emerson did not recognize the antagonism between abstraction and action that later critics would impose on him.

But why did Emerson see fit to address the issue of slavery? His preoccupations in the earlier "Wide World" journals show a young man devoted to pondering his role in life, particularly as it addressed attention to duty and charity. Realizing this, at the end of "Wide World" 7, Emerson adds the following concluding comments: "I have come to the close of the sheets which I have dedicated to the Genius of America, and notice that I have devoted nothing in my book to any *peculiar* topics which concern my country" (*JMN* 2:39, emphasis added).

Two days later, on November 6, 1822, Emerson begins "Wide World" 8. As usual, he offers a dedication, but this time he deconstructs the very idea of a dedication in language reminiscent of what will appear later in the opening of *Nature:* "To glory which is departed, to majesty which hath ceased, to intellect which is quenched—I bring no homage,—no, not a grain of gold. For why seek to contradict the voice of Nature and of God, which saith over them, 'It is finished,' by wasting our imaginations upon the deaf ear of the dead? Turn rather to the mighty multitude," Emerson suggests, and in doing so he chooses "one from the throng. Upon his brow have the Muses hung no garland. His name hath never been named in the halls of Fashion, or the palaces of State; but I saw Prophecy drop the knee before him, and I hastened to pay the tribute of a page" (*JMN* 2:40–41).

Emerson then begins to address the peculiar topics he has avoided in previous journals, transporting himself to this mighty multitude through a dreamlike experience, visiting "many old and curious institutions," clearly contemplating "the brilliant spectacle of an African morning" (*JMN* 2:41). Emerson envisions a man hunting a leopard, which he shoots dead with an arrow. While trying to claim his kill, Emerson sees several families going to a nearby river to cast their nets. Suddenly, the people are themselves captured by "men dressed in foreign garb":

> these surrounded the fishers, and bound them with cords, and hastily carried them to their boats, which lay concealed behind the trees. So they sailed down

the stream, talking aloud an[d] laughing as they went; but they that were bound, gnashed their teeth and uttered so piteous a howl that I thought it were a mercy if the river had swallowed them.

In my dream, *I launched my skiff to follow the boats and redeem the captives.* They went in ships to other lands and I could never reach them, albeit I came near enough to hear the piercing cry of the chained victims, which was louder than the noise of the Ocean. . . .

Canst thou ponder the vision, and shew why Providence suffers the land of its richest productions to be thus defiled? Do human bodies lodge immortal souls? . . . Confess that there are secrets in that Providence, which no human eye can penetrate, which darken the prospect of Faith, and teach us the weakness of our Philosophy. (*JMN* 2 : 41–42, emphasis added)

Having thus launched his skiff, Emerson's proceeding career did follow the boats, finding better and better ways to free the captives.

Two days later, on November 8, 1882, Emerson reflects on his dream, admitting that "nobody now regards the maxim 'that all men are born equal,' as any thing more than a convenient hypothesis or an extravagant exclamation. For the reverse is true,—that all men are born unequal in personal powers and in those essential circumstances, of time, parentage, country, fortune" (*JMN* 2 : 42–43).

The sympathetic reader of Emerson would like to stop reading here. After all, he declaims the evils of slavery, declares how it weakens even our philosophy, and he embraces the mission to launch his own skiff and sail about trying to secure the redemption and freedom of these captives. Yet Emerson adds to his dream reflection: "Nature has plainly assigned different degrees of intellect to these different races, and the barriers between are insurmountable." He continues by noting that "This inequality is an indication of the design of Providence that some should lead, and some should serve." Society upholds this very design, where inequality is "not only the direct and acknowledged relation of king & subject, master & servant, but a secret dependence quite as universal, of one man upon another, which sways habits, opinions, conduct" (*JMN* 2 : 43). This attitude is addressed later by the principle of self-reliance when Emerson suggests the possibility of one's reliance upon the opinions of others as swaying and supporting the attitude that some are providentially slaves. However, is this sufficient to justify one's enslavement of another human being? Emerson does entertain several arguments attempting to justify slavery, but ultimately dismisses them, urging that "No ingenious sophistry can ever reconcile the unperverted mind to the pardon of *Slavery*; nothing but tremendous familiarity, and the bias of private *interest*" (*JMN* 2 : 57). As we will see below, Channing's own opening lines on a tract on slavery—"The first question to be proposed by a rational being is, not what is profitable, but what is Right"—also eschews crude material interests.

This commentary on slavery implies that, while slavery was a barbarous institution that impoverished society, it was only an effect of a greater cause that he seemed more intent upon examining; that is, the broad issue of human freedom rather than the specifics of the deprivation of such freedom through racial bias. He had written in these passages, for example, "For if he is himself free, and it offends the attributes of God to have him otherwise, it is manifestly a bold stroke of impiety to wrest the same liberty from his fellow" (*JMN* 2 : 58). In other words, slavery could be addressed by asserting the general freedom of individuals, all individuals, and, through a kind of trickle-down theory, those enslaving others would discontinue the enslavement. This type of thinking was indebted to Channing: if society would prefer to promote individual freedom, then freedom would become more widespread. As such, Emerson perhaps believed that slavery as an institution could end as the result of a philosophical point—although slavery had impoverished philosophy.

The commentary on slavery does not stop here, however. Granted, these are the most specific passages devoted to the topic, but students of Emerson know that his tendency toward abstraction requires of his readers attention to the broader claims he is addressing. What is most curious is the manner in which Emerson challenges traditional notions of right and justice in the remaining "Wide World" journals. In current parlance he offers a deconstruction of justice as it takes place in America, and this provides the germ of what will be addressed later in the 1855 "Lecture on Slavery."

After several pages of commentary on slavery, Emerson shifts gears: "This is all that is offered *in behalf* of slavery," he says; "we shall next attempt to knock down the hydra" (*JMN* 2 : 49). This comment is vital to appreciating Emerson's larger program for social progress. Slavery was admittedly "the worst institution on earth" (*JMN* 2 : 57), the largest, ugliest head on the many-headed hydra. But slaying this evil beast, for Emerson, involved not merely decapitating one of the several heads, but striking a blow to the very body of this evil.

As was his custom, Emerson would write notes in large capital letters at the bottom of his journal books. The opening passages on slavery, for instance, contained footers that read "Slavery" and "Omnipotence." His comments about the hydra leads to another section titled "Moral Law" and another titled "Justice." In this latter section Emerson questions the on-ward path of progress toward perfection referred to earlier, as if his note-books have had the effect he so desired: waking him from easy slumber. The consummation may not be so easy. As he continues his entries, Emer-son recognizes the limited extension of progress through his deconstruc-tion of justice as it regards slavery:

> If an ignorant man were carried from his Closet to the prisons and peni-tentiaries of a vast kingdom and shewn a multitude of men confined and scourged and forced to labour, and informed that this was the act of the gov-ernment, if he knew nothing more of that state and perhaps foolishly con-ceived that its limits extended no further than the walls wherein he stood, it would be a very plain Conclusion that this government was a savage and out-rageous tyranny; while perhaps at that very moment the government was the most perfect and beneficent in the world. Our rash conclusions from the dark side of human affairs are analogous to these, and like these are to be corrected by broader views of the system which we misunderstand. (*JMN* 2:52–53)

In this worldview, good and evil exist simultaneously, slavery being the most "peculiar" example of evil. While the existence of evil can be under-stood as a necessity in the world, according to a system that allows it as a kind of crucible to test individual free will, slavery cannot be viewed as a necessary evil within this system for it only marks the failure of humanity to shine through. Nonetheless, Emerson preserves his idealism by ending "Wide World" 8 on a positive note, concluding "America hath ample in-terval to lay deep & solid foundations for the greatness of the New World" (*JMN* 2:72).

This theme of more perfect foundations, key in the essays of *Nature* to come, begins "Wide World" 9 by refuting that "the world's dark barba-rism, or darker vice, should be the best idol that the intellect can set up" (*JMN* 2:75). Anticipating the charge of youthful optimism, he writes, "It is not the freak of a youthful or Utopian imagination to anticipate more from the future than the past has produced." While he admits that "Man in many trials has failed" (*JMN* 2:76–77), America differs because it "is daily rising to a higher comparative importance & attracting the eyes of all the rest of the world to the development of its embryo greatness"—words that seem reminiscent of the early Puritans such as John Winthrop who saw America as the fulfillment of sacred history, the New Jerusalem. Admonishing later that "History will continually grow less interesting as the world grows bet-ter," Emerson suggests that history is most important at what he calls "true

epochs," periods of "those successive triumphs which age after age the
communities of men have achieved[,] such as the Reformation, the Revival
of letters, the progressive Abolition of the Slave-trade" (*JMN* 2:90).

Emerson was devoted to the gradual progress of the world; one might
say that this endeavor is a constant preoccupation among the breadth of
topics addressed in his "Wide World" journals. Indeed, in an April 8, 1823,
entry Emerson remarks with extreme candor, "There *is* a huge & dispro-
portionate abundance of *evil* on earth. Indeed the good that is here, is but
a little island of light, amidst the unbounded ocean. What mind therefore
(that is stirred by ardent feelings) looks over the great desart of human life
without fervently resolving to embark in the cause of God & man?" (*JMN*
2:115). Over thirty-one years later, in a letter to his brother William on
January 17, 1855, he still conceives of slavery in the same manner. "I am
trying hard in these days to see some light in the dark Slavery question to
which I am to speak next week in Boston," he says in regard to his "Lecture
on Slavery." "But to me as to many tis like Hamlet's task imposed on so
unfit an agent as Hamlet"(*L* 4:484).

In "Wide World" 11 Emerson addresses why the moral obligation to
ameliorate this preponderance of evil is not met, and he assigns one word
to answer it: apathy. Later in his career he exchanges "unbelief" for this
term but the meaning is similar. Time and experience clarify the role of
obligation and duty, Emerson makes clear, when he writes, "We learn more
accurately the number & nature of our duties, we see more clearly, the con-
nexion & symmetry of all the parts of the moral world. We see that goodness is better than greatness; we learn that goodness & beauty are one. I
know there are deplorable instances to the contrary but I believe that, *in
general*, the tendency of habits of thought & reflexion is decidedly propi-
tious to morals" (*JMN* 2:157).

This said, it would be unfair to characterize Waldo as apathetic to social
ills, for he was very aware of the broader scope of evil in the world, and it
was to its demise that he devoted himself from the start. In a sense counter-
ing claims by Rowe that his aesthetic dissent was fruitless, Emerson suggests that the breadth of his endeavors address a better future: "In the
perfectly confident hope of future indulgence, the labourer toils. The hope
of the lover is not apathy. Political & literary ambition are not apathy.
Hope is so strong that on it is founded the uninterrupted sedulous labour
of many years." So strong are Emerson's feelings about hope that he says,
"Remove hope, & the world becomes a blank & rottenness" (*JMN* 2:163).
Thus, hope itself is reform-minded. Through and through, Emerson pre-

sents a kind of pragmatic approach: "If the past were presented to our hearts in all its dark reality relieved by no contrasted Hope for the future, men would rebel in spirit against the Providence which placed them here & had darkened their lot with such deep and damning shades. Why does omnipotence, they would murmur, send the poor slave of its power into this wide prisonhouse to run the selfsame round of madness & sorrow that the long train of generations have run already" (*JMN* 2 : 164). To affirm his approach, Emerson adds, "If Hope be the beautifier that out of such darkness creates such light; it must needs have potent energy" (*JMN* 2 : 164).

But already by "Wide World" 12, kept from 1823 to 1824, Emerson's maturation is seen. What he appreciated so much about Socrates were two complementary tendencies: to ground virtue on a single principle, and to appeal to people in a populist manner. In an entry just before the Christmas of 1823, on December 21, Emerson asks what will be perhaps the most profound question he will address in his work as a whole: "Who is he that shall controul me? Why may I not act & speak & write & think with entire freedom? What am I to the Universe, or, the Universe, what is it to me?" To answer this question, he considered each individual as a solitary prisoner in the wider prisonhouse of society. He goes beyond the present and creates a mightier community that is Hope itself, the Hope of the future and the future of Hope: "Is society my anointed King? Or is there any mightier community or any man or more than man, whose slave I am? I am solitary in the vast society of beings." After listing all manner of possible social associations, Emerson claims "I disclaim them all" (*JMN* 2 : 190).

With the last "Wide World" entry on August 11, 1824, eight months later Emerson began another notebook labeled "Notebook XV," and there he declares: "Our nature has a twofold aspect[,] towards self & towards society[,] and the good or evil[,] the riches or poverty of a man is to be measured of course by its relation to these two" (*JMN* 2 : 344).

In writing about slavery and duty, even fleetingly in a young man's notebook, Emerson approached a topic that would, within a full generation, tear the country apart. Indeed, thirty-nine years after his "Wide World" 8 journal entries, Emerson would turn, as he often did, to this vexing topic. In an 1851 journal entry he addresses America's "fathers" and its current sons:

> In the weakness of the Union the law of 1793 was framed, and much may be said in palliation of it. It was a law affirming the existence of two states of civilization, or an intimate union between two countries, one civilized and Christian, and the other barbarous, where cannibalism was still permitted ...

and the law became, as it should, a dead letter. It was merely there in the statute-book to soothe the dignity of the man-eaters. And we Northerners had, on our part, indemnified and secured ourselves against any occasional eccentricity of appetite in our confederates by our own interpretation, and by offsetting state law by state laws. (*JMN* 11:354–55)

About midway between the essays and journals of the early 1820s and the one from 1851 quoted above, as Gougeon points out, Emerson delivered his first antislavery speech, in November of 1837. However, as Gougeon makes clear, Emerson's "major concern was not so much the evil of slavery as the preservation of the principle of free speech which was threatened," so Emerson thought, "by an almost universal repression of abolition oratory." When addressing "the actual problem of slavery," Emerson preferred to present an "exhortation to his audience to be mindful of immediate moral problems as well as the remote sin of slavery." What's more, Gougeon comments, Emerson "also called for a sympathetic understanding of the slaveholder and his plight." To say the least, Gougeon concludes, "The entire performance was a severe disappointment to the abolitionists." The reason is clear: precisely because Emerson's "consideration remained on the level of moral abstraction."[9] What we find is that while Emerson devoted serious thought to slavery as an abstraction, several years remained before he began speaking out on slavery as a concrete reality. The question is, what happened to Emerson between the 1820s and the 1850s?[10]

Channing's Influence

Emerson seems to have gained a positive outlook on social progress during his Harvard years, undoubtedly influenced by William Ellery Channing.[11] While many have rightly pointed to Daniel Webster's defense of the Fugitive Slave Law in his infamous speech of March 7, 1850, as spurring Emerson toward collective action, moving beyond what Gougeon called "moral abstraction," Channing's influence was as great, extending beyond his death in 1842. His principle of "moral suasion," as Gougeon discusses in *Virtue's Hero*, seems to have initially dissuaded Emerson from external, philanthropic involvement that smacked of collective social activism.[12] Ultimately, Emerson reacted against both Webster and Channing.

Emerson's Bowdoin Prize essay owes to Channing at its very start. On the subject of slavery, we find Channing saying in the first lines of his 1835 essay on the topic: "The first question to be proposed by a rational being is, not what is profitable, but what is Right. Duty must be primary, prominent, most conspicuous, among the objects of human thought and pursuit. If we cast it down from its supremacy, if we inquire first for our interests, and then for our duties, we shall certainly err."[13] This duty is the chief good, of which Channing notes: "There is but one unfailing good; and that is, fidelity to the Everlasting Law written on the heart, and re-written and re-published in God's Word" (*ELP* 317). Writing itself for Channing is acting out of his sense of duty because "There are times when the assertion of great principles is the best service a man can render society"; this he says in the face of a society in which the moral law has been "made to bow to expediency" (*ELP* 318). Given the fact that individuals motivated by profit upheld slavery, Channing placed great expectations upon these individuals to reform themselves. According to Channing, all duty must be directed toward the slaveholders who are reached in a roundabout manner: the emphasis of moral principles and "The deliberate, solemn conviction of good men through the world, that slavery is a grievous wrong to human nature, will make itself felt. To increase this moral power is every man's duty. To embody and express this great truth is in every man's power; and thus every man can do something to break the chain of the slave." In short, Channing suggests that slaveholders should peacefully and graciously give up the bond over their slaves. He goes so far as to state, echoing Emerson's claim in the 1820s, that "there is no subject, now agitated by the community, which can compare in philosophical dignity with slavery." (*ELP* 321).

However naïve Channing's views may seem now in regard to abolition, he is most emphatic that change cannot occur as the result of outside, "foreign" intervention, but that it must terminate by an internal decision, the remnant of his belief in "moral suasion." He declares, "To the slave-holder belongs the duty of settling and employing the best methods of liberation, and to no other. We have no right of interference, nor do we desire it" (*ELP* 393). Here Channing presents duty ambivalently. Duty is to do what is right, something we are bound to enact, but the means of achieving this is through verbal influence *directly* (speaking rather than acting out), and through acting morally *indirectly*. After all, he continues, "It is by calm, firm assertion of great principles, and not by personalities and vituperations, that strength is to be given to the constantly increasing reprobation of slavery through the civilised world." Channing suggests that founders like Franklin and Jay participated in such conversations, specifically as members of abolition societies "immediately succeeding the adoption of the Constitution." We can write all we want, he seems to say, but actual speaking against slavery is more important: "Speech has wings, as well as the printed word. Sometimes the living voice is more quickening than the press" (*ELP* 402, 404).

Channing's penultimate chapter in his essay is devoted to abolitionism, an activity whose evolution Channing is wary of. It meant one thing for Franklin and Jay, he says, and it has changed now "to promote Immediate Emancipation" (*ELP* 405). Given his notion that "gradual influence" is the best, anything smacking of immediacy will be abhorrent. In fact, Channing pointedly comments that "they have sought to accomplish their objects by a system of Agitation; that is, by a system of affiliated societies gathered, and held together, and extended, by passionate eloquence" (*ELP* 408–9). One might wonder about the harm of such action, but Channing declares unequivocally that "The age of individual action is gone. Truth can hardly be heard unless shouted by a crowd. The weightiest argument for a doctrine is the number which adopts it." So Channing argues for having a large number of people speak against slavery, relying on the kindness and morality of the community to see the truth, so to speak, precisely because of the decline of individual agency.

Channing is more attentive to the means rather than the ends in his approach: "We ought to think much more of walking in the right path than of reaching our end," he says. "We should desire virtue more than success" (*ELP* 411). But the problem with his approach is that it promotes apathy and ambivalence, something to which Emerson was opposed. For Channing, those denied their basic rights should be put on hold until we can have a polite conversation about the situation. If we act rashly or immediately to change the situation, we run the risk of being less than virtuous—albeit in the face of great evil.

When he becomes even more specific in his critique of immediate action on the part of the abolitionists, one can hear the similarity between Channing and Emerson. First Channing writes of the wrong approach: "The forced, artificially excited enthusiasm of a multitude, kept together by an organisation which makes them the instruments of a few leading minds, works superficially, and often injuriously." He then proposes the right path: "The chief strength of a Reformer lies in speaking truth purely from his own soul, without hanging one tone for the purpose of managing or enlarging a party. Truth, to be powerful, must speak in her own words, and in no other's; must come forth, with the authority and spontaneous energy of inspiration, from the depths of the soul" (*ELP* 412).

In the end, Channing wanted civil discourse on the subject to occur, politely mentioning the evils of slavery concerning a recognizable higher law that contravenes slavery. As a result, those contravening the higher law would stop doing so, but only after the "enlightened people" voiced their opinion that, indeed, such a challenge to the higher law had been committed. If this cannot occur, then more talk, Channing's "passionate eloquence," is necessary: "One great principle, which we should lay down as immovably true, is, that, if a good work cannot be carried on by the calm, self-controlled, benevolent spirit of Christianity, then the time for doing it has not come" (*ELP* 411).

For Emerson it became clear by the 1850s that polite discourse would only go so far and that the time would never come.

Skepticism and Antislavery

By 1844, the time of the publication of *Essays: Second Series,* Emerson's unbridled optimism for the future was tempered, and he began a period of relative crisis and doubt. The ideas characterizing this period are summed up in his pivotal essay, "Experience" (1844). The emphasis on the ability of the soul to cause significant change is called into question. Emerson never sought government to provoke change; indeed, he even questioned the ability of the church toward this end. He invested nearly all his faith in individuals, whom he believed, in their creativity, would ascertain how to manifest their "moral suasion" toward positive ends.

However, he begins "Experience" by questioning originality. In fact, the ultimate animus, the individual's soul and its reflection of the greater Soul that connects us all, Emerson seemed to doubt as well. Souls are separated from their objects, Emerson ponders, and have no connection to the everyday. Yes, the Soul must be spiritual and not tied to the mundane, but it must also be directed toward influencing the everyday. This occurs because of the extent to which we are unable to transgress the bounds of the everyday, to lift ourselves beyond it. Instead, we live in a world of illusion, Emerson says, and we not only seem to live in a dream but in the dream of a dream, waking up from one illusion into another, the result of seeking to understand only that which is right in front of us. Emerson is also afraid that we no longer seek that which is beyond us—which is, after all, the Soul. As a result, evidence is needed for everything, Emerson laments, even the spiritual, which should provide its own evidence. Because of this, we remain on the brink, on the edge of some great ocean, never able to step across.

Despite this skepticism, Emerson does present a direction we should take. Concentrate on the flashes of light, he says, concentrate on the ineffable, what he referred to earlier as Hope. This skepticism emanated from the precarious position in which Emerson found himself: one of the most heinous affronts to the improvement of society was slavery, which many of his self-reliant friends had spoken out against. But would not collective action, even if directed toward something noble such as the abolition of slavery, contradict his principle? Emerson's emphasis upon viewing the world as "Philosophically considered" (*cw* 1:8), his line from *Nature*, left him with little option but to continue to treat his principle purely as a triumph of speculative discourse, as a moral abstraction.

Ultimately, Emerson generally stayed away from even smaller, more concentrated forms of community—the skiff in "Wide World" 8 was always preferable to the ship. While he was comfortable living in the small community of Concord, surrounded by friends and family, he was not interested in the Brook Farm experiment (1841–47), the venture of several friends and like-minded Transcendentalists. The list of eminent members is well known, as is the parody of it in Hawthorne's *Blithedale Romance* (1852). In declining to participate, Emerson's language is important: "I do not wish to remove from my present prison to a prison a little larger," he said in a journal entry, adding, "I wish to break all prisons" (*JMN* 7:407–8). Even later, after the passage of the Fugitive Slave Act, he would write something similar in declining to speak directly to abolitionist concerns: "I have quite other slaves to free" (*JMN* 13:80). These comments return us to the groundwork established in the early 1820s.

Was it possible that slavery was not merely an abolitionist concern, but a self-reliant concern as well? On principle, Emerson believed in a universal, transcendent approach to social reform, the result of individuals hearing the dictates of a universal Mind and Soul that no single person or group could claim as their exclusive domain. What is most important to recognize, however, is that it was only after Emerson would see *literal* prisons to be the greatest living hindrance to the smashing of all those *figurative* prisons—slavery the most immediate and horrific example—that the interpretation of his own principle evolved.

Undoubtedly, Emerson wanted to help perfect society. While a great part of what Emerson seems directed toward is the perfection of the soul, he needed to realize the practical impediments to reaching the universal mind and soul for other individuals whose histories differed. Although the skepticism that developed after 1844, defined implicitly in "Experience," may have awakened a paradigmatic shift in interpreting self-reliance, it is necessary to go back to 1838 to see the working out of the order of the soul and the social impediments to its perfection. Indeed, in the most controversial address from this period, he described the complicity of the church in detracting from the soul's perfection.

Emerson first addresses the role that the mind plays in relation to the soul in the 1838 "Divinity School Address." There he suggests that the mind needs to be open, revealing "the laws which traverse the universe, and make things what they are." Unfortunately, the way in which we view or interpret these laws is marked by "our imperfect apprehension" that can only see things "tend this way or that, but not come full circle." Behind each of these imperfect views are "infinite relations, so like, so unlike; many, yet one" (*cw* 1:77).

All laws, in other words, contain the divine Law. However, "These laws refuse to be adequately stated. They will not by us or for us be written out on paper, or spoken by the tongue. They elude, evade our persevering thoughts, and yet we read them hourly in each other's faces, in each other's actions, in our own remorse." In short, they defy inscription on anything but the individual's soul. But how do we read and see these things? Emerson's response is that "The intuition of the moral sentiment is an insight of the perfection of the laws of the soul. These laws execute themselves. They are out of time, out of space, and not subject to circumstance" (*cw* 1:77). No, the individual cannot become perfect, but the closer to perfect the individual gets, the more the law reveals itself.

Souls, however, do not teach one another; they provoke one another, the very definition of community for Emerson. "Truly speaking," he writes, "it is not instruction, but provocation, that I can receive from another soul." The religious sentiment, then, is not a dogma or a doctrine but the understanding of our interaction with one another, our provocation of one another—be they good or bad provocations. This, for Emerson, is tied to faith. We must believe in the ability to influence one another and to control and to produce positive provocations; we must believe that we are all connected, part of one Soul. If not, then "The doctrine of divine nature being forgotten, a sickness infects and dwarfs the constitution" (*cw* 1:80); that is, the sickness infects what unites, or does not unite, us all.

Unfortunately, as Emerson sees it, "The eye of youth is not lighted by the hope of other worlds." But the soul is the key: "In the soul, then, let the redemption be sought. In one soul, in your soul, there are resources for the world" (*cw* 1:89)—and, one assumes, all the new worlds to be imagined. Ultimately, Emerson admits, we "shall see the world to be the mirror of the soul" (*cw* 1:93). What do we see? What kind of soul does our world and our worlds have?

Over time, Emerson liked less and less the world presented to him. His emerging evolution nonetheless took a positive direction, for by 1844 he began to modify the practical application of self-reliance by speaking out on the issue of slavery. Over the course of a decade, Emerson's rhetoric would reach a fever pitch by 1855, all the while maintaining his several constituent tenets drafted in 1841 and the early attention to duty in the 1820s. What changes is that Emerson allows for the eternal law to shine so brightly on this particular issue that self-reliant individuals can sing in harmony to redeem slavery's captives.

The year 1855 is important for Emerson, since in January of that year he delivered a lecture in Boston on American slavery, one that he repeated in other cities in the following months.[14] Living in and near Boston most of his life, Emerson was rarely in personal contact with the institution of slavery. As suggested above, he had talked of slavery as early as 1821 in his "Wide World" journals kept while a Harvard undergraduate, but these were usually references to a philosophical and social condition. However, Concord friends as well as his family began to bring the issue of slavery closer to home, and he was encouraged to address the subject as more than moral abstraction.

Overall, his fear was of becoming a single-issue thinker; he wanted to be no one's ideologue, for it would transgress his emphasis upon self-reliance and it would also place too much emphasis upon the group over the individual. Nevertheless, the way in which law was being made a mockery of provoked Emerson finally to speak out against slavery. The first major occasion was a speech titled "Address on the Emancipation of the Negroes in the British West Indies," delivered in 1844 on the tenth anniversary of Britain's emancipation of slaves in its colonies. At the start, Emerson gives a long overview of the history of emancipation in the British court and politics, culminating in full emancipation in 1834. He then continues: "this event is signal in the history of civilization. There are many styles of civilization, and not one only. Ours is full of barbarities" (*aw* 19). He sees complicity all around: "What if it cost a few unpleasant scenes on the coast of Africa? That was a great way off," he says sarcastically, adding, "If any mention was made of homicide, madness, adultery, and intolerable tortures, we would let the church-bells ring louder, the church-organ swell its peal and drown the hideous sound" (*aw* 20).

Emerson does point out that the British debated emancipation for a long time and had certain conveniences the United States did not: "I know that England has the advantage of trying the question at a wide distance from the spot where the nuisance exists: the planters are not, excepting in rare examples, members of the legislature" (aw 22–23). But he then goes on to attack his native Massachusetts for tolerating slavery, especially politicians: "Gentlemen, I am loath to say harsh things, and perhaps I know too little of politics for the smallest weight to attach any censure of mine,—but I am at a loss how to characterize the tameness and silence" of senators. He declares that the "government exists to defend the weak and the poor and the injured party; the rich and the strong can better take care of themselves." "This event," says Emerson, "was a moral revolution . . . working not under a leader, but under a sentiment. Other revolutions have been the insurrection of the oppressed; this was the repentance of the tyrant. It was the masters revolting from their mastery" (aw 25–26). With these words Emerson's sense of the moral sentiment moves from a philosophical idea to a practical reality.

For nearly the next twenty years Emerson will be more socially active, continuing to promote self-reliance but doing so in an altered manner. Like Whitman, he never referred to himself or even thought of himself as an abolitionist—this would be too evangelical for him—yet he embraced John Brown as exemplary of self-reliance and began to see how slavery best exemplified the bulwark he confronted in transforming society.

A definite transition occurred after the passage of the Compromise Act of 1850, which contained the Fugitive Slave Act. With this Act, Emerson was brought face to face with slavery, since under its terms no state could legally provide refuge for a slave. The Act further enraged Emerson because of the moral betrayal he felt from Daniel Webster, the Massachusetts senator whose support was key to its passage. An important subject turned into a burning issue.

As he began to speak against slavery, the ambivalence between theory and practice collapsed, as the speech "The Fugitive Slave Law" (1854) exhibits. It opens with Emerson saying, "I do not often speak to public questions. They are odious and hurtful and it seems like meddling or leaving your work. I have my own spirits in prison,—spirits in deeper prisons, whom no man visits, if I do not." But whereas he would have stopped at this point in the past, preferring to speak no more, he then goes on: "I have lived all my life without suffering any known inconveniences from American Slavery. I never saw it; I never heard the whip; I never felt the check on my free speech and action until, the other day, when Mr. Webster, by his personal influence, brought the Fugitive Slave Law on the country" (AW 74). Webster did not author the bill, Emerson continues, but his energy helped it pass.

Emerson continues by attacking the role of government, asking, "What is the use of admirable law forms and political forms if a hurricane of party feeling and a combination of monied interests can beat them to the ground?" (AW 82). Then comes a call for action: "Whilst the inconsistency of slavery with the principles on which the world is built guarantees its downfall, I own that the patience it requires is almost too sublime for mortals and seems to demand of us more than mere hoping" (AW 86–87). Emerson sums up what took place in 1850 and before: "Are you for man and for the good of man; or are you for the hurt and harm of man? . . . whether the Negroes shall be as the Indians were in Spanish America, a piece of money?" Implicitly, Emerson recognizes the connection between colonization and slavery. Passage of the bill "shows that our prosperity had hurt us; and we can not be shocked by crime." In addition, "while we reckoned ourselves a highly cultivated nation, our bellies had run away with our brains, and the principles of culture and progress did not exist" (AW 79–80). Reminiscent of Channing, duty takes precedence over interest.

Very skeptically, Emerson concludes, "The events of this month are teaching one thing plain and clear . . . that papers are of no use, resolutions of public meetings, platforms of conventions, no nor laws nor constitutions any more. . . . You relied on the Constitution. It has not the word slave in it" (AW 82). So, institutions fail us. What of the people? On this account, Emerson is equally skeptical: "I fear there is no *reliance* to be had on any kind or form of covenant, no, not on sacred forms,—none on churches, none on bibles. For one would have said that a Christian would not keep slaves, but the Christians keep slaves. Of course, they will not dare read the bible. Won't they? They quote the bible and Christ and Paul to maintain slavery. If slavery is a good, then is lying, theft, arson, incest, homicide, each and all goods and to be maintained by union societies" (AW 83, emphasis added).

Emerson's conclusion is that "These things show that no forms, neither Constitutions nor laws nor covenants nor churches nor bibles, are of any use in themselves," specifically if they create reliance. Emerson would rather teach people to fish, to follow the biblical parable, than simply have them supplied with fish. His attitude presents the thrust of this piece: "He only who is able to stand alone, is qualified for society. And that I understand to be the end for which a soul exists in this world, to be himself the counterbalance of all falsehood and all wrong" (AW 83). Slavery negates freedom, negates self-reliance, for "Liberty is never cheap. It is made difficult because freedom is the accomplishment and perfectness of a man" (AW 86). At the very end of his remarks he then refers to the theme of unbelief brought up in earlier speeches, ending: "I hope we have come to an end of our unbelief, have come to a belief that there is a Divine Providence in the world *which will not save us but through our own co-operation*" (AW 89, emphasis added). Through these statements, Emerson did not abandon his principle of self-reliance, for he was still devoted to transferring the sovereignty previously located in the person of aristocrats or those privileged by birth to an individual sovereignty where everyone must act as his or her own priest and judge, but he surely modified it, preferring to rely upon the association of like-minded selves to terminate what he deemed an utterly inhumane practice.

The previously unavailable 1855 "Lecture on Slavery" illustrates Emerson's evolution.[15] Though this speech is about slavery, Emerson never brings up the topic directly. Instead, he is concerned with talking about three main issues: the past, the future, and foundations. As he stressed in previous speeches and essays, society gains nothing from blindly holding to the past. What is of value is ascertaining the way in which these old ideas were, in their time, forward looking, directed toward the future. Unfortunately, society acts as if things have been decided once and for all, as if we need no longer continue to adapt to changing conditions. Emerson does believe that there is something unchanging, a basic foundation, but that we have not continued to build on this foundation. The language he uses to refer to this foundation suggests it is a new word for the soul: "Everything rests on foundations," he says, and "Some foundation we must have" (AW 97, 96).

One might think that Emerson was calling for the destruction of the past—and he was. He made this clear from the start of his career as an essayist. Yet he adds to the element of destruction in his "Lecture on Slavery" when he complains, "There is no confession of destitution like this fierce conservatism" (AW 95–96). Trying to maintain the past is as, if not more, destructive than changing the future. The future is to be all about change, is itself changing, and has a positive force behind it. Emerson suggests that it takes more energy to maintain the past, arresting forward-moving development, than it does to override movement toward the future. The maintenance of the past Emerson declares a blindness, and he diagnoses it as emanating from unbelief, lack of faith, and lack of hope.

While Emerson concentrates on the compromised immunity of the United States to defeat the cancerous system of slavery, he opens his "Lecture on Slavery" by encouraging individuals to take a stand on this particular issue, diagnosing the malady for them—and this last point is very important. Previously, Emerson would have been concerned with creating a reliance among his readers by doing their thinking for them. But now he says of slavery, "there is somewhat exceptional in this question, which seems to require of every citizen at one time or another, to show his hand, and to cast suffrage in such manner as he uses" (*AW* 91). Emerson casts his vote by presenting an altered self-reliance: "It is not to societies that the secrets of nature are revealed, but to private persons, to each man in his organization, in his thoughts" (*AW* 102). After developing this point he then adds an important comment, alone marking the ultimate evolution of self-reliance: "whilst I insist on the doctrine of the independence and the inspiration of the individual, *I do not cripple but exalt the social action*" (103, emphasis added). This did not cast Emerson as a professed abolitionist, for he would never fully abandon his own self-reliance, but as an important ally to the cause. Ultimately, the Concord sage modified his stance on this pressing issue, and the implication upon his principle of self-reliance made the evolution much greater.

Conclusion

In the concluding chapter of *Emerson and Self-Reliance* Kateb asks, "Did the failure of the Emersonian theory of self-reliance in the face of the crisis over slavery and the Civil War portend that theory's general inapplicability to ever more dire or complex social circumstances?" (197–98). But how did it fail? It evolved. Consider Emerson's "New England Reformers" (1844) lecture. Here he says:

> We desire to be made great, we desire to be touched with that fire which shall command this ice to stream, and make our existence a benefit. If therefore we start objections to your project, O friend of the slave, or friend of the poor, or of the race, understand well, that it is because we wish to drive you to drive us into your measures. We wish to hear ourselves confuted. We are haunted with a belief that you have a secret, which it would highliest advantage us to learn, and we would force you to impart it to us, though it should bring us to prison, or to worse extremity. (*CW* 3 : 163)

This implies that Emerson was open to an evolved sense of self-reliance as early as 1844. Emerson's principle of self-reliance not only evolved over the course of his antislavery involvement, but it was naturally extended as Emerson's own silence was confuted. Individuality did not mean isolation for Emerson, but was always tied to his other preoccupation: duty. Emerson's individuality approached being an indeterminate concept. We are each, as individuals, to improve ourselves in part as a way of improving one another; thus, there is always a sense of community even in our individuality. However, singular principles upon which all should act are not desired; rather, singular individuals are. An indeterminate concept demands that events and situations be treated on a case-by-case basis. Individuals have the tools with which to decide, but they must act on the basis of an individually derived equation or calculus. If people are denied these tools, social action must provide the tools and the means by which they can be used. The magic of this decision works in a specific instance, but it loses this magical singularity the instant it becomes enforced as ritual. Ultimately, the end is not imitation but the process, the means by which the end was reached—if it is a good end. Thus, the decision derived by separate individuals may, at times, be similar, requiring association not de jure but de facto.

While slavery caused Emerson personally to apply the range of his principles, Kateb still wonders: "if slavery was an exceptional phenomenon, an aberrant system of atrocity, the political events of this century—beginning with World War I—have established atrocity as the norm." As such, Kateb asks, "How, in the face of these horrors, can Emerson's vision of life be compelling?" (*ESR* 198). It is compelling exactly if we see how duty and self-reliance were companion principles. After all, there is a danger in becoming completely mentally self-reliant, Kateb points out: "The possible consequences of maintaining Emerson's conception of mental self-reliance is to turn oneself into a late Roman Stoic for whom mental self-reliance becomes escape and self-consolation, and, more, a self-enclosure that aspires to make the dismal world unreal." This would make no sense for Emerson, who always intended to decrease the conspiracy of society against individuals. Doing so would present a foolish consistency. As Kateb puts it: "We have seen that once confronted with public moral imperatives, Emerson does not hesitate to urge the claims of duty. Of course, he does not say that he suspends his doctrine of self-reliance for the sake of duty" (*ESR* 199). Indeed not, for the two are inextricably tied to one another. Kateb adds that because of duty and self-reliance, "A good person will give himself or herself for some part of the time to a suspension of individuality. Undeniably, even the acceptance of organizational discipline—if one could only find the right organization—can be an enlightening experience." He then concludes, "Periods of turning one's back on oneself may even help one find oneself" (*ESR* 201).

It was Emerson's relationship to the question of slavery that required him to understand his own convictions and even to alter them. Emerson was obsessed with the notion that we are all equally imprisoned, that we are all too reliant on external influences. He believed that we were each confined in far deeper, metaphorical prisons—spiritual, mental, and emotional—which in turn informed the manifest structures within society. Helping to end slavery, a practice fueled by the poisonous attitude of inferiority, would help break other bonds of reliance.

Ultimately, Emerson realized the extent to which self-reliance as a principle is hollow in a society that maintains a legal and constitutional attitude about the inferiority of some its members. While Emerson, for all his radical views, retained rather conservative contemporary attitudes about the role of women and minorities within American society, his thoughts on slavery mark an evolution of these attitudes. Slavery presented Emerson with a visible form of *literal* enslavement. When he appreciated the difference between internal and external prisons, between those of the soul and mind and those of the body, Emerson understood his duty to address the prisons in which others were held, not just those in which he was sentenced.

Emerson, who always intended to decrease the conspiracy of society against individuals, sought to fulfill that duty by promoting individualism. His greatness was to realize and then promote the inextricable connection between self-reliance and duty as companion and guiding principles on the path to find oneself—and to help others find themselves, too.

NOTES

1. John Carlos Rowe, *At Emerson's Tomb: The Politics of Classic American Literature* (New York: Columbia University Press, 1997), 24. Additional references will be cited parenthetically as *ET*.

2. Albert J. von Frank, *The Trials of Anthony Burns: Freedom and Slavery in Emerson's Boston* (Cambridge: Harvard University Press, 1998), 327. Additional references will be cited parenthetically as *TAB*.

3. The recent publication of *AW* helps exemplify this evolution by having gathered together available and previously unavailable material on this topic. See my

review in *South Atlantic Review* 60 no. 4 [November 1995]: 179–82), where some of my points here were originally developed.

4. George Kateb, *Emerson and Self-Reliance* (Thousand Oaks, CA: Sage Press, 1995), xxviii. Additional references will be cited parenthetically as *ESR*.

5. Ralph Waldo Emerson, *Two Unpublished Essays* ["The Character of Socrates" and "The Present State of Ethical Philosophy"] (New York: Lamson, Wolfe, 1895), 77. Additional references will be cited parenthetically as *TUE*.

6. For an overview of Channing's as well as Emerson's connection to the anti-slavery movement generally, see Gougeon's insightful historical background in *AW*, xi–lvi.

7. Emerson undertook a great number of public lectures between 1836 and 1841. "The Philosophy of History" lectures were in twelve parts and began in 1836. Notably, the last lecture, "The Individual," became the germ of both "Self-Reliance" and "History." See *EL* volume 2.

8. The influences on Emerson were considerable, but none seems greater than that of his aunt, Mary Moody Emerson, of whom he wrote in an early Wide World entry, "The religion of my aunt is the purest & most sublime of any I can conceive." He adds later, in a gesture toward self-reliance, that her religion "is independent of forms & ceremonies & its ethereal nature gives a glow of soul to her whole life." Ultimately, "She is the Weird-woman of her religion," Emerson concludes, "& conceives herself always bound to walk in narrow but exalted paths which lead onward to interminable regions of rapturous & sublime glory" (*JMN* 1:49).

Phyllis Cole's recent study, *Mary Moody Emerson and the Origins of Transcendentalism: A Family History* (New York: Oxford University Press, 1998), explores the influence of Aunt Mary on Waldo specifically and Transcendentalism generally, suggesting that "Ralph Waldo Emerson appropriated and assimilated his aunt's language from youth through old age." Cole adds, "At the age of eighteen," when he began his Wide World journals, "he began copying whole letters into his journal as the work of 'Tnamurya' (anagram for 'Aunt Mary')" (9). A kind of companion text is Nancy Craig Simmon's edition of *The Selected Letters of Mary Moody Emerson* (Athens: University of Georgia Press, 1993), which allows us to grasp Cole's point. See, particularly, Mary's January 18, 1821, letter to Waldo, where we find a whole passage by Mary that makes its way into Waldo's 1821 Bowdoin essay (139–40). I am grateful to Cole and Simmons for pointing this out to me.

9. Len Gougeon, "Abolition, the Emersons, and 1837," *New England Quarterly* 54 (September 1981): 345, 354. This essay was later developed as chapter two in Gougeon's *VH*.

10. Marjory M. Moody's essay, "The Evolution of Emerson as an Abolitionist" (*American Literature* 17 [March 1945]: 1–45), which in part inspired this present essay, provides an excellent background to this topic, citing the sum of Emerson's connections to the issue of slavery as well as his comments on them. Also noteworthy is Daniel B. Shea's "Emerson and the American Metamorphosis" in *Emerson:*

Prophecy, Metamorphosis, and Influence, ed. David Levin (New York: Columbia University Press, 1975). Here Shea talks of how Emerson's own personal metamorphosis affected "a version of the American Metamorphosis" (30). See also Leonard Neufeldt, "Emerson and the Civil War," *Journal of English and Germanic Philology* 17 (October 1972): 502–13.

11. One might even suggest that the principle of self-reliance owes a great deal to Channing's notion of "self-culture," presented publicly by Channing in a September 1838 address delivered at Boston as part of the Franklin Lectures. See William Ellery Channing, *Self-Culture* (New York: Arno Press and The New York Times, 1969). In *William Ellery Channing: An Intellectual Portrait* (Boston: Beacon Press, 1955), David P. Edgell suggests that Channing also went through his own evolution. Edgell cites an anecdote from Paul Revere Frothingham that addressed Channing's change: "'[W]hen Dr. Channing used to preach about God and the soul, about holiness and sin, we liked him; that was Christianity. But now, he is always insisting on some reform, talking about temperance or war. We wish he would preach the gospel'" (41).

12. It is worth noting that Emerson chose to speak out on the West Indian emancipation shortly after Channing did (in 1840 and 1841, respectively), and that Channing's previous decision to write the tract *Slavery* (December 1835) was followed by Emerson's decision to speak out on slavery by 1837. Perhaps the nature of Channing's discussions in *Emancipation* (1841), where the very inhumanity of slavery was discussed, albeit again in terms of the West Indian experience, influenced the tenor of Emerson's own writing. Painful as Channing's death in 1842 must have been for Emerson—indeed, the Boston and Concord communities in general—I cannot help but wonder if it also freed Emerson in some sense, allowing him to be more self-reliant from the formidable influence of this man and to be more collectively active.

13. William E. Channing, *Essays, Literary & Political* (Glasgow: James Hedderwick & Son, 1837), 317. Additional references to this work will be cited parenthetically as ELP. See also Channing's *Slavery and Emancipation* (New York: Negro Universities Press, 1968) and "Remarks on the Slavery Question," in a *Letter to Jonathan Phillips, Esq* (Boston: James Munroe, 1839). Eric J. Sundquist positions Channing and his antislavery writing in "The Literature of Slavery and African American Culture," part of his section on "The Literature of Expansion and Race" in *The Cambridge History of American Literature, Volume Two: Prose Writing 1820–1865*, ed. Sacvan Bercovitch (New York: Cambridge University Press, 1995), 281–82. Here he cites Channing's other antislavery writings: *Remarks on the Slavery Question* (1839) and *Duty of the Free States* (1842).

14. In AW Joel Myerson notes in the textual commentary following the writings that "Emerson first delivered his lecture on slavery before the Massachusetts Anti-Slavery Society at the Tremont Temple in Boston on 25 January 1855. He repeated it in New York on 6 February, in Philadelphia on 8 February, in Rochester on 21 February, and in Syracuse on 25 February" (171).

15. This speech is referenced throughout Emerson's "WO Liberty" notebook. Scholars interested in this notebook, volume 14 in *JMN*, have been frustrated that only notes for this speech are referenced. The speech was previously available only as a transcript in newspapers of the cities where Emerson delivered it, notably Boston, Worcester, New York, Rochester, and Syracuse, and in an obscure journal publication of the Boston transcript (see Rollo G. Silver, "Mr. Emerson Appeals to Boston," *American Book Collector* 6 no. 5–6 [May–June 1935]: 209–19, drawn from a January 26, 1855, transcript from the *Boston Evening Traveller*). Lost for some time, the notebook appeared at the Library of Congress as part of the Moorfield Storey Collection (see John C. Broderick, "Emerson and Moorfield Storey: A Lost Journal Found," *American Literature* 38 no. 2 [May 1966]: 177–86). This notebook was also the topic of a dissertation by Patricia G. Barber titled *Ralph Waldo Emerson's Antislavery Notebook, wo Liberty* (University of Massachusetts, 1975). In a personal letter, Len Gougeon commented to me that Barber's thesis that "Emerson was planning a book on the topic of liberty might very well be the case," emphasizing Barber's suggestion "that the publication of John Stuart Mill's *On Liberty* might have affected his plans" (February 23, 1995).

Emerson's Abolition Conversion

"What have I to do with the sacredness of traditions if I live wholly from within?"
—Self-Reliance, 1841

LIVING WHOLLY FROM WITHIN has long been a hallmark of Emersonian Transcendentalism. An emphasis on intuitively perceived values and moral self-reliance resonates throughout his published works. Indeed, for some scholars, it is probably Emerson's defining characteristic and that of the movement with which his name is so often associated. It is not surprising, therefore, that many of these same critics have traditionally maintained that, for the most part, Emerson remained aloof from the major reform movements of his time. He was, in their view, serenely confident in, if not always completely comfortable with, the self-sufficiency of the individual in responding to the challenges of the world. Any compromise of this principle was unacceptable because closer cooperation with society and its various institutions would inevitably lead to a diminution of freedom, independence, and, ultimately, of self. "Society," Emerson warns, "is a joint-stock company in which the members agree for the better securing of his bread to each shareholder, to surrender the liberty and culture of the eater. The virtue in most request is conformity. Self-reliance is its aversion" (cw 2: 29). Indeed, Emerson goes on to point out, in his famous essay on the subject, that the would-be reformers of the day suffer from a conspicuous lack of self-reliance and, hence, are failures. "We want men and women who shall renovate life and our social state," he says, "but we see that most natures are insolvent, cannot satisfy their own wants, have an ambition out of all proportion to their practical force and do lean and beg day and night continually" (cw 2:43).

Despite this strong emphasis upon self-reliance, however, on August 1, 1844, Emerson would reach a dramatic turning point in his attitude toward social reform in America. As the following discussion will demonstrate, his famous address "On the Emancipation of the Negroes in the British West Indies," given that day in Concord, represents a significant departure from his previous position on the question of reform, a departure that would bring him into a de facto alliance with the very reformers who were previously the subjects of some of his harshest criticisms. It is clear from both the speech itself and the new evidence presented in this essay, including a previously unpublished letter from Emerson, that he was profoundly affected, both emotionally and intellectually, by his preparation for this address, as well as by the historical developments that prompted him to give it. The same evidence also clearly demonstrates that this preparation itself was much more extensive than previously thought.

Additionally, the significant array of historical and legal documents Emerson consulted, and his resulting use of them in the speech, shows him to be very much a "connected critic" of American society, that is, one who utilizes existing norms and shared values as the grounds for moral and social criticism.[1] Despite his long-standing commitment to the importance of intuitively perceived values, Emerson would not rely on these alone in waging his first major battle in what would be a long and personal struggle against America's greatest moral and social blight.

Background

In his 1841 address "Man the Reformer," Ralph Waldo Emerson boldly proclaims, "What is a man born for but to be a Reformer." Indeed, throughout his lengthy career as preacher, poet, lecturer, and essayist he strove to improve the moral condition of his society and to function as a "Re-maker of what man has made; a renouncer of lies; [and] a restorer of truth and good" (*cw* 1:156). However, the problem that Emerson faced when engaging the specific issues of reform was what particular role he should personally play. Early on, in a number of lectures, addresses, and journal entries, he expressed his commitment to the notion that reform was always an individual matter. If every person sought conscientiously to reform himself, then the reformation of society would naturally follow. Moral suasion was the preferred instrument in this redemptive process. Emerson also believed very deeply that true reform was never partial because a reformed heart brings with it total renewal, not partial amelioration. Because of these principles, he was very skeptical of reform associations that submerged the individual in a group identity which was, in turn, focused upon singular social ills. Undoubtedly, his Unitarian background was a strong factor in the evolution of these views.[2] Emerson was also leery of those who joined such organizations, the self-appointed social moralizers who took it upon themselves to impose their partial visions of social justice upon others, often without putting their own houses in order first. Collectively, these specific attitudes and other reservations served to separate Emerson for some time from the most dramatic and important reform movement of his age—the cause of abolition. Indeed, many have argued that this aloofness from social causes persisted throughout his lifetime.[3] As noted above, however, Emerson's remarkable August 1, 1844, address, "On the Emancipation of the Negroes in the British West Indies," evinces a significant change in his thinking on such matters, a change that would cause him to forgo his previous reservations and join in an enduring alliance with those organized reformers who actively opposed America's most heinous evil.

Emerson's August 1 address had a long foreground. Although his journals indicate a concern with the problem of American slavery dating back to his Harvard undergraduate days, it was not until November 1837 that he made his first public pronouncement on the topic.[4] The provocation for this address was undoubtedly the recent murder of the abolitionist publisher Elijah P. Lovejoy by an anti-abolition mob in Alton, Illinois, on November 7, 1837. This dramatic event shocked Emerson and other moral reformers because the silencing of Lovejoy's press disabled, both symbolically and literally, the very instrument upon which the persuasionists depended to accomplish their task. Not surprisingly, the focus of Emerson's presentation is on the importance of preserving free speech in a free society (*JMN* 12:151–52).[5]

In other respects the 1837 speech served mainly to confirm the persistence of Emerson's previous thinking on issues of reform. Although he would make another such foray into the realm of special causes with his "Letter to Martin Van Buren" regarding the removal of the Cherokees a year later, he was clearly not pleased with the public role in which such efforts cast him.[6] In his journal at the time he refers to this letter as "A deliverance that does not deliver the soul," and observes that, "This stirring in the philanthropic mud, gives me no peace" (*JMN* 5:479). The reasons for Emerson's distaste with the effort is noted by his wife Lidian in a letter to her sister where she observes that "Mr. Emerson very unwillingly takes part in public movements . . . preferring individual action."[7] In several public presentations in the following years Emerson again and again reiterated his observations on the limitations and shortcomings of contemporary reformers and reform organizations. The myopia of single-issue reformers is noted in a January 1839 lecture titled "The Protest," in which he states, "Every reformer is partial and exaggerates some one grievance. You may even feel that there is somewhat ridiculous in his tenacious oppugnation of some one merely local and as it were cutaneous disorder as if he dreamed, good simple soul, that were this one great wrong righted a new era would begin" (*EL* 3:91).

Another lecture, delivered at the Masonic Temple a year later and titled "Reforms," cautions against the loss of individuality which, in Emerson's view, associated efforts at reform often precipitate. "Accept the reforms," says Emerson, "but accept not the person of the reformer nor his law. Accept the reform but be thou thyself sacred, intact, inviolable, one whom leaders, one whom multitudes cannot drag from thy central seat. If you take the reform as the reformer brings it to you he transforms you into an instrument" (*EL* 260). Speaking directly to reformers themselves, Emerson makes his point with personal emphasis. "Though I sympathize with your sentiment and abhor the crime you assail yet I shall persist in wearing this robe, all loose and unbecoming as it is, of inaction, this wise passiveness until my hour comes when I can see how to act with truth as well as to refuse" (*EL* 3:266).

In "Man the Reformer" (January 25, 1841), a presentation that Emerson delivered in Boston and then published in *The Dial* (April 1841), he would again emphasize the importance of individual action, informed by the principle of love, in bringing about the reform of society. "Love," he says, "would put a new face on this weary old world in which we dwell as pagans and enemies" (*CW* 1:159). It was at this time too that he published "Self-Reliance" in a volume that was at first titled simply *Essays* (1841). This presentation, with its manifest emphasis on the importance of individuality, contains a famous attack on the narrow-mindedness and myopia of many reformers of the time, especially abolitionists. These people Emerson refers to as "angry bigot[s]" whose "incredible tenderness for black folk a thousand miles off" is "spite at home" because these moral busybodies with their "hard, uncharitable ambition" have not yet reformed themselves (*CW* 2:30).

Ultimately, Emerson would present a powerful summary of his philosophy of reform and a frank criticism of the social reformers of the time in his lecture "New England Reformers," which he delivered at Amory Hall in Boston on March 3, 1844. This address was presented in a series of

"Sunday Meetings at Amory Hall" organized by radical reformers including the most prominent associationists of the time. The gathering was
dominated by the presence of William Lloyd Garrison, another of the fea-
tured speakers of the series. Despite the makeup of his audience, or perhaps
because of it, Emerson was unreserved in his criticism.[8] While he ap-
plauded the general movement toward reform in American society, as represented by the numerous organizations, communities, and associations
that promoted it, Emerson also criticized those who did not have as their
goal the comprehensive and universal reform of mankind. These, he said,
are "partial; they are not equal to the work they pretend. They lose their
way; in the assault on the kingdom of darkness, they expend all their energy
on some accidental evil, and lose their sanity and power of benefit" (cw 3 :
154). Indeed, Emerson was painfully candid in addressing the manifest de-
fects of those who sat before him and was clearly frustrated at the unfortunate waywardness of their good intentions. "When we see an eager assail-
ant of one of these wrongs," says Emerson, "a special reformer, we feel like
asking him, What right have you, sir, to your one virtue? Is virtue piecemeal? This is a jewel amidst the rags of a beggar" (cw 3 : 155). Emerson was
particularly pointed in his criticism of the associationists. "If partiality was
one fault of the movement party," he notes, "the other defect was their
reliance on Association" (cw 3 : 155). He was not reluctant to remind the
followers of Adin Ballou, Charles Lane, George Ripley, William Lloyd
Garrison, and others that "no society can ever be so large as one man"; and
while unions are possible, "this union must be inward, and not one of covenants, and is to be reached by a reverse of the methods they use. The union
is only perfect when all the uniters are isolated" (cw 3 : 156, 157).

Not surprisingly, the reformers themselves found Emerson's approach
to the question of reform as less than ideal. To many, his emphasis on inner,
personal reform, and his opposition to organizations and associations,
seemed to be merely an excuse for inaction. As early as 1838 Emerson's
boyhood friend, the activist Boston lawyer Ellis Gray Loring, wrote to him
and observed that he was "sometimes *thought* to teach, that, in the great
struggles between right and wrong going on in society, we may safely &
innocently stand neuter, altogether;—gratifying mere tastes, so that they
be elegant, intellectual tastes,—this is surely a misconstruction of your
words."[9] Similarly, Maria Weston Chapman, one of Boston's leading female abolitionists, was led to comment in a draft article on Emerson that
his character was "rather contemplative than active" and that because of
this he "has been a philosophical speculator rather than a reformer." She

makes particular note that "hundreds of young persons have made him their excuse for avoiding the Anti Slavery battle & talking about the clear light." [10] Emerson's August 1, 1844, "Address on the Emancipation of the Negroes in the British West Indies," however, would indicate a dramatic shift in his approach to the question of reform generally, and the antislavery movement in particular, which would cause reformers who were previously the subjects of Emerson's ire to welcome him to their cause with enthusiasm.

The Address

It is not my intention to present a comprehensive and detailed analysis of Emerson's August 1 speech here. I have done that elsewhere. [11] However, in light of the foregoing outline of Emerson's philosophy of reform as it evolved up to the spring of 1844, it is appropriate to point to certain salient facts regarding the content of the address and the circumstances of its delivery and publication. This speech was exceptional for many reasons. First of all, despite his frequent criticisms of one-issue reformers, the most recent only five months earlier, Emerson now decided to address the specific issue of American slavery. As noted above, he had spoken publicly on this particular subject only once before, seven years earlier, following the murder of Elijah Lovejoy. His subject then, however, was primarily freedom of speech and not slavery per se. The only other instance up to this time where Emerson had spoken to a single social issue was his appeal on behalf of the Cherokees, a performance that he found distasteful, albeit necessary. In either case, prior to August 1, 1844, he had been silent on the slavery issue for more than six years.

The second exceptional aspect of Emerson's August 1 foray into the realm of public polemics is that the gathering that was the occasion for his presentation was sponsored by organized reformers. American abolitionists had been celebrating West Indian emancipation every August 1 since 1834 as a means of promoting the cause of American emancipation. The particular event in Concord was sponsored by the Concord Female Anti-Slavery Society, the membership of which included, among others, Emerson's wife Lidian, as well as Henry Thoreau's mother and sisters. It was the latter who prevailed upon Emerson to actually make the address. [12] The moving force in this group was Mary Merrick Brooks, an ardent Garrisonian and friend to Lidian. [13] Obviously, Emerson, in putting aside his long-standing opposition to reform organizations and associations, now found himself joining in a de facto alliance with them, a development that delighted the abolitionists.[14]

Finally, a third exceptional element associated with Emerson's emancipation address is that it brought him into a cooperative relationship with well-known abolition leaders, the very people whom he previously criticized for their myopia and tendency toward self-aggrandizement. According to an account of the activities of the day by William Henry Channing that appeared in the *New-York Daily Tribune* on August 5 and was later reprinted in *The Liberator* on August 16, Emerson, "The Orator of the Day," was introduced in the morning session by one of the most outspoken abolitionists of the time, the Rev. Samuel Joseph May.[15] Emerson was to be followed in the afternoon by "Messrs. [William] White, [Frederick] Douglass, [Rev. Samuel] May, and others who were present."

Not surprisingly, given his earlier, oft-expressed criticisms of such reforms and reformers, the uniqueness of this somewhat anomalous association did not go unnoticed by the conservative press in Boston. Two weeks after the presentation, for example, *The Liberator* (August 23) reprinted an article from the *Boston Courier* where the writer remarks that "Before we saw notice of this celebration, we were not aware that Mr. Emerson had sufficiently identified himself with the abolitionists, as a party, to receive such a distinguished token of their confidence." Similarly, Nathaniel Rogers, editor of the *Herald of Freedom* and a man admired by Emerson, was pleased that the Concord bard had, apparently, finally brought himself to join "openly and expressly in the anti-slavery movement," and he echoes Maria Weston Chapman's sentiment in observing that, before this, Emerson's "remaining in known *unconnection* (I cannot stop for approved words) with us operated as a virtual discountenance and opposition."[16] Obviously, this was now no longer the case.

At this point one might ask of Emerson, as Emerson once asked of Webster regarding his leadership on the Fugitive Slave Bill, "How came he there?" The reasons are, in fact, many. Initially, one might point to the many historical developments of the time, the most disturbing of which was the application of Texas for entry into the Union as a slaveholding state. Following its declaration of independence from Mexico, Texas first petitioned for statehood on August 4, 1837. Because it was clear that, if accepted, the entrance of Texas into the Union would upset the delicate balance of power between free and slaveholding states, the petition was hotly opposed by abolitionists everywhere. On October 3, 1837, Emerson joined with Ezra Ripley, his venerable step-grandfather, and other citizens of

Concord, in signing a protest against the measure and the inevitable extension of slavery that it would bring about. He would later sign yet other petitions with the same intent and recorded in his journal the observation that Massachusetts should "resist the annexation tooth & nail," and that the "great governing sentiment of the State is anti-slavery & anti-Texas" (*JMN* 9:74, 180). Unfortunately, the momentum in favor of annexation seemed irresistible. On April 12, 1844, under the direction of Secretary of State John C. Calhoun, a treaty was signed that provided for the annexation of Texas. President Tyler urged its approval in Congress and the passage of the measure appeared inevitable to many.[17] With it would come the end of the precarious balance of power that had obtained since 1820 and the Missouri Compromise. Following this, the possibilities for the continued expansion of slave territory, and slave power, were unlimited. As Martin Duberman has observed, referring to the growth of active opposition to slavery, "The real watershed came in 1845, when Texas was annexed to the Union, and war with Mexico followed. The prospect now loomed of a whole series of new slave states. It finally seemed clear that the mere passage of time would not bring a solution; if slavery was ever to be destroyed, more active resistance would be necessary."[18] It is safe to say, given his several journal comments on the matter, that Emerson anticipated this situation by the summer of 1844 and it, along with other developments both personal and social, undoubtedly influenced his decision to become more active himself in opposing the increasingly aggressive evil of slavery.[19]

Emerson was also undoubtedly encouraged to take a more public role by friends such as Margaret Fuller[20] and the example of members of his own family, especially the women. It has already been noted that his wife Lidian was an active abolitionist at this time, as were his mother, Ruth, and his dynamic aunt, Mary Moody Emerson.[21] Also, his brother Charles, who died in 1836, made an outspoken presentation in Concord in 1835 wherein he advocated immediate emancipation, the more radical position among abolitionists at the time.[22] Additionally, Emerson's step-grandfather, the Rev. Ezra Ripley, publicly supported the antislavery cause and on occasion provided his Unitarian meetinghouse for their gatherings (*VH* 25–26).

Last, it must have seemed to Emerson in the summer of 1844 that his preferred method of reform, individual moral suasion, had clearly *not* been effective in ameliorating the appalling evil of American slavery. Indeed, that evil had now become aggressively expansive.

Whatever the immediate motivation, given the evidence that follows, it is clear that once Emerson began his study of the slavery question in preparation for his presentation, for the first time he was brought face to face with the truly terrifying visage of America's greatest moral affliction. His view of slavery would change forever.[23]

Emerson's research on the topic was extensive and detailed. It represents the most intensive engagement with the subject that he had ever undertaken. The address itself, almost 10,000 words in its published form, is the most comprehensive statement he would ever make on the moral, social, racial, economic, and historical aspects of the institution of slavery. In preparing his speech Emerson read from several sources, including Thomas Clarkson's *The History of the Rise, Progress, and Accomplishment of the Abolition of the African Slave Trade by the British Parliament* (1808, 1839) and James A Thome and J. Horace Kimball's *Emancipation in the West Indies: A Six Month's Tour of Antigua, Barbados, and Jamaica in the Year 1837* (1838). In addition to these major sources and those borrowed from Ellis Gray Loring that are detailed later, Emerson also refers in his address to the "recent testimonies" (AW 30) of Joseph Sturge (1793–1859), whose work *The West Indies* (1837) documents the abuses of slaves and apprentices in the West Indies; Joseph John Gurney (1788–1847), the Quaker philanthropist who wrote *Winter in the West Indies* (1840); and the Reverend James Phillippo (1788–1879), a British Baptist missionary to the West Indies whose work *Jamaica: Its Past and Present State* was issued in a second edition in 1843.

The Clarkson work was first published in 1808 and had appeared in a new edition with "remarks on the subsequent abolition of slavery" by Lord Brougham in 1839. Joseph Slater, in his study of two of Emerson's sources for the speech, remarks that this

> large 615-page volume, crammed with facts, depositions, charts, tables, and paraphrases of parliamentary debates . . . is at once history and autobiography. Even today it transmits movingly the simple, powerful, personality of its author and his terrible, triumphant testimony. . . . There is a Smolett-like verisimilitude in Clarkson's account of how he interrogated sailors and slavers in the waterfront saloons of Liverpool, and even in his dogged parliamentary reporting one feels what Conrad called the fascination of the abomination. For a reader of 1844 it must have meant what the record of the Nuremberg Trials meant a hundred years later.[24]

Thome and Kimball's *Emancipation in the British West Indies* was first published in 1838. From this work Emerson learned more about the horrors of slavery, including the dungeons that were attached to every plantation house, the pregnant women forced to work and punished on the treadmill, and a twelve-year-old boy who was made to strip and beat his mother. "As the boy was small, the mother was obliged to get down on her hands and knees so that the child could inflict the blows on her naked person with a rod. This was done on the public highway, before the mistress's door."[25] Information such as this undoubtedly had a major emotional impact on the gentle Emerson, as reflected in the address. The *Tribune* account quotes the following from the speech as delivered.[26]

> If we saw the whip applied to the old men, to tender women, and undeniably, though I shrink to say so,—and pregnant[27] women set in the treadmill for refusing to work, when, not they, but the eternal law of animal nature refused to work; if we saw the runaways hunted with bloodhounds into swamps and hills, and in cases of rage, a planter throwing his negro into a copper of boiling cane-juice,—if we saw these things with eyes, we should wince. They are not pleasant sights. The blood is moral; the blood is anti-slavery; it runs cold in the veins; the stomach rises with disgust, and curses slavery. It becomes plain to all seeing men, the more this business is looked into, that the crimes and cruelties of slavery could not be over-stated.

Passages such as this give the address a uniquely emotional quality. Margaret Fuller, who is known to have criticized Emerson on occasion for his lack of passion,[28] was present at the gathering and was more than satisfied with what she heard. She later noted in her journal that the oration was "great heroic, calm, sweet, fair. . . . So beautifully spoken too! Better than he ever spoke before: it was true happiness to hear him; tears came to my eyes."[29] Similarly, George Curtis, who was a resident of Brook Farm at the time, also heard the speech and reported in a letter to Isaac Hecker that "It was not of that cold, clear, intellectual character that chills so many people, but full of ardent Life." He goes on to speculate that Emerson's "recent study of Anti Slavery history has infused a fine enthusiasm into his spirit & the address was very eloquent."[30] Finally, an account by a Concord woman, which appeared in the *Herald of Freedom*, notes that as Emerson "pictured the infinite wrongs of the colored man and his god-like patience, our hearts swayed to and fro at his bidding, and tears found their way down the cheeks of sturdy men as well as of tender-hearted maidens."[31]

Emerson's study of slavery went well beyond the sources noted above, however, and the evidence indicates that he actually continued his research on the topic for some time after delivering the address, this despite the substantial pressures that were on him at the time to meet the publishing deadline for *Essays, Second Series*. He was also deeply involved in preparing his "Representative Men" lectures series. Nevertheless, as Emerson became more engrossed in his study of the slavery question he specifically requested from Ellis Gray Loring several additional background sources, most of which relate to the legal and historical aspects of slavery. Loring was a longtime friend of Emerson, dating back to their days together at the Boston Latin Grammar School. Like Emerson, Loring also went on to Harvard College, where he distinguished himself as a Phi Beta Kappa scholar. Apparently Loring's independent cast of mind manifested itself early on, and he was dismissed from Harvard in May 1823, along with others who were found guilty of offering "resistance to college discipline." This event, however, did not prevent Loring from pursuing the study of law, and in 1827 he was admitted to the Massachusetts Bar.[32]

Loring was involved in social reform causes for virtually all of his adult life. He was one of the "immortal twelve" who gathered together in the basement of the African Baptist Church in Boston on January 1, 1832, to found the New England Anti-Slavery Society. He was a strong supporter of William Lloyd Garrison and served on the Board of Managers of the Massachusetts Anti-Slavery Society and the Financial Committee that supported *The Liberator.* He, along with David Lee Child (husband of Lydia Maria Child) and Samuel Sewall, often provided legal counsel to abolitionists who requested it.[33] Loring, who, as noted earlier, had once expressed his concern with Emerson's apparent inaction on the slavery question, was more than happy to oblige his request for information. Loring's letter, which appears below in its entirety, is dated August 22, 1844, and is obviously a response to a specific set of questions that Emerson apparently raised either in writing or perhaps orally on one of his visits to Loring's Boston office or home. Emerson incorporated references to each of the issues discussed in Loring's letter in the published version of his address.

Dear Sir:[34]

1. *As to persons imprisoned in N.[ew] O.[rleans] etc.* Mr. Sewall[35] & I have each been instrumental in procuring the release of many blacks imprisoned in N.[ew] Orleans without the allegation of any crime.[36] Not keeping copies of my letters I cannot recollect the *names* of any from Massachusetts: there were however some. I do recollect one young man from Maine, whose name was Luke Thompson. This was in 1840. Mr. Sewall only recollects one name: John Tidd, a Bostonian—8 or 10 years since.—See also Report on Geo.[rge] Odiorne's[37] petition in vol. lettered "Anti Slavery Legislation."

2. *English Act of Emancipation.*[38] It is doubtful whether there is a copy of the

Statute at large in the U.S.—I send you however a very full & trustworthy abstract in the 11th vol. of the Law Reporter.[39] If your object is to get the *language* of the Statute I think I can get you a copy of the most material clauses.—This vol. is the only one I send which it is important to have returned soon. Please send it to me within two or three days & keep the rest as long as you please.

3. *Sommersett's Case.*[40] The Judgment by L[ord] Mansfield[41] is in Lofft's Reports.[42] Lofft is an inaccurate Reporter of small authority but his is the only report of the judgment in this case. The reluctance of Mansfield, pressed on one side by the fearful "consequences" of the decision, & on the other by the growing spirit of liberty, is amusing. Hargrave's argument, in the 'State Trials'[43] is justly celebrated. I send also a vol. entitled "Antislavery Tracts"[44] at the end of which is a case resting in part on the authority of Sommersetts Case, in which its bearing & doctrines are discussed.

4. *Ship Zong.*[45] I send you the authoritative report in this case copied from a rare book which I was not allowed to take. What took place at the trial before the Jury is not fully given; but it is evident from their finding a verdict for the plntf. that the presiding judge *must* have instructed them that the Captain was justified in throwing over Slaves, if the scarcity of water made it necessary for the safety & health of the crew. A new trial was granted, because the full bench did not consider that the evidence supported the allegation of necessity. It is however clearly implied that such necessity may exist. The case was never reported till 1831.

I am sorry that my absence on a journey prevented my hearing your address. I expect much satisfaction from it judging by W.[illiam] H.[enry] Channing's sketch.[46] I do not however like the idea of the "extermination" of the feebler races of men. Mr. Geo. Ticknor's[47] remedy for Slavery is, I have heard, "extermination." This is a cool and summary mode of settling the question. I hope he has more to do than to prove the inferiority of the negro, before he can make it the established doctrine. The negro may be inferior, but a man's a man, for a' that.[48]

Let me thank you for a lesson you gave me some years since. I said that an antislavery meeting at Faneuil Hall, which proved spiritless—a failure to us—, would tell just as well upon the distant public. Your rebuke—which you probably do not remember—has done me good ever since. My truest feelings did not speak when I made that remark; I was, at least, good enough to recognize then & ever after, the truth which you spoke to me. It is due to you & a satisfaction to me to make this acknowledgment.

Truly your friend,
Ellis Gray Loring

Emerson's response to Loring's letter, which is also presented here for the first time, was sent just four days later and indicates clearly that he had already begun a careful study of these sources. As noted earlier, eventually he would incorporate a good deal of the information and legal and cultural commentary that they contain into his published address.

My Dear Sir,[49]

I return The Abridgement of Statutes,[50] with my thanks for your generous & profuse attention to my requests which I fear must have been very troublesome on a busy day. But you have answered them so well, that I only believe you delight to oblige.

Mr. Hargrave's argument is beautiful reading; and the matters that went before & followed after led me far aside from my lesson. I must keep it & Lofft & the other books a little longer, & hope I have not kept them too long.

I have not quite reached in revising my manuscript what touches the destiny of the negro race, & to see whether any offensive or unauthorized expressions occur; they shall certainly be considered, when they appear, in the warm light you hold up to me, if I can make it mine.

Your obliged servant,
R. W. Emerson
Monday night
Aug 26—

Publication History

Emerson's revisions of his August 1 address clearly were undertaken with publication in mind, and the final arrangements he made in this regard provide further evidence of the significance of his new approach to the question of social reform and the best means to achieve it. As it turns out Emerson was presented with two possibilities. Joseph Slater, in his introduction to the Harvard edition of *Essays, Second Series*, points out that when Emerson's publisher, James Munroe and Company, informed him in July 1844 that the book "was not large enough" and that additional material was needed to flesh it out (*CW* 3:xxx) Emerson was faced with a critical choice. He could utilize the lecture that he had delivered at Amory Hall in the spring—eventually to be titled "New England Reformers"—or he could include the emancipation address, which undoubtedly he was working on at the time. As the previous discussion indicates, the two addresses were strikingly different in their approach to the issues of reforms and reformers. Indeed, Slater observes that, while both presentations shared some characteristics such as style and subject matter, their differences are dramatic. "The Amory Hall address," he says, "was an application of 'Nominalist and Realist' rather than a reply to it. Ironic and multifocal, it saw many sides to New England reformism: the heroic and the ridiculous, the brave, the saintly, the tyrannical, the fanatical. At the end," says Slater, "it blended acquiescence and optimism" (*cw* 3:xxix–xxx).[51] By contrast, the West Indian address, notes Slater, "contained no double vision, no even handed judgment of slavery, nothing like the sketch of the universe that Emerson had drawn in 'Nominalist and Realist'; . . . In the Concord court-house that August morning Emerson's voice had been full of blood, whips, licentiousness, bloodhounds, torture, and murder. His words about slave-holders were fierce and abusive . . . and his doctrines as simple and univocal as those of William Lloyd Garrison. He seems," concludes Slater, "to have had no second thoughts about what he had said or how he had said it" (*cw* 3:xxix–xxx).

Because of these dramatic differences, Emerson's eventual choice of "New England Reformers" to complete *Essays, Second Series* seemed inevitable to Slater. The emancipation address was simply not compatible in philosophy or tact with the established content of that volume.[52] The significance of this choice has many important ramifications touching upon Emerson's evolving view of social reform generally and abolition in particular. For example, does the inclusion of "New England Reformers" and the exclusion of "Address on the Emancipation of the Negroes in the British West Indies" suggest Emerson's preference for the former as a more accurate delineation of his views on reform? Or does it ultimately suggest the opposite, namely, that "New England Reformers" represents a position that Emerson had once found philosophically pleasing, but which, after his "conversion" in the summer of 1844, was no longer compatible with his new activist views on the subject? From this perspective the choice of "New England Reformers" for inclusion in *Essays, Second Series* suggests closure rather than preference.[53]

While it is clear from the evidence presented here that Emerson's research on his topic was both extensive and intensive, that he read these materials closely and was deeply moved, both emotionally and intellectually, by the experience, ultimately, one must look beyond 1844 for evidence of a truly lasting change in Emerson's thinking on reform and the best means of achieving it. The salient questions are: Did Emerson continue to address the problem of slavery as a singular and unique social and moral illness? Did he continue to support specific abolitionist organizations in their attack upon this evil? Did he continue his cooperative association with major personalities in the abolitionist movement? A brief review of Emerson's activities in the remaining years of the decade of the 1840s indicates that the answer to all three of these questions is *yes*.

Following the 1844 address, Emerson was praised extensively by abolitionists for his effort. They came to see him as one of their own. Having once broken the ice, in what had been an admittedly chilly relationship, Emerson's alliance with the abolitionists would grow throughout the remainder of the decade, as proslavery forces became ever more aggressive. He came to respect, and even admire, such prominent activists as Garrison, Phillips, Lucretia Mott, and others.[54]

The August 1 address itself would achieve wide circulation among the abolitionists, first through their newspaper accounts and then through the published edition.[55] After completing work on the final manuscript of his address, Emerson, with the enthusiastic support of Henry Thoreau, arranged for the publication of the work by James Munroe and Company in pamphlet form.[56] On September 9, 1844, the *Boston Daily Advertiser* carried an announcement of its availability. Additionally, before the end of the year John Chapman issued a British edition, and Emerson described himself as "very well contented with the handsome pamphlet" (*L* 3:273, 7:609–12).[57]

Not surprisingly, Emerson felt some discomfort in his new role as abolition activist. In December he would tell Thomas Carlyle, who had commented on the "remoteness" of his writing and thinking from real life, "If I can at any time express the law & the ideal right, that should satisfy me without measuring the divergence of it from the last act of Congress. And though I sometimes accept a popular call, & preach on Temperance or the Abolition of slavery, as lately on the First of August, I am sure to feel before I have done with it, what an intrusion it is into another sphere & so much loss of virtue in my own."[58] In a similar vein, he states in his journal around this time, "I do not and can not forsake my vocation for abolitionism" (*JMN* 9:64 n.). Despite his reluctance, however, national events would continue to draw Emerson into a more public role and a de facto alliance with the abolitionists. These events took on a personal character when Emerson's Concord neighbor and friend Samuel Hoar and his daughter Elizabeth (the former fiancée of Emerson's deceased brother Charles) were driven from Charleston, South Carolina, under threat of physical violence. Hoar had been sent to Charleston as an agent of the state of Massachusetts to investigate the mistreatment of Negro sailors serving on Massachusetts ships,

one of the specific issues about which Emerson had complained in his address. Emerson was so upset with this development that he sent a letter to
the *New-York Tribune* (December 20, 1844) praising Hoar for his heroism
in the matter (*L* 7:620). Emerson also attended an indignation meeting in
Concord in January that was called to protest the expulsion, and he complained bitterly of the barbarism of South Carolina (*JMN* 9:161, 173–74).
In the same month he successfully defended Wendell Phillips' right to
speak on the subject of slavery in the Concord Lyceum. In his journal at
the time he describes the fiery abolitionist as "one of the best speakers in
the Commonwealth" (*JMN* 9:102), and following Phillips' address, in
March 1845, Emerson wrote to Samuel Ward and said of the presentation
that he "had not learned a better lesson in many weeks than last night in a
couple of hours" (*L* 8:15–16).

On August 1, 1845, Emerson would again address a large antislavery audience in celebration of emancipation in the British West Indies.[59] The
gathering in Waltham, Massachusetts, was sponsored by the abolitionists
of Middlesex and Suffolk Counties. The *Liberator* account (August 8, 1845)
indicates that "large delegations from Boston and Concord, and considerable numbers from other places in the vicinity attended." The *National
Anti-Slavery Standard*, and Horace Greeley's *New-York Daily Tribune* published detailed accounts of the speech.

The following month Emerson attended a Middlesex Convention in
Concord to protest the annexation of Texas. The convention met again
in October in Cambridge with Emerson once more in attendance. He
brought with him a letter from John Greenleaf Whittier that was read at
the convention and later published in the *Emancipator* (October 1, 1845).
In the letter Whittier praised Emerson for adding his "manly voice" to the
growing chorus of opposition to the institution of slavery (*AW* xxxiii).

In November 1845 Emerson made a more personal protest against racism, which had been the specific subject of his emancipation address four
months earlier. After being informed that the New Bedford Lyceum had
voted not to allow regular membership to blacks, Emerson refused to lecture there. He noted in his letter to the Lyceum, which was later published
with his permission in *The Liberator* (January 16, 1846), that the racist
policy of the Lyceum, "by excluding others, I think ought to exclude me"
(*L* 8:61–62).

In June 1846 the agitation on the slavery issue and the recent advent of
the Mexican War moved Emerson to compose his famous "Ode: Inscribed
to W. H. Channing" where he opposed the absolute separation of North

and South, which was then demanded by many abolitionists who were insisting on a "no-Union with slaveholders" policy. "What boots thy zeal, / O glowing friend," he asks, "That would indignant rend / The northland from the south?" While the poem obviously indicates an area of disagreement with his abolitionist cohorts, the source of that disagreement lies in Emerson's new determination to confront the problem of slavery head on. The "no Union" position articulated by the abolitionists at this time must have appeared to him as tantamount to capitulation, not constructive engagement.[60]

On the Fourth of July 1846 Emerson once again addressed a large antislavery gathering, this one in Dedham, Massachusetts. The gathering was sponsored by the Massachusetts Anti-Slavery Society as a fund-raiser for that organization, and William Lloyd Garrison, James Freeman Clarke, and Wendell Phillips joined him on the platform. In his address Emerson applauds the association of which he was once so critical. "The history of this party of freedom," he says, "seems to me one of the best symptoms, but it is only a symptom. I am glad, not for what it has done, but that the party exists. Not what they do, but what they see, seems to be sublime." But he also offers a bit of gentle persuasion to move them toward a more comprehensive view of reform, something which he obviously continued to see as important despite his own growing dedication to the singular cause of abolition. "I am a debtor," he says, "in common with all well-meaning persons, to this association. I think they have yet lessons to learn, and are learning them. I shall esteem them, as they cease to be a party, and come to rely on that which is not party, nor part, but which is the whole, and which as readily and irresistibly pours itself from one man, as from the most numerous co-operation" (AW 44). Despite such reservations, Emerson's increasing comfort with his new relationship with the abolitionists is reflected in his earlier response to Mrs. Weston's invitation to give the speech at Dedham. Here Emerson notes that he would "cheer [himself] with the generous resources you open of the company of the great & the good at Dedham," and he goes on to indicate that "It is a real consolation in this darkness & disgrace of our politics, to see the vivacity & the growth of that Church of Liberty which you love & which loves you so well. I also am very grateful to you & your fellow apostles" (L 8:82). Following his presentation, and apparently at her request, Emerson provided a copy of his speech to Maria Weston Chapman for publication in the National Anti-Slavery Standard (July 16, 1846).[61] Affirming his commitment to the group and their cause, less than a month later Emerson would deliver his third address celebrating emancipation in the West Indies on August 1, 1846, which was again noted in *The Liberator* (August 7, 1846).[62]

The following month Boston abolitionists were greatly agitated when a runaway slave was seized on the ship *Ottoman* in Boston harbor and, despite vigorous objections, was returned to his master in Louisiana. A public protest meeting was held and Charles Sumner, Wendell Phillips, and Theodore Parker spoke. Emerson, who was unable to attend, provided a letter to the "Kidnapping Committee" that was later published as part of the committee's report. This letter expresses Emerson's shock and disgust at the shipowner's actions and congratulates the committee "for undertaking the office of putting the question to our people, whether they will make this cruelty theirs? and of giving them an opportunity of clearing the population from the stain of this crime, and of securing mankind from the repetition of it, in this quarter, forever" (*AW* 46).

Despite his generally optimistic philosophy, local events like the kidnapping, as well as national developments like the Mexican War, which had erupted in May, depressed Emerson. Partially in response to this depression, on October 5, 1847, he set sail for England, where he would lecture and renew acquaintances with old friends like Carlyle. While there he would also witness the growth of the Chartist movement and in his journal he expresses his support for the ragged protestors who undoubtedly reminded him of his abolitionist friends at home. He observes, "Shame to the fop of philosophy who suffers a little vulgarity of speech & of character to hide from him the true current of Tendency, & who abandons his true position of being priest & poet of those impious & unpoetic doers of God's work" (*JMN* 10:326).

Emerson returned from England in July 1848, apparently somewhat renewed by the experience and more hopeful for the future. Perhaps because of this, when Garrison asked him to speak once again at a celebration of West Indian emancipation on August 3, 1849, he accepted. The gathering was at Worcester, Massachusetts, and, perhaps as a sign of the anxieties of the time, was one of the largest ever held in the Commonwealth, with over 5,000 people in attendance. Once again, the Massachusetts Anti-Slavery Society was the sponsoring organization. Emerson's remarks were brief, perhaps because of a congestion from which he was apparently suffering, but the words were beautiful and heartfelt and Garrison and the other abolitionists were no doubt grateful for his affirming presence. As in his earlier abolition addresses, Emerson here applauds his abolition friends. "It should be praise enough," he states, "for our friends who have carried forward this great work, friends to whom it seems to me always, the country is more and more indebted, that it is the glory of these preachers of freedom that they have strengthened the moral sense, that they have anticipated this triumph which I look upon as inevitable, and which it is not in man to retard" (AW 49). Once again, a full account of Emerson's speech was published in *The Liberator* (August 17, 1849).

Emerson's comments in this final address from the decade of the 1840s inform the nature of his relationship with the abolitionists throughout the turbulent 1850s. The dramatic and distressing developments of the period virtually guaranteed that the alliance between himself and these "friends" would grow even stronger.

The 1850s would open with the passage of the Fugitive Slave Act and other elements of the "Compromise of 1850." This futile effort to defuse the growing tensions between North and South had the opposite effect. Abolitionists, including Emerson, were outraged by the new law and vowed eternal opposition. Emerson's involvement in public affairs would accelerate dramatically throughout the decade as confrontations between pro- and antislavery parties became ever more violent. It would culminate with his stirring defense of the age's greatest abolitionist hero, John Brown. While Emerson's involvement during this period is reasonably well documented, it is clear that his active commitment to organized efforts at social reform had its origins in a stirring address that he presented on an August morning in Concord, sixteen years earlier.

NOTES

1. I have in mind here Richard F. Teichgraeber's use of the term, which he derives from Michael Walzer's *Interpretation and Social Criticism* (Cambridge: Cambridge University Press, 1987). Walzer, Teichgraeber notes, uses the term to "account for a historical phenomenon: the work of a group of actual critics who were neither alienated nor detached from practices and institutions they criticized, but instead criticized from the inside by invoking what they took to be their society's shared values as the grounds for criticism." Teichgraeber, correctly I believe, offers Emerson and Thoreau as "two additional instances" of this phenomenon. (*Sublime Thoughts/Penny Wisdom: Situating Emerson and Thoreau in the Marketplace* [Baltimore: The Johns Hopkins University Press, 1995], pp. xi–xii.)

2. For a discussion of the Unitarian influence, and other factors, on Emerson's early views on social reform, see *VH* 41–49.

3. Among nineteenth-century commentators, Oliver Wendell Holmes is the most prominent in presenting a conspicuously conservative image of Emerson as a man who eschewed social reform activity. In his work Holmes states flatly,

and incorrectly, that "Emerson had never been identified with the abolitionists." *Ralph Waldo Emerson* (Boston: Houghton Mifflin, 1884), p. 304.

Among twentieth-century commentators, Stephen Whicher in *Freedom and Fate: An Inner Life of Ralph Waldo Emerson* (Philadelphia: University of Pennsylvania Press, 1953) insists that, for most of his life, Emerson was withdrawn from public affairs, and that after his negative experience with the "Divinity School Address" in 1838, Emerson's "image of the hero-scholar, leading mankind to the promised land, steadily gave way to the solitary observer, unregarded and unregarding of the multitude" (76).

For a comprehensive discussion of how Emerson's social activism has been treated by biographers and commentators from the nineteenth century to the present see *VH* 1–23.

4. For a comprehensive discussion of the events affecting Emerson's view of the slavery question from 1837 to 1844 see my "Emerson and Abolition: The Silent Years, 1837–1844," *American Literature* 54 no. 4 (Dec. 1982): 560–75; and *VH* 41–85. For the period before 1837, see my "Abolition, the Emersons, and 1837," *The New England Quarterly* 54 no. 3 (Sept. 1981): 345–64.

5. Gerald Sorin, *Abolitionism: A New Perspective* (New York: Praeger, 1972), p. 91. Only fragments of Emerson's presentation survive. They appear in James Elliot Cabot's *A Memoir of Ralph Waldo Emerson*, 2 vols. (Boston: Houghton Mifflin, 1887).

6. The letter is dated April 23, 1838. A complete and fully edited version of this letter, along with other important Emerson reform writings, appear in *AW* 1–5.

7. *The Selected Letters of Lidian Jackson Emerson*, ed. Delores Bird Carpenter (Columbia: University of Missouri Press, 1987), p. 75.

8. According to contemporary newspaper accounts, other speakers in the series, in addition to Emerson and Garrison, were Charles Lane (cofounder of Fruitlands), Adin Ballou (founder of the utopian community Hopedale), Charles Dana (managing trustee of Brook Farm), Ernestine Rose (feminist reformer and freethinker), Wendell Phillips (abolitionist), and Henry David Thoreau, who spoke on "The Conservative and the Reformer." For an excellent discussion of this gathering and related issues of reform see Linck Johnson, "Reforming the Reformers; Emerson, Thoreau, and the Sunday Lectures at Amory Hall, Boston," *ESQ* 37 (1992):235–89.

9. Ellis Gray Loring to Emerson, March 16, 1838, Houghton Library, Harvard University. Quoted with the permission of Harvard University and the Ralph Waldo Emerson Memorial Association.

10. Maria Weston Chapman, draft article on Emerson, 1844, Boston Public Library. Quoted with permission.

11. See *VH* 75–90.

12. Walter Harding, *The Days of Henry Thoreau* (New York: Knopf, 1965), p. 174.

13. Ellen Tucker Emerson, *The Life of Lidian Jackson Emerson*, ed. Delores Bird

Carpenter (Boston: Twayne Publishers, 1980), p. 64. Thomas Blanding, "Beans, Baked and Half-baked," *The Concord Saunterer* 17 no. 3 (Dec. 1984): 47.

14. Emerson's presentation would win praise from many abolitionists, including Maria Chapman, Wendell Phillips, William Lloyd Garrison, and John Greenleaf Whittier. See *VH* 84–88.

15. For an informative account of May's life and his numerous social reform activities, see Donald Yacovone, *Samuel Joseph May and the Dilemma of the Liberal Persuasion, 1797–1871* (Philadelphia: Temple University Press, 1991).

16. Quoted in the introduction to *Essays: Second Series* (*CW* 3:xxv).

17. The Senate rejected the treaty in June. In March of 1845, following the election of John Polk to the presidency, the issue was again brought forward in the Congress. After substantial debate and political maneuvering, Texas was admitted to the Union as a state on December 29, 1845.

18. "The Northern Response to Slavery," in *The Antislavery Vanguard: New Essays on the Abolitionists*, ed. Martin Duberman (Princeton: Princeton University Press, 1965), p. 397.

19. Barbara Ryan, in "Emerson's 'Domestic and Social Experiments': Service, Slavery, and the Unhired Man," *American Literature* 66 no. 3 (1994): 485–508, offers the interesting suggestion that Emerson may also have been prompted to make his address at this time because of the failure of his own "domestic and social experiments," conducted between 1837 and 1844, in which he attempted to bring non-kin servants into his home in a family-like setting where labor and rewards would be shared, not unlike the idealized vision of slavery which apologists for the institution promoted. Ryan notes, "Only after a series of experiments had been tried and found wanting did he accede to friends' pleas to oppose slavery publicly" (487).

Amy Earhart has recently speculated that Emerson's decision to speak out at this time "resulted from a number of contemporary historical developments, including slave insurrection in Haiti and Cuba that was receiving extensive coverage in New England periodicals as Emerson was preparing his address." Abstract, "Slave Revolt, Representative men, and Emerson's 'conversion' to Abolitionism," *Emerson Society Papers* 7 no. 2 (fall 1996): 4.

20. Christina Zwarg sees Emerson's growing relationship with Margaret Fuller and her interest in social reform as an influence in his decision to give the speech. See *Feminist Conversations: Fuller, Emerson, and the Play of Reading* (Ithaca: Cornell University Press, 1995), pp. 136 ff.

21. See *AW* xxiv–xxvii. For the story of Aunt Mary's abolitionism see Phyllis Cole's *Mary Moody Emerson and the Origins of Transcendentalism: A Family History* (New York: Oxford University Press, 1998), pp. 200–245.

22. Charles Emerson, "Lecture on Slavery," April 29, 1835, manuscript, Houghton Library, Harvard University.

23. That the address represents a significant change in Emerson's approach to

the question of reform seems generally agreed upon. Ralph Rusk comments, "His sudden leap into the political arena in aid of the abolitionists had occurred only a few weeks before the publication of the second *Essays*. Then, in his address on emancipation in the West Indies he had seemed to at least one observer to be a new man, not cold, clear, and intellectual but genial and benevolent, smiling as if to defy the world, flesh, and devil. . . . Almost at the moment the second *Essays* came from the press, it seems, he was visiting the extremist William Lloyd Garrison in his office and, at last, respecting him without reservation" (*The Life of Ralph Waldo Emerson* [New York: Columbia University Press, 1949], p. 303).

Maurice Gonnaud speculates that "the reading Emerson did in preparing the speech . . . revealed new and unexpected horizons" and that the speech itself reveals a "new and crucial element" in Emerson's understanding of the Negro and the potential benefits of emancipation (*An Uneasy Solitude: Individual and Society in the Work of Ralph Waldo Emerson*, trans. Lawrence Rosenwald [Princeton: Princeton University Press, 1987], p. 344).

Similarly, Carlos Baker notes that Emerson's "private 'Genius' had long caused him to oppose slavery in fact and in theory without allowing the 'Universal Genius' to persuade him into public utterance on the subject." Eventually, however, Emerson would find his public voice on the subject. "The turning point," Baker suggests, "seems to have come with his historical discourse on 'Emancipation in the British West Indies' given at Concord in August 1844." (*Emerson Among the Eccentrics: A Group Portrait* [New York: Viking, 1996], p. 371.)

Lastly, Richard Teichgraeber states flatly, "There can be no question that Emerson's attitude [towards reform] underwent fundamental modification as he prepared for his Concord Address" (*Sublime Thoughts/Penny Wisdom*, p. 93 n.).

24. "Two Sources for Emerson's First Address on West Indian Emancipation," *ESQ* 44 (1966): 97.

25. Slater, "Two Sources," p. 99.

26. See *New-York Daily Tribune*, 5 August 1844, p. 2, and *The Liberator*, 16 August 1844, p. 129. Emerson's final version of the passage differs somewhat from the newspaper accounts. See *AW* 10.

27. Both the *Tribune* and *The Liberator's* reprint, contain the typo "frequent" rather than "pregnant," which appears in both Emerson's source and his published version.

28. See Charles Capper, *Margaret Fuller: An American Romantic Life* (New York: Oxford University Press, 1992), pp. 328–29.

29. "'The Impulses of Human Nature': Margaret Fuller's Journal from June through October 1844," ed. Martha L. Berg and Alice De V. Perry, in *Proceedings of the Massachusetts Historical Society*, vol. 102, 1990 (Boston: Massachusetts Historical Society, 1991), p. 107.

30. August 4, 1844. Archives of the Paulist Fathers, New York City. Quoted with permission.

31. Quoted by Slater in his introduction to *Essays: Second Series* (cw 3:xxiv).

32. *Loring Genealogy*, ed. Charles Pope and Katherine Loring (Cambridge, Mass.: Murray and Emery, 1917), pp. 255–56. For further information on Loring see my "1838: Ellis Gray Loring and a Journal for the Times," in *Studies in the American Renaissance, 1990*, ed. Joel Myerson (Charlotte: University of Virginia Press, 1990), pp. 33–47.

33. Among his more famous cases was that of the slave child "Med" who was brought to Massachusetts by her mistress. Loring successfully argued before the Massachusetts Supreme Court in 1836 that any slave who is voluntarily brought into the state by his or her master cannot be removed from the state against his or her will. The case established an important legal precedent.

Loring also came to the defense of Abner Kneeland when he achieved the questionable distinction of being the last person to be convicted of the crime of blasphemy in the state of Massachusetts. It was Loring who, together with the elder William Ellery Channing, composed and circulated *Petition on Behalf of Abner Kneeland* in 1838. Among those who signed the petition was Ralph Waldo Emerson who, at the time, was embroiled in the controversy generated by his own recent "heretical" "Divinity School Address."

34. Manuscript, Houghton Library, Harvard University. Quoted with the permission of Harvard University and the Ralph Waldo Emerson Memorial Association.

35. Samuel Edmund Sewall (1799–1888) was an abolitionist lawyer who often defended runaway slaves who were under arrest. He helped Garrison financially in the organization of *The Liberator* and was one of the counselors at the trial of John Brown in Virginia in October 1859.

36. This was a common practice at the time in many Southern ports. For example, Albert Bushnell Hart indicates that "After the unsuccessful Denmark Vesey insurrection of 1820, suspicion was strong against every negro. South Carolina passed a series of laws, commonly called the 'negro seamen acts,' which provided in effect that whenever a ship arrived in port any negroes on board must go to jail, there to stay till the vessel was ready to sail again. Northern states at once protested that their citizens were thus deprived of their 'privileges and immunities'; and the British government made similar remonstrances. After an opinion of Attorney-General Wirt that the law was unconstitutional, South Carolina relaxed the measure against England, but continued it against the northern states." *Slavery and Abolition: 1831–1841* (New York: Harper & Brothers, 1906), p. 277.

In his address, Emerson complains about this situation and refers to Loring and Sewall when he states, "In the sleep of the laws, the private interference of two excellent citizens of Boston has, I have ascertained, rescued several natives of this State from these southern prisons. Gentlemen, I thought the deck of a Massachusetts ship was as much the territory of Massachusetts, as the floor on which we stand. It should be as sacred as the temple of God" (24).

As indicated later, Samuel Hoar would be sent to South Carolina as a commissioner of the state of Massachusetts to investigate this situation, with unfortunate results.

37. According to Walter Merrill, "A man named Odiorne, probably a Boston merchant, became the first vice president" of Garrison's New England Anti-Slavery Society when it was founded in 1832. *Against Wind and Tide: A Biography of Wm. Lloyd Garrison* (Cambridge: Harvard University Press, 1963), p. 58.

38. The Emancipation Act of 1833 effectively abolished slavery from the British Empire. See Betty Fladeland, " 'Our Cause being One and the Same': Abolitionists and Chartism," in *Slavery and British Society: 1776–1846*, ed. James Walvin (Baton Rouge: Louisiana State University Press, 1982), pp. 76, 77, 90; and F. O. Shyllon, *Black Slaves in Britain* (London: Oxford University Press, 1974), pp. 230–31.

In his address Emerson quotes the following from the act: "Be it enacted, that all and every person who, on the 1st of August, 1834, shall be holden in slavery within any such British colony as aforesaid, shall upon and from and after the said 1st August, become and be to all intents and purposes free, and discharged of and from all manner of slavery, and shall be absolutely and forever manumitted; and that the children thereafter born to any such persons, and the offspring of such children, shall, in like manner, be free from their birth; and that from and after the 1st August, 1834, slavery shall be and is hereby utterly and forever abolished and declared unlawful throughout the British colonies, plantations, and possessions abroad" (*AW* 14).

39. Possibly *The Monthly Law Reporter*, 27 vols. (Boston: W. Guild, 1838–66).

40. In 1772 James Somerset, a Negro, was brought by his master from Boston to England. When his master attempted to take him back to America, Somerset sued for a writ of habeas corpus, which Lord Mansfield allowed on the ground that "the state of slavery is of such a nature that it is incapable of being introduced on any reasons, moral or political. It is so odious that nothing can be suffered to support it but positive law." (Hart, *Slavery and Abolition*, p. 52.)

41. William Murray (1705–93), Lord Mansfield, Chief Justice of the King's Bench of Great Britain (1756–88). Emerson clearly admired Mansfield's moral courage in adjudicating slave cases. Edward Emerson notes, "Mr. Emerson honored Lord Mansfield for his decision in the case of Somerset the slave, and contrasted him in his journals with the Boston judges who gave the decision under the Fugitive Slave Law returning Sims and Burns to bondage" (*W* 7:370). (See *JMN* 11: 281 for Mansfield and the American Fugitive Slave Law.) In his August 1 address Emerson says, "There is a sparkle of God's righteousness in Lord Mansfield's judgment, which does the heart good" (*AW* 11).

42. Capel Lofft's report of the Somerset case appears in his *Reports of Cases adjudged in the Court of King's Bench, From Easter Term 12 Geo. 3 to Michaelmas 14 Geo. 3* (London, 1776). See, Shyllon, *Black Slaves in Britain* (London: Oxford University Press, 1974), p. 236.

43. Shyllon notes that "the report of the Somerset Case usually cited is Howell's *State Trials*, Vol. XI and Capel Lofft's report" (p. 236). See also Francis Hargrave's (1741?–1821) *An Argument in the Case of James Sommersett, A Negro, Lately Determined by the Court of King's Bench; Wherein it is Attempted to Demonstrate the Present Unlawfulness of Domestic Slavery in England; to which is Prefixed a State of the Case* (London, 1772). Shyllon observes that "Hargrave's report is quite competent, consisting of a short statement of the facts of the case, and his own learned argument. . . . In a note preceding the argument, Hargrave makes the point that he delivered his argument in Court 'without the assistance of notes'" (pp. 236–37).

44. I have not been able to identify this volume. It is possible that it is simply an ad hoc collection of antislavery materials that Loring had bound for his own use.

45. Refers to a case where a slave ship captain in 1781 ordered 133 slaves who had grown ill to be cast into the sea. Only one survived. The insurance arrangement provided that if the slaves died of natural causes the captain and owners of the ship would suffer the loss, but if they were thrown alive into the sea, under any pretext of safety for the ship, it would be the underwriters' loss. For a detailed discussion of the case see Shyllon, *Black Slaves in Britain*, pp. 184–209.

In his address Emerson notes, "In the case of ship Zong, in 1781, whose master had thrown one hundred and thirty-two slaves alive into the sea, to cheat the underwriters, the first jury gave a verdict in favor of the master and owners: they had a right to do what they had done. Lord Mansfield is reported to have said on the bench, 'The matter left to the jury is,—Was it from necessity? For they had no doubt,—though it shocks one very much,—that the case of slaves was the same as if horses had been thrown overboard. It is a very shocking case'" (*AW* 29).

46. As noted earlier, William Henry Channing (1810–84) published an account of the address in the *New-York Daily Tribune*, August 5, 1844. The letter is dated Dec. 17, 1844. See *The Letters of Ralph Waldo Emerson*, 10 vols., ed. Ralph Rusk and Eleanor Tilton (New York: Columbia University Press, 1939–95), 7:620.

47. George Ticknor (1791–71) one of Emerson's more notable Harvard professors, was strongly anti-abolitionist. Loring's reference to Emerson's use of the term "extermination" in the speech relates to his statement, "If the black man is feeble, and not important to the existing races not on a parity with the best race, the black man must serve, and be exterminated. But if the black man carries in his bosom an indispensable element of a new and coming civilization, for the sake of that element, no wrong, nor strength, nor circumstance can hurt him: he will survive and play his part. . . . The anti-slavery of the whole world, is dust in the balance before this,—is a poor squeamishness and nervousness: the might and the right are here: here is the anti-slave: here is man: and if you have man, black or white is an insignificance" (*AW* 31).

48. From Robert Burn's poem, "For A' That and A' That," *Selected Poems of Robert Burns*, ed. Charles W. Kent (New York: Silver, Burdett, 1901), p. 79. The poem, which refers to poor slaves and other examples of oppressed humanity, was appar-

ently a favorite with abolitionists for that reason. Emerson liked the poem well enough to include it in his collection *Parnassus* (1875), where it appears under the title, "Honest Poverty."

49. Manuscript, New York Public Library, Astor, Lenox, and Tilden Foundations, Rare Books and Manuscripts Division, Lee Kohms Collection. Quoted with permission. The letter is dated Monday night, 26 August, no year. The internal evidence clearly indicates that the year is 1844. Additionally, August 26 was a Monday that year.

50. Possibly the "Law Reporter" referred to in note 42.

51. Emerson expresses this position succinctly at the conclusion of his address. "Our own orbit," he says, "is all our task, and we need not assist the administration of the universe" (*cw* 3:166).

52. In addition to "Nominalist and Realist," and "New England Reformers," the other essays included in the volume are "The Poet," "Experience," "Character," "Manners," "Gifts," "Nature," and "Politics."

53. Christina Zwarg agrees with Slater that because "the shifting tones of 'New England Reformers' . . . bore a greater resemblance to the rhetorical maneuvers of the earlier chapters," and because "the address on the emancipation, by contrast, contained some of Emerson's most unequivocal writings, addressing the slavery issue with uncompromising anger," the former must have appeared to Emerson as the most logical choice. Like Rusk, Gonnaud, Baker, and Teichgraeber, she too goes on to note substantive differences in the two works, especially the "issue of agency," and in this regard she states, "'New England Reformers' provides a thematic closure for the collection [*Essays: Second Series*]" (*Feminist Conversations*, 134).

Robert Burkholder, however, has recently argued against this position on the grounds that "such a radical change in [Emerson's] perspective" is unlikely because "Emerson was not often a close reader, and at this period in his life, when he was putting the finishing touches on *Essays, Second Series* and was deeply involved in preparing the 'Representative Men' lectures, it is at best unlikely that his reading of one or two particular works would have so impressed him as to cause a complete reexamination of long-held views." ("History's Mad Pranks: Some Recent Emerson Studies," *ESQ* 38 [3rd quarter 1992]: 11–12.)

54. After meeting her in Philadelphia in January 1843, Emerson told Samuel Ward, "I have seen Lucretia Mott who is a noble woman" (*L* 7:523). Emerson's praise of Phillips was noted earlier. See also *JMN* 9:136–37. Emerson's estimation of Garrison is summed up in his statement, "I cannot speak of that gentleman without respect"(*JMN* 9:132–34).

55. Speaking of the address, one abolitionist noted that Wendell Phillips "was wont for years to keep it on hand for distribution" (W. J. Potter, "Emerson and the Abolitionists," *Index*, 3 December 1885).

Also, Teichgraeber notes that "the historical significance of the pamphlet edition of Emerson's 1844 address on 'Emancipation in the British West Indies' has generally been underestimated by historians. Its continuing significance in lending cultural legitimacy to the cause of abolition is suggested by the presence of excerpts from the pamphlet in Hinton Rowan Helper's *The Impending Crisis of the South* (Baltimore, 1857). Rowan's volume, which appeared in several editions, was the most elaborate contemporary exposition of the economic case against slavery. Used extensively by the Republican Party as campaign propaganda, one hundred thousand copies of *The Impending Crisis* were distributed by a group of Republican congressmen in 1859" (*Sublime Thoughts/Penny Wisdom*, p. 111 n.).

56. Harding, *Days*, p. 175; L 3:259. The pamphlet is titled *An Address Delivered in the Court-House in Concord, Massachusetts, on 1st August, 1844, on the Anniversary of the Emancipation of the Negroes in the British West Indies*, by R. W. Emerson, Published by Request (Boston: James Munroe and Company, 1844).

57. Chapman also issued a British edition of *Essays, Second Series*. The American edition was published by James Munroe and Co. and advertised as "published and for sale" in the *Boston Daily Advertiser* of October 19, 1844 (L 3:264 n.).

58. *The Correspondence of Emerson and Carlyle*, ed. Joseph Slater (New York: Columbia University Press, 1964), p. 373.

59. The address, "Anniversary of West Indian Emancipation," can be found in AW 35–38.

60. For a comprehensive analysis of this poem and its relationship to Emerson's evolving abolitionism see VH 114–17.

61. See L 8:84. The speech itself can be found in AW 41–44.

62. No record of this presentation survives, other than the notice in *The Liberator*.

HAROLD K. BUSH

Emerson, John Brown, and "Doing the Word": The Enactment of Political Religion at Harpers Ferry, 1859

TRUE AMERICANS don't just talk; they must constantly be "up and do-ing," willing "to act, that each to-morrow / Find us farther than today." This progressive and pragmatic ideology informs what was likely the most beloved and well-known poem of the American nineteenth century, Henry Wadsworth Longfellow's secularized hymn "A Psalm of Life":

> Not enjoyment, and not sorrow,
> Is our destin'd end or way;
> But to act, that each to-morrow
> Find us farther than today . . .
>
> Life is real—Life is earnest— . . .
> Let us then be up and doing, . . .
> Still achieving, still pursuing![1]

We might well ask, why was Longfellow's poem so culturally powerful and pervasive? Frederick Douglass, for example, quoted from the poem in his most famous speech, "What to a Slave is the Fourth of July?" (1852). There, Douglass argued that the true "eternal principles" that were "seized upon" by the founding fathers must be reapplied to the contemporary American scene:

My business, if I have any here to-day, is with the present. The accepted time with God and His cause is the ever-living now.

> "Trust no future, however pleasant,
> Let the dead past bury its dead;

197

Act, act in the living present,
Heart within, and God overhead."[2]

In his three-pronged directive to "seize" the eternal principles of the
founding revolutionary fathers, perform God's will, and "act in the living
present," the "ever-living now," Douglass invoked what was rapidly becoming the dominant ideology of the American antebellum renaissance.
Certainly, Douglass's own rhetorical project was deeply indebted to the historical fact that he had been a slave and had made a stand of public defiance
against the "slave power," a stand memorably documented in the Covey
episode in the 1845 version of his *Narrative*. Such public moves in which
"the speaker incarnates the argument" constitute a rhetorical form known
as "enactment."[3] That is, writers and rhetors enhance the rhetorical power
of their arguments when they are willing not only to voice them but to
enact them, to "incarnate" them.[4]

The strategic value of investing rhetorical speech with practical action
became a central feature of the regnant American myth throughout the
early nineteenth century. Thus, for example, for the myriad church-related
societies of the early nineteenth century, the key "objective was to 'do
good': to assist the poor, convert the heathen, and lift up the fallen."[5] What
Carla Peterson has recently shown to be the burden of numerous African
American women can be expanded to include much of middle-class American culture of the antebellum period: the overpowering desire to become
not just hearers, but also "doers of the word." As Peterson argues, "for
these and other activists . . . speaking and writing constituted a form
of doing."[6] Moreover, the shift in American Christianity elaborated by
Peterson is just one prominent example of an even broader shift in Western
philosophy: as one historian puts it, "the movement . . . towards the positing of some dynamic and practical version of what Schopenhauer calls
'the will.'"[7]

The call in America to "do the word" was aimed not merely at the religious but generally at all "true American citizens," meaning that what had
begun as a Christian principle of sanctification had become subtly transformed into a patriotic national initiative by which the Union would even-
tuate in a better place for all. Preachers regularly began calling for the closure of what one theologian has called the "sanctification gap": that is, the
disturbing trend among multitudes of American citizens who had asserted
their Christian faith and yet had not committed themselves to the lifelong
quest toward holiness and Christian perfection in the Wesleyan tradition.[8]

The widespread Christian call to live in fuller holiness, made throughout much of the American church, was duplicated by a similar yet more secular call to close the sanctification gap inherent among the believers in what we might term an authentic American repentance. True American repentance comprised an act of rebellion against corrupt authority that commenced with an individualized, public "declaration of independence" at a specific and identifiable point in time.[9] The religious critics disdained the "easy conversion" that had manifested among Christian believers; similarly, other cultural critics castigated the "easy conversion" by which so-called Americans claimed to have "repented" and become truly American but in fact had continued living the sorts of lives that indicated a betrayal of fundamental American creeds and values. As a result of this perceived sanctification gap among both Christians and American citizens, a heightened sense of repentance was sounded forth by various spokespersons, including members of marginalized populations such as slaves and ex-slaves, many of whom drew on revolutionary and biblical models to enact endless new manifestations of an authentically American repentance. Through countless reenactments of the "Declaration of Independence," the namesake document began taking on a new life of its own as central American fundament.

Beginning from about 1827 to 1831, as some historians have argued, a cultural shift took place by which many localized African American voices began to merge into a more nationalized public voice.[10] In particular, African American men such as David Walker (whose *Appeal* was published in September 1829) and Nat Turner (who led a slave uprising in August 1831) enacted a revolutionary impulse that drew significantly upon America's Declaration myth. This increasing African American emphasis on revolutionary rhetoric and at times armed resistance to tyranny emerged in a period of unprecedented mob violence and rioting throughout many of America's major cities. Boston, New Haven, Detroit, Newark, Camden, and Buffalo all were scenes of rioting from 1826 to 1834. Riots related to issues of race also occurred in these years in Providence, Philadelphia, New York, and Cincinnati.[11] The explosive growth of violence was noted by many observers: a committee of the New York Assembly, for instance, remarked that a "spirit of anarchy and insubordination has been waked in our land"; while the attorney general of Massachusetts lamented that a "wicked and furious spirit" was at work in the American citizenry.[12] Regarding racial incidents, the bloody riots of Philadelphia in August 1842 caused Robert Purvis to associate the "wantonness, brutality and murderous spirit" of the mob with the African American citizenry's "utter and complete nothingness in public estimation."[13]

David Walker's political vision must be considered in light of both this shocking and pervasive growth in mob violence and the emergent African American revolutionary voice. Walker was himself never a slave; but his father was, and Walker's powerful sense of Christian mission and God's ordained call on his life deeply informs his rhetorical project. In essence, Walker's *Appeal* argues for the full humanity of the Negro and thus for his inclusion into the precepts of the Declaration. Jefferson's prediction—that the Fourth of July (or more specifically, the Declaration that is celebrated on that day) would be to the world "the signal of arousing men to burst the chains" enslaving them—is echoed and expanded in the heart of Walker's message: "I appeal to Heaven for my motive in writing—who knows that my object is, if possible, to awaken in the breasts of my afflicted, degraded and slumbering brethren, a spirit of inquiry and investigation respecting our miseries and wretchedness in this *Republican Land of Liberty! ! ! ! !*"[14] Walker frankly urges his readers to enact their own form of independence by violent resistance, a striking appeal in 1829: "the man who would not fight under our Lord and Master Jesus Christ, in the glorious and heavenly cause of freedom and of God . . . ought to be kept with all of his children and family, in slavery, or in chains, to be butchered by his *cruel enemies.*"[15] Walker also invokes the domestic slave uprising of Denmark Vesey in 1822 and the insurrection in Haiti that began in 1791, both of which were frightening references for antebellum whites.[16]

In effect, Walker's literary production is one of the first and best of the endorsements of African American armed resistance to slavery. Not surprisingly, Nat Turner's insurrection of August 1831 was linked directly to Walker's *Appeal.* Turner's rebellion (due largely to Turner's and others' subsequent mythologization of it) came to be accepted by many as an ingenious enactment of the central American myth of the Declaration insofar as it symbolized an open hostility against corrupt tyranny. The mythic brilliance of Turner's momentous rebellion lay in the fact that it fully "embodied the spirit of the Age of Revolution," especially in his assertion that slaves, like the founding colonists, inherently held a "right of revolution."[17] Moreover, Turner, like Walker before him, continually claimed that he was motivated by a spirit, or "enthusiasm," emanating from God: "the Lord had shewn me things that had happened before my birth. . . . I was intended for some great purpose. . . . [M]y superior judgment . . . was perfected by Divine inspiration. . . . Having soon discovered to be great, I must appear so, and therefore studiously avoided mixing in society, and wrapped myself in mystery, devoting my time to prayer and fasting." [18]

In Turner's depiction of the state of American society, he stands as the prophet of God's judgment announcing in visionary language the coming of a cosmic battle through which a newly ordered America will emerge free and victorious: "there were lights in the sky to which the children of darkness gave other names than what they really were—for they were the lights of the Saviour's hands, stretched forth from east to west, even as they were extended on the cross on Calvary for the redemption of sinners." Turner even asserts that his mission, ordained by God, was announced to the nation via a recent astronomical phenomenon: "the eclipse of the sun last February." An appeal to the heavens as providing signs of God's impending judgment is in keeping with numerous biblical passages that do the same, perhaps most notably the apocalyptic book of Joel. According to Turner, God supposedly scheduled the commencement of judgment on a particularly telling date: "it was intended by us to have begun the work of death on the 4th July last." [19] Turner and Walker have much in common, but I would like to draw particular attention to the way they both conjoin the biblical apocalypse of God's judgment against slavery with the nationalistic celebration of the Declaration. It is of interest, for example, that Turner would assert that God planned to knit into his apocalyptic plan the decidedly powerful American symbol of the Fourth of July. This rather ingenious rhetorical assertion has much in common with the age-old American urge to wed the civil and religious realms, thus making it a classic reformulation of the American jeremiad.

Within the deeply Christian ethos of the antebellum period, rhetors like Turner and Walker hoped to convey that their political agendas were endorsed by the Almighty. However, the construction of the core of American ideology in the antebellum period was hardly limited to participation of African American male speakers and writers. Indeed, the quintessential declaratory enactment was surely that undertaken by John Brown and his fatalistic followers at Harpers Ferry, Virginia, in October 1859.[20] Or at least, that is how countless Northern rhetors attempted to represent Brown and the symbolic effect of his doomed raid. These rhetors included the most prominent abolitionists of the day, including Douglass, Wendell Phillips, and William Lloyd Garrison, as well as many famous literary figures such as Bronson Alcott, Henry Thoreau, Lydia Maria Child, and William Ellery Channing. Elizabeth Cady Stanton, for instance, claimed that she was ready to "consecrate" her own sons "to martyrdom, to die, if need be, bravely like a John Brown." Perhaps Douglass put it most succinctly: "How shall American slavery be abolished? . . . The John Brown way."[21]

This essay will consider briefly the refiguring of Brown by his many supporters. More particularly, I will outline the rhetorical apologia as created by one of Brown's most fervent admirers, Ralph Waldo Emerson, the admirer whose own artistic achievement would in the end have the most profound and far-reaching impact on Brown's refiguring. On the level of public policy, Emerson's endorsement of Brown was tantamount to a confession of personal abolitionist views; but as Len Gougeon and others have recently shown, this view had come forth long before 1859. However, Emerson's endorsement and indeed his mythologization of Brown's raid must be understood as transcending the mere public policy issue of slavery in the United States. Additionally, Emerson's championing of Brown, whose bravery and defiance emphasized the acts of the individual will and the powerful rhetorical effects those acts were capable of having, both responded to and fostered the emerging mythic American ideology, one that itself championed the Declaration of Independence as redemptive entrance into a purely American repentance.

Emerson's initial reaction to the news of Harpers Ferry was hesitant and negative: in a letter to his brother, he opined that Brown had "lost his head."[22] Shortly thereafter, however, Emerson began singing the praises of Brown as Christian martyr and champion of liberty. Indeed, Emerson seemed willingly to romanticize Brown to the level of a prophetic embodiment of a truly American "political religion."[23] This role was one that Brown was fully cognizant of and in fact actively fostered through his words and deeds while jailed. Emerson's powerful evocation of Brown as a representative "true" American simultaneously foregrounded God's violent and apocalyptic judgment upon the sinful South (and the complicit North), Brown's rhetorical connections with the Puritan and Revolutionary fathers, and Brown's embodiment of a "romantic" will to power that responded to a need for a national martyr through whom there might come a national repentance. These themes were not peculiar to Emerson, but in fact were widespread, and they are themes that were prefigured throughout much of Emerson's earlier career. Tellingly, in 1875 Emerson called Brown retrospectively "one of the two best examples of eloquence" in American history (ranking him with the war's other martyred hero, Abraham Lincoln), an opinion that can only make sense if we take into account not so much Brown's writings or speeches but his powerful rhetorical enactment of an American political religion to which his words pointed. Such was the truest kind of eloquence, claimed Emerson, a fact powerfully proven by the subsequent cultural response of Brown's (and Lincoln's) many "hearers."

A key similarity between Turner's rebellion of 1831 and Brown's raid of 1859 is that, coincidentally, both of these cataclysmic events were accompanied by spectacular displays in the skies overhead. Such astronomical phenomena had long been associated by Bible-reading cultures with apocalyptic movements in history. A key verse of Scripture in this regard is Joel 2:30: "I will display wonders in the sky and on the earth. . . . before the great and awesome day of the Lord." Jesus draws upon this crucial passage in describing His second coming (Matt. 24:29–31), and Peter alludes to the same remarks in Acts 2 at the pouring out of the Spirit of God at Pentecost, the definitive signal of a new era.[24] Given such a spiritualized understanding of these phenomena, it was appropriate that Turner should prominently note that his uprising came on the tail of a solar eclipse. Likewise, it seemed particularly inauspicious to many residents of the northeastern United States that throughout the period between the capture of John Brown on October 16 and his execution by hanging on December 2, 1859, "a meteor shower dazzled the Northeast and was widely reported in the press." The *Berkshire County Eagle*, reporting one particularly powerful meteor display, "recalled, as did other newspapers, the Nat Turner insurrection of 1831." As Kent Ljundquist has shown in a brief but fascinating article about this prolonged meteor light show, several major authors, including Herman Melville, Henry Thoreau, and Walt Whitman, were not only aware of the event but likely "responded to the same natural phenomenon by endowing it with metaphysical significance."[25]

Although Ljundquist does not mention Emerson's response, it would be surprising indeed if he were not aware of the meteor displays. Further, if Emerson were to speak of them, one would expect that he, echoing the authors mentioned above, might also endow them with "metaphysical significance." Certainly this attitude is demonstrated at times in his sermons during his public ministry. On at least one occasion, for instance, he refers to the well-known passage from Joel mentioned above when he describes his listener as "stretching forward to an infinite hope, the citizens in trust of a future world. . . . [who] are born to live when the sun has gone down in darkness and the moon is turned to blood" (*CS* 1:60). Like his forebear Jonathan Edwards, Emerson often "suggests that nature is a metaphor for moral conditions," and his sermons are replete with references to a variety of natural phenomena as "expressions of omnipotence" and perhaps warnings of God's coming wrath.[26] Before we discount these as mere religious flourishes from a bygone season of Emerson's youth, I should like to begin my analysis of Emerson's defense of the captured hero by quoting at some length the passage with which Emerson opens his "Speech at a Meeting to Aid John Brown's Family":

> I share the sympathy and the sorrow which has brought us together. Gentlemen who have proceeded me have well said that no wall of separation could here exist. This commanding event that has brought us together,—the sequel of which has brought us together—eclipses all others which have occurred for a long time in our history, and I am very glad to see that this sudden interest in the hero of Harper's Ferry, has provoked an extreme curiosity in all parts of the republic, in regards to the details of his history. Every anecdote is eagerly sought, and I do not wonder that gentlemen find traits of relation readily between him and themselves. One finds a relation in the church, another in the profession, another in the places of his birth. He was happily a representative of the American public. Captain John Brown is a farmer, fifth in descent from Peter Brown, who came to Plymouth in the Mayflower, in 1620. All the six have been farmers. His grandfather, of Simsbury, Connecticut, was a captain in the Revolution. . . .
>
> He believes in two articles—two instruments, shall I say—The Golden Rule and the Declaration of Independence [applause]; and he used this expression in conversation here. "Better that a whole generation of men, women and children should pass away by a violent death, than that one word of either should be violated in this country." There is a Unionist. (AW 117–18)

In stating that the "commanding event" of Brown's raid "eclipses" by its cosmic significance all other recent political events in America, it is probable that Emerson is here alluding to the contemporary heavenly signs just as Melville, Thoreau, and Whitman did. It becomes even more probable when we consider that the date of the speech, November 18, 1859, came immediately after a massive fireball over northeastern skies. The appearance of the dazzling sight on November 15 was covered extensively in papers published on November 17: the *Boston Atlas and Daily Bee* of that date, for instance, in a story headlined "A Startling Meteoric Display in New York," described the display in biblical proportions as "a fiery scimitar, or the flaming sword that, in the hands of the avenging angel, drove our first parents out of Eden." [27] The wording is suggestive of various scriptural passages such as Isaiah 34:4: "My sword is satiated in heaven, Behold, it shall descend for judgment upon Edom, And upon the people whom I have devoted to destruction. The sword of the Lord is filled with blood."

More generally, Emerson's opening passage is remarkable in that it brings together a number of the important themes that he developed throughout his defense of John Brown, his rhetorical fight against slavery, and even earlier in his often-ignored sermons of his ministry at Second Church in Boston.[28] Besides the apocalyptic sense of God's impending judgment that is invoked by references to signs in the heavens such as the meteor, three other thematic features are most prominent here and throughout Emerson's material on Brown. Together, these features form the framework of Emerson's conception of an American political religion.

First, Emerson insists that Brown is a Puritan New Englander. He misrepresents Brown in this respect, however, when he states that his descendent Peter Brown came over on the Mayflower in 1620; this had become a rather common mistake about Brown that Emerson (and Thoreau) had accepted and propagated uncritically.[29] As one historian has noted, these are merely a few of a long "series of exaggerations and extrapolations which leads Emerson to 'transcend' the historical facts toward his ultimate apotheosis of John Brown, the transcendental hero."[30] Emerson goes on to call Brown's courage an example of "perfect puritan faith" much the same as the faith that brought "his fifth ancestor to Plymouth Rock." These comments find their precedent in a reverence for Puritan New England, a theme seen throughout Emerson's antislavery speeches, and indeed a noticeable element as early as his sermons of 1826–32. Emerson's connection to and development of the Puritan tradition can be seen throughout much of his career, particularly his use of the mode of the jeremiad, and his ardent inclusion of a fictive Puritan connection in his defense of Brown would only seem to reemphasize this connection.[31] Emerson's jeremiadic scorn regarding the fallenness of Boston as symbol is a central aspect of his "Address to the Citizens of Concord" in 1851: "the fame of Boston . . . the eloquence of the Christian pulpit, the stoutness of Democracy, the respectability of the Whig party, are all combined to kidnap [the runaway slave]" (*AW* 56). The strong emphasis on the wedding of civil and religious law, a major theme of the jeremiad mode of Puritan rhetoric, is seen throughout the speeches: "[America is] a Republic professing to base its laws on liberty, and on the doctrines of Christianity" (*AW* 92); "[Boston is] the heart of Puritan traditions in an intellectual country" (*AW* 93); "every man of worth in New England loves his virtues. . . . [W]e confide the defence of a life so precious, to all honorable men and true patriots, and to the Almighty Maker of men" (*AW* 110). In summary, says Emerson, Brown is "a fair specimen of the best stock of New England. . . . Our farmers were Orthodox Calvinists, mighty in the Scriptures"; and archetypal Brown, like David and several of the other Old Testament prophets, as a boy was "set to keep sheep . . . bareheaded and barefooted, and clothed in buckskin" (AW 122, 121). In describing Brown, Emerson crucially draws upon the "cult of the Puritan Fathers," and in so doing he succeeds in revitalizing "the Puritan prophecy of America redeemed in time and place: He declares that 'the fear of God in the community . . . is the salt that keeps the community clean' and is the very 'foundation' of society." [32]

Second, and related to the concept of Brown as Puritan New Englander, Emerson emphasizes Brown as spokesperson for American political religion by underscoring his prophetic office as defender of the Declaration. In the lengthy quotation above from the speech of November 18 in "Meeting to Aid John Brown's Family," Emerson claims that Brown believed in only "two articles—two instruments, shall I say—The Golden Rule and the Declaration of Independence" (AW 118). A short time later in the same speech, Emerson invites his listeners to identify strongly with Brown's political and religious philosophy, appealing to "every man who loves the Golden Rule and the Declaration of Independence" (AW 119). Emerson's conjoining of the preeminent creed of the New Testament with the fundamental dogma of the American nation is another rhetorical act of political religion. It is worth noting the cagy use of the term "instrument" with regard to the Declaration: this legal term is suggestive of the philosophical battle at the time over the Declaration's actual status as a legal instrument, an argument being made by various important affirmers of the Declaration, including Abraham Lincoln. "Instrument" as a term is also suggestive of Brown's frequent claim that he was an "instrument in the hands of God." [33] Finally, this important speech ends with a third reference to the idealistic document of liberty and equality: Emerson praises "A Vermont judge, Hutchinson, who has a Declaration of Independence in his heart" (AW 120). By ascribing to a particular person the characteristic of having fully internalized the Declaration, Emerson is suggesting that this sacred American document, like the Gospel, can be "inscribed" on a person's heart: "I will put My Laws upon their heart, And upon their mind I will write them" (Heb. 10:16; see also Jer. 31:34).

Emerson's invocation of and reverence for the Declaration in this central speech only repeats his emphasis on it earlier in his career. Such rhetorical flourishes hearken back to the sermons, such as the magnificent July Fourth oration delivered on July 5, 1829, at Second Church:

It has pleased God in His providence to distinguish our country in great and important respects. Fifty three prosperous years have elapsed since the Declaration of American Independence. . . . the Christian has peculiar reason to rejoice in an event that he can't help regarding as the fruit of Christianity. . . . I cannot but rejoice that our anniversary is full of honour, is the memorial of virtue of a self-devoted Christian struggle, where a whole people sympathized and suffered, and many a noble martyr gave up the ghost—*for a principle.* (*CS* 1:312)

Perhaps the most powerful reference to the Declaration, and certainly a passage that is a tour de force among all of Emerson's antislavery writings, is in the "Fugitive Slave Law" oration of 1854: "You must be citadels and warriors, yourselves Declarations of Independence, the charter, the battle, and the victory" (AW 83). It is a classic Emersonian figure and is similar to a figure employed by ex-slaves such as Frederick Douglass in naming the practical actions taken by slaves to free themselves and to assert their humanity: runaway slaves are patriots who "acted out the Declaration of Independence."[34] In addition, Emerson's statement alludes to the announcements of Jesus Christ of His own status as incarnation of the transcendent: "I am the Bread of Life"; "I am the resurrection and the life"; "before Abraham was, I AM" (John 6:35, 11:25, 8:58). Just as Christ implores His followers to manifest the truth of His gospel, Emerson challenges his listeners to incarnate the Declaration. Tellingly, he follows up this bold proclamation with a quote from Cromwell: "We can only resist the superior training of the king's soldiers, by having godly men." This reference both underlines the power of godliness over secular military and political might as well as again placing Emerson's resistance to slavery squarely within a Puritan tradition.

Third, Emerson sketches Brown as a sort of general embodiment of idealism, romantic action, and the will to power. Emerson, like his friend Thomas Carlyle, can be understood as a spokesman for the romantic commitment to a gospel of power that is in direct confrontation with its greatest enemy: "a world in which 'ennui'—lack of will—had become a major threat to human action."[35] A "de-transcendentalized" version of Emerson would stress his desire to engage directly with society and its ills, thereby transforming it; it is of course a version that is in direct contrast with the more traditionally "transcendental" Emerson of introspection, disengagement, and mystical individualism.[36] Just as the Declaration reprimanded the tangible political and economic tyrannies imposed by the King of England, Emerson rebuked the conformity and cowardice he witnessed among his ostensibly democratic and Christian fellow citizens in the new nation. Emerson's anger, which seethed against the patriarchal, deadened formality of the Unitarian religious tradition, has long been the subject of scholarly attention: for instance, according to Joel Porte, Emerson suffered from a "sublime discontent" that finally issued, in the summer of 1838, in Emerson's "self-definition through defiance and dissent." [37]

Finally, and again like the original Declaration, Emersonian ideals must issue in action, often violent in nature. As Bertram Wyatt-Brown puts it, for Emerson, Brown had "reanimated the spirit of Yankee idealism by violence"; Brown's raid had "endowed antislavery with a virility that its long association with Sunday school ethics, missions to the 'heathen,' women's causes of temperance and equality, and the New England 'priestcraft' had seemed to deny." [38] This virility, or what one historian has called Brown's association with a "cult of martial virtues," is perhaps best exemplified by Brown's obsession with several heirlooms that he commandeered from Lewis Washington, great-grandson of George Washington's half brother: a sword presented to the first president by Frederick the Great and several pistols given by Lafayette. Brown clung to these items, hoping thereby to be associated with the revolutionary hero. [39] "This veneration of the martial virtues . . . created myths from historical events. . . . [and] had a profound impact on the historiography of Brown's raid, elevating the untutored, distracted author of that military fiasco into a symbol of martial heroism." [40] Much of Emerson's response to Brown derived from a veneration of violent action and martial virtue.

In addition, Emerson admired Brown as a personification of moral action, which he considered the essence of Christianity. He had long since rejected historic Christian dogma; nevertheless, he always "continued to find great importance in the 'uses' of his first hero—and still representative 'great man'": Jesus Christ. [41] Emerson's direct comparison of the heroic captain with Jesus, as it turned out, was the aspect of his material on Brown that proved by far the most controversial, for obvious reasons. In his Boston lecture of November 8, 1859, entitled "Courage," Emerson made a statement about Brown similar to if not identical to the following: "[He is] The Saint, whose fate yet hangs in suspense, but whose martyrdom, if it shall be perfected, will make the gallows as glorious as the cross." In fact, it is not altogether clear what Emerson actually said; and yet the wording is crucial because it has to do with Emerson's comparison of Brown to Jesus on the cross. Did he say "as glorious as" the cross, as was widely reported; or did he simply say that Brown would make the gallows "glorious, like a cross," as most early historians had it? [42] For most of today's readers, the offense of the metaphor seems slight; but for staid New Englanders and other Northerners in 1859, such remarks were cataclysmic indeed. Emerson, when challenged by an acquaintance for the exact wording, cagily replied, "That's about what I said": he seemed to understand the significance of the allegation and couched his response accordingly. [43]

In any event, this single remark initiated a highly inflammatory attack from many quarters against the already controversial public figure. Emerson was labeled an "anti-slavery fanatic" by the *Boston Post*, and his well-known comparison of Brown with Jesus brought him much notoriety during a lecture tour in Ohio and Indiana during February and March of 1860. [44] The *Cincinnati Enquirer* of Feb. 1, 1860, considered Emerson's elevation of Brown "blasphemous," "traitorous," and "a public scandal," and demanded a boycott of his lecture in that city. [45] His appearance in Lafayette, Indiana, later in the same week raised a similar ruckus: "A disposition to startle by clap trap and *ad captandum* expressions is charged upon him. It will be recollected that his glorification of John Brown, in which he asserted. . . . that his execution had rendered the scaffold no less sacred than the cross, called forth some very severe rebukes from the press of the country." [46] The upshot of these selections is the fact that Emerson's remarks had by this time been widely publicized throughout the North, marking him as a key witness of the work of John Brown. Furthermore, and more to the point, Emerson's mythologized version of Brown had become widely associated with a questionable, perhaps even blasphemous attempt to raise him to the level of religious hero, like Jesus. Significantly, Emerson's rhetorical constructions were severely attacked in many news accounts as such: they were seen by many as little more than "clap trap and *ad captandum* expressions." For Emerson, however, the association with Jesus was crucial to an understanding of Brown's greatness as a romantic hero of moral action.

More generally Emerson's cumulative remarks about his fallen hero characterize Brown as the incarnation of the American political religion, and to that end he defends Brown in Christlike terms as the quintessential "Unionist." Brown is able, unlike most men, to "use [his] eyes to see the fact behind the form" (*AW* 119), a point that emphasizes Brown's spiritual sight through revelation of the Spirit: "buy from me . . . eyesalve to anoint your eyes, that you may see" (Rev. 3:18; see also I Cor. 2:10). Brown, according to Emerson, typifies "the love that casts out fear" (*AW* 123), an allusion to John's claim that "There is no fear in love; but perfect love casts out fear" (I John 2:18). Finally, Emerson compares Brown's teachings favorably with those of Jesus in the following pregnant passage about Brown's reverence for "The Golden Rule and the Declaration of Independence": regarding these as co-equal codes, it is "Better that a whole generation of men, women and children should pass away by a violent death, than that one word of either should be violated in this country." Brown's allusion in this stylized quotation is to Jesus' Sermon on the Mount, wherein He argues that He "did not come to abolish the Law, but to fulfill it": "not the smallest letter or stroke shall pass away. . . . Whoever then annuls one of the least of these commandments, and so teaches others, shall be called least in the kingdom" (Matt. 5:17–19).

The upshot of Brown's revision and expansion of this passage (and of Emerson's deployment of it in this key speech) is to elevate the Declaration to a position comparable to God's transcendent Law, and to prophesy that the violation of the Declaration, like the violation of the Law, will bring about the vengeful wrath of a holy and blameless God. Tellingly, the promise of bloody reprisal showed that "even in a hotbed of transcendentalism such as Concord, the American taste for violence was evident."[47] In Emerson's view, this joining of the sacred words of Jesus and the by-now sacred Declaration of the Revolutionary fathers constitutes the ultimate task of the politically religious patriot: "There is a Unionist," Emerson declares; and thus Brown, now "happily" mythologized into "a representative of the American republic," "the founder of Liberty" who like Jesus is be honored for his "singleness of purpose," a "romantic character absolutely without vulgar trait; living to ideal ends," is metamorphosed into a new messiah who "eclipses" all other incarnations of the American political religion (AW 117, 121, 122, 117). These lengthy passages from "Speech at a Meeting To Aid John Brown's Family" show why that oration deserves to be ranked as the most powerful Emersonian statement on John Brown. Furthermore, its concise yet rhetorically sophisticated elaboration of Emerson's view of an American political religion supports its elevation to an even higher status than it has previously been given among Emerson's writings.

Given such a reappraisal of these antislavery pieces, one is confronted with an eagerly social Emerson. Recent Emerson scholarship has been preoccupied with the paradox of the Transcendental Emerson vis à vis the social Emerson, a conflict that broaches the question of whether Emersonian "dissent" can have any social consequence, or whether such an attitude is merely "aesthetic dissent" with no social effect. For example, John Carlos Rowe, in the opening section of his recent *At Emerson's Tomb*, plainly states that "Transcendentalism reveals itself to be at fundamental odds with the social reforms. . . . Emersonian transcendentalism and political activism in mid-nineteenth-century America were inherently incompatible." Specifically, he rejects Sacvan Bercovitch's concept of an "enabling, fundamentally poetic 'paradox' at the heart of Emerson's thought"; more generally, Rowe brings up what has become a crucial obsession of Emerson studies. While the dispute will surely go on, my own suggestion for retreat from this seeming quagmire of critical paradox is suggested in another comment made by Rowe: "Emerson's political writings from 1844 to 1863 remain so profoundly divided internally between transcendentalist values and practical politics as to be practically useless, except as far as the value of their political rhetoric might be measured."[48] This is precisely the point, and Rowe's wording here betrays the fact that he has underestimated the significance of his own offhand remarks. While he claims that Emerson's political writings were "useless," the "except" points to the one undeniable value that they surely had. Rowe is understatedly correct in seeking the value of Emerson's political rhetoric and how it might be measured. Again, the Geertzian concept of religion as a system of "symbols which . . . establish powerful, pervasive, and long-lasting moods and motivations" is directly related to Emerson's political speeches and writings, even more so in light of his enlistment and depiction of an emergent American myth centered on political religion.[49]

Emerson can be considered more of a religionist than a philosopher— or, more precisely, a political religionist. This phrase joins the transcendental with the practical, just as Emerson's social commentary often did, and it is in this direction that a possible solution to the problem posed by Rowe and others may be found. Rather than trying to solve what appears to be a false dilemma regarding the "true" interpretation of Emerson (is he Transcendentalist or social reformer?), we would do better to embrace the ambivalence itself as inherently American and as inherently Emersonian. In this sense, Emersonian wrestling with the sacred versus the secular or the transcendental versus the practical and social is very much like the earlier "Puritan dilemma" encountered by John Winthrop, sketched so ably by Edmund Morgan, and suggested recently as a key to understanding Emerson by Wesley Mott.[50] Indeed, as Mott has argued, it is not too much to claim that the "sermons and their legacy reveal that Emerson's place in the Puritan tradition is even more central than has been supposed."[51] Much the same can be stated about Emerson's defense of, and perhaps even poetic obsession with, the beleaguered Captain John Brown.

A view of Emerson that focuses on his "de-transcendentalized" nature is no more accurate than one that speaks solely of his transcendental aspects. Emerson embraced both poles of the paradox. Surely this is why, in 1875, he ranked Brown with Lincoln retrospectively as "the two best examples of eloquence" in American history. Like Lincoln, Brown sealed his fate as Transcendental hero with a violent and public death that emerged as ameliorative martyrdom. Both were committed to identical idealistic and sacred written creeds, particularly the Declaration of Independence and the Sermon on the Mount. Such was the truest kind of eloquence, claimed Emerson; and its essence was its ability to join such transcendent idealism with public practice. Rowe is surely correct to point out that Emerson's political writings were "profoundly divided internally"; yet Emerson championed Brown and Lincoln precisely because their rhetorical speeches and acts were able to join both realms. Each quintessentially expressed and incarnated the American political religion as envisioned by Emerson. Not only did each echo the call of Jesus to "lay down your lives" for the sake of the gospel Americana, but both became sacramental and sacrificial "doers of the word" by fully enacting their idealized love through death. Symbolically, they marked the beginning and the end of the War of Secession to an almost uncanny extent. Brown's prophetic entrance upon the scene was announced by the skyward brilliance of the meteor showers; Lincoln was fatally wounded on Good Friday less than a week after the surrender, and passed heavenward on Easter Sunday. Brown and Lincoln thus became the key postmortem participants in a deeply American root paradigm of martyrdom and sainthood that itself was rooted in the life, death, and resurrection of Jesus.[52]

Such root paradigms, by extension, allow us to get at "the fundamental assumptions that undergird society."[53] The assumptions being made about John Brown by many prominent Americans at the time of his death, including but certainly not limited to Emerson, indicate a strong desire to bridge the gap presupposed by the Puritan dilemma. These observers were aware that "only John Brown actually brought insurrectionary action and antinomian ideals together as a conscious, aggressive, and dynamic part of the abolitionist movement."[54] Bronson Alcott memorialized Brown in similarly paradigmatic terms at a sympathy meeting in Boston on the evening of December 2, 1859, a meeting which was attended by Emerson, Thoreau, and many others:

> O Patriot True! O Christian meek and brave!
> Throned in the martyr's seat henceforth shall sit;
> Prophet of God! Messiah of the slave![55]

Whatever else we might notice about these exemplary remarks of the time, Alcott fundamentally desired to link Brown's work as "Patriot true" with his character as "Christian," "martyr," "Prophet," and "Messiah." In so doing, and in so echoing the previous rhetorics being fashioned by Emerson, Thoreau, Douglass, Phillips, Garrison, Cady Stanton, and many others, and indeed anticipating the subsequent tropes of Lincoln and a cast of thousands, Alcott betrayed his deep attachment to what can only be considered the root paradigm of the distinctly American political religion. Above all, Americans must be "doers of the Word" and thereby fully enact the American political religion.

NOTES

1. Henry Wadsworth Longfellow, "A Psalm of Life" [1838], *The Norton Anthology of American Literature*, 2nd ed., ed. Nina Baym et al. (New York: Norton, 1985), 1319–20.

2. Frederick Douglass, *The Life and Writings of Frederick Douglass*, vol. 2, ed. Philip Foner (New York: International, 1950–75), 188.

3. Karlyn Kohrs Campbell, "Style and Content in the Rhetoric of Early Afro-American Feminists," *Quarterly Journal of Speech* 72 no. 4 (Nov. 1986): 435, 444.

4. See Harold K. Bush Jr., *American Declarations: Rebellion and Repentance in American Cultural History* (Urbana: University of Illinois Press, 1999).

5. Dorothy Sterling, *We Are Your Sisters: Black Women in the Nineteenth Century* (New York: Norton, 1983), 105. Similar points are made in Nancy Cott, *The Bonds of Womenhood* (New Haven: Yale Univ. Press, 1977).

6. Carla L. Peterson, *"Doers of the Word": African-American Women Speakers and Writers in the North (1830–1880)* (New York: Oxford Univ. Press, 1995), 3.

7. David Simpson, ed., *German Aesthetic and Literary Criticism: Kant, Fichte, Schelling, Schopenhauer, Hegel* (New York: Cambridge Univ. Press, 1984), 161. See also p. 80: "The general tendency observable in the history of philosophy between Kant and Hegel or Schopenhauer [is] roughly speaking a movement from an emphasis on knowledge to an emphasis on will."

8. Richard F. Lovelace, *Dynamics of Spiritual Life: An Evangelical Theology of Renewal* (Downers Grove, IL: InterVarsity, 1979), 232–35. General surveys of antebellum Wesleyan-style revivalism are documented in Timothy L. Smith, "Righteousness and Hope: Christian Holiness and the Millennial Vision of America, 1800–1900," *American Quarterly* 31 (spring 1979): 180–98; William G. McLoughlin, *Revivals, Awakenings, and Reform: An Essay on Religion and Social Change in America, 1607–1977* (Chicago: University of Chicago Press, 1978); Perry Miller, *The Life of the Mind in America: From the Revolution to the Civil War* (New York: Harcourt Brace, 1965), 49–58, 64–84; and Robert Handy, *A Christian America: Protestant Hopes and Historical Realities* (London: Oxford Univ. Press, 1971).

9. This concept is fleshed out in great detail in my book *American Declarations*, where I refer to it as the American *Metanoia*.

10. See Celeste Michelle Condit and John Louis Lucaites, *Crafting Equality: America's Anglo-African Word* (Chicago: University of Chicago Press, 1993), esp. 77.

11. See John M. Werner, *Reaping the Bloody Harvest: Race Riots in the United States during the Age of Jackson 1824–1849* (New York: Garland, 1986), esp. 299.

12. Werner, *Reaping the Bloody Harvest*, 18.

13. Ripley et al., "Introduction," 19.

14. David Walker, *David Walker's Appeal, in Four Articles; Together with a Preamble, to the Coloured Citizens of the World, But in Particular, and Very Expressly, to Those of The United States of America*, [1829] (New York: Hill and Wang, 1965), 2.

15. *David Walker's Appeal*, 14.

16. Eric Sundquist has described the resonant image of Haiti as "the trope of San Domingo," a signifier that had become by 1829 "the fearful precursor of black rebellion throughout the New World. . . . a prophetic simulacrum of events feared to lie on the horizon of American slavery." See Sundquist, *To Wake the Nations: Race and the Making of American Literature* (Cambridge: Belknap Press, 1993), 32.

17. Sundquist, *To Wake the Nations*, 36, 47. Sundquist goes on to describe Turner's accomplishment as peculiarly American in the sense of Emersonian "representativeness": "In his rhetorical crusade against slavery . . . or even in his millenarian uprising against it . . . the slave rebel, one could say, became most American." See also Edmund S. Morgan, *The Challenge of the American Revolution* (New York: Norton, 1976), esp. 139–73. Turner, who deployed "the accents of the Declaration of Independence and the Rights of Man," openly appealed to the reigning ideologies of the American Revolution in justifying his violent acts; see Eugene Genovese, *From Rebellion to Revolution: Afro-American Slave Revolts in the Making of the New World* (New York: Random House, 1979), 49.

18. See the "Confessions of Nat Turner" taken from Henry Irving Tragle, ed., *The Southhampton Slave Revolt of 1831: A Compilation of Source Material* (Amherst: University of Massachusetts Press, 1971), 306ff. Quotes above are from pp. 306–7. I shall also simply state my affinities with Sundquist's basic view of Turner's controversial "authorship" of this text, the intricacies of which are beyond the scope of this chapter. In short, I agree that Turner, to an unknowable extent, did assert some authority over the transcribed text published by Thomas Gray, and the text he helped create must be considered to some degree a highly ingenious rhetorical performance with certain political ends in mind.

19. "Confessions of Nat Turner," 309, 310.

20. The variant spelling of the town (Harpers or Harper's) continues to be problematic, and I will use the former throughout this essay.

21. Paul Finkelman, "Manufacturing Martyrdom: The Antislavery Response to John Brown's Raid," in Finkelman, ed., *His Soul Goes Marching On: Responses to John Brown and the Harpers Ferry Raid* (Charlottesville: University of Virginia Press, 1995), 61, 60.

22. Ralph L. Rusk, *The Life of Ralph Waldo Emerson* (New York: Columbia Univ. Press, 1957), 408.

23. The concept of an American political religion has a long and somewhat checkered past: in particular, basic discussion can be found in Robert Bellah, "Civil Religion in America," *Daedalus* 96 (1967): 1–21. This conception of religion owes a debt to Clifford Geertz, who defined religion as "(1) a system of symbols which acts to (2) establish powerful, pervasive, and long-lasting moods and motivations in men by (3) formulating conceptions of a general order of existence and (4) clothing those concepts with such an aura of factuality that (5) the moods and motivations seem uniquely real": see Geertz, *The Interpretation of Cultures: Selected Essays* (New York: Basic Books, 1973), 90. Thus Geertz, by describing "a system of symbols which acts," is closely aligning the work of religion with the rhetorical process of "enactment" as defined by Campbell.

24. Numerous other biblical passages along these thematic lines might here be mentioned, including many allusions to heavenly wonders throughout the Book of Revelation. The mass suicide in March 1997 by the so-called Heaven's Gate cult in southern California is a shocking reminder of the powerful resonance that the appearance of such heavenly phenomena, in that case the Hale-Bopp comet, still is capable of commanding among participants of various strands of American culture. For further elaboration about America's historic and continuing fascination with "signs in the heavens above," see Daniel Wojcik, *The End of the World as We Know It: Faith, Fatalism, and Apocalypse in America* (New York: New York Univ. Press, 1997), esp. pp. 175–208.

25. See Kent Ljundquist, "'Meteor of the War': Melville, Thoreau, and Whitman Respond to John Brown," *American Literature* 61 no. 4 (Dec. 1989): 675, 676, 675.

26. Wesley T. Mott, *"The Strains of Eloquence": Emerson and His Sermons* (University Park: Pennsylvania State Univ. Press, 1989), 130. The theme of "nature as a metaphor for moral conditions," of course, prefigures much of Emerson's later works, including *Nature*.

27. Ljundquist, "'Meteor of the War," 677.

28. See Mott, *"The Strains of Eloquence"*, especially 113–42; and Susan L. Roberson, *Emerson in His Sermons: A Man-Made Self* (Columbia: University of Missouri Press, 1995).

29. On this mistake (based partly on Brown's own studied art of deception), see Gilbert Ostrander, "Emerson, Thoreau, and John Brown," *Mississippi Valley Historical Review* 39 (1953): 722; and Oswald Garrison Villard, *John Brown, 1800–1859: A Biography Fifty Years Later* (Boston, 1910), 10.

30. John J. McDonald, "Emerson and John Brown," *New England Quarterly* 44 (1971): 382.

31. On Emerson's use of the jeremiadic mode in the sermons, see Mott, *"The Strains of Eloquence"*, esp. 127–29 and 151–55.

32. Mott, *"The Strains of Eloquence"*, 155.

33. Bertram Wyatt-Brown, "'A Volcano Beneath a Mountain of Snow': John Brown and the Problem of Interpretation," in Finkelman, ed., *His Soul Goes Marching On*, 22.

34. Frederick Douglass, *Frederick Douglass' Paper*, Sept. 29, 1854.

35. Michael Lopez, "Transcendental Failure: 'The Palace of Spiritual Power,'" in Joel Porte, ed., *Emerson: Retrospect and Prospect* (Cambridge: Harvard Univ. Press, 1982), 129.

36. A summary and analysis of recent attempts to "de-transcendentalize" Emerson is in Michael Lopez, "De-Transcendentalizing Emerson," *ESQ* 34 no. 1 and 2 (1988): 77–139; a much briefer and earlier discussion of this trend is in Lawrence Buell, "The Emerson Industry in the 1980's: A Survey of Trends and Achievements," *ESQ* 30 no. 2 (1984): 123–29. Also see T. Gregory Garvey, "Two Faces of Emerson: A Review of Recent Books," *College Literature* 25 no. 1 (winter 1998), 261–75.

37. For a reading of Emerson as heroic leader of a revolutionary war against patriarchy and champion of antinomianism, see Joel Porte, *Representative Man: Ralph Waldo Emerson in His Time* (New York: Oxford Univ. Press, 1979). Barbara Packer, in *Emerson's Fall: A New Interpretation of the Major Essays* (New York: Continuum, 1982), emphasizes Emerson's essays as contending with the stultifying fears and intellectual tyrannies that plagued antebellum American culture, especially in light of such idealistic statements as the Declaration and the Bill of Rights. General information about this crucial period of Emerson's life is found in Rusk, *Life of Emerson*, 249–74; Gay Wilson Allen, *Waldo Emerson: A Biography* (New York: Viking, 1981), 268–318; John McAleer, *Ralph Waldo Emerson: Days of Encounter* (Boston: Little, Brown, 1984), 234–70; and Maurice Gonnaud, *An Uneasy Solitude* (Princeton: Princeton Univ. Press, 1987), 236–47. The quote is from Porte, 91.

38. Bertram Wyatt-Brown, *Yankee Saints and Southern Sinners* (Baton Rouge: LSU Press 1985), 125.

39. Robert E. McGlone, "Forgotten Surrender: John Brown's Raid and the Cult of Martial Virtues,' *Civil War History* 60 no. 3 (1994): 189, 192.

40. McGlone, "Forgotten Surrender," 187.

41. Mott, *"The Strains of Eloquence"*, 32.

42. A brief recapitulation of this controversy is provided in McDonald, "Emerson and John Brown," 386–87; see especially footnotes 27–29. Len Gougeon also remarks on this controversy in his historical background in *AW* xlvii.

43. McDonald, "Emerson and John Brown," 387.

44. Gougeon, *AW* xlvii. See also David Mead, *Yankee Eloquence in the Middle West* (East Lansing: Michigan State Univ. Press, 1951), 48–49.

45. Mead, *Yankee Eloquence*, 49.

46. *Lafayette Daily Journal*, February 4, 1860.

47. Wyatt-Brown, "Volcano," 23.

48. John Carlos Rowe, *At Emerson's Tomb: The Politics of Classic American Literature* (New York: Columbia Univ. Press, 1997), 21, 24, 22.

49. Geertz, *Interpretation of Cultures*, 90. For extensive discussion of the rhetorical power of Emerson's vision on 1854 Boston, see *TAB* 322–33.

50. Edmund S. Morgan, *The Puritan Dilemma: The Story of John Winthrop* (Boston: Little, Brown, 1958). Mott refers to Morgan's version of Winthrop in *"The Strains of Eloquence"*, 114.

51. Mott, *"The Strains of Eloquence"*, 143.

52. See Charles Joyner, "'Guilty of Holiest Crime': The Passion of John Brown," in Finkelman, ed., *His Soul Goes Marching On*, 296–334. See in particular 299–301, where Joyner draws upon the cultural anthropological works of Victor Turner to build upon his theory of "root paradigm." Turner's important discussion of this concept, along with an extensive development of his influential theory of "social drama," is found in *Dramas, Fields, and Metaphors: Symbolic Action in Human Society* (Ithaca: Cornell Univ. Press, 1974).

53. Joyner, "'Guilty of Holiest Crime,'" 301.

54. Wyatt-Brown, *Yankee Saints and Southern Sinners*, 103.

55. Joyner, "'Guilty of Holiest Crime,'" 315.

Part Four

EMERSON'S THOUGHT AND THE PUBLIC SPHERE

DAVID M. ROBINSON

Emerson's "American Civilization": Emancipation and the National Destiny

EMERSON BASED HIS EARLY THOUGHT on the soul's direct experience of divinity and portrayed with dramatic intensity the arrival of moments of illumination and sudden spiritual insight. By the early 1840s he came to recognize the tenuous, unpredictable nature of these experiences and the unstable quality that they brought to the individual's ability to sustain an ongoing purpose and faith. His dissatisfaction with the "flash-of-lightning faith" (*cw* 1:213) based on moments of ecstatic but unpredictable illumination grew during the 1840s, yielding a new orientation toward social relationships, ethical action, and political reform. By the 1850s this shift had resulted in a much more pragmatic and action-oriented philosophy and had brought his focus increasingly to bear on political criticism and the analysis of broader social trends. This new emphasis is apparent in *English Traits* (1856) and *The Conduct of Life* (1860) and in several political addresses prompted by his increasing concern over the slavery issue.[1]

Even though he had distinguished himself as an advocate of self-reliance and radical individualism, he found it more and more necessary to address the social aspects of experience in his later works and to take with increasing seriousness the questions of social organization and social processes. These questions had been pressed on him in the 1840s by friends such as Bronson Alcott, George Ripley, Margaret Fuller, and William Henry Channing, whose interests in utopian communal experiments and forms of radical social theory such as Fourierism set the tone for much of the later discourse of the Transcendentalist movement.[2]

The growing national debate over slavery in the 1850s converged with

Emerson's own reorientation toward social theory, and he began to think about the political imperatives of the slavery impasse and to place the American crisis in larger historical terms, recognizing the continued existence of slavery as a test of the broader moral principles that were the foundation of the democracy. As Eduardo Cadava has argued, "For Emerson, America's unredeemed sin is the persistence of slavery in a nation that was to be founded on the virtues of freedom, liberty, and equality."[3] The conflict over slavery therefore had both moral resonance and enormous historical relevance for Emerson, representing a historical turning point at which the progress of human civilization would be weighed. Emerson's attacks on the Fugitive Slave Law in 1851 and 1854 were an immediate reaction to what he viewed as a dangerous expansion of pro-slavery power; they are impressive oratorical performances, suggesting the depth of his emotional engagement in the politics of antislavery. As the war broke out, he explored the significance of that historical moment in "American Civilization" (1862), a work that shows the interplay of immediate political events and a more comprehensive philosophy of history in his later social thought. The essay establishes an historical framework from which slavery can be viewed and builds to an argument for immediate emancipation, a policy that Emerson presented as both a moral and a political necessity.

"American Civilization" was published in the April 1862 issue of the *Atlantic Monthly*, predating Lincoln's decision on emancipation the following September. In Emerson's *Complete Works* we find the essay divided into two parts. The first part was included as "Civilization" in *Society and Solitude* (1870), a volume published by Emerson after the war and included as the seventh volume of the Centenary Edition of his *Complete Works*. The concluding part appears as "American Civilization" in *Miscellanies*, a collection of his occasional pieces that comprise the eleventh volume of his *Complete Works*. In *Society and Solitude*, "Civilization" helps to complete the depiction of the varied human activity and interaction that Emerson saw as the context for ethical decision making on the part of the individual. The relation of work and technological innovation to moral aspiration is an important theme in *Society and Solitude*, and also in his later work as a whole, where it provides in part his answer to the spiritual malaise that he recorded so memorably in "Experience."

But in *Society and Solitude* only implicit allusions to the repressive and antidemocratic tendencies of the slaveholding South remain in Emerson's more general descriptions of the nature of civilization. Only when we examine "American Civilization" in its originally published form in the *Atlan-*

tic Monthly can we understand fully the connections between Emerson's general views of civilization and his specific concern over the crisis of slavery. In the essay's original form, Emerson's larger views of history and the development of civilization provide the groundwork for his advocacy of emancipation.

Emerson's decision to exclude much of the specific political commentary on slavery and emancipation in *Society and Solitude* raises some important questions about his reputation and political legacy. As Len Gougeon has persuasively documented, Emerson's political reputation was very much in contest in the last decades of the nineteenth century, claimed both by those who wanted him remembered as an active antislavery spokesman, and others, led by Oliver Wendell Holmes, who played down Emerson's abolitionist ties and presented him as a genteel, essentially apolitical sage (*vh* 1–23). Emerson's decision to divide the essay after its original publication may have contributed, whether intentionally or not, to Holmes's more conservative portrait.

Since Emerson did not publish *Society and Solitude* until 1870, well after the war was over, he may have regarded the discussion of the questions of slavery and emancipation as somewhat dated and irrelevant. But his removal of this part of the essay from his larger portrait of civilization also cohered with his persistent self-identification as a scholar who was a reluctant and in some way inappropriate political spokesman. "I do not often speak to public questions;—they are odious and hurtful, and it seems like meddling or leaving your work," he had confessed at the outset of his 1854 address "The Fugitive Slave Law." "I have my own spirits in prison;—spirits in deeper prisons, whom no man visits if I do not" (*w* 11:217). Reluctant or not, he used his rhetorical gifts to enormous advantage as an antislavery spokesman, and though long neglected, his antislavery work is experiencing a significant revival as interest in his later career converges with new interest in cultural studies, political theory, and a reassessment of American political history. His division of "American Civilization" suggests that his own desire to write "permanent" or theoretical essays, rather than occasional essays on the political conflicts of the day, may have contributed to his underestimation as an antislavery spokesman and progressive political thinker.

Emerson's division of the essay can be useful to us now, however, in suggesting his conception of the relationship between the development of human civilization and the immediate crisis over slavery. Emerson saw the

American political crisis as a crisis in human civilization itself, a conviction that added to his determined commitment to the policy of emancipation. In the first part of the 1862 "American Civilization," the part included in *Society and Solitude*, Emerson defines civilization and lists its key characteristics, noting particularly the "moral" basis of its development. This part of the essay is a broad investigation of the philosophy of human history, an attempt to provide a framework within which we can come to see our individual lives as part of a much larger process of the development of the human race.

He begins by defining civilization as "a certain degree of progress from the rudest state in which man is found," connecting it with "the evolution of a highly organized man, brought to supreme delicacy of sentiment, as in practical power, religion, liberty, sense of honor, and taste" (*Atlantic* 502; *w* 7:19).[4] Admitting a certain vagueness or difficulty in specifying civilization precisely, he admits that "we usually suggest it by negations" (*Atlantic* 502; *w* 7:19), noting, from the perspective of the present, what may be lacking from an individual or culture from the present or the past.

In laying out this definition, Emerson was clearly aware that it might serve to justify and reinforce the status quo. A student of history who had often found examples in the past that reproached the present, he was suspicious of a simplistic assumption that the passage of time could unqualifiedly be equated with progress or that the present was in every aspect better than the past. "I was never for a moment the victim of Enlightenment, or Progress of the Species, or the Diffusion of Knowledge Society" (*JMN* 15:81), he wryly remarked in a late journal entry. Even so, his definition of civilization clearly entails a positive view of human advancement through technology; the burden of his argument is that such technological mastery must be accompanied by political and cultural progress, a kind of progress ultimately deriving from moral principle.

Such considerations of human progress were linked in the nineteenth century to issues of cultural and racial difference, and in the opening of "American Civilization," we can discern Emerson's struggle to clarify these issues for himself. He advances the imperialistic assertion of the superiority and privilege of European culture, but also expresses a recognition of the inevitable difficulties and limitations of that viewpoint. Emerson had considered these issues at some length in his earlier *English Traits*, which contains both a portrayal of Anglo-Saxon superiority and a rejection of the determinative nature of racial qualities and classifications. He recognized that despite the extensive theorizing about racial characteristics at that time, the possibility of the eventual intermingling of the races rendered any fixed categories of racial attributes finally meaningless and any sense of racial hierarchies false. This philosophical consideration was also impelled by his disgust with slavery and the Southern racial ideology that justified it.[5]

Emerson argues that "each nation grows after its own genius, and has a civilization of its own" (*Atlantic* 502; w 7:19), a plea for a measure of cultural tolerance, especially when we consider it in its Civil War context. But we also find there a description of the dynamic of progress in which "the savage tribes do not advance,"[6] the measure of civilization being a kind of adaptability, "a facility of association, power to compare, the ceasing from fixed ideas." In such a process, the aggressively adaptive, technologically oriented modern European exerts a power that can overwhelm other cultures. Emerson chose his illustration from the conflict on the American frontier: "The Indian is gloomy and distressed, when urged to depart from his habits and traditions. He is overpowered by the gaze of the white, and his eye sinks" (*Atlantic* 502; w 7:20). Emerson is much less disturbed or critical about this phenomenon than modern readers would expect or hope, presenting this process of colonization and cultural oppression as an inevitable and ultimately positive process.

As Emerson begins to analyze the nature of civilization further, however, he develops a normative description of human society shaped in important ways by the contemporary crisis over slavery. This version of civilization is deliberately cast so as to exclude the South as a region that has not yet achieved the fundamental goal of civilization. As in the ascending ladder of "uses" in *Nature*, Emerson begins his description of civilization on the level of commodity, presenting the benefits to human life and well-being of such developments as adequate housing, effective transportation, satisfying labor, and the accessibility of knowledge and information. He also specifies the "right position of woman in the State" as a criterion of civilization, though he offers less a defense of equal rights than a justification of the necessity of "the influence of good women" to the success of civilization: "a severe morality gives that essential charm to woman which educates all that is delicate, poetic, and self-sacrificing, breeds courtesy and learning, conversation and wit, in her rough mate" (*Atlantic* 503; w 7:23–24).

Emerson's representation of the role of woman, though positive in some senses, also reinforced the existing hierarchy of the genders, associating power with the male and restraint or reserve with the female. But the discussion does initiate one crucial turn in the essay—the shift from the conception of civilization as material advance to the much more central idea that "there can be no high civility without a deep morality" (*Atlantic* 504; *w* 7:26). Emerson had been aiming his discussion toward this shift, and it emerges as his central argument, given urgency by the slavery crisis. "The evolution of a highly destined society must be moral; it must run in the grooves of the celestial wheels. It must be catholic in aims" (*Atlantic* 504; *w* 7:26). Emerson's language taps subtly into the ideology of American exceptionalism, using the sense of a special mission or high destiny, part of the national psyche since the Puritan migration, as a means of underlining his call for a rededication to moral purpose. Such a call to moral purpose would inevitably have been heard by Emerson's audiences as a call to stay the course in the conflict with the South. Emerson was defining the progress of civilization with America's special destiny and tying that destiny to the end of slavery.

Emerson's association of morality with catholic aims was fundamental to his perspective. "What is *moral?*" he asks. "It is the respecting in action catholic or universal ends" (*Atlantic* 504; *w* 7:27). While there is nothing startling or original in this definition, which Emerson attributes to Kant, it has obvious pertinence to the question of slavery, a system of oppression that exploits many for the benefit of the few. Emerson begins to emphasize the importance of "universal ends" by developing an analogy between technological and moral progress. The use of tools and other strategies to perform work uses a greater-than-human strength, employing in our aid the existing powers of the natural world. "That is the way we are strong, by borrowing the might of the elements. The forces of steam, gravity, galvanism, light, magnets, wind, fire, serve us day by day, and cost us nothing" (*Atlantic* 505; *w* 7:28–29). Material progress, largely the result of technological innovation and social organization, is based in the human capacity to direct the existing power of the natural world to specified human ends.[7] Humans must reach outside themselves to tap into a source of power much greater than they are. "Now that is the wisdom of a man, in every instance of his labor, to hitch his wagon to a star, and see his chore done by the gods themselves" (*Atlantic* 505; *w* 7:28).

This same pattern of seeking beyond the self, Emerson argues, is also the basis of moral action, on both an individual and a social level. "And as our handiworks borrow the elements, so all our social and political action leans on principles. To accomplish anything excellent the will must work for catholic and universal ends" (*Atlantic* 505; *w* 7:29–30). A selfless concern for the larger good is therefore the ethical equivalent of the ingenuity that makes technological innovation possible. Each is a reaching beyond the self, a placing of the self within a power that encompasses it, and thereby empowers it more completely.

In emphasizing the necessity of selfless motives in both personal ethics and effective public policy, Emerson returns to the motto "hitch your wagon to a star" (*Atlantic* 505; W 7:30), infusing it now with a much enlarged meaning of moral aspiration. Actions aimed at mere self-betterment will ultimately be self-limiting; "work rather for those interests which the divinities honor and promote,—justice, love, freedom, knowledge, utility" (*Atlantic* 505; W 7:30). When this principle is applied to public policy, it generates laws and institutions that help to cultivate character, strength, and compassion in its individual citizens. "The true test of civilization is, not the census, nor the size of cities, nor the crops,—no, but the kind of man the country turns out" (*Atlantic* 506; W 7:31). Character and moral direction, not wealth and power, mark the achievements of civilization: "the vital refinements are the moral and intellectual steps" (*Atlantic* 506; W 7:32).

Emerson's argument that civilization is ultimately the product of principle and moral action, and only secondarily the result of technological progress, establishes the basis for an arraignment of the American South. The South has failed Emerson's test of civilization because of its perversion of moral principle and political freedom. It is at this point that "American Civilization" becomes more overtly political, the indictment of the South only implied in the final two paragraphs that Emerson retained in *Society and Solitude*.

Emerson offers a number of tests that can be applied to gauge a nation's civility. These tests constitute a series of de facto indictments of Southern wrongs, and they also carry a note of warning to the North, where intellectual freedom was also threatened by the tensions and divisions of the war. Gougeon describes, for example, Emerson's own experience in being shouted down by hecklers while giving an antislavery address in January 1861, a memory which must have informed his commentary on civilized society.[8] Civilization can thus be indicated by the health of the democratic processes in a society. Can the term "civilized" be applied, Emerson asks, to a country where

> knowledge cannot be diffused without perils of mob-law and statute-law,—
> where speech is not free,—where the post-office is violated, mail-bags opened
> and letters tampered with,—where public debts and private debts outside the
> State are repudiated,—where liberty is attacked in the primary institution of

their social life,—where the position of the white woman is injuriously affected by the outlawry of the black woman,—where the arts, such as they have,
are all imported, having no indigenous life,—where the laborer is not secured
in the earnings of his own hands,—where suffrage is not free or equal? (*Atlantic* 506; w 7:33–34)

"Barbarous" is the term that Emerson applies instead to "that country,"
emphasizing that these violations of justice counteract any material attain-
ments. "No advantages of soil, climate or coast can resist these suicidal
mischiefs" (*Atlantic* 506; w 7:34).

As Emerson brings home the weight of this judgment of the South, his
analysis of civilization converges with his sense of America's immediate crisis. It is here that we see the theoretical analysis of the course of civilization
blend most completely with his thinking about the immediate politics of
the antislavery movement. Certainly this essay confirms that key emphases
of Emerson's later thinking were shaped by his response to the American
political struggle over slavery and that he saw his historical moment as a
unique and crucial one. By linking the day's political crises to the larger
development of human civilization, Emerson was able to give a new authority and urgency to his condemnation of the South and also give a renewed sense of purpose to the larger effort for the emancipation of the
slaves.

Emerson found the link between his broader theory of civilization and
his indictment of the South in the related concepts of use, labor, and service, each of which made an important extension and refinement of the
larger principle of morality as a reaching toward some end beyond the self.[9]
"Use, labor of each for all," he argues, "is the health and virtue of all beings.
ICH DIEN, *I serve*, is a truly royal motto. And it is the mark of nobleness to
volunteer the lowest service,—the greatest spirit only attaining to humility" (*Atlantic* 507; w 11:297). The call to the nobility of voluntary service sanctifies the mission of the newly enlisted Union troops, but it has a
further purpose. In identifying the capacity to serve or to be of use to others with the idea of labor, Emerson lays the groundwork for a depiction of
the Southern slavery system as a perversion of labor, and thus a corruption
of the essential ingredient of the moral health of individuals and of society.
The South's construction and maintenance of the slavery system is an attempt "to reverse the natural sentiments of mankind, and to pronounce
labor disgraceful, and the well-being of a man to consist in eating the fruit
of other men's labor" (*Atlantic* 507; w 11:297). This is a crippling distortion

of the energy necessary for any constructive advance in individual culture or in human civilization.

"There is no interest in any country so imperative as that of labor" (*Atlantic* 507; *w* 11 : 297–98), Emerson declares, embracing in this new context an emphasis that had grown in the later phase of his work. "I like not the man who is thinking how to be good, but the man thinking how to accomplish his work" (*JMN* 15 : 462), he commented in his journal, and this emphasis on work as both a source of revelation and a means of moral measurement had enabled the ethical pragmatism that had become his new source of intellectual authority. In the course of this intellectual reorientation, worship had been redefined in terms of work, a commitment to a task that called for patience, craft, and a dedication that effaced self-consciousness.[10]

Emerson thus emphasized the centrality of labor in defining human experience: "Labor: a man coins himself into his labor,—turns his day, his strength, his thought, his affection into some product which remains as the visible sign of his power." The importance of labor to the well-being of the individual and the larger society placed a particular responsibility on the state: "to protect that, to secure that to him, to secure his past self to his future self, is the object of all government" (*Atlantic* 507; *w* 11 : 297). As Emerson makes clear, the security and ownership of one's labor is fundamental to human identity itself; the theft of that labor is a grave wrong, a violation of human integrity and an obstruction to any development or progress in human civilization.

The theft of labor is also a threat, as he noted pointedly, to the livelihood of the working wage-earner. "All honest men are daily striving to earn their bread by their industry. And who is this who tosses his empty head at this blessing in disguise, the constitution of human nature, and calls labor vile, and insults the faithful workman at his daily toil?" In his attempt to portray the Southern slavery system as a threat to the laborer of the South and the North, Emerson even resorts to a racist reference to the eventuality of "servile war, and the Africanization of the country that permits [slavery]" (*Atlantic* 507; *w* 11 : 298). This lamentable reference seems intended to pose the slave as a threat to the Northern worker, and to depict "Africanization" as a kind of corruption or degradation of American culture. It suggests not only that Emerson shared many of the racist assumptions of his time, but that he was also willing to exploit regional resentment and racial fear to mobilize Northern sentiments against slavery.[11]

Emerson's frustration boils up to a central question, generated by the confluence of his analysis of civilization and his observation of the intractability of Southern slavery: "Why cannot the best civilization be extended over the whole country, since the disorder of the less civilized portion menaces the existence of the country?" (*Atlantic* 507; *w* 11:299). What lies behind the question, as a series of further rhetorical questions will illustrate, is the fear that civilization has become weak or powerless, unable to execute or enforce its ideals because of a lack of will or courage. In what has clearly shifted from an analysis of the nature and qualities of civilization to a call to action, he pointedly asks, "Is not civilization heroic also? Is it not for action? has it not a will?" (*Atlantic* 508; *w* 11:299).

This is not, Emerson believes, a situation that can be blamed on a lack of information or argument. The *Edinburgh Review*, he notes, made the convincing case that slavery is bad economy forty years earlier, but such arguments are not persuasive in the face of more narrowly focused economic interests. "Can you convince the shoe interest, or the iron interest, or the cotton interest, by reading passages from Milton or Montesquieu?" (*Atlantic* 508; *w* 11:301). The problem lies in the realm of motivation, not in the realm of information or argumentation. "There are already mountains of facts, if anyone wants them. But people do not want them" (*Atlantic* 508; *w* 11:300).

People do not want the facts—this is perhaps the most painful realization of Emerson's analysis of the slavery crisis, one that calls into question his entire representation of civilization as the product of an inevitable human progress through history. It forces him to face the difficult question of the limits of both reason and motivation, limits that become moral obstacles to the individual and also hinder the progressive development of civilization. Emerson sees a paralysis of the moral will in the country at large, the product of apathetic temperament and material greed. There is only one remedy to that paralysis, an act of public policy that can unleash a surge of new moral power and energy into the country: emancipation. "Emancipation is the demand of civilization. That is a principle; everything else is an intrigue." The effect of emancipation would be to restore the balance that slavery has upset; it "puts the whole people in healthy, productive, amiable position,—puts every man in the South in just and natural relations with every man in the North, laborer with laborer" (*Atlantic* 509; *w* 11:304).

Not only would emancipation set in motion a process of moral recognition and moral motivation, it would also add, Emerson believed, the pressure of a new force on the South, threatening it from within with a complex set of internal conflicts. "Emancipation at one stroke elevates the poor white of the South, and identifies his interest with that of the Northern laborer" (*Atlantic* 510; *w* 11:307). The threat of emancipation is not only that of the slave to his master, but that of the Southern yeoman to the planter class, Emerson argues. Through the claim of the workers, both white and black, for the rightful product of their labor, a new urgency and motivation would be added to the necessity to restore labor and use as fundamental moral categories. Emancipation thus constituted for Emerson the public act that promised to set in motion a restoration of the natural relationship between work and identity, usefulness and reward, labor and freedom.

Emerson would soon see his plea, and that of many other antislavery thinkers, enacted in Lincoln's Emancipation Proclamation of September 22, 1862, an act that Emerson praised soon afterward in a September 1862 address in Boston, published in the *Atlantic Monthly* the following November.[12] Whatever the political calculations behind the act, it stands as one of the nation's great progressive advances. Like a politician concerned with the right "spin," Emerson played down the immediate impact of the proclamation, saying that "it is by no means necessary that this measure should be suddenly marked by any signal results on the negroes or on the rebel masters." But he did emphasize the important impact on national will and national objectives that this shift in public policy could have. "The force of the act is that it commits the country to this justice,—that it compels the innumerable officers, civil, military, naval, of the Republic to range themselves on the line of this equity." Moreover, he understood how the goal of emancipation of the slaves gave the war a moral consecration that the goal of preserving the union of the states, however worthy and politically wise, simply could not do. "This act makes that the lives of our heroes have not been sacrificed in vain. It makes a victory of our defeats. Our hurts are healed; the health of the nation is repaired" (*w* 11:319–20).

Emerson believed that the course of history, and the fate of human civilization, rested on the struggle to end slavery in America. And as a corollary, he believed that the moral soundness of the American nation depended on its ability to free itself from slavery. His philosophy of history and the development of civilization merged dynamically with his perception of what was at stake in the Civil War as the war accelerated, and emancipation was the stroke that refocused the nation's confused moral attention. As he observed, "Life in America had lost much of its attraction in the later years" (*w* 11:318). But as a result of emancipation "we have recovered ourselves from our false position, and planted ourselves on a law of Nature" (*w* 11:320).

NOTES

The author is grateful for research support from the Center for the Humanities, Oregon State University.

1. Len Gougeon has traced in illuminating detail Emerson's increasing involvement with the antislavery cause in *vh* demonstrating the previously overlooked evidence of Emerson's growing commitment to antislavery. Also of importance is *aw*, which brings to light much additional evidence of Emerson's antislavery work. Two other scholars have also recently taken up this issue, with differing emphases. Eduardo Cadava in *Emerson and the Climates of History* (Stanford: Stanford Univ. Press, 1997) has offered analysis of the way that the politics of antislavery shaped Emerson's intellectual development. Anita Hayes Patterson in *From Emerson to King: Democracy, Race, and the Politics of Protest* (Oxford and New York: Oxford Univ. Press, 1997) emphasizes Emerson's importance for later political leaders such as W. E. B. Du Bois and Martin Luther King Jr. but argues that Emerson based his theory of American nationality and collective purpose on racist assumptions growing from his valorization of Anglo-Saxon racial and cultural heritage. For discussion of Emerson's later emphasis on moral purpose, see Merton M. Sealts Jr., *Emerson on the Scholar* (Columbia: University of Missouri Press, 1990); David M. Robinson, *Emerson and the Conduct of Life: Pragmatism and Ethical Purpose in the Later Thought* (Cambridge and New York: Cambridge Univ. Press, 1993); and Michael Lopez, *Emerson and Power: Creative Antagonism in the Nineteenth Century* (DeKalb: Northern Illinois Univ. Press, 1996).

2. For analyses of the social and political aspects of Transcendentalism, see Taylor Stoehr, *Nay-Saying in Concord: Emerson, Alcott, and Thoreau* (Hamden, Conn.: Archon, 1979); Anne C. Rose, *Transcendentalism as a Social Movement, 1830–1850* (New Haven: Yale Univ. Press, 1981); and Richard Francis, *Transcendental Utopias: Individual and Community at Brook Farm, Fruitlands, and Walden* (Ithaca: Cornell Univ. Press, 1997). A full discussion of the rise of Fourierism in America can be found in Charles Guarneri, *The Utopian Alternative: Fourierism in Nineteenth-Century America* (Ithaca: Cornell Univ. Press, 1991). On Fuller's influence on Emerson, see Christina Zwarg, *Feminist Conversations: Fuller, Emerson, and the Play of Reading* (Ithaca: Cornell Univ. Press, 1995); and Charles Capper, *Margaret Fuller: An American Romantic Life, The Private Years* (New York: Oxford Univ. Press, 1992). For the impact of William Henry Channing, see David M. Robinson, "The Political Odyssey of William Henry Channing," *American Quarterly* 34 (summer 1982): 165–84; and for the impact of Ripley, see Charles Crowe, *George Ripley: Transcendentalist and Utopian Socialist* (Athens: University of Georgia Press, 1967).

3. Cadava, *Emerson and the Climates of History*, p. 26.

4. I will cite the original edition of "American Civilization" published in the *Atlantic Monthly* 9 (April 1862), pp. 502–11 as *Atlantic*, and also include the corresponding citation in the *Complete Works* as w. Minor variations between the two versions will not be noted.

5. See Philip L. Nicoloff's discussion in *Emerson on Race and History: An Examination of English Traits* (New York: Columbia Univ. Press, 1961), pp. 118–46; and Robinson, *Emerson and the Conduct of Life*, pp. 115–18. In *From Emerson to King* Patterson stresses the persistence and importance of Emerson's fascination with the Anglo-Saxons and argues that "Emerson's racism is central to his vision of American nationality." She also emphasizes that "Emerson's racist vision of the representative self is essential for his articulation of a call to revolution—what Thoreau (and, much later, King) would designate as 'civil disobedience'" (p. 132).

6. In "Civilization" (*Society and Solitude*) the passage reads: "the savage tribes are gradually extinguished rather than civilized" (w 7:20).

7. For a detailed discussion of Emerson's views of technology, see Leonard Neufeldt, *The House of Emerson* (Lincoln: University of Nebraska Press, 1982), pp. 75–99.

8. *VH* 262–67. Emerson's comments on the requirements of a "civilized" society seem directed principally to the South, but they may also have been shaped by his knowledge of the conflicts over dissenting speech in the decade before the war.

9. The version of "American Civilization" published in *Miscellanies* begins with this discussion of labor.

10. For further discussion of Emerson's view of the redeeming qualities of work, see my discussion of the theme of work in *The Conduct of Life* in *Emerson and the Conduct of Life*, pp. 134–58.

11. For further perspective on the issue of Emerson's views on race, see Nicoloff, *Emerson on Race*, 118–46; *VH* 82–84 and 178–86; Cadava's discussion of Emerson's complicity with nineteenth-century racism and his attempt to deny both race and slavery as "natural categories" (*Emerson and the Climates of History*, 53–70); and Patterson, *From Emerson to King*, 126–55.

12. Emerson's reaction to Lincoln's Emancipation Proclamation was published as "The President's Proclamation" in the *Atlantic Monthly* 10 (November 1862) and w 11:313–26. For further information of his views on emancipation in the context of the outbreak of the war, see *VH* 268–90.13.

STEPHEN L. ESQUITH

Power, Poise, and Place: Toward an Emersonian Theory of Democratic Citizenship

AFTER MORE THAN A CENTURY in which setting constitutional limits on political power has dominated the field of democratic theory, active citizenship has resurfaced as a legitimate topic of theoretical reflection.[1] Today's debate over the contours of democratic citizenship is dominated by three perspectives. Liberal political philosophers, led by John Rawls, have argued that the duties and virtues of citizenship should be derived from prior institutional principles of justice. A good citizen is someone who possesses the virtues needed to act according to these principles and to feel at home in a society whose institutions are ordered by them. Republican and communitarian critics of this liberal view, such as J. G. A. Pocock, Michael Sandel, and Alasdair MacIntyre, object that this is not enough to ensure stability or justice. In addition to the liberal virtues of tolerance and a commitment to play the role of the loyal opposition, citizens also must be committed to certain substantive ideals. For the more historically minded republicans, these are universal ideals of excellence and public service. For communitarians, they are the specific moral or religious ideals of particular communities within the larger liberal tradition.

I want to step outside this intramural debate in order to focus more directly on the democratic content of citizenship. What skills, habits, and dispositions do citizens need to generate political power democratically and to share in democratic public life? I call the conception of political virtue that I favor Emersonian. "Let us be poised, and wise, and our own today," Emerson urged, "amidst this vertigo of shows and politics" (JMN 3:35). It is this notion of "poise" while handling political power that gives Emerson's reflections on the virtues of the democratic citizen their distinct value.

Why burden democratic citizenship with Emerson? While Oliver Wendell Holmes's 1884 characterization of Emerson as a poetic idealist who "accepted his martyrdom with meek submission"[2] probably has been beaten back for the last time, there is still no scholarly consensus on Emerson's status as a political theorist. Some of his defenders, such as Len Gougeon, emphasize his opposition to slavery or, as Christina Zwarg does, his friendship with Margaret Fuller[3] as signs of his political egalitarianism. Others, such as George Kateb and Stanley Cavell, emphasize his commitment to the values of individuality and autonomy.[4] A third, more critical set of commentators, for example, David Leverenz and Christopher Newfield, has found Emerson all too ready to defer to patriarchal and corporate forms of authority rather than elaborate his own theory of popular political participation.[5]

Given these competing interpretations, it would be surprising to find that Emerson had a coherent democratic theory. He did not, and there are several reasons why. Emerson's political views were not entirely consistent, and his feelings toward active political engagement were ambivalent. Instead of exploring these contradictions and trying to reconcile them, Emerson tended to rely on the idea of Nature as an independent synthesizing force of its own. We will see in the next section how this affected his understanding of power and his ability to formulate an egalitarian conception of democratic citizenship.

Despite these shortcomings, Emerson remains a valuable resource for democratic theory because he insisted on the importance of generating, not just constitutionally limiting, political power in a democratic society. Emersonian citizens possess an appreciation of the strengths of character needed to sustain this dual process through hard times.

Emerson himself did not always display this kind of democratic character. Sometimes, especially in his journals, he wrote as if democratic citizenship were a painful chore and public figures were personally abhorrent.[6] Even though Emerson did not formulate a full democratic theory and did not always relish democratic politics, this does not mean that an Emersonian theory of democratic citizenship cannot be constructed, with the help of others such as Dewey and Royce. A theory of democratic citizenship can make good use of three elements of Emerson's work—power, poise, and place—elements that together cannot be found in contemporary republican or communitarian writings.

Power

As Michael Lopez has noted, "the search after power, the goal of empowerment, remains consistent through Emerson's essays," even though the forms that power take vary considerably.[7] This is true of Emerson's understanding of political power as well: power assumes many forms and can be transmuted in several ways. Before examining Emerson's attempts to come to terms with the dynamism and fluidity of political power and its relationship to other forms of power in Nature, we must, as Lopez does, take special notice of the positive valence that Emerson places on power in all its forms. To understand Emerson's interpretation of political power, it is necessary to start with the hold that all power has on us: "And what activity the desire of power inspires! What toils it sustains! How it sharpens the perceptions and stores the memory with facts" (w 10:129).

Unlike democratic theorists today, Emerson underscored the creative and inventive role that the desire for power plays in democratic politics. He was certainly aware of its dangers in *The Conduct of Life* ("This power, to be sure, is not clothed in satin" [w 6:63]), but he believed that without this desire for power there was no predicting or influencing the future in a constructive way. "The same energy in the Greek *Demos* drew the remark, that the evils of popular government appear greater than they are; there is compensation for them in the spirit and energy it awakens" (w 6:62).

It is this desire that Emerson wants to use to mine unequally distributed intellectual and economic resources in the service of a more inclusive democracy. However, to get to this point, Emerson had to struggle with the notion of natural inequalities. The results were not entirely successful.

Journal entries in late 1822 mark out a position against natural equality that Emerson tried to come to terms with long into his adult life:

> I believe that nobody now regards the maxim 'that all men are born equal,' as any thing more than a convenient hypothesis or an extravagant declamation. For the reverse is true—that all men are born unequal in personal powers and in those essential circumstances, of time, parentage, country, fortune. The least knowledge of the natural history of man adds another important particular to these; namely, what class of men he belongs to—European, Moor, Tartar, African? Because Nature has plainly assigned different degrees of intellect to these different races, and the barriers between are insurmountable. (*jmn* 2:42–43)

Emerson did struggle with this view, sometimes mightily.[8] In *English Traits* he held that "Race in the negro is of appalling importance" (cw 5:26) even though at an Abolitionist rally in 1845 he had doubted their "hopeless inferiority" in light of the "facts collected in the United States and in the West Indies" (aw 36). In private the long journal entry quoted above was repeatedly qualified. "Slavery," he wrote, "is an institution for converting men into monkeys" (*JMN* 5 : 295).

The more Emerson felt that racial inequalities were the product of institutions like slavery, the more active he became in the abolitionist movement. However, his faith in Nature kept him from abandoning his earlier views entirely, despite "the impossibility of arriving at satisfaction on the historical question of race" (*CW* 5 : 28).

Differences between rich and poor gave rise to another ambivalence. In "Self-reliance" he wrote that the "mob" that "goes abroad to beg a cup of water of the urns of other men" repelled him (*CW* 2 : 41). Jacksonian democracy was "nonsense" propped up by "public opinion" (*JMN* 3 : 100). "The mass," he claimed in *The Conduct of Life*, "are animal, in pupilage, and near chimpanzee" (*W* 6 : 251), and Emerson was quick to justify their economic misfortunes according to a simplistic doctrine of natural economic growth.[9] However, he was unable to leave it at that. Alongside the famous passage from "Self-Reliance" in which he grudgingly gives up his "wicked dollar" to the poor "through miscellaneous popular charities" (*CW* 2 : 31), we find seemingly contradictory sentiments like this passage from his 1841 lecture "Man the Reformer": "The state must consider the poor man, and all voices must speak for him. Every child that is born must have a just chance for his bread. Let the amelioration in our laws of property proceed from the concession of the rich, not from the grasping of the poor. Let us begin by habitual imparting. Let us understand that the equitable rule is, that no one should take more than his share, let him be ever so rich" (*CW* 1 : 159).

On the equality of men and women, Emerson was again of two minds. Despite his admiration for Margaret Fuller and the influence of his second wife, Lidian, Emerson was unwilling to abandon the idea of woman's angelic nature. "Woman only can tell the heights of feminine nature, & the only way in which man can help her, is by observing woman reverentially & whenever she speaks from herself & catches him in inspired moments up to a heaven of honor & religion, to hold her to that point by reverential recognition of the divinity that speaks through her" (*JMN* 8 : 381). However, no sooner had he written this than he slipped back into the negative stereotype of the obtrusive housewife: "In every woman's conversation & total influence mild or acid lurks the *conventional devil*" (*JMN* 8 : 391).

At once a divine inspiration and the carping voice of social conformity, woman in Emerson's eyes falls short. As Jeffrey Steele says, "Man the Reformer" reveals Emerson's preference for a powerful masculine spirit over woman, the "puny, protected person guarded by walls and curtains, stoves and down beds, coaches, and men-servants and women-servants from the earth and the sky."[10] Even though Emerson believed that the women's movement and the antislavery movement were equally deserving of his support in the mid-1850s, he also believed that women did not want an equal role in public affairs at that time.[11]

Is there an Emersonian conception of equality? We could, of course, settle for something like the equal potential for self-reliance—that "unattained yet attainable self" Emerson suggests all individuals can and should strive for. There is something of the poet and the hero in all of us, he argued in *Essays: First Series* (cw 2 : 5). Even the masses, he claimed in "Considerations by the Way," if they can be decomposed, have this potential: "To say then, the majority are wicked, means no malice, no bad heart in the observer, but, simply that the majority are unripe, and have not yet come to themselves, do not yet know their opinion" (cw 6 : 252). If we choose this conception of Emersonian equality,[12] then we are likely to set aside Emerson's particular views of natural racial, economic, and gender inequalities as unworthy of him.

One alternative to this reading of Emerson is that his blind spots and inconsistencies represent a bias in the underlying concept of the "attainable self." Exactly what is to be attained through self-reliant thought and action? Self-reliance is not a universal value but rather a cultural value that is specific to early-nineteenth-century patriarchal, commercializing society. Even if Emerson was unhappy with the emerging mass society,[13] he still resisted experiments that called into question possessive individualism, in particular, socialist experiments, and balked at a more fluid, feminist conception of identity.[14] The underlying concept of equality that his more specific conception of an equal potential for self-reliance rests upon is, on this reading, deeply flawed.

There may be a kernel of truth in these readings of Emerson. He sometimes did think of self-reliance as a Kantian ideal that all rational persons were capable of striving for, especially in thought. Regardless of where they started, they could do a better job thinking for themselves. They could improve their Nature, even if they could never achieve equality of results. At other times, he seemed simply to refuse to take feminist and socialist values seriously, hiding his cultural biases behind the concept of Nature.

However, I am suggesting another way to read Emerson's appeal to Nature that emphasizes its place in a democratic theory of power. In this sense Nature represents the external reality of raw materials and uncultivated ground to which individuals stand in creative antagonism, and it also represents the products that people create out of these natural sources as well as their own capacities, skills, and dispositions that they bring to this relationship with Nature (*cw* 1 : 7–8). Nature, then, provides a variety of resources, including our own abilities, out of which power can emerge and be shaped. When tapped in this way, Nature generates additional sources of power that will follow certain "laws," and when power is used in accordance with these laws by people with the "desire for power," the possibility of generating political power and a more inclusive political domain exists. The process of generating political power from Nature and other intellectual and economic resources is not a simple progression, but it does follow certain patterns, and these are what Emerson calls laws of power.

Emerson's laws of power do not predict with certainty. They connect the cooperative generation of political power to other natural and human resources through the medium of human character. This is not an esoteric secret. Even ordinary citizens can see how intellectual and economic power works its way through densely knotted limbs, succeeds itself along new circular lines, and never swings too far in one direction before moving back in the other. Once they have grasped these laws of power and seen how power depends in part on human character, Emerson believed, they will be in a position to generate greater political power and a more inclusive political domain.

This ability to grasp the laws of power is itself rooted in Nature, but it is not merely a matter of drill and sheer concentration any more than it is a radiant quality of individual greatness that enables citizens to make use of intellectual and economic resources. The more citizens honestly discuss their own shortcomings and personal stakes, the more capable they will be of grasping of the laws of power, tap into intellectual and economic resources, and finally expand the political domain within the shifting boundaries of these laws.

In the essays "Compensation" and "Circles" Emerson describes these patterns or laws of power.[15] In the former essay he claims that "each thing is a half, and suggests another thing to make it whole." This built-in "polarity" can be traced back to human nature. It is not just that human beings are made up of contradictory traits but that actions and compensatory reactions originate in our orientations toward ourselves and others. When we have done someone an injustice, for example, we speak fearfully, and the fear that we will be called to account soon makes us hated for what we did. We condemn ourselves in our own words—not explicitly, but in our tone and phrasing. Only when we are aware of the fact that our own powerful acts produce a true image of our own worth can we speak more plainly and honestly. Power's compensatory swings begin with our own fearfulness, and by grasping its psychological origins we are in a better position to control it.[16]

In "Circles" Emerson then extends this analysis of power along a second axis. In opposition to the law of polarity is the law of "swift circumscription." Every action has a tendency to be superceded by a greater action; every object is impermanent. Again, what drives this process is something deeply rooted in human character. "We thirst for approbation, yet cannot forgive the approver. The sweet of nature is love; yet if I have a friend I am tormented by my imperfections." As the circles of our friends are redrawn so that we do not have to confront the fearsome thought that old friends might see through us, we rationalize our actions by underlining the others' shortcomings. An even wider circle is then needed to avoid our imagined deficiencies, and we soon forget that it was our own deficiency, our own fear of disapproval, that forced us outward in the first place.

There is no way out of this process of "swift circumscription" and no way to avoid power's "polarity." When Emerson says that "life is a search after power," he does not mean, as Hobbes did, that we are at the mercy of these natural laws. On the contrary, by grasping how power naturally works, we can better adjust our efforts to obstacles: "All power is of one kind, a sharing of the nature of the world. The mind that is parallel with the laws of nature will be in the current of events, and strong with their strength" (w 6:56). According to Emerson, Nature is a rich source of material to be used by creative human powers and at the same time a harsh, determining force in our lives: "all kinds of power usually emerge at the same time; good energy, and bad; power of mind, with physical health; the ecstasies of devotion, with the exasperations of debauchery" (w 6:63–64). Nature's magazine of powers, good and bad, are there to be used. Properly used when Nature resists our efforts, these powers take us deeper into, not beyond, our ordinary experience.

In one sense, then, Emerson was a determinist but not a fatalist. "Thus we trace Fate, in matter, mind, and morals,—in race, in retardations of strata, and in thought and character as well. . . . If Fate follows and limits power, power attends and antagonizes Fate" (w 6:21–22). Necessity hoops us in, but our capacity to tap into natural forms of power makes freedom possible. What powers are at our disposal and how are we to use them to counter our fate within the laws of polarity and circumscription?

Emerson often praised catlike dexterity and plain hard work. In these acts he claimed to find "the miraculous in the common" (cw 1:44). Human beings are equally capable, he argued, of making useful products, if not equally pleasing poetry. Consistent with this, Emerson was quick to find fault with those who accumulated wealth and power parasitically and did not, as Locke would say, leave enough for others to use productively: "Every man is a consumer, and ought to be a producer. He fails to make his place good in the world, unless he not only pays his debt, but also adds something to the common wealth" (w 6:85). When unequal private wealth does not contribute to the "common wealth" in this material sense, it is unnatural.

What troubles Emerson so much about giving a "wicked dollar" to charity is that it represents a kind of political alienation for the giver, not so much dependency for the receiver. If you have the money, it is much easier to pay someone else to take care of the anonymous poor than it is to understand their lives yourself. But when intellectual and economic powers are used in cooperation productively, the process can be of value to rich and poor alike.[17] What it takes to do this is not a selfless commitment to philanthropy or utopian socialism, Emerson believed, but a certain kind of poised, cooperative effort.

Can the poor afford to wait for this direct relationship with their benefactors? Is it really their responsibility to help others overcome their political alienation? What guarantee do they have that once the rich and poor alike have understood Emerson's laws of Nature, they will be better off economically or politically? Emerson does not take up this line of questioning. Instead, he asks another question that he thinks is prior to these. What kind of character will be needed by all democratic citizens if they are ever going to be ready to take up these matters? Without it, no statute or constitutional provision can protect the weak from economic exploitation and political disenfranchisement.

Poise

"Experience" was written in 1844, when Emerson was coming to terms with the death of his son and the need to take a stronger public stand against slavery. It was a time when poise was more than a matter of political etiquette for him.

For Emerson poise became that peculiar political virtue that enables citizens to handle themselves and the things they have formed out of Nature when they do not have the luxury of starting from scratch. Democratic politics is precisely the kind of experience Emerson describes when he says that we find ourselves in mid-stride on a staircase and with no clear memory of how we came to be there. This is the feeling democratic citizens continually experience as they are forced to change the rules of the game in order to cope with unforeseen circumstances and ironic twists of fate.

The distinctive feature of Emersonian poise is the way it enables citizens to respond to this fearsome challenge. Poise is an orientation toward power—"the vertigo of shows and politics"—that enables citizens to express their desire for power creatively and cooperatively without losing sight of the subtle ways in which this peculiar desire also clouds their vision and makes them deaf to the dynamics of power in a democratic society. Emersonian poise enables democratic citizens to engage, sometimes openly and other times covertly, in the pervasive power struggles that run through democratic politics without losing their balance or their ear for the sound of the "switch" in their own voices.[18] "There is a sort of climate in every man's speech," Emerson wrote in his journal, "running from hot noon, when words flow like steam & perfume—to cold night, when they are frozen" (*JMN* 11:52). Poised democratic citizens must be able to register the entire range.

Just as philosophical inquiry depends on the Socratic virtues of honesty and a willingness to submit one's own arguments to critical scrutiny, so democratic political dialogue depends on this Emersonian virtue of poise. Its correlative vices are, on one side, a communitarian self-absorption with identity politics and, on the other, a liberal impatience with the process of political dialogue. The former blinds citizens to the operations of power that maintain the boundaries of their community; the latter encourages citizens to assume that silent acquiescence always means assent.

Political virtue, according to republicans and communitarians, is the ability and disposition of citizens to overcome self-interest for some greater political good. They disagree about what the greater political good is and how an attachment to it can be created. They share, unwittingly, a naive attitude toward power.

Republicans argue that political participation has an intrinsic value that is greater than the value of other competing goods.[19] That intrinsic value may be an individual agonistic one: competing for political recognition in itself is more exciting and challenging than the pursuit of private wealth or theoretical knowledge. Another possibility is that political participation is valued more highly because it is the most gratifying form of collective activity. Discussing and addressing public issues together has an intrinsic value higher than participating in family or economic activities.

To realize the intrinsic values of political participation, other interests have to be limited. Republican citizens must have the skills to participate in politics, and they must be disposed to use these skills even at the expense of their economic and social interests. These abilities and dispositions that constitute republican political virtue can be nurtured gradually through participation in voluntary associations or, if need be, ingrained through an austere military regimen. In either case, the rhetorical and deliberative republican skills of political engagement and the attachments to honor, glory, and political debate do not come naturally. Furthermore, they are not skills and dispositions that all can or should aspire to. Republican citizenship, since Machiavelli, is active but not egalitarian.

Unlike republican political virtue, Emersonian poise does not rank political participation above other human activities or reserve it for a chosen few. Emerson himself never romanticized politics. On the contrary, he believed that "Every actual state is corrupt" and legislation an "after-work, a poor patching" that is better repealed than left standing (*w* 3:142, 140–41). At the same time he was able to recognize and respond to urgent political demands. Witness his reaction to the Fugitive Slave Law and Webster's defense of it: "These things show that no forms, neither constitutions, nor laws, nor covenants, nor churches, nor bibles, are of any use in themselves. The Devil nestles comfortably into them all. There is no help but in the head and heart and hamstrings of a man. Covenants are of no use without honest men to keep them; laws of none but with loyal citizens to obey them" (*AW* 83). Emerson does not categorically reject laws and political institutions, but he forcefully underscores their limits as adequate instruments for solving deep social conflicts. This ambivalence towards politics in Emerson results from his understanding that power takes shape in the hands of democratic citizens and that they can neither do without it nor give themselves over to it entirely.[20]

For example, to face the poor and do one's share with one's own hands takes more poise in the Emersonian sense than to pay someone else to do the work. It takes poise to join with the poor, without sermonizing, and understand how the dominant forms of power oppressing them can be harnessed constructively. Poise is not a political virtue in the sense that republican civic virtue is; it is not a capacity to resist economic and social interests for the sake of political participation. Poise is a way of getting closer to the effects of power in order to see the potential for using it constructively as well as to understand its debilitating statist tendencies. Emerson does not reject philanthropic institutions categorically, and Emersonian poise does not require that we reject state-run welfare programs in a mass democratic society. What poise involves is firsthand experience with the institutions designed to help the poor so that these problems can be addressed more knowledgeably as they arise. This holds for donors and taxpayers as well as administrators and bureaucrats; they cannot hope to understand the way power operates through these institutions and within the economy more broadly without encountering those they want to help where they want to help them.[21]

Furthermore, to be effective, this act of composing oneself to come to grips with power cannot be done alone.[22] Emerson's treatment of "representative men" illustrates how poise should work as a form of collective resistance against the beguiling images of powerful experts and leaders.

Even the most-admired public figures are flawed, Emerson argued, and we should not think of them as role models. "Bonaparte," for example, "was the idol of common men because he had in transcendent degree the qualities and powers of common men." At the same time, "this exorbitant egotist narrowed, impoverished, and absorbed the power and existence of those who served him" (*cw* 4:147). The Emersonian model of poised resistance to this idolatry is the "sturdy lad from New Hampshire or Vermont, who in turn tries all the professions, who teams it, farms it, peddles, keeps a school, preaches, edits a newspaper, goes to Congress, buys a township, and so forth, in successive years, and always like a cat falls on his feet" (*cw* 2:43). This is no recluse. His "professions" put him in touch with Nature but also require that he master the art of conversation. He knows how to buy and sell, how to engage the reading public, how to hear as well as speak with his congregation, and finally how to represent them in debate on the floor of Congress. Emerson wants citizens to recognize the complexity of power through a wide range of on-site conversations: "When each new speaker strikes a new light, emancipates us from the oppression of the last speaker to oppress us with the greatness and exclusiveness of his own thought, and then yields us to another redeemer, we seem to recover our rights, to become men" (*cw* 2:184). Because "Our conversation with Nature is not just what it seems" (*w* 6:311), we must be willing and able to engage with "each new speaker." In an age of specialized knowledge democratic citizens should avoid condescending to those they think know less than they do and deferring uncritically to experts. How can ordinary citizens contest expert knowledge and also avoid the arrogance that their own professions sometimes breed? Emerson's solution is not mysterious. Only someone who has conversed with farmers, with congregants, with students, and with legislators on an equal footing and in their own terms is going to have this kind of poise. To hold our own ground, we must be "a bundle of relations, a knot of roots" (cw 2:20). In this sense self-reliant citizens should depend upon others. They need sources of encouragement but also honest sounding boards that enable them to hear how they sound to others.

Taken literally, of course, Emerson's longing for "sturdy" citizens who can switch jobs was increasingly obsolete when he wrote and is now relevant only for laid-off workers who are bounced from one entry-level job to another.[23] What is still useful in Emerson's vision of this catlike figure is the notion that he, unlike Napoleon, represents the dialogical skills that democratic citizens need to engage others whose experience differs dramatically from their own. You do not have to be a farmer, merchant, teacher, or elected politician to converse with these people. What you have to be is someone ready to listen carefully to what they have to offer and listen hard for the sounds of condescension in your own voice as you question them.

Sometimes this will be easier than others. For example, when you depend directly on the voluntary cooperation of another to satisfy your own interests, you can't just go your separate ways without giving something up that is important to you. But Emersonian poise also pertains to situations where it is not immediately clear that people share each other's fate. Where the issues are national or international in scope, then it is not at all clear that Emerson's talkative "lad" could persuade those who are not his neighbors that they are all in it together. Can poise really do us much good where the parties are not already on speaking terms and committed to a common enterprise?

Place

Geographically and psychologically, Emersonian political virtue begins locally. Poised citizens can pick up on local accents and customs different from their own that can either obstruct or facilitate more cosmopolitan ends. In this respect Emersonian poise differs radically from contemporary communitarianism, which sheers off the jagged edges of actual political experience. The localness of Emersonian political virtue is not a matter of being faithful to the ethical norms of a small community. It refers to a way of taking in and being engaged with the political world, what John Dewey would call "experiencing"[24] political power, starting with the first circle of relations that surround us and gradually moving out from there.

To make the contemporary relevance of local Emersonian poise clearer, however, we have to extend Emerson in directions later mapped out by Dewey and Josiah Royce.

In late January 1841, Emerson delivered the lecture "Man, the Reformer," his response to the "challenge of George Ripley's Brook Farm commune and to Orestes Brownson's critique of transcendentalism."[25] According to David Jacobson, in this lecture Emerson argued that "the site of politics is local" and "consistently advised his readers to attend to the issues of their own community before going far and wide in search of political causes."[26] Unlike these nineteenth-century communitarians, Emerson's localism was not hostile to larger political causes or national political institutions. Consider, for example, Emerson's encounter with the Fugitive Slave Law. He begins his March 7, 1854, address on this topic regretfully acknowledging in an aside that he had never really witnessed slavery and qualifying his own authority to speak as an expert on this subject. "The one thing not to be forgiven to intellectual persons is not to know their own task, or to take their ideas from others and believe in the ideas of others. From this want of manly rest in their own, and foolish acceptance of other people's watchwords, comes the imbecility and fatigue of their conversation. For they cannot affirm these from any original experience."[27]

Just as Emersonian poise is a prerequisite but not a substitute for effective institutional solutions to poverty and oppression, so too is local engagement a prerequisite but not a substitute for an understanding of and involvement in national issues. National politics can be heady, and to avoid being either enchanted or repelled by power on such a large scale, Emersonian poise must first be developed locally.

John Dewey recognized this relationship between citizenship and place: "Unless local communal life can be restored, the public cannot adequately resolve its most urgent problem, to find and identify itself." Dewey ended this passage on what it means for citizens to find themselves as a body politic by invoking Emerson: "We lie, as Emerson said, in the lap of an immense intelligence. But that intelligence is dormant and its communications are broken, inarticulate and faint until it possesses the local community as its medium."[28] Local participation does not simply educate the public by giving it access to more fine-grained information. Local participation is the "medium" out of which a coherent public identity grows because it is here that citizens learn how to ask each other political questions about who they are and what forms of power they value. Without these questions, access to more information is meaningless.[29] Without this locally educated "immense intelligence," frustration will quickly set in, strategic openings will be exploited too forcefully, tempers will flare, and quieter voices will be ignored. Emerson's language in the passage Dewey refers to is less explicit than Dewey's—he prefers the images of climatic and alluvial change to direct discussion. But "society" is still for him a "troop of thinkers," and what attracts "capital or genius or labor" is "a city like New York, or Constantinople" (w 6:61).

The local character of political virtue is also captured by Josiah Royce's concept of provincialism. The "new and wiser provincialism" that Royce advocated was, he claimed, "no mere renewal of the old sectionalism." Rather than dividing people, provincialism "makes people want to idealize, to adorn, to ennoble, to educate, their own province." [30] Then provincialism can work as an antidote to three political problems, in this way directly engaging power.

First, argued Royce, by giving citizens objective reasons for taking pride in their local institutions, provincialism enables them to give strangers a share in this common wealth. Royce calls this assimilation, but it is not assimilation in the homogenizing and self-denying way we tend to think of it today. By becoming more loyal to their local democratic institutions— the libraries, the public parks, and the schools as well as the elective offices—citizens become more capable of "assimilating to our own social order the strangers that are within our gates." [31] Provincialism enables citizens to convince strangers already in their midst that the demands of local democratic citizenship are worth it. Provincialism gives citizens the wherewithal to persuade others to become fellow-citizens when they could remain resident aliens. It is the poise citizens need to resist the temptation to exclude or denigrate others.

The second danger that provincialism wards off is what Royce called "leveling," or social conformity. Provincialism, he believed, helps citizens identify this destructive form of power and counteract it through the pride they have in the local cultural institutions they have built. [32] Similarly, provincialism can counteract the "greatest danger of popular government," that is, the "spirit of the mob." [33] Cautiously relying on the work of Le Bon, Royce suggested that the mob psychology that can undermine order in democratic society can be avoided by pride in the value of one's local political institutions. Unlike assimilation where provincialism generates a new form of creative power, in leveling and mob psychology provincialism serves as an antidote to destructive forms of power. In these two cases provincialism represents the poise not to be carried along with the crowd— that is, not to conform to its pedestrian or violent ways.

The local nature of poise that allows citizens to take advantage of their latent "immense intelligence" can be distinguished from the communitarian virtues that philosophers such as Alasdair MacIntyre have called attention to. For communitarians, roughly speaking, individual identity and the effective pursuit of individual conceptions of the good depend on membership in a community that has more in common than simply a set of liberal procedures for solving problems of distributive justice. Without the support of a substantive moral or religious community a person cannot sustain coherent individual life plans and agree to social schemes for redistribution.[34] Conversely, political virtue in these substantive communities should enable citizens to support the basic structure of the community not just for the community's own sake but also for the sake of their own individual projects and identities.

Unlike civic republicans, communitarians do not value political participation as the highest form of human activity. They value political order because without it their deeper, shared moral commitments and their individual conceptions of the good would be unrealizable. What communitarians and republicans share is a conception of political virtue that is inattentive to the peculiar dynamics of power. Republicans glorify the exercise of power, whereas communitarians romantically yearn for a community in which the power to include will never have to be used to exclude. The latter's vision of a harmonious political community or a set of harmoniously interconnected communities myopically overlooks the way that forming and sustaining even the most law-abiding communities always involve violence or the threat of violence against those, inside and out, who do not share the community's moral commitments.[35]

How exactly does poised participation in local politics cultivate a more critical orientation toward power? As I have already suggested, awakening democracy's "immense intelligence" is a matter of teaching citizens how to ask the right questions. The city neighborhood famously described by Jane Jacobs suggests one possibility.[36] Children growing up in this environment learned how neighbors who were also strangers took care of, questioned, and disagreed with one another civilly without any professional duty bearing down on them. More generally, Christopher Lasch has suggested, neighbors learn how to ask questions of one another, make arguments, and agree to revisit their disagreements. This "quasi-public forum" and other neighborhood meeting grounds do not constitute voluntary associations in the Tocquevillian sense because they do not exist to serve a single purpose.

They have the more diffuse end of encouraging the political virtue of "decency" in conversation.[37]

Lasch has been fairly criticized for idealizing these local institutions and the folks who frequent them. Simply coming out in favor of decent conversation is hardly enough, given the mixed record of the populist movements Lasch aligns himself with.[38] But the political virtue of Emersonian poise does not require this kind of idealization of "provincial" life. To cope with the alluring and frightening complexities of power on a larger scale, democratic citizens need an education in power that makes sense of their immediate world. There is no guarantee that they will gain this poise and their "immense intelligence" awakened by confronting the political conflicts that run through their own backyards. Sometimes the locals get it wrong, and the elites Lasch excoriates for abandoning faith in them do step in just in time. Without this experience the dangers Royce describes (widespread nativism, conformity, and demagoguery) are more likely to get the better of both. The elites Lasch presumptively criticizes are more likely to be of help when they also have had a share in creating and maintaining the local institutions Royce praises. For example, simply holding public hearings on new administrative regulations without having had some experience trying to make local institutions work may only polarize the local community and encourage violent local opposition.[39]

Conclusion

More still remains to be done if Emerson's treatment of power, poise, and place are to form the basis of a theory of democratic citizenship. Focusing on local politics becomes harder as the news media trivialize local concerns and transform national politics into entertainment. Spotting the forces that drive faraway local conflicts requires that citizens understand complex descriptions of these conflicts. However, only their own local political experience can prepare democratic citizens to understand these descriptions and critically discuss issues such as war or trade agreements. Otherwise, they can only repeat the platitudes and cliches that pass for a national debate, as reports from the front sail by them.

Democratic citizens should be able to discuss the generation as well as the constitution of power without denigrating their opponents as power grabbers and deluding themselves that they are somehow above power politics. This kind of civility and self-awareness depends upon a degree of humility that can be learned. Democratic citizens are educated, not born; and their education is an education in the protean ways power courses through their own lives.

It is also an education that begins on familiar ground. Democratic citizenship doesn't stop here, but it must start here. Only on local terrain do citizens have a chance to experience the compensatory and circular patterns of power and learn that through these patterns they do often depend on the willing cooperation of those they disagree with. It is this kind of experience that will give them the imagination to see how larger circles of power are bound together.

Finally, democratic citizens must be capable of discussing differences in power and morality, and this includes listening to how they sound to each other in the heat of these conversations. Everyone does not have to speak in the same stripped-down vernacular. It is hard to imagine what such a political Esperanto would sound like. Instead, citizens should strive to listen for the accents in their own voices that they had not been aware of before and that their opponents often had good reason to notice.

Emerson's skills as an orator have long been appreciated.[40] It is not clear what kind of listener he was. If his journal entries are any indication, he spent a lot of time talking silently to himself when in the company of those he found fault with and rehashing this silent conversation in his mind later. The skills and attitudes of a democratic citizen are much different. Such a person is not just poised and anxious to hold forth on great public issues, and prepared, in words Emerson used to describe Montaigne, "to shoot the gulf."[41] The democratic citizen I have in mind is attentive to the way power echoes in his or her own voice and can be used to forge political connections with others, however tenuous and temporary.

Emerson sometimes reached out in this way by writing letters, making statements of public support, and even giving monetary contributions. That he also often found this psychologically hard to do does not diminish the importance of this kind of political virtue for democrats today. It reminds us just how demanding democratic citizenship can be. Again from "Experience": "Never mind the ridicule, never mind the defeat; up again, old heart!—it seems to say,—there is victory yet for all justice; and the true romance which the world exists to realize will be the transformation of genius into practical power" (cw 3:49). In Richardson's words, "Experience" is an essay about "the impossibilities, miscarriages, and mortgagings of power," but it is not a "defeated essay." While "the fire within may be modest," it may still be "sufficient" to illuminate the complex centrality of power in democratic politics.[42]

NOTES

1. Will Kymlicka and Wayne Norman, "Return of the Citizen: A Survey of Recent Work on Citizenship Theory," *Ethics* 104 no. 2 (January 1994): 352–81. Before this, one would have to go back to Rousseau and Hegel to find major political theorists who placed citizenship at the center of their work.

2. Oliver Wendell Holmes, *Ralph Waldo Emerson* (Boston: Houghton Mifflin, 1884), p. 408.

3. Christina Zwarg, *Feminist Conversations: Fuller, Emerson, and the Play of Reading* (Ithaca: Cornell University Press, 1995); cf. Jeffrey Steele, *The Representation of the Self in the American Renaissance* (Chapel Hill: University of North Carolina Press, 1987).

4. This line of interpretation, arguably the most popular today, began with Stephen E. Whicher, *Freedom and Fate: An Inner Life of Ralph Waldo Emerson* (Philadelphia: University of Pennsylvania Press, 1953). See especially George Kateb, *Emerson and Self-Reliance* (Thousand Oaks, CA: Sage, 1995); and Stanley Cavell, *Conditions Handsome and Unhandsome: The Constitution of Emersonian Perfectionism* (Chicago: University of Chicago Press, 1990).

5. David Leverenz, *Manhood and the American Renaissance* (Ithaca: Cornell University Press, 1989); and Christopher Newfield, *The Emerson Effect: Individualism and Submission in America* (Chicago: University of Chicago Press, 1996).

6. "Even when Emerson engaged in political struggle with characteristic passion, his journals and letters reveal the distrust tinged with irritation that forms of collective action continued to evoke in him even when they seemed clearly necessary." Maurice Gonnaud, *An Uneasy Solitude: Individual and Society in the Work of Ralph Waldo Emerson*, trans. Lawrence Rosenwald (Princeton: Princeton University Press, 1987), p. 408. I am indebted to T. Gregory Garvey for reminding me of this contradiction in Emerson's life.

7. Michael Lopez, *Emerson and Power: Creative Antagonism in the Nineteenth Century* (De Kalb: Northern Illinois University Press, 1996), p. 10.

8. Even though he wrote to President Van Buren in April 1838 protesting the relocation of the Cherokee, "Like many other moralists and reformers, he was not yet convinced that blacks and other minorities were altogether equal in their ability to compete in society. If they were not self-reliant, any effort to establish their social equality through external agitation and moral suasion would be for naught. This thorny question would plague him for some years" (AW xix).

9. "Wealth brings with it its own checks and balances. The basis of political economy is non-interference. The only safe rule is found in the self-adjusting meter of demand and supply." "Wealth" (w 6: 105).

10. Quoted in Jeffrey Steele, *The Representation of the Self in the American Renaissance* (Chapel Hill: University of North Carolina Press, 1987), p. 102.

11. See the comments on Emerson's 1855 lecture "Woman" before the Boston women's rights convention in Christina Zwarg, *Feminist Conversations*, pp. 259–61.

12. For example, Stanley Cavell, *Conditions Handsome and Unhandsome: The Constitution of Emersonian Perfectionism* (Chicago: University of Chicago Press, 1990).

13. Mary Kupiec Cayton, *Emerson's Emergence: Self and Society in the Transformation of New England, 1800–1845* (Chapel Hill: University of North Carolina Press, 1989).

14. In *Feminist Conversations*, Zwarg argues that Emerson was sympathetic to Fourier's vision of socialism and Fuller's fluid, relational conception of the self.

15. Elsewhere I have discussed these laws of power and how they might be applied to contemporary issues and events; see *Intimacy and Spectacle: Liberal Theory as Political Education* (Ithaca: Cornell University Press, 1994). The argument there is that liberal theorists have appropriated only one side of Emerson, the oculocentric individualist, and have ignored his potential as a democratic theorist of power. Emerson's place in what I call the liberal tradition of humanistic corporatism is similar in some respects to the critical interpretation offered by Christopher Newfield (in *The Emerson Effect*), who uses a related term, "corporate individualism," to describe the liberal tradition.

16. Emerson invokes the law of compensation or polarity in "Politics" in *Essays: Second Series* (cw 3:123–24) and "Power" in *The Conduct of Life* (w 6:68–69). An indicative phrase in the former, and repeated slightly altered in the latter, is "Wild liberty develops iron conscience."

17. On Emerson's nontranscendental conception of use, see Lopez, *Emerson and Power*, chapter 2.

18. "You kin feel a switch in his hand when he's talkin' to yuh." Zora Neale Hurston, *Their Eyes Were Watching God* (Urbana: University of Illinois Press, 1979), p. 78.

19. "The Republican revisionist reading has replaced Lockean liberalism with civic humanism. Part Aristotle, part Cicero, part Machiavelli, civic humanism conceives of man as a political being whose realization of self occurs only through participation in public life, through active citizenship in a republic. A virtuous man is concerned primarily with the public good, *res publica*, or commonweal, not with private or selfish ends." Isaac Kramnick, "Republican Revisionism Revisited," *American Historical Review* 87, no. 3 (June 1982): 630.

20. "Human life is made up of the two elements, power and form, and the proportion must be invariably kept if we are to have it sweet and sound." Emerson, "Experience" (cw 3:38).

21. Habitat for Humanity's home-building program is an example of this kind of proximate help.

22. The danger of "self-centeredness" for virtue ethics in general is discussed in David Solomon, "Internal Objections to Virtue Ethics," in *Midwest Studies in Philosophy* vol. 13, *Ethical Theory: Character and Virtue*, eds. Peter A. French, Theodore E. Uehling Jr., and Howard K. Wettstein (Notre Dame: University of Notre Dame Press, 1988), pp. 428–41.

23. I am indebted to Charles McCracken for raising this objection. In the lecture "Man the Reformer," Emerson shows a clear preference for agrarian work and hopes that if more people benefited from it, "the advantages which arise from the division of labor" could be usefully reclaimed. The journal entry for April 7, 1840, expresses a similar view. "I see with great pleasure this growing inclination in all persons who aim to speak the truth, for manual labor & the farm. It is not that commerce, law, & state employments are unfit for a man, but that these are now so perverted and corrupt that no man can right himself in them, he is lost in them *he* cannot move hand or foot in them. Nothing is left him but to begin the world anew, as he does who puts the spade into the ground for food. When many shall have done so, when the majority shall admit the necessity of reform, of health, of sanity in all these institutions, then the way will be open again to the great advantages that arise from the division of labor. & a man will be able to select employments fittest for him without losing his selfdirection and becoming a tool" (*JMN* 7:342).

24. Dewey's theory of experience is complex. The central insight, for my purposes, is that experience involves a reciprocal relationship between energetic doing and receptive undergoing. When the two are combined with imagination so that they form a bounded whole, Dewey seems to think experiencing is on the right track, aligned with Nature. See John Dewey, *Art as Experience* (New York: Perigree Books, 1980); and *Experience and Nature* (Chicago: Open Court, 1994).

25. Robert D. Richardson Jr., *Emerson: The Mind on Fire* (Berkeley: University of California Press), p. 345.

26. *Emerson's Pragmatic Vision: The Dance of the Eye* (University Park: The Pennsylvania State University Press, 1993), p. 81.

27. Reprinted in *AW* 73, and textual commentary, p. 170. At other times Emerson seemed to be uninterested in this need for local concreteness. See his earlier "Address to the Citizens of Concord" on May 3, 1851, on the Fugitive Slave Law, reprinted in *AW* 53, and textual commentary on p. 164, which served as a campaign stump speech for John Gorham Palfrey, a member of Congress on the Free Soil ticket. In this address Emerson begins with a mild regret that he has been forced into politics by recent events despite "a duty to shun" such activities. Then, in the second paragraph he grounds his subsequent remarks. "We do not breathe well. There is infamy in the air. I have a new experience. I wake in the morning with a painful sensation, which I carry about all day, and which, when traced home, is the odious remembrance of that ignominy which has fallen on Massachusetts, which robs the landscape of beauty, and takes the sunshine out of every hour."

28. John Dewey, *The Public and Its Problems* (Denver: Alan Swallow, 1927), pp. 216, 219.

29. See Christopher Lasch, *The Revolt of the Elites and the Betrayal of Democracy* (New York: Norton, 1995), pp. 162–63.

30. Josiah Royce, *The Philosophy of Loyalty* (New York: MacMillan, 1924), p. 245.

31. Josiah Royce, *Race Questions, Provincialism, and Other American Problems* (New York: MacMillan, 1908), p. 71.

32. *Ibid.*, p. 79.

33. *Ibid.*, p. 91.

34. For example, Michael J. Sandel, *Democracy's Discontent: America in Search of a Public Philosophy* (Cambridge: Harvard University Press, 1996). See also Shlomo Avineri and Avner de-Shalit, eds., *Communitarianism and Individualism* (New York: Oxford University Press, 1992); and Will Kymlicka, *Liberalism, Community, and Culture* (New York: Oxford University Press, 1989).

35. Robert M. Cover, "Violence and the Word," *Yale Law Journal* 95 (1986): 1601–29.

36. Jane Jacobs, *The Death and Life of Great American Cities* (New York: Vintage, 1961).

37. Lasch, *The Revolt of the Elites and the Betrayal of Democracy*, pp. 99, 117–28.

38. It is important that the historical record on populism be kept straight; Lasch's theoretical arguments often threaten to understate the unhappy chapters in this record. See Michael Kazin, *The Populist Persuasion* (New York: Pantheon, 1995). However, it is also important to avoid collapsing Lasch's arguments for localism with communitarian and republican arguments which, as I have suggested, do not focus on the need for a political education in power. For an example of this kind of overkill, see Stephen Holmes, *The Anatomy of Antiliberalism* (Cambridge: Harvard University Press, 1993), pp. 122–40.

39. See, for example, the mainstreaming and inclusion of handicapped students in public education in Joel F. Handler, *The Conditions of Discretion: Autonomy, Community, Bureaucracy* (New York: Russell Sage Foundation, 1986).

40. Donald E. Pease, *Visionary Compacts: American Renaissance Writings in Cultural Context* (Madison: University of Wisconsin Press, 1987).

41. Putting words in Montaigne's mouth, Emerson wrote, "So, at least, I live within compass, keep myself ready for action, and can shoot the gulf, at last with decency." "Montaigne; or, the Skeptic" in *Representative Men* (cw 4:94–95).

42. Richardson, *Emerson: The Mind on Fire*, p. 403.

Contributors

HAROLD K. BUSH is assistant professor of English at Saint Louis University. He is author of *American Declarations: Rebellion and Repentance in American Cultural History* (Illinois, 1999), which contains a chapter titled "Emerson as Myth."

PHYLLIS COLE is associate professor of English and Women's Studies at Pennsylvania State University, Delaware County. She has published critical articles on the Transcendentalists in journals such as *Studies in Romanticism* and *ESQ: A Journal of the American Renaissance*, as well as in several collections of essays. Cole is author of *Mary Moody Emerson and the Origins of Transcendentalism: A Family History* (Oxford, 1998).

STEPHEN L. ESQUITH is professor of philosophy at Michigan State University. He is author of *Intimacy and Spectacle: Liberal Theory as Political Education* (Cornell, 1994), the editor of *Political Dialogue: Theories and Practices* (Rodopi, 1996), and author of articles on justice, democracy, and political education. His most recent work is on mass violence and democratic transitions, including "Toward a Democratic Rule of Law, East and West" in *Political Theory* (June 1999).

T. GREGORY GARVEY is assistant professor of English at SUNY-College at Brockport. He has published articles on Emerson, Frederick Douglass, and Catharine Sedgwick, among others.

ARMIDA GILBERT has published on Emerson and women's issues, and on other areas of the American Renaissance in *American Literature, Studies in the American Renaissance, Nineteenth-Century Prose, Victorian Periodicals Review, Byron Journal, Emerson Society Papers*, and *The Biographical Dictionary of Transcendentalism*. She teaches at East Georgia College in Statesboro, Georgia.

LEN GOUGEON, Professor of American Literature at the University of Scranton, is the author of *Virtue's Hero: Emerson, Antislavery and Reform* (Georgia, 1990) and coeditor (with Joel Myerson) of *Emerson's Antislavery Writings* (Yale, 1995). He currently serves as president-elect of the Ralph Waldo Emerson Society and is at work on a book-length study of Emerson and the Civil War.

LINCK C. JOHNSON is professor of English at Colgate University. He is the author of *Thoreau's Complex Weave: The Writing of "A Week on the Concord and Merri-*

mack Rivers," with a Complete Text of the First Draft (Virginia, 1986); the historical introduction to *A Week* in the Princeton edition of *The Writings of Henry David Thoreau* (Princeton, 1980); and numerous essays and reviews. The essay published here is drawn from a book he is writing on Emerson and Thoreau in relation to antebellum reform.

SUSAN L. ROBERSON is assistant professor of English at Alabama State University. She is author of *Emerson in His Sermons: A Man-Made Self* (Missouri, 1995) and is the editor of *Women, America, and Movement: Narratives of Relocation* (Missouri, 1998).

DAVID M. ROBINSON is Oregon Professor of English and distinguished professor of American literature at Oregon State University. He is author of *Apostle of Culture: Emerson as Preacher and Lecturer* (Pennsylvania, 1982); *Emerson and the Conduct of Life* (Cambridge, 1993); and *World of Relations: The Achievement of Peter Taylor* (Kentucky, 1998). He is author of the chapter on "Emerson, Thoreau, Fuller and Transcendentalism" for *American Literary Realism* and is currently serving as president of the Ralph Waldo Emerson Society.

JEFFREY A. STEELE, professor of English at the University of Wisconsin-Madison, is author of *The Representation of the Self in the American Renaissance* (North Carolina, 1987), and editor of *The Essential Margaret Fuller* (Rutgers, 1992). He is also author of essays on nineteenth-century American literature, including "Transcendental Friendship: Emerson, Fuller, and Thoreau" in *The Cambridge Companion to Ralph Waldo Emerson* (1999).

MICHAEL STRYSICK is visiting assistant professor of English at Wake Forest University. He offers courses in American and ethnic American literature, cultural studies, literary criticism, and film. He has published articles in *Cultural Critique*, *Romantic Review*, and the *South Atlantic Quarterly*. He is finishing a book manuscript titled "Feudal America: Literature, Community, and the Politics of Social Change."

Index